In Memory

Of

William V. Totman

The
CONFEDERATE NAVY

The CONFEDERATE NAVY

The Ships, Men and Organization, 1861-65

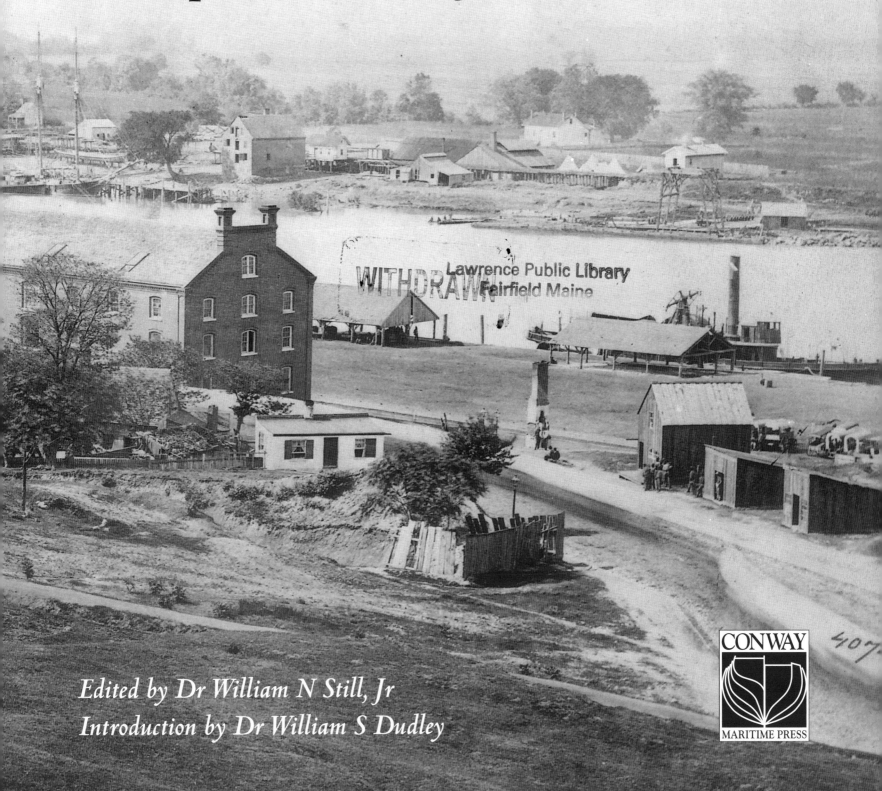

Edited by Dr William N Still, Jr
Introduction by Dr William S Dudley

CONWAY MARITIME PRESS

© Conway Maritime Press, 1997

First published in Great Britain in 1997 by
Conway Maritime Press
an imprint of Brassey's (UK) Ltd
33 John Street, London WCIN 2AT

Telephone: 0171 753 7777
Fax: 0171 753 7795
E-mail: brasseys@dial.pipex.com
Web: http://www.brasseys.com

ISBN 0 85177 686 8

*A CIP catalogue record for this book is available
from the British Library.*

The images of *H.L. Hunley* (pp 63, 209)
are strictly copyright and are published by
kind permission of the South Carolina
Hunley Commission.

Jacket Illustration
Richmond by Moonlight, 1863 is reproduced
courtesy of WRM Graphics, Inc,
Cleveland, Ohio 44122, USA

Project Editor: David McLean
Picture Researcher: Robert Holcombe
Designer: Peter Champion
Typeset in Centaur by York House
Typographic, London
Printed and bound in Italy by LEGO SpA

The contributors

Dr Robert M Browning, Jr is currently the Chief Historian for the United States Coast Guard. He is the author of *From Cape Charles to Cape Fear: The North Atlantic Blockading Squadron during the Civil War* and is writing a book on the South Atlantic Blockading Squadron.

Dr Norman C Delaney is Professor of History at Del Mar College, Corpus Christi, Texas. Since publication of his award-winning biography of John McIntosh Kell in 1973, he continues his research on the Confederate commerce raiders and other aspects of Civil War naval history.

Robert Holcombe is Director of the Confederate Naval Museum, Columbus, Georgia. Holds a degree from East Carolina University. Author of *Notes on the Classification of Confederate Ironclads*, 1980. Articles on Confederate warships published in *Warship International* and other journals.

Dr Harold D Langley is Curator of Naval History, Emeritus at the Smithsonian Institution's National Museum of American History in Washington DC. Since 1967 he has published monographs, chapters in books and articles relating to aspects of the social history of the US Navy.

Professor Raimondo Luraghi, Emeritus at the University of Genoa, Italy, has written several books on the American Civil War and the Old South. The latest one is *A History of the Confederate Navy* ,1996 which has been awarded the 'Roosevelt Naval History Prize'.

Dr Maurice Melton is Associate Professor of History at Andrew College, Cuthbert, Georgia. He has been writing on the South and the American Civil War since 1968, and today lives in Columbus, Ga., near the Old Confederate Navy Yard and the Naval Ironworks.

Dr Royce Shingleton is Professor of History at Darton College in Albany, Georgia. He has written fifty articles and book reviews and three books on Southern and Civil War history, including biographies of Southern naval officers John Taylor Wood and John Newland Maffitt. In 1992 he was the subject of a bibliographic essay in the *Naval War College Review*.

Dr William N Still, Jr was Professor of History and Director of the Program in Maritime History and Nautical Archeology at East Carolina University, North Carolina, until his retirement in 1994. He has written extensively on American maritime history, winning the Harry Truman award for outstanding research in American history in 1989. He now lives in Hawaii.

David M Sullivan is the author of *The United States Marine Corps in the Civil War: The First Year* and more than 50 articles on Confederate States and United States Marine Corps history.

The publishers wish to thank the following institutions and individuals who kindly made available illustrations for this book and helped to locate sometimes obscure material:

Alabama Department of Archives and
  History, Montgomery, Alabama
Atlanta Historical Society, Atlanta, Ga.
Boston Public Library, Boston, Mass.
Confederate Museum, Charleston, SC
Connecticut State Library, Hartford, Conn
Florida State Museum, Tallahassee, Florida
Georgia Historical Society, Savannah, Ga.
Library of Congress, Washington, DC
Mariner's Museum Newport News, Va.
Monroe County May Hill Russell
  Library, Key West, Florida
Museum of the Confederacy, Richmond, Va.

National Archives, Washington, DC (NA)
Naval Historical Center, Washington, DC
Robert M Strozier Library, Florida State
  University, Tallahassee, Florida
South Carolina Hunley Commission,
  Columbia, SC
South Carolina Institute of Archaeology
  and Anthropology, Columbia, SC
Tennessee State Library and Archives,
  Nashville, Tennessee
The Woodruff Museum of Civil War
  Naval History, Columbus, Ga
  (WMCWNH)

George M Brooke
Dan Dowdey
Robert G Elliott
Steve Freeman
Brooks Hamm

James Harris
Robert Holcombe
Katherine Hosch Jessup
Margaret Key
Samuel Lawson
Ron Marlett
Senator Glenn McConnel
Robert A Moses
Andrew H Parker
Charles V Peery
B Ramsay Powell
C B Pritchett, Jr
Ann Thom Williamson Roberts
Sidney H Schell
Dale Snair
Elizabeth S Steen
Adelaide M Trigg
Albert W Weems, Jr

CONTENTS

Chapter Seven
SEAMEN, LANDSMEN, FIREMEN AND COAL HEAVERS *by Dr Royce Shingleton*. *133*

Chapter Eight
THE MARINES *by David M Sullivan* *147*

Chapter Nine
SHIPBOARD LIFE *by Dr Harold D Langley* *175*

Chapter Ten
STRATEGY AND TACTICS *by Dr Norman C Delaney*. *193*

Chapter Eleven
OPERATIONS *by Dr William N Still, Jr.* *214*

INTRODUCTION

by Dr William S Dudley

Director of Naval History, United States Navy

The advent of this institutional study devoted to the history of the Confederate States Navy, with various chapters authored by specialists in their fields, is a notable publishing event. For while a number of narrowly focused studies on the Southern war at sea have been published, very few that cover the entire subject have seen the light of day. Before the 1960s, only the massive early work by J Thomas Scharf, *History of the Confederate States Navy: From Its Organization to the Surrender of Its Last Vessel* (1887) had stood the test of time, but its dated sources, its flawed presentation, the discovery of new sources of documentation, and the advance of historiography due to the outpouring of works during the centennial of the Civil War have brought about a new interest in the accomplishments of the Confederate States Navy. Raimondo Luraghi's recently published synthesis, *A History of the Confederate States Navy* (1996) is a remarkably exhaustive work of narration and analysis by an Italian military historian whose diligent research has produced a fine contribution to the field after nearly thirty years of study.

Much is owed to the works of the editor of this volume, Dr William N Still, Jr, who has produced a series of original books and articles which, taken together, can be said to have brought about a renaissance in Civil War maritime and naval scholarship. His overall emphasis has been on the naval organization, logistics, and technology with which the South fought its more industrialized opponent at sea. The Civil War at sea was not a confrontation of battle fleets but one of technological and logistical challenges.

The history of the Southern cause at sea cannot be told by a rollicking narration of sea battles because they were few and for the most part were not conducted on the high seas, but rather in the bays, sounds and rivers of the Old South. Rather, this history is the account of Southern ingenuity and a Confederate awareness that even the industrialized North had failed to exploit what a rapidly expanding European naval technology, by 1860, had begun

to reveal. Dr Still's studies are exemplified in such works as *Confederate Shipbuilding* (1969), *Iron Afloat: A History of the Confederate Armorclad* (1971), and articles such as 'Selma and the Confederate States Navy', *The Alabama Review* (January 1962). Still's works and teaching career have stimulated others to follow his example, and even Professor Luraghi admits that his own study owes a great deal to the pioneering work of his American counterpart. It should not be surprising that Dr Still's contribution in the present volume springs from the inspiration of bringing the essays of others together in a way that essentially demonstrates advances in specialized knowledge about the Confederate States Navy that developed in the wake of his own path-breaking studies.

There is a good reason for the current interest in the Confederate States Navy among naval scholars and intelligence experts who study the military aspirations of the less-developed nations of the world as they contend with the technologically advanced, diverse, and more numerous ships and aircraft of the Western European and United States navies. During the years 1861–1865, the Confederate Navy utilized technological surprise against a burgeoning Union Navy. The 1850s generation of steam-driven frigates of the US Navy were still constructed of wood and were therefore vulnerable to attack by armoured and ironclad ships armed with rifled cannon and by spar torpedoes carried by gunboats and submarines, to say nothing of contact and electrically detonated mines. That even ironclads could be sunk by mines was several times demonstrated by Confederate specialists in mine warfare. The Southern naval threat ultimately failed, but its defeat demanded a huge effort by the US Navy and many Northern lives and ships were lost in the process. This lesson is not lost on those who find themselves partisans of small navies with sparse resources. During the Civil War, one mine sank the powerful monitor USS *Tecumseh* off Fort Morgan, Alabama, and in recent times, the nearly fatal mine damage to US warships USS *Princeton*, USS *Samuel B*

Roberts and USS *Tripoli* in the Persian Gulf galvanized the American mine warfare community into action, demanding more numerous and more capable mine-countermeasures ships, equipment, and personnel. In the hands of a resourceful enemy, a cleverly deployed 'cheap' threat can be very costly indeed for the larger, more capable, but less-prepared naval force if attacks against it are carried forward with audacity. That is but one of the lessons to be learned from the American Civil War at Sea.

How and why the Confederate Navy was able to confront and frustrate the US 'Union' Navy for as long as it did is the principal theme of this book. The subject-matter ranges widely, starting with a background essay by Raimondo Luraghi covering the secession crisis, the establishment of a navy department, the establishment of state navies, and the outbreak of war. Robert M Browning, Jr, historian of the US Coast Guard and known to us for his study of the US Navy's North Atlantic Blockading Squadron, explains how the Confederate Navy Department was established and operated and describes the relationship between the Confederate Congress and the Navy, and how the Navy Department managed its far-flung operations. The wide variety of Confederate ship types and their technical characteristics is analysed in depth by Robert Holcombe, director of the Civil War Naval Museum in Columbus, Georgia. Maurice Melton, author of *The Confederate Ironclads* (1968) and a specialist on the Savannah Squadron, discusses the South's shipbuilding facilities and manufacturing plants. He details how the Confederacy overcame many difficulties in its drive to construct ironclad ships but in the end met intractable problems, such as shortages of iron, rail transport, and manpower. Royce Shingleton, biographer of Captain John Taylor Wood, CSN, expounds upon the sources of Confederate naval officers, their shift of allegiance from Union to Confederacy, the gradually developed training of younger officers, and personnel logistics, the working of the seniority system, the need for uniforms, the staff corps, and the conditions under which officers worked. In another chapter, Shingleton examines the way the Confederate Navy's sailors were recruited, trained, rated, and disciplined. The Confederate Marines receive a similar treatment from David M Sullivan who expands on the knowledge base provided by the late Ralph Donnelly.

Harold D Langley, a former Smithsonian Institution curator of naval history, devotes his considerable expertise on a view of how Confederate sailors spent their lives at sea, ranging from matters such as daily routine to health, discipline and desertion. Another naval scholar, Norman C Delaney, the biographer of Commander

John McIntosh Kell, CSN, looks at the Confederate Navy through a different prism, that of strategy and tactics, emphasizing the Navy's efforts to distract the Union ships from their blockading assignments by destructive raiding in the world's sea lanes by foreign-built raiders, the obstruction of river navigation, and the development of types of guerrilla warfare at sea. In a concluding chapter, editor Still provides an overview of Confederate naval operations in the Atlantic Ocean, Gulf of Mexico, and western rivers, and even the trackless Pacific Ocean where CSS *Shenandoah* virtually destroyed the Union's whaling fleet late in the war.

In the final analysis, this well-organized collection of essays demonstrates that the Confederate Navy made a valiant but futile effort to overcome the lack of infrastructure, a system of procurement and recruitment priorities that favoured the Confederate Army, and delay-producing bureaucratic conflicts. Initially, international sentiment favoured the South, but foreign governments such as Great Britain and France were unwilling to translate that sentiment into definitive action harmful to the North. Individual Southern naval officers made life-consuming efforts to provide a naval service worthy of the name. The resources of the Union were too great and the Northern naval strategy of denying the South the control of the river systems that penetrated to the core of the Confederacy ultimately slowed the flow of supplies to a trickle.

On the other hand, this volume demonstrates how the South's contributions to naval technology made a lasting impression that reverberated into the twentieth century. In the years immediately following the war, Secretary of the Navy Mallory's visionary precepts, ironclad, armoured, and steel-hulled warships became standard equipment in the world's most advanced navies. Sea mines were the most successful weapon used against US Navy ships, more than sixty Union vessels, some of them armoured, were sunk by Confederate mines. Although the Confederate submarine *H.L. Hunley* was not a CSN invention, and was manned principally by both Confederate Navy and Confederate Army volunteers, this revolutionary submarine ultimately sank the blockading steam frigate USS *Housatonic*, providing an effective portent for the future of naval warfare. The editor of this volume and the authors of these essays have provided a splendid new focus on aspects of the Confederate States Navy that will provoke thought, discussion, and further research. Several of the chapters are themselves deserving of book-length treatment. Despite some inevitable overlap and repetition always to be found in topically arranged chapters in a multi-authored book, time will show that the substance of this volume makes a solid contribution to the historiography of the Civil War.

PREFACE

by Dr William N Still, Jr

The American Civil War is the most popular topic in United States history. The reasons why are complex but as the historian James McPherson in his bestseller *Battlecry of Freedom* wrote, 'The Civil War is by far the most vivid and dramatic and violent single event in [American]...history'. The continuing popularity of this subject can be demonstrated in numerous ways. In 1990 more than fourteen million people viewed the initial TV showing of Ken Burns' eleven-hour series 'The Civil War'. More than 50,000 books have been written about the conflict at a rate of several hundred a year. Several popular magazines as well as two learned journals discuss this topic. Clubs known as CIVIL WAR ROUND TABLES exist throughout the United States with a total membership of more than a quarter of a million participants. Interest in this war does not end at the United States border. The Southern Skirmish Association in the United Kingdom gives £150 a year to the high school student who writes the best essay on America's war. A magazine about the Civil War is published in Belgium and an organization called 'The Confederate Headquarters of Europe' is located in Zurich.

Despite the impressive interest in this conflict on the part of the general public and historians alike, the naval side has been somewhat neglected. This is particularly true of the Confederate States Navy. Only one comprehensive history of the Confederate Navy, Raimondo Luraghi's *A History of the Confederate States Navy*, has been published since 1887 and it originally appeared in Italian in 1993. Professor Luraghi's study is excellent, but in a general work such as this some topics are only briefly discussed.

The present book is an attempt to fill some of these gaps while at the same time presenting a balanced study of the Confederate Navy. A topical approach has been utilized as the most effective means of covering the subject matter. Inevitably at times this approach seems superficial and it has also resulted in a certain amount of unavoidable overlapping and redundancy. Books could and have been written on many of the topics presented in chapter form here. Some of the chapters are based on original research, others synthesize the available published literature, but all of them include some original material and interpretations.

We would like to thank the staffs of all the libraries and institutions that have helped us in various ways preparing this book. The Woodruff Museum of Civil War Naval History (formerly the Confederate Naval Museum) in Columbus, Georgia is due our sincere gratitude for acting as a clearing house for much of the material and illustrations included in this work. Thanks also go to Conway Maritime Press and particularly to editor David McLean for working with us to get this study published.

NOTE:

The Union Navy was officially the US Navy but the phrase is used for clarity.

Chapter One
BACKGROUND

Secession of the Southern States

The nature and the causes of the events that, in 1860, generated the disruption of the American Union – and that compelled many a naval officer to take the momentous decision of resigning from service in the US Navy to join the new Confederacy – constitute, even to-day, a bone of contention between historians with no sign of abating.

Undoubtedly, such events had their roots in the American past. Indeed, since the early era, the English colonies in the New World – gravitating around the two distinct centers of New England and the South (Virginia) – had been growing according to different lines of development, culturally, economically and socially, so as to give birth to two different civilizations and, more recently (at least in the case of the South), to a different national consciousness.[1]

The South's road to secession has been widely studied: enough to say that the manifold grievances of the Southern states against the North seemed to concentrate, in the late 1850s, around the issue of slavery. The South (or, at least, its most cultivated and thoughtful citizens) did by no means underrate the negative, even shameful, side of the 'peculiar institution': indeed, it had been in the South that the first tentative proposals for emancipating the slaves and getting rid of the institution had taken place. Yet (and this is the point) the explosion of the industrial revolution in the North had exacerbated all the motives of conflict with the emotive agrarian South. Among them, not to be underrated, was the issue of free trade versus protectionism: one which would have momen-

tous consequences on the naval side of the forthcoming war.

The North – pushed by the needs of its process of industrialisation – was tired of a rather loosely connected Union. It wanted instead a strong, centralized, protectionist organism: the 'great Republic', as Abraham Lincoln would have it. Of course, in the North's eyes, slavery was not only immoral, it was anti-economic, a residuum of a backward era, a substantial obstacle to the building of that national market (as well of goods as of labour and capital) which was indispensable to the achievement of the industrial revolution.

Historian Eric Foner, in a seminal book, has clearly stated the new credo of the industrial North: 'free soil, free labor, free men.'[2] The fantastic growth of the Northern industrial plant required an ever wider pool of cheap labour; consequently, workmen had to be 'free' to become wage earners and not tied down by any sort of bondage.

This, together with the European crisis of 1848–50, increased to enormous proportions the influx of immigrants from the Old World (449,432 in 1851 alone). All those people went almost exclusively to the Northern states: the existence of slave labour kept them clear of the South, both because they could not compete with bonded workmen, and because of their natural repugnance to slavery.

Such an increase of population in the Northern states, other than giving birth to nativist currents which do not concern us here, stimulated the march westward, adding fuel to the movement of freesoilers, who wanted slavery (and black men) out of the Territories by any means.

Montgomery, Alabama, first capital of the Confederacy; A view from across the Alabama River. (*Harper's Weekly*)

Since the best way to get rid of bondage and to keep both Southerners and their slaves out of the Territories was to attack the 'malignant tree' of slavery at its roots, the uproar against the 'peculiar institution' increased in the North, scaring Southerners, by contrast, into an almost blind, irrational defense of slavery, which, in the past, they had instead widely criticized.

The candidacy to the office of President of the United States of Abraham Lincoln, who was, right or wrong, considered an anti-slavery man (he was certainly not an abolitionist: yet he was substantially a free-soiler) spread more panic among the inhabitants of the Southern states, already terrorized beyond any reasonable measure by John Brown's raid.

If not an abolitionist, Lincoln was surely the supporter of a strong central government, which would not admit the survival of localisms, such as 'states' rights'; and he was determined to stop the institution of slavery from spreading into the Western Territories which, according to his own words, were to be reserved for 'free white people', which was also the aim of free-soilers. In addition, Lincoln was a staunch defender of protectionism and its tariffs.

At any rate, the South was now persuading itself that the recent events threatened to reduce it to an inferior status, similar to that of a colony. Be it as it may, a wave of emotions and irrational feelings now swept the country: everybody seemed to have forsaken the capability of remaining cool and reasonable. Secession seemed to Southerners the only solution: as Abraham Lincoln, the new President of the United States, had polled no votes south of the Mason-Dixon line, angry and frustrated Southerners decided to play the fateful card of independence.

This would, most probably, generate an armed conflict, which would be a war between a strongly industrialized country and an agrarian one, only partly industrialized. This would, of course, weigh heavily on the naval side of the forthcoming war.

Yet, on December 20, 1860, a Convention elected by the people of South Carolina, meeting in Charleston, voted unanimously an ordinance of secession: Mississippi, Florida, Alabama, Georgia, Louisiana and Texas followed suit. On February 4, 1861, a Convention of the seceded states met in Montgomery, Alabama, in order to give birth to a new Southern Confederacy; on February 8 a provisional Constitution of the Confederate States of America was approved.

Formation of the Confederate Government

The new Confederacy existed, for the time being, only on paper. It had no Government, no President, no Departments, nothing. Truly, on February 9 a Committee had been elected for drafting a permanent Constitution; yet, it was impossible and dangerous to wait for it to complete its job. What was the North doing? This was a time of almost intoxicating illusions. Many were still reiterating the shibboleth of the North as 'a nation of shopkeepers who would not fight': yet, the majority of the men assembled in Montgomery were under no illusion. The Southern independence would never be achieved cheaply. The threat from the North was a real one. Still, very few, if any, understood that the true strength of the North – which would, in the end, prove formidable – derived exactly from its being 'a nation of shopkeepers', capable of waging a modern, industrial kind of warfare.

This, in turn, evidenced the high priority of organizing the defense of the Confederacy. Therefore, under the provisional Constitution, Congress (born from a transformation of the constitutional Convention) was given the power to raise armies and 'to provide and maintain a Navy'. For this purpose a series of Standing Committees were created, among them a Naval Affairs Committee.

Yet, the new Navy (and the new Army) had no Commander-in-Chief nor Secretaries. However, the provisional Constitution authorized Congress to wield executive power until the election of a President of the Confederate States of America (CSA). Therefore on February 14 the Committee on Naval Affairs sent telegrams to naval officers native to the South inviting them to resign from the US Navy and to proceed to Montgomery. Following the invitation, on February 19, former Captains Lawrence Rousseau, Duncan N Ingraham and Victor M Randolph and Commander Raphael Semmes met in Montgomery with the Committee on Naval Affairs, to establish the guidelines for the building of a thus far non-existent Confederate Navy.

Indeed, the new Commander-in-Chief had been elected unanimously by Congress since February 9: he was former Senator Jefferson F Davis, from Mississippi. Yet, owing to the poor rail communications of the South (something which, to heedful observers, might have sounded ominous) he was not inaugurated until February 18.

Jefferson Davis's personality has been so much discussed by historians that there is no reason to add here further fuel to the quarrel. Undoubtedly he did not lack military experience. During the Mexican War he had commanded a Mississippi Volunteer Regiment, and fought gallantly at Buena Vista where he had contributed to winning the day and had been seriously wounded. Secretary of War of the United States, he had also covered for a while the charge of Acting Secretary of the Navy.

Talking before Secession to the future US Admiral David Dixon Porter, he had even boasted that the future Southern Confederacy would have 'a Navy to be proud of'. Moreover, the man who was to become Secretary of the Navy of the Confederacy, Stephen Russell Mallory, would speak of him always in a laudatory way.

Yet it seems that President Davis would not interfere with naval matters because he would always consider such problems as secondary ones, giving the highest priority to the Army; this, of course was negative to the full development of naval effort; yet in a way it was helpful because the Navy would be able to develop with little or no interference from the President. It may be because of this (and, certainly, because Davis always trusted Mallory) that the Secretary of the Navy, together with the Postmaster General Reagan, was the only member of Davis's Cabinet who kept his office throughout the whole war.

Meanwhile, on February 20, Congress at last instituted the Navy Department; therefore President Davis was able, on the 25th, to nominate the Confederate Secretary of the Navy; he was former Senator Stephen R Mallory, from Florida. On May 5,

Jefferson Davis. President of the Confederate States of America. (Library of Congress)

putting aside some opposition coming from fire-eaters who considered him a moderate (which he was) and a union man (which he was not, at least after the election of Abraham Lincoln), Congress confirmed the appointment.

Mallory was then 49 years old, having been born in 1812 at Key West, Florida. His mother, an Irishwoman, soon widowed, having sent him to a Pietist school, raised him as a Roman Catholic, which he continued to be all his life, albeit rather mildly. At any rate, his adherence to the Catholic Church was reinforced by his marriage, in 1838, with Angela Moreno, of a prominent Catholic Creole family from Pensacola.

Since his youth, he had practised law, specializing in maritime problems, such as between shipowners and the local organizations of 'wreckers', very active in the dangerous waters of south Florida and the Keys. An active Democrat, he was considered a moderate, with few secessionist ideas. In 1851 he won a seat in the US Senate, in place of the local Senator, David Yulee, considered by many an extremist.

In Washington he had pursued his studies on naval matters which, in 1854, brought him the Chairmanship of the US Senate Committee for Naval Affairs. As such, he worked actively to modernize the US Navy. Always abreast with the most recent innovations both in shipbuilding and in naval science, he worked energetically to reinforce the Navy by six steam frigates, six first-class steam sloops and several more of the second class: all ships powerful, modern and looked at with envy and concern by foreign navies. Ironically, Mallory was reinforcing the US Navy, against which he would later fight almost empty-handed.

Another initiative by Mallory had been his attempt to promote a project, already discussed by Congress, concerning the building of an ironclad warship for the defense of New York harbor. In this he failed yet his initiative shows his interest in the latest armoured vessels. Mallory was also the main promoter of a so-called 'Naval Retiring Board', intended to prune the Navy of old, bureaucratic and frequently unsuitable personnel. The Board's work was in the main useful to the Navy; yet it hurt many people who became sworn enemies of Mallory. Since one of them was the naval scientist Matthew Fontaine Maury, a man incapable of forgiving or forgetting and eventual Confederate naval officer, it may be said that Mallory made for himself a series of future headaches.

When Mallory was able, at last, to start work as Confederate Secretary of the Navy (his appointment met a delay, because it had to win over some opposition) he had around him literally nothing. Only on March 8 did the Confederate provisional Congress approve a limited number of personnel to work with him: a Chief Clerk, four Clerks and a Messenger. On March 11 Congress approved the organization of the Navy Department, to

The swearing in of Jefferson Davis as President of the Confederacy at Montgomery, February 18, 1861. (*Harper's Weekly*)

be based on four Bureaux (Office of Ordnance and Hydrography, Office of Orders and Details, Office of Medicine and Surgery, Office of Provisions and Clothing) and a commander of the Marine Corps. Now the structure of the Navy Department was ready: the problem was that, at this moment, no Navy existed.

Establishing a navy

To establish a Navy, the Confederacy needed three things: personnel, ships and – first and foremost – money. Indeed, without money, ships or men the new Navy would run the risk of being compelled to surrender even before being born. This was the starting point.

The system put up by the Confederate authorities to finance the naval effort was cumbersome and far from efficient. The Navy Department never had a portfolio nor its own budget. In practice, Secretary Mallory had to submit to the standing Committee for Naval Affairs of the provisional Congress (then, after the regular Assembly was elected, to Committees in both the Senate and the House) his estimates for normal and extraordinary expenditures; Congress would (it was hoped) approve them; then the Secretary had to get the money in time for any single expense from the Treasury by means of something like draft letters.

Such a system created a whole series of delays, misunderstandings and unending haggling with the Treasury Department. This was certainly not the fault of Secretary of the Treasury, Christopher G Memminger; it happened because the strictures of Confederate finance were, in effect, thrown upon the shoulders of the Navy, with disastrous results. Owing to this, the Navy would have during the war very close relations with the Treasury Department: more close than with those of War or of State.

The most dramatic points of interference between the Navy and the Treasury Department were mainly three: money, personnel and skilled labour. First of all, there was the very policy followed by the Confederate Treasury to finance the war. When the conflict started, Secretary Memminger had to face the bitter fact that 67.5 per cent of specie reserves remained in Federal hands, whereas the Confederacy had only a meagre 32.5 per cent. Still worse; such reserves were in the vaults of Southern banks which the Confederate Government dared not touch, trying instead to make do with what was in the several mints of Louisiana: barely $600,000. This was indeed very little, since the first estimate of

appropriations needed by the Navy alone, up to February 4, 1862, amounted to $2,065,110.

The Treasury was in a quandary. Recourse to taxation was almost impossible, since (obviously) the Confederacy had had no possibility of establishing a war tax system before the outbreak of hostilities. Memminger, to mobilize the specie reserves of the banks, floated a so-called 'Specie loan', intended to drain up what specie were in the vaults. Unfortunately, the banks were scarcely responsive because they feared, not unreasonably, running the risk of going bankrupt if they remained without specie reserves; the Treasury succeeded in obtaining no more than $8-9 million. This would be the small capital which the Navy Department would have to count on for its multifarious expenditures abroad (to buy or to build warships, heavy naval guns, ammunition, powder, garments and medical stores). Furthermore, the Navy would always have to share budgets with the Army.

Yet the South had an immense wealth in cotton. Its annual production amounted to 4,500,000 bales. At 11.5 cents per pound, it had been exported in 1860 for $184,400,000. The Treasury tried to tap such enormous wealth by means of a so-called 'produce loan', to be subscribed in cotton, tobacco, rice and sugar. It was a conspicuous failure, yielding no more than 417,000 bales of cotton. Indeed the planters, almost without cash to pay their debts, were scarcely responsive. Still, here too, the 417,000 bales of cotton would in the future be the initial base for the Navy Department to finance its activities abroad by means of tendering the so-called 'cotton certificates', granted by such a small cotton reserve.

Of course, had the 'produce loan' been successful, the problem of selling the goods abroad would still remain. Since the North had declared the blockade of Southern coasts, only the Navy might protect such exporting of cotton. Yet the Confederate Navy did not exist, at least for the time being: to buy war vessels abroad, it needed money; to get money, it was necessary to sell the cotton abroad. No sales of cotton on the world market, no warships; but, no warships, no protection to the exporting of cotton, which would become almost impossible.

This is just an example of the terrible difficulties generated for the Navy by the strictures of the Treasury Department: the fact that Mallory, notwithstanding this, would succeed in buying and building war vessels, to put them afloat and to challenge the enemy on the sea, was in itself a miracle.

Still, there was, for a while, a remote possibility of placing a large amount of cotton abroad. George Alfred Trenholm, banker

Firing on Fort Sumter, April 12-13, 1861. (*Harper's Weekly*)

and financier from Charleston, South Carolina, and a sincere Southern patriot, understood that the British East India Company was selling ten of its steamers, four of large size and six smaller, all with iron hulls, and capable of carrying some heavy guns. The cost of buying them would be $2 million, equal to 40,000 cotton bales. Trenholm's proposition was that the Confederate Government buy such steamers; they would then enter the Southern ports with weapons, ammunition and any other goods useful to the Confederate war effort; then transport abroad as much cotton as possible, to pay for future acquisitions. The project however came to nothing: the steamers had a draft of more than 10ft, which left them unable to enter the majority of Southern ports. In addition, the policy of exporting cotton on a large scale was fast becoming unrealistic, since it was impossible to defy public opinion which endorsed the idea of embargoing cotton in order to generate a famine of such impact in Europe, that, it was hoped, the maritime powers would act and raise the blockade declared by the Union. Even if the Confederate Government did nothing (other that putting on cotton an export duty of ⅛ cent per pound) to actuate an embargo, such an idea was highly popular. In turn, the Government did not dare to disclaim it clearly, so that the dangerous idea that there was an 'embargo' on exporting cotton lingered for a long time.

After that of money, the second problem for the Confederate Navy was personnel. Since the South was mainly an agrarian area, it lacked the basic ingredient for recruiting seamen: a good merchant marine. Out of a tonnage of 5,539,812 tons of freighters possessed by the United States, the South had barely 500,000,

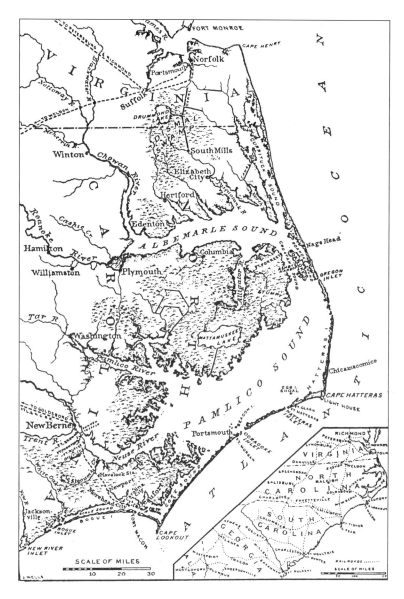

The coastal sounds of North Carolina. (*Battles & Leaders*)

and many belonged to Northern owners. New York State had 1,740,940 tons; New England alone owned 1,839,158. As far as warships were concerned, Southern naval officers, before resigning their commissions to join the Confederacy, felt obliged by their sense of honour and duty to deliver their vessels to the US Navy, their rightful owner. In addition, the few sailors available had been hastily enlisted into the Army, which felt heavily outnumbered by the Union forces and was desperately looking for any kind of human resource, so that now Mallory had to fight an extremely difficult battle (and not rarely a losing one) to get them back.

Fortunately, the Officer Corps did not present such problems. Out of 2,234 naval officers of the US Navy and Marine Corps,

Southerners accounted for 671. Of them 321 tendered their resignation and cast their lot with the Confederacy; 350 Southerners remained loyal to the Union. It is interesting to observe how much the allegiance to the old flag was stronger in the Navy than in the Army. This was, perhaps, because naval officers, serving, as they did, normally far from home and in contact with foreigners, had a more direct sense of fealty toward the Union as a whole than toward their native states.

In time, a problem which became very serious was that of pilots. The coastal charts of the Civil War era were imprecise at best; therefore pilots were indispensable for navigating coastal and inland waters. Yet pilots – all of them civilians – were in part of Northern origins, and unwilling to serve the Confederacy with any sense of duty; others did not want to risk their lives and performed their tasks, at best, in a lukewarm way. The Confederate Navy never entirely solved the problems of pilots; yet many of them behaved as true Southern patriots, and those at Wilmington – which would become the main port of entry for blockade-runners – were subject to military discipline.

Last – yet by no means the least – there would be the problem of the shortage of skilled labour. The South lacked the distinctive characteristics of modern industrial societies: a vast amount of financial capital for investment and an array of skilled workmen, what sociologists would call 'the industrial reserve army'. This feebleness was integral to the South, so that a true remedy to it was simply impossible without a complete upheaval and overthrow of the whole social fabric, from top to bottom (including the 'peculiar institution'); yet in such a case the Old South would simply cease to exist. It was exactly what the Northern enemy wanted and was fighting for.

When these problems had to be faced, the capital city of the Confederacy was no longer in Montgomery. The secession of Virginia, on April 17, 1861, had carried with it a strong pressure for the transfer of the capital from Montgomery to Richmond. As correctly argued by General J F C Fuller, it was to be a strategic blunder, especially on the naval side. Montgomery was far from the enemy lines of penetration, almost impervious to offensives from the sea. Richmond was on the main inland line of operation for the enemy, barely some 80 miles from Washington, DC; far worse, Virginia was everywhere penetrated by deep waters and rivers, one of which, the James River, would become what the Tago river had been for Napoleon during the peninsular campaign in Spain: the lethal wound through which the overwhelming naval power of the enemy would mortally affect the terrestrial one.

Indeed, the James became something far more deadly than the Tago, since in its case the wound almost reached the very heart of the Confederacy.

Yet it was almost impossible to resist the force of attraction of the Virginian magnet; home of Presidents, mother state of George Washington, Thomas Jefferson, Patrick Henry and John Marshall, Virginia was a symbol, indeed a banner for the whole South.

Nevertheless, there was some opposition to the transfer; only on May 21, 1861 did President Davis inform Congress by special message that the bill shifting the capital to Richmond had been signed. The President then left Montgomery and went to Virginia.

Mallory departed from Montgomery on May 31 and reached Richmond on June 3, tormented by burning attacks of gout; there he established his office (and, indeed, the whole Navy Department) on the second floor of a brick building facing Capitol Square between Franklin and Main Streets (with the entrance on Ninth). This building, which does not survive today, had been the seat of the Mechanics Institute and was now allocated to the military Departments of the Southern Confederacy.

Captain John K Mitchell commanded naval forces at the battle below New Orleans, April 1862. He was later the chief of the Bureau of Orders and Details 1862-4 and afterwards commanded the James River Squadron 1864-5. (Scharf, *Confederate States Navy*)

President Davis, Secretary Memminger and the Department of State had their seats not far away in a handsome stone building facing Capitol Square from the south, which had been the old Custom House (and is now, fairly extended with new wings, the seat of the Main Post Office of Richmond).

From his office Mallory would lead – for four dramatic years – the naval effort of the Confederacy; there he set immediately to work to 'launch' the Navy.

Starting with the nightmarish problem of money, Mallory asked immediately that $2m be sent to Great Britain, to cover the costs of ten gunboats for coastal defense, either to be bought or built anew. Yet the Secretary of the Treasury had not such money at hand and Mallory had to content himself by sending $600,000; $400,000 in letters of change on London and $200,000 credited by the banker and businessman George Alfred Trenholm, from Charleston, South Carolina, on his firm in Liverpool: Fraser, Trenholm & Co. This last sum was got only through the patriotism of Alfred Trenholm who supported the operation with his own money.

What also contributed to the troubles of the Navy Department was the inflation which soon became ruinous. Unwilling (or unable) to finance the war effort by means of taxation, the Confederate Government soon made recourse to loans (which was still the best way) and to printing more and more notes, which was the way to economic disaster. This, in time, would have dire consequences for the Confederate Navy: steadily increasing inflation rendered valueless any estimate, raised the cost of foreign exchange to unbelievable peaks, and hindered and disturbed the acquisition and building of ships.

Through the whole life of the Confederacy, Secretary Mallory had to contend with such problems, which absorbed much energy and time, which would have been far better spent by fighting against the enemy.

The state navies

Buying and building were indispensable, because the Confederate Navy received very little, if anything, from the short-lived state Navies.

South Carolina, the first state to secede, had soon to take good note that its coastal population was seriously scared by the expected danger from the sea and wanted to be protected. This attitude is revealing: from the very heyday of 'Southern

Louisiana State Navy Gunboat *Governor Moore*. (*Battles & Leaders*)

independence' the sea was instinctively felt by people as sinister and threatening.

The Legislature tried to relieve such concerns by creating a so-called 'Coastal Police' appropriating for this $150,000. Governor Pickens, therefore, acted quickly by buying three small screw-propeller steamers to be based at Charleston, Beaufort and Georgetown and ordering Army officers to make sweeping inspections and provide for a wholesale reinforcement of shoreline fortifications, another revealing symptom of the forthcoming war of land against sea.

All in all, the South Carolina Navy was a poor enterprise. Despite being put under the orders of old and experienced Captain Duncan N Ingraham, it was pitifully small, being composed of only the old sailing revenue cutter *Aiken*, one gun; tug *James Gray* (re-christened *Lady Davis*), a couple of small sailing-boats, formerly in the Lighthouse Service, and three little steamers (*Catawba*, *Gordon* and *Seabrook*), each with a small-caliber gun and fitted out haphazardly.

Between January 8 and 11, 1861, Mississippi, Florida and Alabama seceded. The first one gave up from the very beginning any idea of building a state Navy, instead, entering resolutely the way of 'land against sea', Mississippians occupied Ship Island, off Biloxi in the Gulf of Mexico, and put some heavy guns on the hills of Vicksburg.

This occupation soon came to nothing. Even if Ship Island had a definite strategic importance (well understood, in time, by Pierre le Moyne d'Iberville, the founder of the French empire in Louisiana who christened it the *Ile du Mouillage*), the Mississippians were unable to defend it, essentially because they had no naval force of any kind. So, in spite of the excellent fortifications built there by the Confederacy, the island had to be abandoned.

As for the big guns at Vicksburg, the consequences were worse. The news that the Mississippians had placed batteries dominating (and, in fact, closing) the great river, started a general alarm and violent protest among the Midwestern states which considered the free navigation along the Mississippi as vital to them. Since the Midwest – primarily agrarian – had a long tradition of political alliance with the South, broken down only recently by the rise of the free-soilers movement, anything which might hurt its susceptibility should have been spared: so the initiative of the Mississippians contributed surely to push Midwesterners more and more toward the side of the Union.

The state of Florida had one of the only two navy yards captured by the South: Pensacola. Still, it was a small gain, as Pensacola was more of a coaling and repairing station than a fully-fledged navy yard . Worse, Pensacola Harbor was blocked by a Union presidium on Santa Rosa Island, supported by US war vessels. The only ship the Floridians were able to seize was a small schooner of the Coast Survey and the wreck of the unfinished ship *Fulton*.

Alabama, which had seized the forts that protected the strategically important Mobile Bay, acquired a revenue cutter and a tug of the Lighthouse Service: almost nothing.

Possibly the most significant was the Georgia Navy. Georgia, 'the Empire State of the South' seceded on January 19. Six days later the decision was taken to buy or build three steamers; yet only two were acquired: the sidewheeler *Savannah*, 406 tons displacement and armed with one 32pdr, and another sidewheeler, the *Huntress*, bought in New York, 500 tons. At any rate, Georgia did not lack experienced officers: old and respected Captain Josiah Tattnall was commissioned Flag Officer in command of the small naval force.

Louisiana did not manage to put together more than two revenue cutters, yet the important forts that protected New Orleans were promptly seized. Texas, the last Southern state to join the early secession on February 1, had to content itself with a single revenue cutter.

Captain Beverly Kennon, Louisiana State Navy. Commander of *Governor Moore*. (*Battles and Leaders*)

When two more coastal states, Virginia and North Carolina, joined the Confederacy, they too were unable to contribute anything more than a handful of small vessels. Virginia, in particular, seized two passenger steamers, later to be transformed into the Confederate gunboats *Patrick Henry* and *Jamestown*, and the tug *Teaser*; North Carolina gave the Confederacy four little vessels, each with a small gun.

Luckily, the Virginia Militia had seized the extremely important Gosport Navy Yard, at Norfolk. The Union sailors put the buildings and the ships inside to the torch before abandoning the navy yard ; yet the fuze applied to the explosive charge intended to blow up the dry dock did not burn and the large dock fell intact into Confederate hands. In time it would permit the South to build and launch its first ironclad.[3]

All in all, the few state Navies put together no more than a dozen of small auxiliary warships with some 12 to 20 guns – not even the armament of a single US sloop of war.

To sum up, the Confederate Navy did not receive from the Southern states any significant naval force: it might be concluded that only the relative lack of preparation of the Union Navy and the consequent slowness of the Federal Authorities to act, saved the Southern state Navies from being swept away at a single stroke.

The war begins

What, instead, the seceded states did successfully was a twofold action: first, they promptly seized the numerous fortifications (with some exceptions) built along the coast and at the mouths of rivers by the US Government; secondly, they started, more or less immediately, the building of new forts, earthworks and shore batteries to complete that almost impregnable line which would in the end contribute to protect the heartland of the Confederacy from invasion by sea.

So, in fact, without any discussion or decisions from above, the Confederate naval way of war took from the start the shape of the fight of land against sea, *mer contre terre*, to quote the keen judgement of the French Admiral Lepotier.[4] This goes a long way to show how the Confederates 'felt' almost instinctively the sea as a mortal threat to their country and acted in consequence.

Indeed, the American Civil War in its naval aspect was certainly the first conflict between major powers in which one (in this case, the Union) possessed, from the very beginning, an almost total command of the sea. This is to be always kept in mind, if one wants to understand the naval strategy and operations of the Civil War.

Yet the Confederacy – and its Secretary of the Navy – were by no means cowed by such a grim situation. Instead, the Secretary decided to make the most of the situation. And there were numerous opportunities to be seized by the Confederate Navy.

First of all, the formidable naval power of the Union was still in big part only potential. On paper, the US Navy was intimidating: 90 vessels, of which 40 were steamers (and, some of them, technically up-to-date). Yet the 50 sailers were obsolete, to be used mainly as floating batteries; 16 steamers were either docked for repairs, or still being built. This reduced the ships ready for duty to 24, of which 19 were scattered all over the world, from the Mediterranean to Brazil, the East Indies and Japan.

So, it was clear that the naval war machine of the Union need-

South Carolina State Navy Gunboat *Marion.*
(*Harper's Weekly*)

ed some time to display its full strength: an advantage – if marginal – for Secretary Mallory's plans.

In the second place, the infant Confederate Navy had no burden of old, obsolete ships, so that it could start immediately by building the most advanced and modern war vessels. (Or try to do it: the backwardness and the limitations of the Southern industrial infrastructure would be a formidable obstacle along the way.)

Confederate naval strategy in its evolution will be examined later in this book, but it is worth stressing that, at the beginning of the naval war, Secretary Mallory took a momentous decision that would turn out to be a true stroke of genius: to play the trump card of technical surprise against the somewhat old-fashioned Union Navy. Since the Confederacy would – obviously – be able to buy or to build only a limited number of ships, those should be the most modern afloat: ironclads, armed with rifled guns capable of firing armour-piercing projectiles.

Mallory was fully aware of the formidable progress in the field of ordnance and shipbuilding. Rifled guns were not yet adopted by the world's navies; as far as ironclads were concerned, they were either old-fashioned vessels with some protection, considered as complementing a fleet, and not its backbone, or heavy, almost

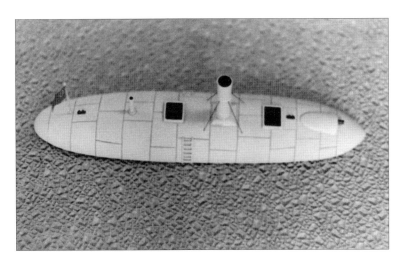

CSS *Manassas*, a model of the first ironclad to see action in the Civil War at Head of Passes, Mississippi River, October 12, 1861 (Robert Holcombe)

immovable floating batteries, intended mainly to shell land fortifications from the sea.

Such had been the French floating batteries like the *Lave*, *Tonnante* and *Dévastation*, as well as their British kin, used successfully to shell and reduce the Russian forts of Kinburn on the Black Sea. On the other hand, the ironclad steam frigates, like the *Gloire* and her followers, adopted by the French Imperial Navy thanks to the genius of Naval Constructor Stanislas Charles Henri Dupuy

CSS *Milledgeville*, a model of a typical late-war ironclad with shortened casemate and extra armour. (WMCWNH)

de Lôme, and the *Warrior* and similar ones in the Royal Navy, were certainly, in a sense, modern revolutionary ships: yet they still had full sailing rigs, and were not intended (very much because of the blindness of politicians and naval chiefs) to be the backbone of the fleets.

Mallory's dramatic purpose was to fight wood with iron. In other words, the ironclad warship was intended to be the 'technical surprise' which would confound and frustrate the enemy. True, at least initially, the wonderful intuition of Mallory was wrapped in a dangerous illusion: that the technical surprise of the ironclad would not only enable the Confederates to meet the challenge of the enemy, but also to field what was supposed to be the 'ultimate weapon', capable of winning the war at a single stroke. In time the able Secretary would understand the limits and the true possibility of ironclads and use them to the best effect; also that 'ultimate weapons' do not exist, because the enemy was soon able to build his own ironclads.

The second surprise card which Mallory intended to play from the beginning of hostilities was that of light, fast cruisers, equipped by the Navy and manned by naval personnel, unleashed on the high seas to attack and destroy enemy commercial shipping. This would astonish a world where, after the Paris Declaration outlawing privateering,[5] everybody was under the illusion that the war on maritime trade was no longer possible or rewarding.

Meanwhile the Secretary was undertaking the adoption of rifled guns, previously unused in naval warfare, on a wide scale, yet this was not the most deadly weapon he was envisioning.

Since the beginning of naval warfare, men had sought the means of striking enemy vessels under the waterline. Such a blow would be a fatal one; yet the obstacles along the way were

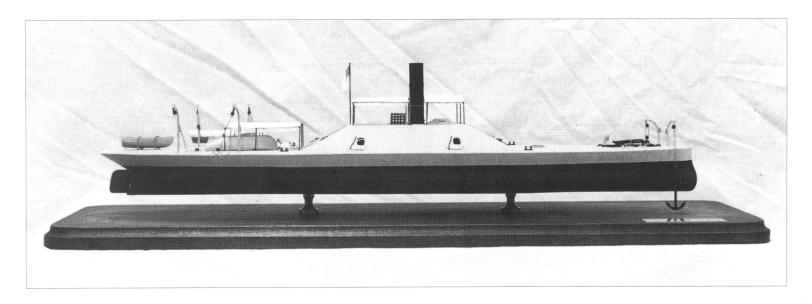

tremendous. It was only at the end of the eighteenth century that the Americans David Bushnell and Robert Fulton were able to develop and experiment with submarine boats. At the same time the state of explosive devices drew both scientists and naval men toward the less complicated and cheaper mine warfare. The invention of the electrical battery by Alessandro Volta as well as the progress in chemical devices helped to solve the problem of initiating explosions.

Like the ironclad warship and the rifled gun, mines (then called 'torpedoes') were by no means invented by the Confederates; they had already been utilized here and there: yet 'thanks to the progress of technology, as well as to the ingenuity of their scientists...'[6] they were able to use such weapons on a scale never before seen in naval war.

When the war started, Mallory was already working on his new, surprise weapons. In the field of commerce raiding he, as a realist, moved along two ways: to have some fast cruisers built in Europe and, meanwhile, to launch at least one from Confederate seaports. The same approach was followed for ironclad vessels.

The missions to Europe were entrusted to two men, one to procure cruisers, the other ironclads. As frequently happens in human affairs, the first one was a near genius; the second, in the main a failure.

The first to move was Lieutenant Commander James D Bulloch. By May 9, 1861, he had received from Secretary Mallory a letter of instruction, ordering him to proceed to Europe, there to get in touch with the firm of Fraser, Trenholm and Co (the British Agency of George A Trenholm) to receive the money sent by the Department in order to buy or to order two fast cruisers

7-inch Brooke rifle model on a shifting pivot carriage, rigged as it would appear with an ironclad's casemate. (WMCWNH)

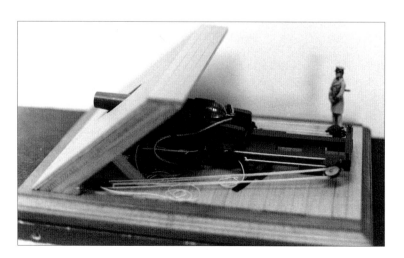

for commerce destroying. Bulloch, without knowing it, was a follower of Napoleon's maxim: 'I might lose a battle, but I never lose a minute', and started immediately by the night train to Louisville, Kentucky. There he carefully destroyed any compromising papers, then, since 'neutral' Kentucky had both borders wide open, passed into Union territory and proceeded to Detroit, observing everywhere active preparations for war. From Detroit he crossed into Canada, went to Montreal by rail and there embarked on the passenger steamer *North American*, landing in Liverpool on June 3. Thus began the incredible enterprise which would carry the Confederate cruisers *Florida* and *Alabama* (and later the *Shenandoah*) to their fantastic careers over the oceans of the world.

Secretary Mallory's other European envoy was Lieutenant Commander James H North, who received the task of buying – or ordering – an ironclad war vessel. Unlike Bulloch, North lacked energy and initiative, and was a rather narrow-minded man. His mission was a failure, and, in the end, Bulloch had also to tackle the problem of ironclads. But that is another story.

Yet at the beginning the Confederacy had none of the powerful ships projected by Mallory. To patch up some naval defense, small squadrons of little, improvised gunboats were brought together and entrusted to able naval officers. The forts, earthworks and coastal batteries were initially armed with some of the big guns found at the Norfolk Navy Yard when it was captured by the Confederates. These (about 1,000) were in the main old smoothbores, almost obsolete; yet, Commander A B Fairfax, CSN, Ordnance Officer at Norfolk, succeeded in rifling some of them, making them acceptable for the time being.

Unfortunately, these guns would soon prove ineffective: when, on August 29, 1861, a Union Squadron commanded by Commodore Silas H Stringham appeared off Hatteras Inlet, North Carolina, the guns of Confederate Forts Hatteras and Clark proved no match for the powerful ordnance on board the Federal ships and after a heavy bombardment the forts had to surrender. The same occurred to Forts Walker and Beauregard at Port Royal, South Carolina, attacked on November 5 by a Union Squadron under Flag Officer Samuel F Du Pont; they too, unable to withstand the Federal fire, had to raise the white flag. Only when the new rifled cannons, requested by Mallory, took over coast defense, would Confederate fortifications become almost impregnable.

Summing up, one may say that, in the main, the initial part of the naval war – during 1861 – proved almost a disaster for the Confederate Navy and, indeed, for the Confederacy itself.

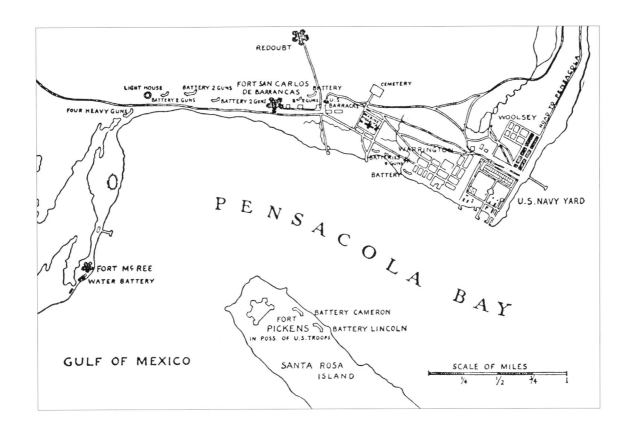

W̲arrington Navy Yard, Pensacola, Florida. (*Battles & Leaders*)

Yet, if one considers that the South had to negotiate that dangerous period when the Union dominated the seas with almost no opposition, managing to survive until the new deadly weapons envisaged by Secretary Mallory were ready to enter the struggle, then one might conclude that the action of building improvised forts armed with improvised guns and protected by improvised obstructions and improvised small gunboats, had indeed some success. The Confederacy survived and the CS Navy, too, survived with serious – but by no means fatal – wounds. And in the following spring some of the new weapons were ready and the aspect of naval warfare changed.

Indeed, one might even argue that it was not so much the CS Navy that succeeded in surviving that lethal period, it was the Union Navy which, in spite of its spectacular successes, was not able to exploit its tremendous advantage, striking a mortal blow to the Confederacy by a fully-fledged invasion by the sea. Yet, whoever makes such an observation, would forget that amphibious strategy had not yet been developed. The keen minds of the Union Navy chiefs, mainly that of 'Captain' Gustavus Vasa Fox and the members of the Blockade Board, would soon 'invent' this kind of deadly warfare which would be used on a large scale against the Confederacy and, in time, bring the US armed forces to such striking victories as were achieved in World War Two and in Korea; and this 'invention' sprang from the experiences of Stringham's and Du Pont's expeditions. In other words, as the Confederacy would soon discover, new weapons and new kinds of warfare do not rise suddenly; they require time and thought.

Unfortunately for the Union Navy, when the planned amphibious operations would at last be ready to start in full, the Confederate Navy would be ready to meet them and – with the exception of New Orleans – would stop, if not always defeat them.

The Confederate States and the world

Whereas Mallory was planning his revolutionary naval strategy and his futuristic weapons, the President of the Confederacy, as well as Prseident Lincoln, had started the war at sea with two acts worthy of a past – and well dead – era.

First, Confederate President Jefferson Davis, in order to

answer Lincoln's Proclamation of April 15 which declared the existence in the South of a 'state of rebellion' calling forth 75,000 militia to suppress it, invited by proclamation on April 19, anybody who wanted to arm and equip private vessels to raid Union commerce, to apply for Letters of Marque. The same day President Lincoln answered in his own turn by proclaiming the blockade of Southern coasts.

The proclamation of privateering proved clearly that President Davis had no knowledge of the recent evolution which was to change naval warfare for ever.

Let us examine this issue more closely. Privateering was an old-fashioned kind of war, centuries old. In the era of sailing ships (when the oceans were, so to say, 'wider', communications slow and distances difficult to encompass), in times of war, the stronger power usually declared a so-called 'paper blockade' reserving for itself the right of making it effective where and when it was deemed necessary. In the unending conflict between Great Britain and France, for example, it was all but impossible for the Royal Navy to keep a permanent array of warships along all the French coasts. Sailing ships were totally dependent on winds and they had normally to keep clear of enemy coasts where they risked being lost in dangerous gales. Yet British ships reserved to themselves the right to stop on the high seas any merchant vessel and to search it for contraband.

The blockaded power (usually France, but also Spain, Portugal, even the United States) reacted by launching a swarm of privateers to prey on the British freighters. The British, in turn, did not refrain from privateering: in Halifax, Nova Scotia, English privateers had their warehouses, even a bank for the profits of their 'honest' toil.

Privateers, as the word suggests, were privately-owned vessels, who received Letters of Marque from a legitimate government. They had to conduct their operations according to international rules, were enabled to capture only enemy shipping or goods and, in such cases, they had to place on board the captured vessel a prize crew and send it to a friendly or neutral port where a Prize Court would judge the capture. If the ship (or the cargo) seized was condemned, the privateer was authorized to sell it at auction and pocket the prize money.

Privateering was an institution characteristic of an era of immense seas and difficult communications. Now the tremendous increase in population, trade and merchant shipping, as well as the advent of the steam engine and the improvement in ship speed, had, so to speak, made the world 'narrow'. Since 1840, when

Samuel Cunard had established his transatlantic line, speedy and luxurious packet steamers crossed the Atlantic; in 1858 the first transatlantic cable had been laid, even if with little success. Economic interests formed a tight network all around the world. It was now virtually impossible to conduct privateering without hurting the interests of a non-belligerent.

Therefore in 1856, after the Crimean War, seven European naval powers (Great Britain, France, Russia, Austria, Prussia, Turkey and Sardinia) meeting in Paris, signed a Declaration intended to regularize naval warfare. Under it, privateering was outlawed, as well as paper blockade. Indeed, the Declaration of Paris established that any blockade, to be acknowledge and accepted by neutrals, must be 'effective', that is, kept by means of a continuous line of warships all along the enemy coast.

The United States, invited to sign the Declaration, refused to do so unless the so called 'Marcy Amendment' (from the name of the Secretary of State) was added. This Amendment would have exempted from seizure any kind of goods, not contraband, even if they belonged to enemy powers. In this way naval war would have been virtually limited to warships and any action against enemy commerce would be outlawed.

Many neutrals received the Marcy Amendment with favour, but not, of course, the main signatories of the Declaration. Therefore the United States refused to sign.

Now the major maritime powers, Great Britain and France, were presented with two acts violating the Declaration of Paris: the launching of a fully-fledged privateer war from one side, and a blockade (which looked a 'paper' one) from the other. In effect the two American Presidents were toying with fire: it was true that the United States had not signed the Declaration; yet Great Britain and France did sign it, and to incur their wrath looked a very risky business indeed.

The initiative by President Davis was quelled rather quickly and easily. To conduct their venture, privateers needed to be accepted into neutral ports, as the Confederate ones were soon blockaded. Yet neutrals, according to the principles established in Paris, closed their ports to Southern privateers who, consequently, had to give up their short-lived activity.

On his side, the US Secretary of State William H Seward, now sent in an application from the United States to sign the

CSS *Nashville* **at Southampton. First Confederate warship to visit European waters.** (*Harper's Weekly*)

THE REISSUE OF

HARPER'S WEEKLY.
A
JOURNAL OF CIVILIZATION.

VOL. VI.—No. 268.]   NEW YORK, SATURDAY, FEBRUARY 15, 1862.   [SINGLE COPIES SIX CENTS.
[$2.50 PER YEAR IN ADVANCE.

Entered according to Act of Congress, in the Year 1862, by Harper & Brothers, in the Clerk's Office of the District Court for the Southern District of New York.

The "Dauntless."   The "Moulton."   The "Nashville" in Dock.   The "Tuscarora."

THE "NASHVILLE" AND "TUSCARORA" AT SOUTHAMPTON, ENGLAND.—[SEE PAGE 107.]

Declaration of Paris. Yet, since President Lincoln had threatened to hang Confederate privateers as pirates, the maritime powers, which, by supporting such an action, risked being dragged into the war against the South, flatly refused. The issue was resolved by President Davis who threatened to hang as many Union prisoners as were the privateers eventually executed by the Union authorities. Therefore the North resigned itself to grant privateers the status of prisoners of war.

More serious and ominous was the question of blockade. Since the Union Government never did recognize the Southern Confederacy as an effective power (even if only *de facto*), it considered that blockading it was, at best, a dubious issue. Indeed, it seems impossible to blockade a non-existent country. In such a case, a Government compelled to face an insurrection usually resorts to closing the rebel ports. Yet here another question arose: was it possible to declare closed (and to effectively close) any port along a coast 3,550 nautical miles in length? Obviously not. The British Foreign Office even made a discrete step in Washington to persuade the Union authorities that such a 'closing up' was impossible, therefore unacceptable.

So, blockade it had to be. The Union Government declared the blockade, basing its decision on the need to make a reprisal against privateering. Yet almost immediately, Her Majesty's Government issued a proclamation of neutrality dated May 14, 1861, which acknowledged the existence of the Confederate States as a *de facto* Government, yet without establishing any diplomatic relations with them. France (which had been contacted by British authorities, so that the two maritime powers would act in concert) followed suit with an analogous declaration by the Imperial Government. As a matter of fact, the French Foreign Minister, Antoine Edouard Thouvenel, had already informed the Union Government of its intention through the Ambassador.

The uproar in the North was immediate: Great Britain (yet not France) was branded as a double dealer, accomplice of the South, supporter of the rebellion, etc.

Nevertheless, the line followed by the two major maritime powers was absolutely logical, prudent and, indeed, more favourable to the North than to the South. Before acting, the British Foreign Minister, Earl Russell, had carefully consulted the Attorney General, whose opinion had been very clear: had the North tried to establish one-sidedly a blockade against the South, that is, against a 'non-existent' power, Great Britain would have been unable to acknowledge it, risking being dragged into the war, this time on the Southern side. The only way out was to reconnoi-

ter the Southern Confederacy, albeit only for blockade purposes, so that it would be possible to acknowledge the blockade *provided* that it conformed to the principles of the Declaration of Paris, or was an effective and not a paper one. On their side, the Confederates had to give up privateering. In other words, the acknowledgment of the Confederacy as a *de facto* power derived solely from the need to accept the Northern blockade as a legal one, so as to avert the danger of a general conflict.

The conclusions to be drawn from all this were appalling and ominous. Twice Great Britain and France had seen opening in front of them the awful chasm of a general war. Indeed, such was now the political and economic entanglement of the world that mankind in those anxious days of May 1861 ran the risk of a world war fifty-three years ahead of its time.

At any rate, the British proclamation of neutrality said more. It was intended to forbid any mixing up of British subjects in the American Civil War; yet it did so without specifying the rules but making reference to an Act of some thirty years before, the Foreign Enlistment Act. This in time would be the source of much misunderstanding between Great Britain and the United States and, in the end, turn into damage for the Southern cause as far as Confederate shipbuilding in Great Britain was concerned.

As a matter of fact, the Foreign Enlistment Act was a document of the past, approved by the British Parliament in 1819 to help to solve old problems, now all but dead. Its aim had been to stop British citizens from entangling themselves in the several insurrections of Latin American colonies against Spain, then allied to Great Britain.[7] As such, the Act was supposed to be a purely 'municipal' law, with no international character. Inasmuch it was far from clear. As far as warships were concerned, the Act asserted that no one was permitted to '...equip, furnish, fit out or arm... any ship or vessel... that... shall be employed in the service of any foreign Prince'.[8]

Of course, the Act did not specify what characterized a ship as a man-of-war: therefore, the wily Bulloch (who had hired a prominent British lawyer) requested that no weapon (not even a penknife) would be on board the ships he was having built in Great Britain.

Now, the activity of both Confederate and Federal agents in Great Britain, intended to secure any kind of weaponry, was such that the Government was soon compelled to scrutinize more attentively the Foreign Enlistment Act in order to establish once and for all whether it could or could not be considered as a document of international law. In the first case (municipal law only) the Government had the right of enforcing (or not enforcing) it according only to its needs and judgment; yet in the second case (international law) the Act would become binding and its application compulsory.

In the end, this was the final interpretation, which rebounded against the Confederate Navy (the seizure of the so-called Laird rams), whereas the Union continued to buy all kinds of weapon and ammunition in Great Britain, practically without hindrance.

The fact was (as correctly pointed out by Wilbur D Jones[9]) that there was another Act which the Government chose not to enforce: the Customs Consolidation Act. According to it, several goods '...may, by proclamation or Order in Council, be prohibited... to be exported', and the Act listed the following items: 'arms, ammunition & gunpowder, military & naval stores & any articles which Her Majesty shall judge capable of being converted into... military or naval stores.'

This Act gave to Her Majesty's Government ample discretion to enforce or not to enforce its provisions; and the British chose not to enforce it, mainly not to hurt the enormous economic interests involved in the production and marketing of weaponry and military stores.

Yet the Customs Consolidation Act did not concern ships or vessels of any kind: those fell under the umbrella of the Foreign Enlistment Act, when the British Government (also under the menacing pressures of the US authorities) decided to consider it as international law.

So Confederate shipbuilding in Great Britain would in time be stopped and the ships seized; whereas the Federal Government (which did not need ships) was able to buy weapons and ammunitions *en masse*. As a matter of fact, the seizure of Confederate ships took place after the Southern defeats at Gettysburg and Vicksburg and the open threat of war from the Union Ambassador to Britain, Charles Francis Adams. As usual God (and the British Government) favoured the biggest battalions.

Nor did British subjects refrain from making money through the blockade. Soon special British firms organized companies for maritime trade through blockade-running. Even special ships were built for the purpose: low, speedy, with powerful engines fuelled by the best coal which made little smoke; they soon yielded handsome profits. It was calculated that one such ship, which was lost after only eight trips, nevertheless yielded a profit of 700 per cent!

Of course, British blockade-runners were by no means concerned with the needs of the beleaguered Confederacy: only with their profits. So, they filled their holds with products which were light, took but little space, could command high prices and, should a Union shell reach the hold, did not risk blowing up the ship. So, they would carry Champagne, silks, perfumes, etc. All things which were of no use to the Confederate war effort and drained the Confederacy of its limited resources.

To forestall such a situation, the Confederacy began to put afloat blockade-runners owned by several Government agencies, among which the Confederate Navy had a prominent part, mainly furnishing officers and crews, but also contributing its own blockade-runners. Among the best Southern naval officers who successfully practised blockade-running were John Newland Maffitt, Robert R Carter and John Wilkinson.

Even the Governor of North Carolina, Zebulon B Vance, purchased a fast ship which, renamed the *Advance*,[10] made many successful trips, so that North Carolina troops could be supplied with large quantities of clothing, shoes and weapons. Yet in the long run this created friction with the Navy Department, mainly over problems of fuel, always scarce.

The second initiative by the Confederacy solved the problem at source – albeit, too late. This bold policy amounted to no less than the nationalization of foreign trade. If the Confederacy was to survive, blockade-runners had to stop carrying useless luxuries and start bringing in weapons, ammunition and military stores which the Confederacy's poor industrial base could not turn out in quantities capable of competing with the gigantic and modern Northern industrial machine.

Therefore, on February 6 and March 5, 1864, Congress, under strong pressure from President Davis, approved two Acts forbidding any further imports of luxury goods and monopolizing, under control of the Confederacy, the exports of cotton, tobacco, sugar, molasses, rice and any military or naval store. Any blockade-runner, either coming in or departing, had to put half of its cargo space at the Government's disposition. Inside the Confederacy all cotton had to be sold to the authorities which put a military officer, Colonel Thomas L Bayne, in charge of buying it, with an appropriation of $20 million.

The results were immediate, and from that moment the Confederacy received, through blockade-running, almost all the military supplies needed to wage war.

As for foreign relations, the second country with which the CS Navy established close relation was France. The Imperial Government was conducting a complicated and risky policy of military intervention in Mexico; the Federal Government and President Lincoln were resolutely against such a policy, therefore the French Government nurtured the idea of assuaging the South which, however, was by no means favourable either.

Yet from this, in part, rose the attempt by the Confederate Navy to build ironclads in France; but this is another story and will be discussed elsewhere in this book. Suffice it to say that the attitude of Napoleon III toward the Southern cause was not motivated only by his involvement in Mexico. The Emperor was a complicated man, and – maybe as an old-time liberal – felt a sympathy toward peoples struggling for their independence. Such feelings were irrational ones, and were always looked at with suspicion by his collaborators who tried to bring him back to the ground of sound policy.

At any rate, the Confederacy succeeded in time in organizing in Paris what should have become their naval Command in European waters, with Commodore Samuel Barron as Flag Officer at Sea. The organization was complete, with even a board to examine midshipmen. Unfortunately, the fleet Barron should have commanded never materialized, as both the British and French-built ironclads were in the end seized, with the exception of the *Stonewall*, which was clearly a case of too little, too late.

Be that as it may, the only European major power which sided resolutely with the North was Imperial Russia. Significantly, in 1863, when the Czarist generals cruelly crushed the Polish insurrection, the North sided with Russia, whereas the South was wholeheartedly on the Polish side. The Russians even sent their naval squadrons to visit Union seaports in New York and San Francisco, there to be ready to operate against British and French Navies, if a general war would explode from the Polish question. Yet this was not communicated to the Federal authorities. No general war came for the time being: Europe and the world had to wait another fifty years.

At any rate, nothing came for the Confederacy from the international stage: no foreign recognition, no substantial help. The North was too strong, and nobody wanted to get entangled in the American conflict. The Confederate Navy Department exploited to its best the possibilities and the openings offered by the European theatre: the building and putting afloat of commerce-destroying cruisers was in itself a success, mainly achieved by that extraordinary man, James D Bulloch and a courageous handful of others.

A second, deadly weapon wielded by the Union against the South was war propaganda. In spite of the highest capabilities of Henry Hotze, Confederate war propagandist in Europe, the South was fighting a losing battle: the stain of slavery which the North was able to rivet upon the Confederacy proved in the end successful in persuading European public opinion to keep clear of the Southern cause.

Professor Raimondo Luraghi

Chapter Two

THE CONFEDERATE STATES NAVY DEPARTMENT

On April 12, 1861, when the opening shots of the Civil War boomed across the harbor of Charleston, South Carolina, the Confederate States of America had only a paper navy, the Confederate States Navy having existed for less than two months. The Confederate Congress initially acted on February 14, 1861, by authorizing a 'Committee on Naval Affairs.' Six days later, on February 20, they created the Navy Department and on the following day, seven weeks before the opening hostilities, President Jefferson Davis appointed Stephen Russell Mallory to head the fledgling Department. Upon taking office Mallory not only faced the prospect of building a navy from the ground up, but he would have to prepare it for immediate warfare with the United States. Mallory began his term on an unequal footing with his Union counterpart Gideon Welles because he not only had to administer a navy, but he also had to create one. One of Mallory's contemporaries summed up the Secretary's plight by writing that he was 'like a chieftain without a clan, or an artisan without tools of his art'.[1]

To achieve success Mallory would have to forge a naval force that could accomplish three major tasks. First, he would have to find a way to break or neutralize a Union naval blockade. He would eventually have some success by building blockade-runners abroad and by contracting space on board British-owned steamers that could run the blockade. Secondly, he would need to defend the South's coastal waters, keep the Southern ports open, and its interior waterways clear of Union naval vessels. The Confederate Navy enjoyed limited success in denying the Union Navy control of these important waterways by converting steamers and by building gunboats, torpedo boats and ironclads. Last, he would be

Stephen R Mallory, Secretary of the Navy. (Naval Historical Division)

compelled to find a way to interrupt the North's shipping and disrupt the Northern economy. He again enjoyed partial success by building and converting vessels to attack the North's seaborne commerce.

Without the semblance of a navy each one of these tasks would be difficult to overcome or implement even under the best circumstances and, Mallory faced many handicaps. The Southern coast stretched thousands of miles and contained 189 harbors, inlets and rivers. Each of these entrances offered the Union Navy access to the Southern states. The dearth of natural and maritime resources that the South possessed compounded the prospects of success. The Southern states had many small vessels and riverboats but few large steamers. It had only two large naval shipyards, both pre-war navy yards that state troops had captured in the early weeks of the war. The South also lacked a developed industrial infrastructure. Skilled mechanics, managers and labourers were not much more numerous than the few rolling mills and machine shops scattered about the region. The South had only a single industrial site that could boast of making a large marine engine. Equally as damaging, many of the raw materials needed to forge the Navy would be competitively sought by the Army. Other resources lay scattered about the South, were too limited, or under-developed transportation made them inaccessible.

The Confederate Congress might have made a difference, but throughout the war it remained stingy and never appropriated funds for the Navy to overcome these problems. In fact, the naval budget for 1861–2 was only about 4 per cent of the entire Confederate budget. The Union Navy for the same period received nearly 9 per cent of the Federal budget but it represented about three times more than the Confederate naval appropriations. In these appropriations for the Government departments the Confederate Congress granted only the executive mansion less money.[2]

The doctrine of states rights only made matters worse. This philosophy would cause the South's resources to be misdirected, hoarded, or wasted, thereby nullifying their benefit for the Confederacy as a whole. Mallory and the Department laboured to overcome these handicaps for four years.

President Davis's choice for his Secretary of the Navy is recognized by many historians as the best appointment of his entire cabinet. Mallory and Postmaster John Reagan were the only men specifically suited to their cabinet duties. In fact, Mallory was the only original cabinet member who brought prior experience to the job. Furthermore, Mallory remained in the cabinet during the entire war. As other men came and went Mallory continued to be one of Davis's most trusted friends and advisors.

President Davis had originally favoured Louisiana Congressman John Perkins for the post of Secretary of the Navy. In all likelihood Davis appointed the Key West, Florida, native not only for his experience and naval background but to give geographical balance to his cabinet. Ironically, the delegation from his home state of Florida raised the greatest opposition to his appointment. They felt that Mallory had not shown enough early enthusiasm for the secession movement and they also blamed him in part for the loss of the Pensacola Navy Yard and the capture of Fort Pickens.

Mallory brought a variety of knowledge and experience to the job. Born in Trinidad, Mallory lived briefly in Mobile, Alabama and New York before his parents settled in Key West. He had experience with small vessels and had commanded a longboat during the Seminole War. At the age of 19 he took the job as Collector of Customs in this booming port town, showing a great deal of initiative, and maintaining a routine of personal study for four years. Mallory, who could speak three languages, passed the bar in 1840, and began practicing Admiralty law in Key West. In 1851 he was elected to the Senator's seat from Florida and during his term as Senator he served on the Committee of Naval Affairs and became chairman of the Committee in 1855. While serving on this committee he actively strove to make the United States Navy larger and showed great interest in ship design, ordnance and innovation.[3]

Although his background did not necessarily prepare him for such a lofty post in the Confederate Government, Mallory was more than equal to the task. He seemed flattered by the appointment and began with confidence and zeal; nevertheless some of his contemporaries felt that he did not look the part of a statesman. Mary Chesnut thought Mallory was 'witty' and 'refined' but recounted that after a few glasses of wine he would confide highly personal stories to her guests. His rather plain round face masked his keen mind and his passion for learning, while his fondness for food and wine exacerbated his ruddy complexion.[4]

Mallory, more so than any other cabinet member, retained the confidence of the President during the entire war and enjoyed relatively little criticism from his peers because few of the Confederate leaders expected much from the Navy. Primarily because Jefferson Davis had little interest in naval affairs, Mallory ran the Department with minimal interference from the President. This allowed him free reign to co-ordinate all the activities of his subordinate bureau chiefs, and set policies, priorities and strategy. Davis's confidence in Mallory, however, did not keep the President from issuing orders directly to naval officers without passing them through the chain of command. For instance, in April 1862, Davis bypassed Mallory and issued direct orders to obstruct the Elizabeth River when he felt that Union forces threatened the Gosport Navy Yard.[5]

President Davis often exhibited his indifference to naval matters but usually showed his Naval Secretary courtesy and respect.

Mechanics Institute in Richmond, which housed the Navy and other government departments. The building was located on 9th Street, opposite Capitol Square. (*Richmond Dispatch*)

Davis's preoccupation with Army matters continually took precedence over those of the Navy. Davis often allowed his inner feelings or his exasperation for naval concerns to show. General Josiah Gorgas, chief of the Army Ordnance Bureau, wrote in his diary that Davis 'sneers continually at Mr. Mallory and his Navy, and is at no pains to conceal his opinions before the secretary.'[6]

Most of the members within the Confederate high command thought highly of Mallory. Judah P Benjamin, General Joseph E Johnston, and several congressmen remained close friends. There were others, however, who had an equally low opinion of the Secretary of the Navy. General Gorgas, one of Mallory's most outspoken critics, felt that the Secretary lacked 'earnestness and devotion to duty. He is too good company and too generally informed to be worth much at any one thing, tho' a man of undoubted ability.' While acknowledging Mallory's intelligence and talents Gorgas also felt that he was 'obnoxious.' Blockade-runner captain John Wilkinson, likewise did not have many compliments for Mallory. After the war he wrote that Mallory was 'incompetent.'[7]

The Navy Department staff

Civil War era staffs pale in comparison with the support personnel required by modern military organizations. The Confederate Navy's staff remained small throughout the war. Initially, the US custom-house in Richmond, Virginia, served as office space for the Department. The Navy's offices, however, were situated on the second floor because the Navy was not considered as important as the War Department. The staff had barely moved in when permanent offices were leased in the Mechanics Institute in Richmond. The staff included a chief clerk and a correspondence clerk who directly assisted Mallory in his daily administrative tasks. In addition, as many as five clerks and a messenger maintained the steady stream of directives and orders necessary to keep the Navy running smoothly. As the work of the Department grew, the Confederate Congress allowed Mallory and his bureau chiefs more clerical help.[8]

Mallory filled his days with meetings and corresponding with the various commands, bureaux and agents. At times he also went riding with President Davis to the battle front where he discussed policy and advised the President. Mallory's most important administrative assistant was Edward M Tidball of Winchester,

Edward M Tidball, Chief Clerk, CS Navy Department. Tidball, along with 2nd clerk Z P Moses, travelled extensively throughout the South during the first two years of the war negotiating contracts for warship construction. (Robert Manning Strozier Library, Florida State University)

Virginia. For about a dozen years before the war, Tidball served as a clerk in the United States Bureau of Ordnance and Hydrography. Tidball has been described by contemporaries as dapper, precise and orderly – a perfect combination for an office manager. Tidball did not perform the same role as an assistant Secretary of the Navy. He rarely signed any official correspondence and he was only infrequently mentioned in the letters. In 1863, Mallory added Midshipman Clarence Cary to his staff. Cary served as the Secretary's aide but seems to have acted more as

a social director. He spent his days in the office reading Union newspapers for intelligence information.[9]

The greatest single oversight in the Confederate naval organization was the lack of an assistant Secretary of the Navy. The Confederate Navy would have benefited by having another key administrator to help perform the Department's requisite and often demanding management tasks. Mallory would have profited by having someone who could have helped him to formulate plans and take care of some of the necessary political responsibilities. Due to this administrative oversight, Tidball's qualities were even more essential to the smooth running of the Department.

The bureaux

By an Act of March 16, 1861, the Confederate Congress provided the Navy Department with four bureaux. The four included: the Office of Ordnance and Hydrography, the Office of Orders and Detail, the Office of Provisions and Clothing, and the Office of Medicine and Surgery.[10] This organization would leave some of the bureaux with overlapping authority and sometimes with duties so diverse that the staffs would be hard pressed to fulfill their responsibilities. Gideon Welles of the Union Navy foresaw these very problems and by his recommendation an Act of Congress split his department from five bureaux into eight.

The most important of the Confederate Navy bureaux was the Office of Orders and Detail. Its principal job was to handle all the personnel issues, maintaining records of assignments, posts afloat and ashore, and duty stations. This office actively archived and maintained the records of all transfers, desertions, discharges and deaths. These records included the men's grades, their time in service, their duty stations, and the nature of their service either ashore or afloat. In addition to these tasks, the Office of Orders and Detail also handled courts martial and courts of inquiry. The functions of this department proved to be a marked improvement over that of the Union Navy's handling of these matters, where the officers applied direct to Gideon Welles for personnel actions and resolutions.[11]

The Office of Orders and Detail established the officer complement of ships and kept them filled with trained men. This office administered the paperwork for about 5,000 officers and men. The bureau had a position entitled 'register,' who kept a file on each unassigned officer as well as all the correspondence that

Navy' served as the legal foundation for general courts martial, summary courts martial and courts of inquiry in the Confederate Navy.[13]

The man who headed the Office of Orders and Detail was usually a senior officer in the service, and, because of this position, he often advised Mallory. This Confederate officer really had more authority than is suggested by the title. Without a formal position of assistant Secretary of the Navy, the chief of the bureau, in some ways served in a similar capacity. Due to the importance of the position and the almost daily interaction with Mallory, the chief of this bureau used this relationship to obtain an operational command. Franklin Buchanan, who commanded the *Virginia*, French Forrest, who commanded the James River Squadron, and John K Mitchell, who also became the commander of the James River Squadron, all held this post at one time during the war.[14]

Initially, matters of construction and repair and yards and docks fell under the Office of Ordnance and Hydrography. A naval reorganization in June and July 1863 gave the Office of Orders and Detail an unusual adjunct responsibility. At this time the bureau inherited, until the end of the war, the responsibility

Zalegman P Moses, 2nd Clerk, CS Navy Department. (Robert A Moses)

Captain Sidney Smith Lee, Gen. Robert E Lee's older brother, was in command of Orders and Detail at the war's end. (Library of Congress)

related to the officer's duty, including applications for service, charges or complaints lodged against him, reasons for leaving a previous service and reasons for declining service. Remarkably, despite all the paperwork that the office maintained, it functioned for most of the war with only one assistant officer, one chief clerk and one register. The office added two additional clerks in 1864.[12]

The Office of Orders and Detail did not attempt to break new ground in dealing with courts martial and courts of inquiry. When the Confederate Navy looked to establish a legal foundation for punishments for officers and men, it had to look no farther than the system used by the Union Navy. With minor revisions, 'An Act for the Better Government of the United States

A model of the CSS *Stonewall*, the only one of the European ironclads to reach Confederate hands. (WMCWNH)

for ship's equipment, the outfitting of ships, the management of the ropewalk at Petersburg, receiving ships and the naval stations. This included the management of the stock of stores, anchors, water, sails and masts, and fuel. The added logistical responsibilities thus basically paralleled portions of the duties of two of the US Navy's bureaux – Construction and Repair and Equipment and Recruiting. Despite the creation of the positions of Chief Constructor and Chief Engineer, the Office of Orders and Detail continued to handle coal and equipment matters with the exception of ordnance.[15]

The only industrial concern managed by the Department of Orders and Detail during the war was the ropewalk at Petersburg, Virginia. It began operation in January 1863, and made cotton rope, tarred rope and cordage for both Army, Navy and civilian uses. It was very profitable for the bureau, providing rope for the Navy at no cost.[16]

Originally both the Office of Ordnance and Hydrography and the Office of Provisions and Clothing handled the Navy's contracts for coal. The former stockpiled it and arranged for transportation to the field while the latter dealt direct with the mines to ship coal to the ordnance works. In the reorganization in the summer of 1863, the Office of Orders and Details took all responsibility. As a consequence all commanders, ashore and afloat, ordered coal through this office.[17] Despite the reorganization, the South's meagre resources could never meet the demands

and a shortage of coal plagued the Confederacy during the entire Civil War.

The Navy Department relied on the Army's Niter and Mining Bureau for the important strategic resources of niter, metals and coal. The Department shipped Alabama coal to its naval stations in Mobile, Savannah and Columbus. Coal from the Egypt mine in North Carolina travelled to Wilmington and Charleston, and Virginia area mines supplied the Navy's needs in Charlotte and Richmond.[18]

The Office of Ordnance and Hydrography had by far the greatest diversity of duties. Its plethora of responsibilities included supervision of manufacturing, design, purchasing, distribution and all other aspects of ammunition and guns. It set allowances for ordnance training activities, it recorded the performances of every gun in the Department and it passed this information, as necessary, to the Army. The Department further administered ordnance stores, navigational instruments and equipment, and charts. Additionally, the bureau also oversaw the construction and maintenance of docks and navy yards. Despite the numerous responsibilities of this bureau, all of the administrative matters were handled by an extremely small staff consisting of the chief of the bureau, one officer who acted as inspector of ordnance, one chief clerk, one clerk, one messenger, and one draftsman.[19]

The bureau had several separate divisions that had a great impact on the Confederate war effort. The Confederacy's mine warfare programme fell under the Office of Ordnance and Hydrography but the programme realistically operated as an independent division. Named the Torpedo Bureau, it was established in October 1862. It grew in importance as technology improved and these 'infernal' weapons became more reliable and deadly. Matthew Fontaine Maury spawned the creation of this division but it did not receive the early support of the Department. For some time Mallory remained sceptical that mines (or torpedoes as they were then known) could be used for defensive purposes. Maury initially began his work with the State of Virginia Ordnance Department which later transferred to Confederate Government control. In August 1861, after witnessing successful experiments, the Confederate Congress appointed Maury to oversee the mine's development. After developing a successful weapon, the programme stagnated because Maury would not approach Mallory for the funding to increase testing and development. The Secretary of the Navy, on the other hand, did not have enough personal interest in the weapons to initiate their widespread use, Mallory eventually realized the value of the weapons and gave his

CSS *Patrick Henry,* part of the James River squadron, served as the naval academy's school ship. (Ron Marlett)

support. Maury travelled to Europe on special service in late 1862, and his replacement, Lieutenant Hunter Davidson, oversaw the weapon's development into an extremely successful and technologically advanced state.

The Department established mine stations at Richmond, Wilmington, Charleston, Savannah and Mobile, and scattered smaller commands throughout the Confederacy. The Torpedo Bureau also employed inventors and artisans in Europe to assist in the development of advanced weapons. The success of the mine revolutionized naval warfare, enabled the Confederacy to thwart Union naval activity, and also gave Mallory and the Department some positive accomplishments to balance the numerous failures.

The Confederate naval school ship *Patrick Henry* also fell under the control of the Office of Ordnance and Hydrography. The school's superintendent Lieutenant William H Parker formerly taught seamanship at the US Naval Academy. Eighteen instructors taught approximately fifty midshipmen the necessary skills to develop them into officers for the Confederate Navy.[20]

One of the more important adjunct duties of the bureau and one not generally recognized was the maintenance of aids to navigation in the South. The Confederacy had begun the war with a Lighthouse Bureau under the control of the Treasury Department. The Treasury Secretary quickly picked Commander Raphael Semmes, who had held a similar position with the Federal Government, to head the bureau. Before Semmes could make any contribution as the head of the Lighthouse Board, the Navy Department tasked him with the more important duty of commanding the commerce raider CSS *Sumter.* Within months the Confederate lighthouse keepers began extinguishing the lights to prevent the Union vessels from benefiting from their beacons. In

Captain Duncan N Ingraham. Ingraham was the first officer to command the Office of Ordnance and Hydrography before transfer to Charleston. (Scharf, *Confederate States Navy*)

house on Smith's Island at the mouth of the Cape Fear River, and to erect some type of aid to navigation on the 60ft-high battery platform at New Inlet on the Cape Fear. Seventy men helped Wilkinson to carry out these functions until he left for another command afloat. While Wilkinson oversaw this office the tactics of blockade-runners improved and vessel casualties diminished. But the inexperienced assistants left to perform this job never managed to carry out the intentions of the Navy Department.[22]

The first officer in charge of the Office of Ordnance and Hydrography was Captain Duncan N Ingraham. In December 1861, Commander George Minor replaced him. Minor's assistant John M Brooke became the chief of the bureau in March 1863, and remained in this position until the end of the war. In 1861, he designed the Brooke rifle, one of the most successful innovations of the war. This heavy artillery piece was regarded as an equal to any that the Union produced. In the early summer of 1863, the Confederate Navy assumed control of the gun foundry at Selma, Alabama, to manufacture the rifled Brooke guns. Besides the Tredegar Iron Works this factory was the only other industrial site that manufactured large ordnance for the Confederacy.

The third bureau, the Office of Provisions and Clothing, handled all the tasks associated with providing food, clothing and the necessary stores and miscellaneous items required by naval personnel. Due to the interaction with contractors and the possibility of fraud, the business of the bureau had similar checks and balances to those the Union Navy found necessary to implement later in the war. The paymasters could not be involved with the purchase of supplies nor with any of the contracts of the Navy Department. Neither could they receive any gratuity for their services. These checks on the paymasters and the fact that they could be court martialed insured that the Confederate Navy was virtually free of corruption. Not a single paymaster was found guilty of fraud or default during the war.

The bureau managed a ration system that was similar to that used in the Union Navy. For most of the war the Confederate Navy had an abundance of food and even lent food to the Army. Commanding officers of ships and shore units approved requisitions prepared by the paymasters and assistant paymasters and forwarded them to the bureau. The relationship between the commanding officers and the paymasters was unique. The paymasters served as the local representative of the chief of the Office of Provisions and Clothing. Since the chief of the Bureau outranked all of the local commanding officers, the paymasters had the ability to change or reject a requisition made by the commanding

addition, lenses and sometimes even lighthouses were dismantled to prevent the Union forces from using them. The system of lights in the South lapsed into obscurity and inactivity until the Office of Ordnance and Hydrography felt a need to re-establish some system of lights in the South's major ports.[21]

In March 1864, the bureau assigned Lieutenant John Wilkinson to establish a system of lights, buoys and other aids to navigation in Wilmington, North Carolina. Wilkinson, who had years of experience on the Coast Survey, opened an office of the bureau with broad powers. He examined pilots and vessels, assigned pilots to blockade-runners, supervised steamers carrying Government cotton, established port regulations and even created a lifesaving service to save cargoes and men from stranded vessels. The Confederate Government instructed him to relight the light-

officer or the local commander. While this might have led to problems between the local commanders and the bureau's pay-masters, the system seemed to have worked well, with few or no difficulties.[23]

The Confederate pay branch had two ranks of commissioned officer: paymaster and assistant paymaster. All eleven paymasters appointed at the outbreak of the war had seen service in the United States Navy as pursers. These men served at the most important shore stations and on the major naval staffs. Not one of the appointed assistant paymasters, however, had had prior experience in naval service.[24]

Persons seeking a commission as an assistant paymaster had to be between 21 and 30 years old. The Department required these men to pass an examination before a board of three paymasters in order to show that they could keep the ship's books. In addition, the candidate had to submit letters of recommendation testifying to his good character. Both paymasters and assistant paymasters required bonding.[25]

A paymaster who had more than twelve years of service had equal rank with a commander, and one with less time ranked with a lieutenant. Promotion from an assistant paymaster to the rank of paymaster was by seniority. An assistant paymaster with over five years ranked below a lieutenant and one with less than five years was next after a master. A third grade of pay officer was clerk to a paymaster. Clerks served by appointment, not by a commission. Ranked equal to a midshipman, the paymaster's clerk had to be 18 years old, and received an appointment by the ship's captain upon the recommendation of the paymaster. This appointment could be terminated by the captain if the paymaster requested it.[26]

Civilians served as naval agents for the Office of Provisions and Clothing. These men purchased all the items required by the Navy Department from uniforms for the men to sundry items and fresh food. They made contracts direct with the manufacturers and suppliers of the goods and also late in the war established factories to supply the various needs of the Department. The naval agents also provided transportation for individuals under orders and dispersed money to pay for other travel claims.

Naval storehouses held the stores of the paymaster's department while the agents shipped much of the material direct to the several commands. The Department had three naval storehouses: one at Albany, Georgia, a second at Mobile, Alabama, and the most important one at Charlotte, North Carolina. Supply departments in the local areas supplied the commands, naval stations and yards with materials needed on a regular basis.

The Office of Provisions and Clothing did not oversee the purchase, storage, and delivery of all goods. The Office of Orders and Detail retained the authority to purchase and distribute rope, wood, coal and sails for vessels. In addition, the Office of Ordnance and Hydrography managed all the ordnance and navigational instruments. The Marine Corps and Office of Surgery also administered both the purchases and the distribution of the supplies needed by their own bureaux.[27]

The Chief of the Bureau, Paymaster John De Bree, had seen service in the United States Navy for 44 years before his appointment. He is reported to have been conservative and increasingly more dependent on Paymaster James A Semple, who moved to the office in Richmond after the destruction of the ironclad *Virginia*. Semple, a son-in-law of ex-President Tyler, had served in the United States Navy for seventeen years. Admired by everyone, he evidently carried the bureau by his extreme competence and his aggressive nature. In April 1864, Semple became the bureau chief and retained this position until the war's end. To perform the necessary administrative tasks to account for items, procure clothing, supplies and food, De Bree and Semple had only one chief clerk.[28]

Semple and De Bree organized the bureau to stockpile as much food and clothing as possible. In 1864, the bureau had about four to eight months supplies of the most important products stowed in the depots, naval stations and other storage sites in the South. The Navy also directed meat packing and set up clothing shops to make woollens, blankets and shoes at Richmond, Mobile and Savannah.[29]

During the war the bureau chief and the paymasters found interesting expedients to fulfill the needs of the Navy. When they found provisions becoming scarce they used tea, molasses, coffee and sugar, items that the Department had in surplus, to make exchanges and to barter for items needed. When the Army monopolized all the mills that made clothing, De Bree had canvas shoes made in Mobile, Alabama, and contracted with firms abroad for shoes, blankets and clothing for the men.[30]

The Navy Department increasingly relied on goods from abroad to fill the needs of the men. Mallory began shipping bales of cotton on naval account and also purchased interest in some blockade-runners. The purchase of the *Coquette* in September 1863 to bring in supplies and carry out cotton to pay for it, gave the Department even more flexibility in its procurement of supplies. Despite these expedients, however, the Navy became increasingly reliant on the Army for domestic procurement.

The Office of Medicine and Surgery was the last of the four

bureaux. This office supervised the purchase of medicine and medical supplies and attended to the health needs of the men by supervising their hygiene and diet. The surgeon in charge of the bureau was Dr William A W Spotswood, a navy veteran of 25-years service. A contemporary described him as a 'brawny, gray-haired six-footer, rough and ready in ways and looks, but a gentle-hearted man'. The bureau's office in Richmond had only one chief clerk and one purveyor to perform the clerical work. The purveyor, Robert Lecky, was a chemist and apothecary who supervised the manufacture, purchase and distribution of the medical supplies. Most of the activity of the bureau was carried out by the bureau's 113 personnel which included 22 surgeons, 15 assistant surgeons, 9 assistant surgeons for the war and other staff at the medical stations and naval hospitals. All the surgeons and most of the assistant surgeons had served in the United States Navy. The Office of Medicine and Surgery was fortunate to have ample supplies of medicines, surgical equipment and hospital stores – compliments of blockade-runners.[31]

Within the Navy Department there existed other semi-autonomous elements that remained outside the four bureaux but that still fell under Mallory's control. The chief engineer and the naval constructor also operated outside the bureaux and served as their own administrative departments. The Confederate Marine Corps was designed as a field unit for specialized combat but fell under Mallory as a matter of convenience. The Confederate Congress authorized 8 captains and 29 lieutenants for this branch of the service. The Corps remained small, however, and only 19

Admiral Farragut's Federal fleet fighting past the forts below New Orleans, April 1862. (detail of illustration on page 225-WMCWNH)

lieutenants were ever appointed. A colonel served as commandant and his assistant was a lieutenant colonel. The staff included an adjutant, a major, a sergeant major, a quartermaster sergeant and two clerks. The Marine Corps headquarters was not in the Mechanics Institute with the other offices of the Navy Department but at 115 Maine Street in Richmond.[32]

The Confederate Navy made a distinction between staff and line officers. Staff officers were naval constructors, surgeons, paymasters and chief engineers who took rank and precedence with each other. All of these officers, however, were restricted in their right to command outside their own corps. Staff officers could not hold command afloat. Only specifically granted authority could alter this regulation.[33]

The Navy Department and Congress

The Navy Department's relationship with the Confederate Congress was often like a ship on stormy seas. Mallory had several enemies and detractors in the Congress but it was President Jefferson Davis's unpopularity that hurt the Department as the President's enemies struck at Davis through Mallory. One of the most bitter enemies of the Department, Henry S Foote, a Congressman from Tennessee, led attacks against both Mallory and the President throughout the war. Foote waged his own personal feud by opposing the President on nearly every issue and remained a strong opponent of Jefferson Davis, the war effort, and, as a consequence, the Navy Department.

The fall of New Orleans, in April 1862, was a severe blow to the Confederacy and the Navy. The successful thrust up the Mississippi River and the capture of the city by the Union forces compelled Confederate authorities to burn the incomplete iron-clads *Mississippi* and *Louisiana*. Charles M Conrad, another Congressional opponent of Mallory, and whose extensive holdings of land in New Orleans had been captured, led a personal attack on the Navy Department. He began his assault by introducing a bill in Congress to abolish the Navy and to transfer its functions to the War Department. This bill was rejected and a vote of censure for Mallory was likewise defeated. In mid-August 1862, he and a core of dissatisfied Congressmen successfully began a congressional investigation to look at the Navy's 'inadequacy'.[34]

The Naval Investigating Board convened over the opposition of Albert Gallatin Brown, the Chairman of the Congressional

Committee on Naval Affairs. All of the proceedings and the in-depth investigations of the Department deeply hurt Mallory. Fortunately he did not have to appear in person but the nature of the proceedings required him to send documents to defend his actions. He also found it necessary to counsel others who would testify. Unfortunately for the South, Mallory would be forced to deal with the hearings at a time when he was still trying to forge the foundation of a navy for the Confederacy. The investigation thus served not only as a destructive force aimed at the Navy Department but it also proved to be divisive for the Confederacy.

The five-member committee examined three major questions. What had the Department done to defend New Orleans? Had it done everything possible to complete the ironclads *Louisiana* and *Mississippi*? And last, could the loss of these ironclads be the fault of the Department? Most of the hearings focused on the loss of the *Mississippi*. The proceedings clearly showed that Mallory and the Navy Department had strongly urged the contractors to finish the ironclad. Mallory had likewise instructed Commander John K Mitchell to intercede and employ workers to finish the ironclad if necessary. What became abundantly evident is how poorly the defenses of New Orleans had been handled – a prelude of things to come, as similar problems would be encountered throughout the war by the Confederate Government. The investigating committee eventually concluded that the Navy Department had not been at fault and Mallory even received some praise for his efforts.[35]

Mallory and the Department also had a cadre of supporters in Congress during the war. The chairman of the Committee of Naval Affairs remained a staunch supporter of Mallory and stood by him during the investigation. He worked throughout the war with Mallory to promote the Navy and strongly supported his efforts to buy ironclads in Europe. Brown defended the Navy's actions in the final months of the war, when a Congressional proposal suggested that the Naval Committee determine whether naval operations should be curtailed and the Department's appropriations be suspended. Brown refused to allow this to happen.

Building and maintaining a navy

The Navy began the war without a single warship. Enterprising individuals seized the old steamer *Fulton*, six revenue cutters, three slavers, two lighthouse tenders, and a couple of privately-owned steamers, but these would not adequately serve as a sufficient nucleus for a fighting force. Early in the war some of the states created their own naval organizations, and these naval assets, with some hesitancy, were transferred to the Confederate States Navy Department to become the core of the Department until a building programme could be implemented.

Building a navy would be one of Mallory's greatest challenges. His former experience as the chairman of the Naval Affairs Committee gave him at least a foundation of the experience necessary. As chairman he had overseen the transformation of the United States Navy from sail to steam and witnessed the adoption of shell guns, iron ships and a more progressive administration. His time would be divided between administering the Confederate Navy Department, building a navy, and creating the infrastructure to support its logistical needs and operations.

During the Civil War, naval manufacturing centers sprouted in Charlotte, North Carolina, and Petersburg, Virginia. Rolling mills developed in Selma, Alabama, Richmond, Virginia, and Atlanta and Macon, Georgia. But to have any hope of success, the shipbuilding centers at Norfolk, New Orleans and Memphis had to be fully utilized. Mallory found this latter job virtually insurmountable due to a number of factors – among the most critical was a shortage of raw materials that kept the shipyards idle. None of the South's shipbuilding centers ever realized their full potential because all three were wrested from Confederate hands early in the war. Mallory's efforts to build a navy were also thwarted by industrial concerns that would not risk business ventures with the Confederate Government, while others would take months to retool their operations in order to perform the necessary heavy industrial work.

Mallory immediately approached Congress for appropriations to fund the building programmes necessary to get the Navy off the ground. Given the dearth of facilities, the time required to build large warships, and the need to develop an infrastructure to launch an immediate building programme, Mallory initially told Davis that he intended to buy ships abroad rather than try to build them in the South.[36] Interestingly, Mallory did not immediately embrace the building of technologically advanced weapons. He had to be convinced by other officers that ironclads, torpedo boats and mines would be beneficial, but once he made up his mind he avidly promoted these weapon systems.

Mallory, though, quickly made the sound decision to build ironclads. He promoted the building of armoured ships capable of withstanding shot and shells. He saw the 'possession of an iron-armoured ship as a matter of first necessity'. He realized that

Chief Naval Constructor John L Porter. Primarily known as co-designer of the ironclad *Virginia (Merrimack)*, Porter planned the majority of the warships built in the Confederacy. (Mariners' Museum)

an ironclad could engage with success any vessel in the United States Navy and thus neutralize the North's superior numbers of warships. Mallory believed that naval battles between wooden ships would prove to be 'simply contests in which the question, not of victory, but of who shall go to the bottom first, is to be solved.'[37]

With his acquisition policy set, there were still many problems to overcome. The Navy Department faced a bureaucratic handicap because it had no Bureau of Construction, Equipment, and Repair similar to that of the Union Navy. The Confederate Navy was hamstrung from the beginning of the war because the responsibilities for the logistical care of ships were divided between two bureaux. Originally the Office of Ordnance and Hydrography managed construction and repair matters, while the Office of Orders and Detail oversaw the details of ship's equipment. Acting constructors also had supervised the various building projects of the Navy Department without a recognized chief. John L Porter initially served as the South's naval constructor without the proper title or authority.

Porter learned the shipbuilding trade at his father's shipyard in Portsmouth, Virginia. He served with the U S Navy in a civilian capacity and drew numerous designs of armour-plated warships and other vessels of war and received an appointment as a naval constructor in 1859. Porter resigned his commission and after serving for a short time with Virginia's naval forces was appointed to supervise the operations at the Norfolk Navy Yard. Here he drew plans for ships for the Department and examined plans drawn by the other naval constructors. Lt John M Brooke, William P Williamson and Porter converted the hull of the *Merrimack* into the CSS *Virginia*. After the destruction of this ironclad, Porter supervised construction at the Rocketts Navy Yard and regularly advised Mallory concerning building matters. When necessary he travelled to supervise or examine work in progress at the various building sites in the South. The Department held Porter responsible for the hull shapes, steering gear, decks, small boats and the ships' furnishings.[38]

In September 1862 Porter asked Mallory to establish officially the Office of Chief Naval Constructor. Mallory sent a request to the Chairman of the Committee of Naval Affairs in the Confederate Senate the same day. Congress authorized the President to appoint a man to this office under the supervision of the Secretary of the Navy. The Secretary turned all responsibilities concerning naval construction over to the chief constructor at this point by general order. In April 1863 Congress gave Mallory the authority to appoint Porter to this position. Porter, however, did not receive his formal appointment until January 7, 1864. Curiously, Porter as Chief Constructor did not fall administratively under any of the bureaux and instead he and his two assistants reported direct to Mallory.[39]

Proposals poured into the Department from interested contractors, naval officers, Congressmen and other persons. Mallory did not have the experience nor the temperament to review all the proposals and these were turned over to the Chief Constructor. Once the ironclad became the premier naval weapon of the South,

Engineer-in-Chief William P Williamson (Ann Williamson Roberts, great granddaughter)

Mallory felt he needed advice from several men. In February 1864 he established a board of naval officers to submit their opinions and recommendations for building ironclads.[40]

The naval constructors in the Confederate Navy yards worked under the direction of the commandants of the yards and had general supervision regarding the building and repairing of vessels as well as supervision over the masters and workmen and the materials used in the yards. They generally handled the muster of the mechanics, defective materials, examination of vessels and the requisitions and returns.[41]

Another semi-autonomous element of the Navy Department was the Department of Steam Engineering which fell under the auspices of the Chief Engineer William P Williamson. Born in Norfolk, Williamson studied mechanical engineering in New York and later worked at the Gosport Navy Yard. By 1842 he super-vised the machine works there and by October of that year was appointed a chief engineer in the US Navy. At the outbreak of the war he refused to take an oath of allegiance and after a short imprisonment, and dismissal from the Navy, he became the senior engineer in the Confederate Navy on June 11, 1861.

Mallory appointed William P Williamson as the Chief Engineer in April 1862. Like the Chief Naval Constructor, Williamson reported direct to Mallory. Williamson served as the Engineer-in-Chief until the war's end. His broad responsibilities included the acquisition, installation or alteration, design and operation of all the warships' engines and boilers. He also conducted and supervised all the trials and inspections and had some supervision of the chief engineers stationed at the yards, naval stations, naval works and in the James River Squadron who were under the direct command of the local commanding officers.[42]

Despite the lack of co-ordination between the states and the Confederate Government and the dearth of mechanics, naval facilities, rolling mills, and raw materials, the South did have many successes. Works in Richmond produced six marine engines and the naval works in Charlotte, North Carolina, Augusta and Atlanta, Georgia, and Selma, Alabama, produced large amounts of guns, ordnance and forgings for the Navy. By May 1863, Mallory had under construction twenty-three gunboats — all but three being ironclads. It is an amazing feat that the South built as many ironclads as it did, given the burdens it faced. Mallory and the Department had to overcome an insufficiency of skilled workmen that kept the industrial complexes producing at a fraction of their capacities. The indiscriminate draft of the Army robbed the industrial plants of their skilled labour. The South lacked materials for shipbuilding, and suffered a dearth of tools, machinery and iron working shops to accommodate the industrial needs of the shipbuilding industry. The Confederate nation did manage to build a respectable number of warships but only a fraction of that necessary to change the fortunes of the war.[43]

The Navy Department and operations

The acts that established the Navy Department and the four bureaux failed to provide for an Assistant Secretary of the Navy. This office in the Union Navy, filled by Gustavus Vasa Fox, allowed Gideon Welles greater freedom to pursue critical and time-sensitive issues of the Department. Mallory did not have this luxury. Without an assistant who could handle a portion of the day-to-day business concerning strategic and technical matters, Mallory had to handle these himself. By necessity, Mallory allowed his officers great discretion in tactical situations. He usually issued general orders and left the details to be handled by the local commanding officer. An Assistant Secretary of the Navy could have overseen the operational matters, freeing Mallory to oversee other responsibilities. Working with Congress on appropriations and interaction with the other executive offices proved to be a full-time job.

When the war began, the chain of command to the field was direct from the Secretary of the Navy to the area commander who disseminated the Department's policy and its instructions. In 1863, Mallory split the responsibility between the forces afloat and the station commanders, and began to issue orders direct to either the commanding officer of a station (usually a flag officer), or to commanding officers of navy yards, naval stations and shore establishments. The responsibilities of these two normally remained separate and distinct except in cases of 'great emergency'.[44]

Mallory opposed the traditional method of choosing the most senior officer for command. He chose Franklin Buchanan to command the *Virginia*, when officers senior to Buchanan had applied. In order to stop them interfering, he appointed Buchanan as officer-in-command of the James River – keeping the position of captain unfilled. Thus when Buchanan took command he would not face any interference from an officer senior to him. This situation worked well and in 1863 the Department divided the command structure between shore and commands afloat. This allowed Mallory to pick aggressive and junior officers for command afloat more easily.

The Confederate Navy had as many as fourteen naval stations during the war. They served as administrative and logistical entities, each bound to specified geographical boundaries prescribed by Mallory. The station commander frequently oversaw recruiting, the storehouses, hospitals, marine detachments, ordnance works and naval construction within his command. He received all the local requisitions and handled the administrative matters as well as inspected the commissioned vessels in port. The station commander did not, however, have control over the Navy yards unless instructed by the Secretary of the Navy.[45]

With dual commands in close proximity, the organization did require co-ordination to work well. Since neither local commander would have authority over the other, there existed a potential for

problems. This organizational situation required the station commandant to furnish stores, personnel and repairs to vessels for the officer afloat. Usually the officer afloat was much younger in age and experience, and junior in permanent rank. The distinction between naval stations and yards was vague, and the chain of command often confused. Frequently, the stations and yards within a single geographical area fell under the command of a single officer. Officers did not always recognize this prescribed separation and senior officers sometimes assumed or exceeded their authority over junior officers. Remarkably, however, little conflict arose over this organization.[46]

Included in this organization was an operational command in Europe. In the autumn of 1863, Mallory assigned Samuel Barron to the command of a newly formed squadron. From his home in Paris Barron commanded and directed the activities of Confederate vessels in the Atlantic Ocean, which at the time comprised only the cruisers *Florida* and *Georgia*. This organizational expedient failed and the squadron seems to have disappeared as quickly as it formed. As the ranking officer he served as the Flag Officer Commanding Naval Forces in Europe. He found that he had no more success than those under him in obtaining warships for the Confederacy. By 1864 he had largely failed to be a decisive force in Europe and had little to do except tend to the administrative tasks of the numerous officers awaiting assignments to the Confederate cruisers.[47]

The administrative paperwork of the commanding officers was not extremely burdensome. Regulations required that they made quarterly returns to their immediate superiors, accompanied by monthly reports if in Southern waters and bi-monthly reports if abroad. Also required of the commanders in charge of a fleet or squadron were semi-annual reports and monthly returns of the state and condition of the fleet.[48]

The staffs of the commandant of a station might consist of a lieutenant as an ordnance officer and aide, a paymaster, an engineer and a surgeon. The commandant routinely sent reports concerning naval construction, ordnance, supplies, naval hospitals, receiving ships and the marine detachment. The flag officer afloat co-ordinated the activities of the naval batteries ashore and the ships assigned to the squadron, and, in addition, handled personnel matters of the ships and batteries attached to his command.

Mallory received more criticism for operational problems and deficiencies than for any other issue. Critics continually felt that the Department had failed its missions. When issuing orders or instructions, Mallory often acted indecisively and issued vague and unchangeable instructions to his subordinates. For example, Mallory never decided how to use the ironclad *Virginia*. He issued Flag Officer Josiah Tattnall instructions so general that the flag officer never had any firm concept of the course of action that the Secretary wished him to take. Neither Buchanan or Tattnall ever knew whether the ironclad was to be an offensive or defensive weapon nor exactly what the Department expected of them. Mallory's interference with the naval operations just before the fall of New Orleans also showed the Secretary's lack of decisiveness.

Mallory could also become quite emotional over operational issues. In 1864 he had several times ordered an opening to be made in the James River obstructions at Drewry's Bluff so that the ironclads could operate below them. His subordinates failed to execute these orders and weeks went by before a hole was blasted to allow the ironclads downstream. A clerk in the War Department witnessed one of Mallory's outbursts and noted that 'Mr. Mallory's usual red face turned purple'.[49]

Operations abroad

The successes and failures of the Navy Department's operations abroad had a great impact on the outcome of the war. The predations of the commerce raiders are well known but it was the acquisition of these and other vessels and the procurement of important strategic goods and supplies that kept the Navy operational. Due to the poorly developed industrial infrastructure of the South, Mallory realized that it would be some time before manufactured goods could be made in sufficient quantities to prosecute the war. Initially Mallory sent men to New York, Philadelphia, Baltimore and Canada to secure any suitable ships that could be converted into warships for the Confederacy. Realizing that the South needed a navy immediately, Mallory proposed to send officers to Europe on special service to scour the foreign arsenals for accouterments, uniforms, arms, cannon, gunpowder, ships, marine engines and other supplies necessary to carry on a full-scale naval war against the Northern states. On May 10, 1861, the Confederate Congress initiated operations abroad by appropriating $2m to purchase or construct one or two warships in European shipyards.[50]

Mallory believed that the European powers would support the Confederate cause and would grant the Confederacy international recognition. He also believed that the South would be able to pur-

Commander James D Bulloch. The most successful of the naval agents sent abroad, Bulloch was responsible for securing *Alabama*, *Florida*, and numerous other ships for the Confederate Navy. (Scharf, *Confederate States Navy*)

chase all of its wartime needs abroad. On May 9, 1861 the South's most successful agent, James Dunwoody Bulloch, left the South for service overseas. Bulloch was born in Savannah, Georgia, and entered the US Navy as a midshipman in 1839. He eventually rose to the rank of lieutenant before resigning in 1854. For the next eight years Bulloch saw service with commercial mail ships and in January 1862 Mallory appointed him a civilian agent for the Navy Department. Due to Bulloch's energy, resourcefulness and his great initiative, Mallory later appointed him to the well-deserved rank of commander. This advancement caused a great deal of excitement, discontent, jealousy and criticism among the Confederate naval officers more senior to him.[51]

Commander James H North. The first naval officer sent to Europe, North was instructed to purchase or build ironclad warships for the Confederacy. He was not as successful as Bulloch. (Charles V Peery)

In May 1861, both Bulloch and agent James H North travelled to England. North had resigned his lieutenant's commission in the US Navy in January and was appointed to the same rank in the Confederate Navy. North previously travelled through New York, Philadelphia and Baltimore looking for ships for the Confederacy, but with no success. This trip would be a portent of the future as North would be the least effective of all the European agents.

Mallory's interest in technology led him to instruct Bulloch continually to purchase the most advanced weapons systems and vessels for the Confederacy. He wanted Bulloch to consider buying British Armstrong guns, submarines and the armoured turrets of one of Britain's foremost naval innovators, Captain Cowper Coles. One of Bulloch's first tasks was to get a shipload of military supplies through the blockade, so he purchased the steamer *Fingal* and carried an important cargo of military supplies into Savannah.[52] Bulloch's absence, however, left the European theatre without a leader for five months.

Important for the South, in order to contest the control of the seas, was the purchase of steam warships. Mallory's agents during the war would procure torpedo boats, gunboats, tenders and supply ships. They purchased and built long-range steamers for commerce raiding, fast steam blockade-runners and ironclads. The process of getting them out of the host countries, however, had varying success.

As senior officer, Bulloch co-ordinated the Confederate business in Europe until Samuel Barron arrived in the fall of 1863. The staffs assigned to Europe were incredibly small. Bulloch and the other agents operated by doing much of the business themselves. Bulloch began with midshipmen assistants but found them inadequate and asked for and later received two lieutenants. All the agents generally kept 'simple' records. They filed contracts and vouchers of each transaction. Bulloch initially had only a single clerk but later hired a bookkeeper. His office consisted of a space with a desk furnished by Fraser, Trenholm & Company, the Confederacy's chief financial partner throughout the war.[53]

Regular and timely communications between Mallory and the agents remained an impediment during the entire war. Long-range communications disrupted the co-ordination of the foreign agents. Delayed and intercepted correspondence crippled any hopes of an efficient organization, endangered secret projects and strained relationships between not only the Secretary and his agents but also between the agents themselves. There were times when the information in naval communiqués had to be protected and the men abroad used a cipher system to conceal their messages. They retained a small dictionary and another similar edition went to the Navy Department. When it became necessary to send sensitive information in code, the first number of the code told on which page the word could be found. The second number denoted the word's place on the page from the beginning of the text. Mail came by blockade-runners but also through couriers who brought regular mails and secret dispatches through Halifax, Nova Scotia, and New York into the Confederacy.[54]

By far the greatest handicap that the agents faced was paying for their purchases. There was little that the Navy Department could do to change this situation. Initially the Confederate Congress authorized the building of as many as six steamers, but both Bulloch and North found that when they arrived in Europe that they could buy nothing due to a lack of cash. Bulloch made his initial visits to dockyards, factories and weapon salesmen but wasted this time because nothing could be purchased on credit. The lack of funds allowed Bulloch to sign contracts for only two steamers. Mallory could not solve the problem because he could not secure specie and sent Treasury notes, the only form of security he could get from the Secretary of the Treasury. The European banks initially refused to accept anything but cash.[55]

The situation worsened because the Confederacy had no central finance officer in Europe to co-ordinate the purchasing activity of the numerous agents. To pay for its purchases, the Navy Department sent specie, but it was a risky business to send such large sums through the blockade. For a commission of 1.5 per cent, the Confederate Treasury could deposit bonds or specie with Fraser, Trenholm in Charleston. The company then sent letters of credit to Liverpool to fund the activities of the Confederate agents. Eventually the Confederate Government had no choice but to raise funds through the sale of cotton. Mallory was the first in the Confederate Government to use cotton certificates as a means of exchange.[56]

In the winter of 1862 Mallory sent George N Sanders to Europe to act as an agent to dispense the certificates for the construction of a combination mail packet and cruiser, but the idea was scrapped in order to fund the building of the cruiser *Canton*. The Navy Department began shipping cotton to Europe to pay the debts it had incurred, but unfortunately, the accounting procedures for the Confederate agents had no built-in flexibility. Cotton came through the blockade earmarked for specific accounts, producing a situation that left some of the accounts with surpluses of money while others lacked the funds necessary to pay the contractors for their work. Eventually, all the Confederate funds would be turned over to Treasury Department agent Colin J McRae to be dispersed in the best interest of the Government.

The success of the commerce raiders *Alabama* and *Florida* prompted Mallory to instruct Bulloch to purchase four more raiders. A secret act of Congress appropriated £2 million sterling for the construction of ironclads in 1863. Mallory left the details of the building of the warships abroad to the expertise of his agents. This was reiterated when he wrote to Bulloch that he should oversee the construction and the details in Europe 'untrammeled by instructions' from the Secretary.[57]

Matthew Fontaine Maury also travelled to Europe in the fall of 1862. Maury brought something to Europe that none of the other agents possessed – a reputation. Well-known as an oceanographer, whose scientific work with wind and tides had already won him international acclaim, Maury could not hide his presence so he worked completely in the open. His activity helped to raise the South's prestige abroad. Maury planned to make purchases for the Government but also intended to modify the financial system by establishing the use of cotton bonds to finance Confederate operations.

In the summer of 1862 Lieutenant George Terry Sinclair arrived on the European scene on 'special service.' Originally Mallory had sent him to replace North. Slow communications, however, complicated the issue and North remained abroad. Had Sinclair replaced North, the lines of authority would have been clear. Instead, Bulloch had the impression that Sinclair came as a private contractor. Sinclair had arrived in Europe with enough cash to pay for the construction of an entire cruiser. But Bulloch thought that this sudden embarrassment of wealth compromised his position. Bulloch had contractors working on other projects awaiting payment and Sinclair, who suddenly showed up with cash, undermined the chain of command in Europe. Since Sinclair's authority came direct from Mallory it was the Secretary of the Navy who failed to grasp the situation. This illustrates the fact that Mallory never developed a clear and defined line of authority in Europe. The Navy Department agents operated in confusion and remained uncertain and unclear of the specific intentions of the Department. Mallory made matters far worse by sending abroad private contractors to buy ships on speculation for the Confederacy. With so many men competing for similar goals, it is amazing that the Confederate agents did as well as they did.

The private contractors sent by Mallory competed direct with the naval agents. They offered to secure ships and deliver them to a Navy representative in international waters for a price arranged in advance. The contractor pocketed any profits from the deal. The problem of a lack of money precluded any contract ship from ever being delivered. Unfortunately, the activity of these men showed up in the pages of the London press which referred to the men as Confederate agents. The activity of private contractors drove Bulloch to despair and he asked Mallory to stop sending them to Europe.[58]

As the war continued, the agents found that getting the finished warships to sea was made more difficult because of the diligent work of American consuls and their spies. US diplomatic agents used the British Foreign Enlistment Act, which prohibited any citizen from arming, manning or equipping a ship for the use of a belligerent nation, to prevent ships from being transferred to the Confederacy. After the British seized the Birkenhead rams, the Confederate agents began to look towards building blockade-runners and steamers capable of conversion into warships instead of large war vessels.[59] Here the Confederacy had great success. Several Confederate Government agencies and departments owned or had partial ownership in over sixty such vessels. These vessels allowed the Confederate Government greater access to the specific supplies and war materials necessary to keep its armies in the field.

The Navy Department throughout most of the war showed little interest in blockade-running and preferred instead to construct commerce raiders, ironclads and marine engines. Nevertheless, the Department had converted the steamers *Stono* and *Oconee* as blockade-runners, although neither met with any success. Bulloch purchased the steamer *Coquette* in Glasgow; she had a 10ft draft, could carry 1,000 bales of cotton and had a better than average career. The Navy Department also negotiated an arrangement with Crenshaw Collie & Company to reserve one quarter of the space in the four twin-screw steamships *Dee*, *Ceres*, *Vesta* and *Hebe*, and the paddlewheel steamer *Venus*. The company approached Mallory to provide naval officers for the enterprise but the Secretary, who had allowed his officers to command only select Government-owned runners, refused.[60]

In April 1864 President Davis approved an agreement made by the Treasury, War and Navy Departments pertaining to the purchase, transportation and sale of cotton, tobacco and naval stores. The agreement centralized the control of these activities and solved many of the self-inflicted problems caused by the efforts of the separate departments. The Navy Department was tasked with the planning, building and sailing of the steamers, and agent Colin McRae sailed to Europe to manage the finances for this project. Later agreements with other companies expanded the role of blockade-running even further.

Overall, the Confederate building projects in Europe met with mixed success. The few cruisers that the agents managed to get to sea had a crippling effect on Union shipping. Likewise the blockade-runners built for the Confederate Government helped to keep the Confederacy supplied with war *matériel*. But the Confederate Government waited far too long to become involved in the building and operations of blockade-runners. By the time the Confederacy had these vessels in full-scale production, money was scarce and the Union had implemented the blockade effectively.

The Confederacy thus never managed to import or export enough *matériel* to satisfy its needs.[61]

Critical blame can be cast on Mallory who failed to recognize how this might have altered the war. He never seriously considered that the Navy Department should take control over blockade-running activity. By committing meagre resources and by employing naval officers sitting ashore waiting for commands, Mallory might have made blockade-running a much more regular and successful activity and solved one of the Confederacy's greatest problems of the war.

Conclusion

During the Civil War the fortunes and failures of the Navy Department rested, in part, upon the shoulders of Stephen Mallory, as his administration was the guiding force that shaped the Navy. While Mallory was always an energetic administrator, he was far from aggressive. Mallory was partially hamstrung because he could not count on the complete support of Jefferson Davis. Perhaps his greatest deficiency was his failure to pressure the President to obtain the resources essential for the successful operation of the Navy. In addition, the members of Congress who openly opposed Mallory added to the public feeling that the Army was more important to the war effort. Fortunately, the severe critics of Mallory and the Navy Department were not numerous.

Mallory's managerial style was also a factor in bringing success or failure to the Navy. He did not have all the skills or the experience he needed to be the consummate Secretary of the Navy. He failed to bring about the proper organizational changes necessary to make the Department function as it should. While he was reliable, methodical and extremely conscientious, he demonstrated that he had difficulty prioritizing his problems and frequently revealed lapses in decisiveness. He did, however, grow with the responsibility thrust upon him in 1861, and, without doubt, the Navy Department was managed better than any other Confederate executive department.

The Navy struggled for the entire war needing greater resources, extra manpower, skilled mechanics, larger budgets, better manufacturing facilities, and dependable transportation for goods and supplies. The Confederate Navy rarely received assistance from the Army or even President Davis to solve these deficiencies. The Army and Navy Departments never developed a good working relationship during the conflict. For most of the war, both branches competed for manufactured products, manpower and skilled mechanics, and the Army usually obtained the lion's share of these important and increasingly scarce strategic resources. This fettered the Navy's building efforts and operations. President Davis, who could have resolved many of these problems, failed to intercede. Mallory is also at fault because he failed to convince the President that his intervention was important.

One of the greatest weaknesses of the Navy was the organizational failure to establish a specific bureau for logistics. No department oversaw all the activities of the shore facilities, construction, repair, and maintenance. The division of these duties between the Office of Ordnance and Hydrography and the Office of Orders and Detail greatly hampered the already strained operational efforts of the Navy.

Logistical inadequacies also developed into one of the Confederate Government's greatest problems. The Navy Department could have solved some of the South's import and export difficulties by nationalizing blockade-running — arguably one of the Confederate Government's most successful programmes. Naval blockade-runners demonstrated that they were the most efficient and had the lowest loss-rate from capture of any of the blockade-running vessels.

Despite the problems that shackled the Confederate Navy, Mallory and the department accomplished a great deal during the war. The 670-ship Union Navy failed to capture Richmond, Charleston, Savannah or Wilmington until the Confederacy was in its death throes. While some historians have portrayed Mallory as something of a dreamer and a romantic, he is better described as a progressive and innovative thinker. His ironclad projects, the use of torpedoes, the development and manufacture of the Brooke gun and the use of the *David* torpedo boats were all successes that went beyond the early war expectations of the Navy.

In the spring of 1861, when the initial plans were made by Confederate leaders to prosecute the war, few would realize that many of the fortunes of the conflict would hinge on the success and failures of the Southern naval forces. Mallory seemed to have been one of the few men who saw the potential impact that the navies would have in the war's outcome. He showed remarkable resourcefulness and initiative in office. His greatest achievement was his establishment of a navy in the 'crucible of war'. This was a remarkable achievement without the benefit of a developed industrial base or the infrastructure to support this activity. The South managed to build technologically advanced warships, and put more than 130 of them into service during the war. While this is only about 20 per cent of the Union Navy's total, it is comparable to the number built by the United States Navy Yards during the same period. The Confederate Navy did a credible job of holding off this numerically superior force for four years.

Even though the President often showed contempt for the Navy, he trusted Mallory and the Secretary remained a close friend and advisor to Davis. Mallory rode on the train that carried the President and the cabinet members out of Richmond just before the arrival of Union troops. Looking out the window, Mallory sighted the James River Squadron's ironclads only hours before they were destroyed. Mallory referred to them as 'chained and sulky bulldogs' which seems to be an appropriate analogy for the entire Confederate Navy Department's limited and hampered operations during the American Civil War.[62]

Dr Robert M Browning Jr

Chapter Three

TYPES OF SHIPS

The nineteenth-century naval revolution and the Confederate Navy

The creation of the Confederate Navy Department coincided with a remarkable period of transformation in the tools of naval warfare. In 1861 the centuries-long reign of the wooden wind-powered warship was in decline. Steam was slowly supplanting sail, advances in ordnance were rendering unprotected wooden hulls obsolete, and iron was seen as the shipbuilding material of the future as the structural limitations of wood were reached. Even experimental underwater weapons were demonstrating their potential as the industrial revolution fuelled rapid changes in naval technology during the first half of the nineteenth century.

The first technical innovation to significantly influence warship design was the steam engine. Initially applied to commercial ventures, by the second decade of the nineteenth century sidewheel steam machinery was being placed in naval vessels. The first practicable steam warship was USS *Demologos*. Completed in 1815 to a design by steamboat pioneer Robert Fulton, *Demologos* was propelled by a single paddlewheel mounted between twin hulls.

Crimean War naval battle scene: bombardment of Kaleh Redoubt. (*Illustrated London News*)

HMS *Warrior.* (CPL)

Intended for the defense of New York harbor, the War of 1812 ended before her completion and she never saw active service. In 1827, the Greek sidewheel *Karteria* became the first purpose-built steam warship to engage in combat when used against the Turks during the Greek War of Independence. The success of *Karteria* and other naval steamers during the 1820s helped dispel concern over the initial shortcomings of early steam propulsion so that by the following decade the merits of the new technology had been widely accepted by the world's major navies.

Deficiencies in the combat effectiveness of the early sidewheel warships, notably the exposure of the propelling machinery to gunfire and a significantly reduced armament resulting from the space and weight requirements of the propulsion system, were largely rectified by the development of the screw propeller in the late 1830s. By the outbreak of the American Civil War the wooden screw warship, with its machinery placed safely below the waterline, had replaced the sailing man-of-war as the supreme weapon afloat.[1]

The greatest stimulus to warship design in the pre-Civil War years was provided by the introduction of a practical shell gun system for shipboard use. Prior to the shell gun's perfection a delicate balance prevailed between ship and gun, with combatants rarely sinking the other by gunfire. This stand-off resulted from the dominant artillery of the period, the muzzle-loading smoothbore gun. Firing a solid non-explosive roundshot, this weapon often lacked the power to penetrate the thick wooden walls of the era's warships. The explosive shell's ability to fragment and even ignite wooden hulls upset this parity and provoked a revolution in naval construction by spurring efforts to find effective methods of protecting ships from the shell's destructive force.

Shipboard shell-firing guns, mostly in the form of inaccurate high-trajectory mortars and howitzers, had been used periodically since the early days of artillery but were considered impractical because of the perceived danger from the accidental explosion of the shells. In the early 1820s French army officer Henri-Joseph Paixhans advocated a standardized naval ordnance system based on large-caliber shell guns capable of horizontal fire. Accordingly, Paixhans developed a 22cm, 80pdr shell gun and successfully tested it against a decommissioned warship. The extensive damage

French Navy *Gloire.* (CPL)

caused to the target ship clearly established the destructive power of the shell against wooden hulls and resulted in approval of Paixhans's system for use by the French Navy in 1824.[2]

The shell gun's success led Paixhans and others to promote the use of iron cladding for ships as a defense against the shell, but little was done other than experimentation. The first attempt at building an armoured warship occurred in America in 1842 when Robert L Stevens convinced Congress to allocate funds for the construction of a 1,500-ton armourclad steamer of his own design. Though this powerful vessel was never completed, its funding and construction momentarily placed the United States in the forefront of naval technology.

The Battle of Sinope in 1853 demonstrated for the first time in combat the destructiveness of the explosive shell against wooden warships. At Sinope, a Russian fleet consisting of nine warships armed in part with shell guns scored a signal victory when it destroyed all but one of a thirteen-ship Turkish squadron. Following this action France and Britain joined forces with Turkey against Russia in the Crimean War, A year later, the powerful effect of shells against unarmoured wooden vessels was repeated during the bombardment of Sevastopol, when Russian forts armed with shell guns severely mauled several of the attacking allied fleet. Sinope and Sevastopol revived French and British interest in developing means to protect warships and led to new experiments. As a result, the French developed plans for a steam-powered floating battery clad with 4in of iron plate and authorized the construction of five the year following Sinope. The British followed with orders to build five additional vessels based on the French plans.[3]

Three of the French batteries were successfully tested in battle in 1855, when they participated in an attack on Russian

fortifications at Kinburn, in the Black Sea Dnieper approaches. Anchoring within 1,000 yards of the forts, the ironclads withstood four hours of heavy fire with minimal damage and casualties, and played an important part in their reduction. This first combat trial of ironclads proved the worth of armour against shell and accelerated the change from wood to iron by the world's major navies. The French responded to the lessons of the Crimean War with *Gloire*, the first seagoing ironclad warship, and the British countered with the iron-hulled armourclad *Warrior*. By the outbreak of the American war over fifty armoured vessels were built or building in Europe and a fundamental change in naval construction was well underway.

Newly appointed Confederate Naval Secretary Stephen R Mallory was keenly aware of the naval revolution in progress. As chairman of the US Senate's powerful Naval Affairs Committee from 1853 to 1861, Mallory was a strong and knowledgeable proponent of a progressive naval force. He supported funding for the Stevens battery and he encouraged development of new and innovative naval weapons. He promoted the construction of a series of modern sail and steam gunboats that, ironically, were to give the US Navy an important edge at the outbreak of the Civil War. And he worked diligently to reform the service in personnel and disciplinary matters. Thus, when empowered to produce a navy for the fledgling Confederacy where none before existed, Mallory's knowledge of worldwide naval matters gained from his Senate experience would serve him well.[4]

Wooden gunboats

When established on February 21, 1861 the Confederate Navy Department possessed not a single warship nor the means to quickly build one. Mallory's first task upon confirmation as naval secretary the following month was to fund and assemble a viable naval force to counter the US Navy. On March 13 he submitted to Congress an appropriations bill for the operation of the Navy Department which included an estimate for the construction or purchase of ten steam gunboats for the coast defenses of the Confederate States. This act was approved by Congress and signed into law by President Jefferson Davis three days later. Although Mallory considered converted gunboats inferior to those purpose-built, he believed that 'the expediency and policy of purchasing rather than building vessels at this time are obvious',[5] and immediately directed officers to seek vessels in both Southern and

HMS *Northumberland,* a five-masted ironclad (CPL)

Northern ports suitable for alteration to warships. The first vessels acquired as a result of this action were apparently the steamers *Huntress, Sumter,* and *McRae,* purchased during the month of April. Attempts to acquire ships in the North were effectively ended by the outbreak of hostilities between the two factions on April 12 when Fort Sumter was fired on. Mallory also began acquiring, usually by purchase, altered gunboats which had formed the navies of several of the seceded states prior to their joining the Confederacy. Vessels belonging to the navies of Alabama, Georgia, Texas, South Carolina, North Carolina and Virginia, were procured in this way. The converted gunboats were a mixed lot, ranging in size from the 250ft sidewheel *Patrick Henry* mounting ten guns, to tiny screw tugs, like the 87ft *Lady Davis,* carrying only two small cannon. None were considered proper warships though many, like *Sumter,* provided yeoman service beyond reasonable expectations. By July 1861 about one dozen of these makeshift men-of-war comprised the fledgling Confederate States Navy.

Early on Secretary Mallory had committed the Confederate Navy to technological innovation in an effort to offset the the numerical supiority of the Union Navy. Yet on July 10, one day before he issued instructions that activated the transformation of the captured steam frigate USS *Merrimack* into the armoured ram CSS *Virginia,* Mallory ordered the building of two conventional

wooden gunboats on the Gulf coast. By so doing he launched what was to become, ironically, the Navy's largest warship construction programme. Mallory's reasons for initiating a building policy that directly contradicted his stated preference for a technologically superior navy are uncertain. Having considerable knowledge of foreign naval developments from his Senate days, he doubtless understood the experimental nature of building armoured warships in America and refused to place total reliance on an untested weapons system; other factors likely entered into the decision as well. But for whatever reason or reasons, Mallory's midsummer directive initiated a massive programme which eventually projected the construction of at least 115 conventional wooden warships.

Gunboats produced by the construction programme fell into three broad categories: (1) a group of at least four sidewheel, sail-rigged steamers; (2) a series of screw gunboat classes designed by Chief Naval Constructor John L Porter; and (3) a class of small screw gunboats conceived by Comdr Matthew Fontaine Maury. The first vessels commenced were those ordered by the naval secretary in July. Mallory initially instructed Captain Rousseau at New Orleans to build one gunboat at that city and another at Mobile, but within a week an additional ship at both places was requested. These four vessels were sail-rigged sidewheel steamers 196ft x 38ft (not including paddleboxes) x 14ft and were designed to mount upwards of ten guns. At New Orleans, the

HARPER'S WEEKLY
A JOURNAL OF CIVILIZATION.

Vol. V.—No. 229.]　　　NEW YORK, SATURDAY, MAY 18, 1861.　　　[SINGLE COPIES SIX CENTS.
$2 50 PER YEAR IN ADVANCE.

Entered according to Act of Congress, in the Year 1861, by Harper & Brothers, in the Clerk's Office of the District Court for the Southern District of New York.

South Carolina State gunboat *Lady Davis*, later taken into Confederate Navy service. (*Harper's Weekly*)

private contractor John Hughes constructed *Bienville*, while Naval Constructor Sidney D Porter produced *Carondelet*. Contractor William Otis and Naval Constructor Henry Bassett, respectively, built *Gaines* and *Morgan* at Mobile. All four vessels were commissioned, though the New Orleans duo were destroyed shortly after completion when the city fell to Union forces in April 1862.

In late September 1861, at nearly the same time as the big sidewheelers were being laid down, Mallory ordered Captain

French Forrest to build two gunboats at Gosport Navy Yard, near Portsmouth, Virginia. This directive apparently resulted in the gunboats *Hampton* and *Nansemond*, which were completed just before the Confederate evacuation of the Hampton Roads area the following May. Although dimensional data is sketchy, the *Hampton* was descibed by a crewman as being about 116ft long and 18ft in beam. Depth of hold was not given but is thought to be about 8ft. Both boats were propelled by twin sawmill-type engines turning a single screw, and armed with two pivot guns — one forward and the other aft. It is unclear if *Hampton* and *Nansemond* were originally meant to be sail-rigged but apparently neither was so fitted during their active service careers. *Nansemond* (and probably

A model of the CSS *Gaines*, one of four sidewheel gunboats ordered to be built from the keel up in the summer of 1861. (Sidney H Schell)

Hampton) received extensive modifications during the war. An 1865 sketch of the former depicts a small pilot house, protective shields against small arms fire, and other structures on the gun deck.

Between October 3 and November 4, a trio of gunboat classes designed by constructor Porter were contracted for. All three classes shared the common charateristic of a 10ft depth of hold and propulsion provided by steam and sail. At least two of the classes (the two largest) were twin screw, with the steam machinery located in the extreme stern. These vessels had lengths between perpendiculars and moulded beams, respectively, of 110ft x 18ft, 130ft x 30ft, and 150ft x 25ft.[6]

Only one of the 110ft class is known to have been ordered, when the Navy Department contracted with the shipbuilding firm of Ollinger and Bruce of Bagdad, Florida, near Pensacola, on November 4. Designed to carry two pivot guns, a 10in smoothbore and a rifled 32pdr, this vessel had been launched but was still incomplete when destroyed to prevent its capture in March 1862. Two of the 130ft gunboats were contracted for: one with David S Johnston of Saffold, Early County, Georgia, on October 19, and another with Martin and Elliott of Elizabeth City, North Carolina, on October 22. Although the Martin and Elliott vessel was destroyed before completion to prevent capture, Johnston's boat, the *Chattahoochee*, went into service January 1, 1863. The *Chattahoochee* class gunboats were designed to carry three masts and mount two pivot and four broadside guns. The largest of the three

Porter gunboat classes, both in size and in numbers, was the 150ft *Macon* class. These craft were intended to be rigged with two masts and mount an armament of four broadside and two pivot guns. Contracts were let for at least seven of the 150ft gunboats. Of these, only *Macon*, built by H F Willink at Savannah, Georgia, and *Peedee*, built by the Navy on the Peedee River, South Carolina, were completed.

In early November, as the last of the 10ft depth gunboats were being contracted for, the Navy Department invited Norfolk shipwrights William A. Graves and Nathaniel Nash to submit proposals for constructing one gunboat each designed by Naval Constructor Porter. The contract proposal gave their dimensions as 112ft x 20ft x 8ft, and described them as being propeller-driven with two masts and gaffs. Except for the sail rig, these small craft were similar to the gunboats conceived by Matthew Fontaine Maury and then being designed. In late November Graves signed a contract to build one vessel, evidently to this design; apparently other boats were later added to the contract. Two, *Dixie* and another unnamed, were nearing completion when Norfolk was evacuated by the Confederates the following spring and were destroyed. The Navy accepted Nash's offer to build two of the gunboats in early December. One was captured unfinished by Federals and completed as the US Army gunboat *General Jesup*. The other was possibly the CSS *Drewry*, which was towed to safety up the James River and completed at Richmond.

150ft gunboat class as designed, 1861. (Robert Holcombe, from original plans)

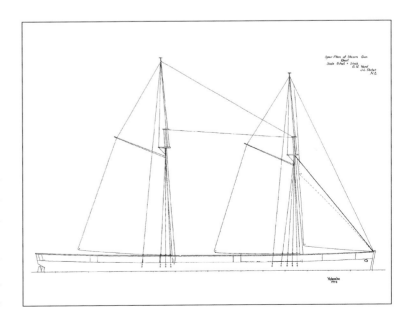

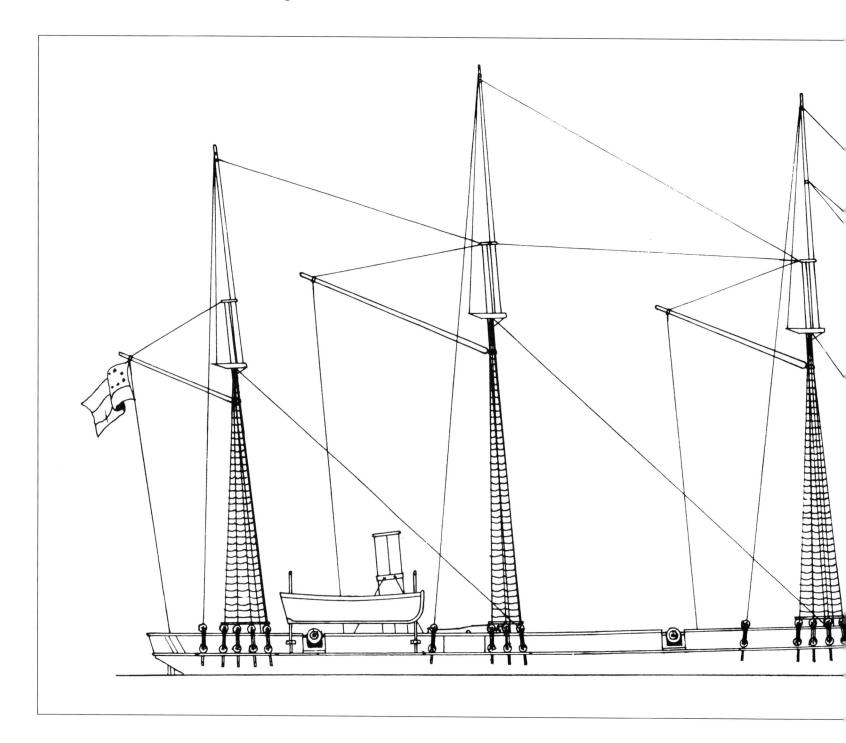

130ft gunboat CSS *Chattahoochee*. (WMCWNH)

The most ambitious of all the Confederacy's warship con-struction programmes – wooden or ironclad – was that conceived by Cmdr Matthew Fontaine Maury, the great oceanographer of the pre-war era. Since the early 1840s Maury had advocated a navy based on the premise that squadrons of small, light-draft gunboats, quickly and cheaply produced, were equal or superior to large warships carrying the same number and type of armament.

As planned by Maury, these boats were to operate in divisions of ten, guarding the Southern coastline and attacking in swarms when opposed. Largely because of Maury's popularity and politi-cal influence, the Confederate Congress passed a bill on December 23, 1861, authorizing $2 million for the construction of one hundred such gunboats.[7]

The initial plan for the Maury gunboats called for a single screw-propelled gunboat measuring 106ft loa x 21ft x 8 ft, with a draft of 5ft. A slightly larger version, with a length of 112ft loa and a draft of 6ft, was later adopted. The gunboats were designed

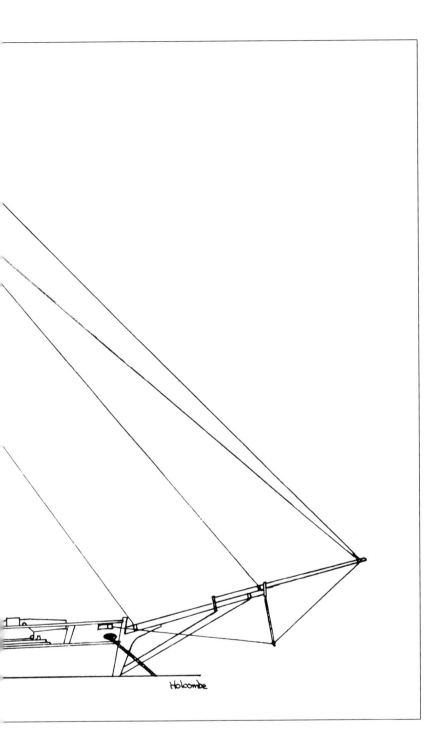

Holcombe

The Battle of Hampton Roads brought Maury's programme to a sudden halt. *Virginia's* triumph on March 8, 1862, and her subsequent battle with USS *Monitor* the following day, conclusively demonstrated the superiority of iron over wood. As a result, many who had supported the gunboat programme because they believed the ironclad to be an untested weapon in ship-to-ship combat, were convinced otherwise. Soon afterwards Congress suspended the gunboat appropriation, with the exception of the fifteen already under construction, and applied the remaining balance to the building of ironclads. Maury's ambitious plans for masses of tiny warships guarding the Southern coastline thus came to an end, smothered finally by the rapid changes occurring in naval technology

Later in the war two small screw gunboats designed for two guns and intended for use in the shallow North Carolina sounds were laid down on the Roanoke River. One, a 91ft steamer, was captured unfinished at the war's end at Halifax, and the other, named *Fisher* (81ft x 17ft x 6ft), was seized unfinished in 1865 at nearby Edwards Ferry.

In keeping with Mallory's wish to have warships built abroad, two iron twin-screw steamers designed for coastal defense at Wilmington were ordered from Denny Brothers, Dumbarton, Scotland, in September 1864. Built under cover names *Ajax* and *Hercules*, these vessels measured 170ft x 25ft x 12ft 6in and were intended to carry an 8in and a 9in rifle. *Ajax*, to be renamed *Olustee*, sailed for Nassau the following January but failed to reach a Southern port before the war ended. *Hercules*, ultimately to be *Vicksburg*, never reached Confederate hands.[8]

Privateers and commerce raiders

The destruction of an adversary's maritime commerce is a common strategy utilized by a weaker naval power in time of war. The Americans effectively used commerce raiding, or *guerre de course*, against Great Britain's large and indispensable merchant fleet during the Revolution and the War of 1812; for similar reasons the Confederacy employed the same strategy against Northern shipping during the American Civil War. Using both privateers and commissioned naval warships, commerce raiding proved in some respects to be the South's most successful naval weapon.

Privateers were privately owned vessels which operated as warships under a government license, or letter of marque, which allowed them to prey on enemy merchant ships for prize money.

to carry a rifled 32pdr forward and a 9in smoothbore aft, but in practice this varied. In particular, the 32pdr rifle was often replaced with a 6.4in Brooke rifle.

At least thirteen Maury gunboats were contracted for in early 1862 and as many as fifteen are believed to have been laid down. *Isondiga*, built by Krenson and Hawkes at Savannah, and *Torch*, started by F M Jones at Charleston but completed as a torpedo ram by Army Captain F D Lee, are the only two known with certainty to have been completed. *Yadkin*, completed at Wilmington in 1864, is another likely candidate but verifiable documentation is lacking.

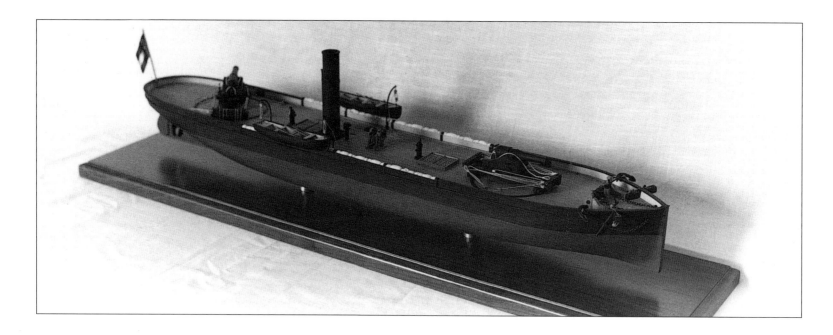

Maury gunboat, a model of the class as intended by Commander Matthew F Maury. (WMCWNH)

Privateering had long been a staple of naval warfare, but in 1856 the Declaration of Paris outlawed the practice and placed restrictions on commerce raiding in general. Of the major powers, only the United States and Spain refrained from signing the agreement. Thus when faced with the need to quickly raise a naval force and carry the war to the Northern states on the high seas, President Jefferson Davis felt unrestrained when he offered letters of marque to interested citizens of the new Confederacy in his proclamation of April 17, 1861. About fifty applicants responded to the President's call but only a few of those receiving letters of marque actually took to the seas. Most privateers were small sailing vessels but several large steamers, like the 175ft five-gun sidewheeler *Calhoun*, also engaged in the practice. Several of the more unusual privateers were the 34ft submarine *Pioneer* and the Civil War's first ironclad warship, the ram *Manassas*. Nearly forty prizes were taken by privateers, the brig *Jefferson Davis* being the most successful with nine captures. The tightening Federal blockade, which prevented easy egress of Southern ports for adjudication of prizes, caused most privateer owners to switch to the more lucrative blockade running trade, and the practice essentially ended by the second year of the war.[9]

The commissioned cruisers of the Confederate Navy proved considerably more successful at commerce raiding than did the private vessels. As early as April 26, 1861 Secretary Mallory expressed a desire to place fast lightly armed commerce raiders on the high seas. His motives were two-fold: to ravage the enemy's carrying trade thereby disrupting the economy and morale of the North, and to weaken the blockade by compelling the enemy to

The Confederate Privateer *Petrel*, sunk on her first cruise by USS *St. Lawrence*, July 28, 1861, without taking a prize. (Naval Historical Center)

CSS *Alabama,*
the most successful of
the commerce raiders.
A photograph taken at Singapore,
December 1863. (Tennessee State Library and Archives)

detach ships in pursuit of the raiders. Although the steamer *Habana* had been purchased earlier at New Orleans and rapidly converted into the cruiser *Sumter*, Mallory believed that suitable commerce raiders could not easily be acquired or constructed in the South and that they must be obtained overseas. The following month, with one million dollars appropriated by Congress, Mallory began sending officers abroad to secure suitable vessels. The most successful of these procurement agents was Cmdr James D Bulloch of Georgia. Operating out of Liverpool, Bulloch carefully skirted the British Foreign Enlistment Act (which prohibited the equipping and manning of ships-of-war by belligerent nations in British territory) and quickly contracted with English builders William C Miller & Sons of Liverpool and John Laird, Sons and Company of nearby Birkenhead for two purpose-built, steam

propeller raiders based on modified Royal Navy gunboat plans. Miller's vessel was to be 184ft 6in x 27ft 2in x 14ft, while Laird's was to be somewhat larger at 210ft x 32ft x 17ft 3in; both ships were designed to mount eight guns. Commissioned the following summer as *Florida* and *Alabama*, these soon-to-be-famous ships possessed the necessary speed to outrun more powerful warships, an armament sufficient to match any enemy that might catch them, wooden hulls for ease of repair in distant, primitive ports, and a full sailing rig and lifting screw mechanism to extend their cruising range. These were ideal characteristics for prosperous commerce raiding and helped to make *Florida* and *Alabama* the two most successful Confederate cruisers. Indeed, Bulloch's sound judgement and skillful diplomacy served the South well; *Florida* and *Alabama*, along with his later purchased acquisition *Shenandoah*,

A model of the CSS *Florida*. (Florida State Museum, Tallahassee)

accounted for over 60 per cent of all captures made by Confederate commerce raiders. The distinctive twin-funnelled *Florida*, under the command of Cmdr John Newland Maffitt and later Lieut John M Morris, made a successful two-year cruise during which she took thirty-seven prizes and spawned three satellite cruisers which captured nearly two dozen more. *Florida's* career ended when she was illegally captured in neutral Brazilian waters by the USS *Wachusett* in October 1864. Under the legendary Raphael Semmes, *Alabama* embarked on a similar two-year cruise which took her from the Atlantic Ocean to the South China Sea. During this period she sank, bonded, or ransomed sixty-nine ships, including the USS *Hatteras* - the only United States warship sunk on the high seas by a Confederate cruiser. The US sloop *Kearsarge* finally caught and sank *Alabama* after a 1 hour 27 minute ship-to-ship duel off Cherbourg, France, on June 19, 1864.[10]

Additional commerce raiders were contracted for in Great Britain and France by Bulloch and other naval agents. Cmdr George T Sinclair arranged with James and George Thomson of Clydebank, Glasgow, for the construction a 230ft screw cruiser to be named *Texas*, while Bulloch contracted for at least another six

potential raiders. Two, the 250ft twin-screw *Black Warrior* and *Waccamaw*, were being built by William Denny Brothers, Dumbarton, Scotland. Four others, 220ft screw corvettes to be commissioned *Georgia*, *Louisiana*, *Mississippi* and *Texas*, were ordered from Lucien Arman of Bordeaux, France, who sub-contracted two of the ships to another French builder, J Voruz of Nantes. For a variety of reasons, including stricter enforcement of neutrality laws, none of these vessels reached Confederate hands.

Whenever possible suitable ships were purchased in Britain and altered to cruisers. In April 1864 James Bulloch acquired the 220ft fast sail/steam merchant ship *Sea King* for conversion to cruiser warfare. As *Shenandoah* she embarked on an epic, globe-circling cruise that took her as far as the Arctic Ocean where she destroyed a considerable portion of the New England whaling fleet. Not learning of the war's end until August 1865, *Shenandoah* returned to Liverpool and was turned over to the English authorities on November 6, 1865. She was the last Southern warship to fly the Confederate ensign. Following Bulloch to England in 1862, Cmdr Matthew Fontaine Maury purchased two vessels for the Confederacy. In early 1863 he bought the 212ft iron-hulled, screw merchant steamer *Japan* and had her converted to the raider *Georgia*. After a brief cruise in the Atlantic, which resulted in nine captures, *Georgia* was decommissioned and sold because of her general unsuitablity for cruiser warfare. Maury next purchased the 200ft ex-Royal Navy gunvessel *Victor*, a bark-rigged, screw steamer that had been built during the Crimean War and decommissioned soon afterwards. Renamed *Rappahannock*, she left Britain in late November 1863 to receive armament and stores from the unsatisfactory *Georgia* off Morocco, but put in to Calais, France, when her machinery failed. There she ran afoul of French neutrality concerns and served as a store and station ship until decommissioned and sold in March 1865.

The Confederates also converted several prize ships into satellite cruisers. The brig *Clarence* was commissioned on the high seas following her seizure by *Florida* in May 1863. After making several captures *Clarence* was set afire and her crew and stores transferred to the more suitable prize bark *Tacony*. In turn, *Tacony* suffered a similar fate in favour of the small fishing schooner *Archer*, following a successful cruise which resulted in fourteen prizes. Federal forces ultimately recaptured *Archer* off the coast of Maine, but not before *Florida*'s three subsidiary raiders had taken twenty-one prizes. On June 20, 1863 *Alabama* captured the bark *Conrad* in the south Atlantic off Brazil. Finding the vessel to be fast and well suited for commerce raiding, the Confederates armed and commissioned her. As *Tuscaloosa* she captured two ships but was later seized at Simon's Bay, South Africa, for allegedly violating English neutrality laws. Although these charges were later disproved, *Tuscaloosa* never served the Confederacy again.

Despite Mallory's opinion that proper commerce raiders could only be obtained abroad, several ships were acquired in the Confederacy and converted into productive high seas cruisers. In the spring of 1861 *Habana*, a 170ft auxiliary screw steamer built in 1859 at Philadelphia, was acquired at New Orleans and altered by Raphael Semmes into the Confederate Navy's first ocean raider. Commissioned *Sumter*, she engaged in a brief six-month cruise and netted eighteen prizes. She was later sold to private interests for blockade-running. About five months after *Sumter*'s purchase the Confederates acquired the 215ft sidewheel passenger steamer *Nashville* at Charleston and armed her for commerce raiding. After brief service in that capacity, during which she took two prizes and became the first Confederate warship to visit an English port, *Nashville* was also sold to private parties for blockade running. Later in the war two English-built, twin-screw blockade-runners, the 175ft *Edith* and the 220ft *Atalanta*, were purchased and armed at Wilmington. Renamed *Chickamauga* and *Tallahassee* (later *Olustee*), both made successful raids along the northeastern coast of the United States. *Tallahassee/Olustee* reverted to blockade-running as

Chameleon in late 1864 and survived the war, while *Chickamauga* served as an armed element of the Wilmington squadron until scuttled on the evacuation of the city in February 1865.

Later in the war the Navy Department attempted to build several commerce raiders in the Confederacy. In early November 1863 naval Secretary Mallory requested an appropriation from Congress 'for the construction of four steam cruisers of the class of the *Alabama* and *Florida* in the Confederate States' at a cost of $2.5 million. A navy yard was established at McIntosh Bluff, Alabama, on the Tombigbee River above Mobile, but no additional information has been found on the construction of these vessels. [11]

Armoured vessels

Navy Secretary Mallory's desire to rely on new and innovative technology to counter the numerical superiority of the US Navy prompted Congress to appropriate $2 million on May 10, 1861 for the purchase or construction of ironclads in Europe. A week later Mallory ordered Lieut James H North abroad with instructions to secure one or two such vessels. If possible North was to purchase the French armoured frigate *Gloire* or another vessel of the same description; if unobtainable, he was instructed to have

CSS *Sumter*, one of the first vessels purchased by Mallory for conversion to a warship. (Semmes, *Memoirs of Service Afloat*)

built two similar ironclads mounting six or eight heavy guns. Soon after North left for Europe, Mallory decided to construct an ironclad in the Confederacy. After a series of meetings with naval officers John M Brooke, John L Porter, and William P Williamson to evaluate potential designs, Mallory elected to convert the remains of the USS *Merrimack* into an ironclad as the most expedient method of obtaining the desired warship. A 275ft screw frigate built in 1856, *Merrimack* had been burned and sunk by retreating Union sailors when Gosport Navy Yard, Virginia, was evacuated the previous April. Although her upper works had been completely consumed by fire, *Merrimack*'s lower hull and steam machinery were relatively unharmed.[12]

On July 11, Mallory ordered the transformation of the ex-Union warship to proceed. Based on plans developed by Brooke and Porter, a strong wooden casemate, or shield, with rounded ends was constructed on *Merrimack*'s hull. This house-like structure's sides and ends were approximately 2ft thick and angled at 35° to the horizon. The Confederates initially planned to cover the casemate's exterior with three layers of 1in iron but 4in laminated plate was applied instead when ordnance experiments demonstrated that the lighter armour could be penetrated at close range by 8in and 9in smoothbore guns. Additional armour would cover the hull below the knuckle (the junction of the casemate and the hull), while a 2in thick iron grating on the casemate roof (often referred to as the spar deck) would provide light, ventilation, and protection to the gun deck below. The ironclad's designers had chosen the casemate structure because of its simplicity. With few industries in the South geared to naval construction at the beginning of the war, the casemate offered an ease of fabrication that the more complex, conventionally armoured ship then building in Europe could not match. Moreover, by inclining the

P rofile of CSS *Virginia.* (Robert Holcombe)

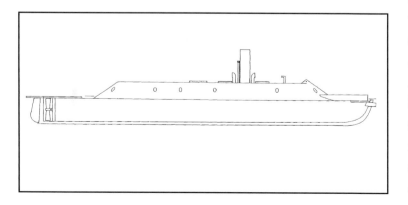

casemate's sides the Confederates believed that resistance was appreciably increased over the near vertical sides of the seagoing European ironclads.

Ten muzzleloading cannon within the armoured casemate comprised the vessel's ordnance. Six of these were 9in Dahlgren shell guns, part of *Merrimack*'s original armament. The remaining guns consisted of two 6.4in and two 7in calibre rifles designed specifically for the armourclad by Lieut Brooke. The 7in rifles were pivot-mounted in the extremities of the casemate and designed to fire on the vessel's centerline or from port and starboard quarter ports. The remaining guns were mounted in broadside, four to a side. As an additional offensive weapon, a 1,500lb cast iron ram was attached to the stem about 3ft below the waterline. The vessel's most unusual characteristics were her submerged extremities, which were purportedly designed to provide speed, bouyancy and protection to the hull. As the conversion neared completion in early 1862, Secretary Mallory capped *Merrimack*'s metamorphosis by christening her *Virginia.*

Despite poor speed, wretched manoeuverability, and an excessive draft of 21ft (later increased to 23ft), *Virginia*'s auspicious performance against Union naval forces at Hampton Roads, Virginia, in March 1862 established her as the prototype of Southern ironclads. Her ram bow, sloped wooden casemate covered with laminated armour plate, and combination of broadside and pivot guns – which included rifled cannon – became characteristic features of virtually every armoured ship built by the South. On the other hand, *Virginia*'s rounded casemate ends and submerged hull extremities were aberrations not seen on another operational Confederate ironclad.

In addition to *Virginia* at least three other ironclads were transformed from existing ships during the first year of the war: *Manassas*, *Baltic* and *Eastport*. Two others, *Atlanta* and *Mobile*, were commenced during the second year of the war when suitable vessels became available for the purpose. The most successful of these conversions were *Manassas* and *Atlanta*. The unorthodox *Manassas* was altered from a twin-screw tow boat by having a lightly armoured, convex 'turtle-back' shield built over her main deck. Armed with only one gun, she was intended primarily as a ram. *Atlanta* was converted at Savannah from the stranded British-built blockade runner *Fingal* into one of the strongest ironclads built in the South during the first half of the war. Along with her powerful Scottish steam engines, *Atlanta* was equipped with four Brooke rifles of 6.4 and 7in caliber, a ram bow, and later had a spar torpedo mounted on her bow. *Atlanta*'s greatest defect was her excessive

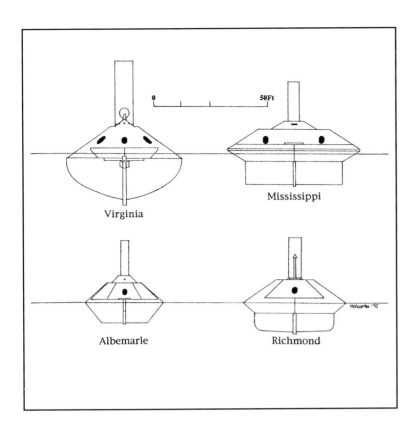

A comparison of ironclad hull types. (Robert Holcombe)

draft of about 16ft, which caused her grounding and capture in June 1863.

While the conversion of *Merrimack* was still under way, five ironclads were begun from the keel up: *Georgia, Louisiana, Mississippi*, and sisters *Arkansas* and *Tennessee (I)*. With the exception of *Georgia*, the designs of these vessels reflected an offensive policy inititaly advocated by Mallory which required ironclads capable of operating on the high seas and attacking Union blockaders. Although their designs varied, all shared one or more common characteristics of a heavy armament of ten or more guns, excessively large dimensions, and unorthodox features in their manner of construction and/or means of propulsion. The unconventional arrangements of several of these vessels demonstrated a lack of experience in naval architecture by their designers. *Louisiana* was conceived and built at New Orleans by veteran steamboat builder E C Murray of Kentucky, and several aspects of the vessel's construction, notably the use of longitudinal bulkheads within her hull and paddlewheels for propulsion, reflect his experience with river craft. Measuring 264ft loa x 62ft x 7 ft, and designed to carry twenty-two guns, Murray's vessel was one of the largest ironclads commenced in the Confederacy. The most unusual feature of

Louisiana was her propulsion system. Four engines and six steam boilers powered two tandem paddlewheels in the center of the hull and two small steering propellers located on the stern quarters. As powerful as this propulsion system seemed at the time, it was insufficient to move the massive hull of *Louisiana* against the swift current of the Mississippi River and she had to be used as a floating battery during the naval battle below New Orleans. Potentially the most powerful of the early purpose-built ironclads was *Mississippi*, designed by brothers Asa and Nelson Tift of Florida and Georgia. Possessing no practical shipbuilding experience, the Tifts conceived a simplified warship design completely devoid of intricately curved hull frames. By using only straight lines, the brothers believed that a warship built according to their precepts could be rapidly produced without the need of skilled shipwrights. The vessel was intended to be 230ft x 58ft x 15ft, and carry eighteen guns behind a casemate plated with 3¾in of iron, but alterations increased her length by 20ft and her ordnance by two guns. *Mississippi*'s propulsion system consisted of three high-pressure engines, sixteen boilers, and three 11ft screws. Although the Tifts were unable to complete *Mississippi* before the fall of New Orleans in April 1862, she was one of the first triple-screw warships designed. The twin-screw sisters *Arkansas* and *Tennessee (I)* were designed by Naval Constructor Porter and built by contractor John T Shirley at Memphis, Tennessee. Smaller than the other early ironclads at 165ft x 35ft x 12ft, they nevertheless carried a heavy armament of ten guns. An unusual characteristic of the class was a casemate design featuring vertical sides, which forfeited the deflecting advantage of angled armour. Their casemate ends were more typically slanted at 35°. Only *Arkansas* was completed, after being taken to Yazoo City, Mississippi, just before the fall of Memphis. Unlike the other early ironclads, *Georgia* was hurriedly built in early 1862 as a steam-powered, floating battery intended to assist in the defense of Fort Pulaski, near Savannah, Georgia, and not for offensive operations on the high seas. In common with the other early vessels, however, she carried a heavy battery of nine guns. *Georgia*'s design is attributed to A N Miller, a Savannah foundryman with little or no experience in naval architecture. When Fort Pulaski fell prior to her completion, *Georgia* served out the war as a floating river battery with machinery too weak to stem the tide.

Successful amphibious attacks on key Southern coastal points during the late summer and early fall of 1861 caused Mallory to shift from an offensive naval strategy to one concerned mainly with defending the Confederacy's vulnerable harbors and rivers.

This new defensive scheme required ironclads that were smaller, more manoeuvrable, and lighter draft than the large seagoing ironclads then under construction. As a result, in early 1862 the Confederate Navy adopted two basic designs which became standard models for most of the ironclads built thereafter. The first of the standardized designs chosen was the *Richmond* class, a group of six-plus ironclads (*Chicora, North Carolina, Palmetto State, Raleigh, Richmond, Savannah* and others unfinished) commenced in the spring of 1862. The single-screw *Richmond* design featured a lower hull of conventional form, with slightly rising floors and a round bilge. At the waterline a solid knuckle, or sponson, protruded 5ft from the hull and protected that vulnerable area from battle damage. Built on the hull was a casemate similar to *Virginia*'s in inclination and thickness of protection, but containing a reduced armament of only four guns: one pivot-mounted at either end and another on each broadside. The designed molded dimensions of the *Richmonds* were 150ft x 34ft x 14ft, while the extreme dimensions were 174ft x 45ft. The intended draft was 13ft, which was a significant improvement over *Virginia*'s 23ft but hardly better than most of the 1861 ironclads.

The built-on knuckle hull form, which Porter claimed to have borrowed from an ironclad plan he had conceived in the 1840s, became numerically the most important configuration used by the Confederate Navy after early 1862. Similarly designed ironclads following the *Richmonds* tended to be stretched versions designed to carry greater firepower. They include the 180ft x 34ft x 14ft *Charleston* class (*Charleston, Virginia II* and others unfinished) designed by Naval Constructor William A Graves, and the Porter-designed 189ft x 34ft x 14ft *Tennessee* class (*Tennessee, Columbia,* and *Texas*). The 250ft x 62ft x 13ft *Nashville* class (*Nashville* and others unfinished) was a sidewheel version developed by Porter in order to take advantage of the widespread availability of riverboat machinery in the South. The designs of these second-generation *Richmonds* often incorporated refinements based on combat and operational experience with the earlier ironclads. Influenced by the shocking capture of *Atlanta* in June 1863, many had an additional 2in of iron (for a total of 6in) added to their casemates as increased protection against the big 15in smoothbore cannon carried by some Union warships. According to several accounts, *Virginia II* carried 8in of iron on her forward casemate end and 6in on the remaining sides. If true she was the most heavily armoured warship built by the Confederacy. Those ironclads receiving extra armour plate invariably had their casemates shortened and often their armaments reduced in order to maintain their designed drafts.

CSS *Savannah, a Richmond-class ironclad. (Robert Holcombe)*

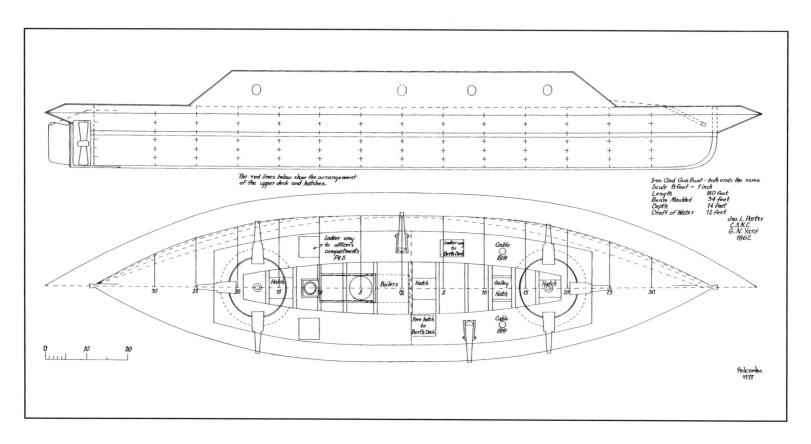

Porter also developed two shallow draft versions of the standard *Richmond* hull form, *Milledgeville* and *Wilmington*. Built on 12ft depth hulls with designed 9ft drafts, both were propelled by twin screws. *Milledgeville* had a short, four-gun casemate covered with 6in of iron, while *Wilmington* had two short casemates, each containing a single, pivot-mounted gun. Neither vessel was completed before war's end. Late in the war Naval Constructor Graves designed an unusual double-ended ironclad that possibly used the *Richmond* hull form. Measuring 220ft x 27ft x 11ft 6in, this vessel had a rudder, two propellers, and a ram on each end so that she could steam in either direction without having to turn around. A single gun was carried in a short casemate plated with an unspecified thickness of armour. Although commenced in 1864 at Richmond by Graves the war ended before her completion.

The second standardized design adopted in conformance to Mallory's new defensive policy was intended for construction at inland sites far from sources of skilled shipwrights. These ironclads had simplified hull forms, usually characterized by flat bottoms and chine bilges. Their scantlings were unusually lighter than those of other classes of ironclad and none carried more than 4in of armour. Warships built to this plan are commonly referred to as diamond hull types because of their diamond-shaped configurations when viewed from end-on. Intended primarily for riverine warfare, most had depths of hold of about 10ft and shallow drafts of around 8ft. With the exception of a single paddlewheel class, all of the diamond hull ironclads were propelled by twin screws.

Four to eight flat-bottomed, light draft ironclads ordered by Mallory in late March 1862 were probably the earliest diamond hull vessels placed under construction. Laid down in the Tidewater region of Virginia, none of these two-gun warships were completed before the Confederate evacuation of the area later that spring. The first diamond hull ironclads to enter service were the sisters *Huntsville* and *Tuscaloosa*. Both were built under contract by Henry D Bassett at Selma, Alabama, in 1862–63. Accurate statistical data on these ships is lacking, but they were estimated to have been 150 to 175ft long and have 7 to 8ft drafts. Each mounted four guns. Two similar ironclads, measuring 160ft x 41ft x 10ft 6in, were commenced on the nearby Tombigbee River but never completed. The *Albemarle* class is considered the quintessential version of the diamond hull ironclad. Consisting of *Albemarle*, *Neuse* and another destroyed before completion at Tarboro, North Carolina, this group of small ironclads was designed by Porter for use in the shallow North Carolina sounds. Original builder's drafts delineate a light draft, two-gun vessel with dimensions of 139ft x 34ft x 9ft, on a 6ft 6in draft, though *Albemarle* and *Neuse* differed slightly from both these plans and each other in size and gun port layout. Typically, both ironclads exceeded the designed draft by about 1½ft. A lengthened four-gun version of the *Albemarle* was also designed by Porter. Built at Richmond as the CSS *Fredericksburg*, she measured 170ft x 40ft x 10ft 10in, on an 8 to 9ft draft.

The centerwheel *Missouri* class, like the standard hull *Nashville*, was conceived by Porter to take advantage of existing high

Blockade-runners in Nassau early in 1864. (*Illustrated London News*)

pressure riverboat machinery, which was better suited for driving paddlewheels than turning screws. Powered by a single, 22ft diameter wheel recessed within and protected by the casemate, the *Missouri*s were designed to be 190ft x 56ft x 9ft 9in, on an optimistic 6ft draft. Their intended armament was eight guns, including a single exposed pivot gun on the short aft flush deck. *Missouri*, built at Shreveport, Louisiana, conformed closely to the original design specs but drew 8ft 6in and carried only three guns; *Jackson*, building at the war's end at Columbus, Georgia, was radically reconstructed while still on the stocks in order to decrease her draft. She was altered to a twin screw configuration with a lengthened hull (c. 225ft loa) and a shortened six-gun casemate. At least two other *Missouri*s were considered but none were apparently started.

In early 1865, the Navy Department approved the construction of a turreted, monitor-type diamond hull ironclad at Columbus, Georgia. Conceived by Chief Engineer James H Warner, this vessel was to be 175ft x 45ft x 9ft and carry two 11in Brooke smoothbores within a 23ft diameter turret protected by 12in of iron backed with 14in of wood. Columbus's capture in April 1865 ended any chance of the Confederate Navy building this warship.[13]

While the Confederacy's efforts to construct ironclads domestically proved remarkably successful, attempts to acquire similar warships abroad were considerably less so. Mallory's first purchasing agent, Lieut James H North, failed in his mission to procure *Gloire* or any other existing ironclad from the French. It was nearly a year after being ordered overseas before he finally initiated the construction of an ironclad from the keel up. In late May 1862 North contracted with J & G Thomson, Glasgow, Scotland, for the building of a large seagoing armoured ram. Variously called the 'Scottish Sea Monster', or *No. 61* (her hull number at the Thomsons' yard), North's vessel seemed a powerful warship. With dimensions of 270ft wl x 50ft x 30ft, *No. 61* was designed to carry a conventional broadside armament of twenty guns on a 20ft draft. Her armour protection consisted of a maximum of 4½in of iron amidships backed with 18in of teak. Although formidable on paper, in reality *No. 61* suffered from an extravagant design which made her unsuitable for work in Southern waters. She was too large, drew too much water, required an excessively large crew of 500, and would be likely to expend immense quantities of fuel once in service. Moreover, because of her obvious warlike characteristics *No. 61* quickly conflicted with British neutrality laws, causing North to terminate his contract with Thomson in late December 1863. The vessel was ultimately sold to the Danish Navy where she operated as *Danmark*.[14]

James D Bulloch, Mallory's most productive foreign agent, contended with problems similar to North's in his efforts to

procure ironclads in Britain and suffered the same disappointing results. In mid-June 1862 Bulloch contracted with Laird's, builders of *Alabama*, for the construction of two armoured rams. Measuring 224ft 6in x 42ft 4in, but drawing only about 15ft of water, Bulloch's two vessels were smaller and better suited to Confederate needs than the North's. They mounted four 9in rifled guns in twin rotating gun turrets protected by 5½in of iron backed with 12in of teak. Their hulls were covered amidships by a 4½in armour belt backed with 12in of teak and an inner layer of ⅝in of iron. A large iron ram projecting about 7ft from the bow added to the vessels' potential offensive power and provided their sobriquet for posterity: the 'Laird Rams'. Screw propulsion and auxilliary sail were to provide an estimated 10kts speed. Bulloch tried to circumvent both British neutrality concerns and close scrutiny by Federal diplomats to insure delivery of the rams to Confederate hands upon completion. He devised an elaborate subterfuge by rigging a sham sale to the Egyptian navy and giving the ships the cover names *El Toussan* and *El Monassir*. The scheme failed, and in October 1863 the rams were detained by the British Government. The following year both were purchased by the Admiralty and became HMS *Scorpion* and HMS *Wivern*.[15]

Even before the Laird Rams were seized the changing political climate in Britain, which was working to the South's disadvantage, had prompted Bulloch to seek ironclads elsewhere. Believing that Napoleon III of France was more favourable to the Confederate cause, Bulloch crossed the Channel in the summer of 1863 and contracted with Bordeaux shipbuilder Lucien Arman for the construction of two small sail/steam rams. Only a few weeks before Arman had reached a tentative agreement with Matthew F Maury to build a 1,358-ton twin-screw ironclad with two armoured turrets for the Confederate Navy, but the plan fell through. Bulloch's rams, to be named *Cheops* and *Sphinx*, were probably similar to Maury's but carried fewer guns and had no rotating gun turrets. At 171ft 10in x 32ft 8in x 14ft 4in draft, they were designed expressly to operate in shallow Southern waters, with some thought to the recapturing of New Orleans. To facilitate manoeuvrability in confined waters, the rams were designed with twin sternposts, screws and rudders which enabled them to turn in their own lengths. Their armament consisted of two 6.4in rifles pivot-mounted in a stationary turret-shaped casemate aft, and a 9in rifle pivot-mounted in the forecastle. A 3½ to 4¾in armour belt backed with 16in of wood protected the hull, while the forecastle and casemate were protected with 4½in plate. A massive ram extended submerged from the bow.[22] In late 1863 Arman was forced to sell the ships when the French Government reneged on an earlier commitment not to interfere with their delivery to the Confederate Navy. *Cheops* went to Prussia as *Prinz Adalbert*, while *Sphinx* became the Danish warship *Staerkodder*. When the termination of the Danish-Prussian war relieved the Danes of their need of *Staerkodder* she was sold back to Lucien Arman. Bulloch was then able to purchase the ram through a prearranged agreement and she was commissioned as CSS *Stonewall* in January 1865 – the only foreign-built ironclad to reach Confederate hands. Unfortunately for the Confederates, *Stonewall* arrived in Havana in May 1865 only to find the Civil War ended. Following transfer to the United States Navy by the Spanish, *Stonewall* was sold to Japan and renamed *Kotetsu*, then *Azuma*. She was the Japanese Navy's first armoured warship and saw combat during the Meiji Restoration War of the late 1860s.[16]

At least two ironclad designs were developed within the Confederacy for construction in Europe. On April 19, 1862, a joint resolution of Congress provided funding for the construction of six sail/steam ironclad rams in Britain in response to a contract between the government and G N Sanders of Virginia. Sanders proposed operating these seagoing ironclads as self-defending freight and mail transports between the Confederacy and Europe. They were also meant to operate as commerce raiders during their cross-Atlantic runs, with Sanders receiving one-third the value of any prizes captured. These multi-purpose screw steamers were planned by Constructor Porter, and measured 234ft x 47ft 6in x 17ft draft. Their intended armament was six to eight guns carried in a short, sponson-like casemate. None were built, as much the result of their ill-conceived mission as with their obvious conflict with British neutrality laws. Three months later, Secretary Mallory instructed Cmdr John M Brooke to prepare plans for a seagoing ironclad to be built abroad. Working with Acting Constructor Graves, Brooke developed a design of unknown dimensions, and drawings were sent to England. Apparently the ship was never commenced for no additional references have been found in surviving naval records.[17]

Blockade-runners

President Abraham Lincoln's blockade proclamation of April 19, 1861 had little initial impact on the South's ability to import needed war supplies. With fewer than fifty serviceable warships, the US Navy was incapable of enforcing a strict blockade of the Confederacy's 3,500-mile shoreline and European cargoes could be shipped direct into Southern ports on large ocean-going merchantmen with little fear of capture. An increasingly restrictive barricade eventually forced a change in the method of carrying out the clandestine trade of blockade-running. Small and fast Southern coastal packets came to be preferred because of their ability to work shallow channels and offshore waters to elude the larger and more numerous blockaders. Lacking the cargo and fuel

carrying capacities of the heavy seagoing ships, these small side-wheel runners were unsuited for the direct transatlantic voyage. Instead, a system evolved whereby goods were brought from Europe to intermediate ports in large neutral carriers, then transferred to the lighter, faster ships for the final dash through the blockade. St. George, Bermuda, Nassau, Bahamas and Havana, Cuba, became the primary trans-shipment points because of their proximity to the major Confederate ports of Wilmington, Charleston and Mobile. Ultimately, a very specialized ship emerged that was constructed specifically for running the blockade. In early 1862, British coastal and cross-channel passenger steamers were beginning to be modified and used as blockade-runners. Built for the most part on the River Clyde, Scotland, these rakish vessels were usually characterized by side paddlewheels, iron hulls, and two or more smokestacks. Because they combined exceptional speed and manoeuvrability with a large cargo capacity on a light draft, the Clyde steamers – and similar types built on the River Mersey – proved remarkably well-suited for blockade-running and quickly became the favoured ship-type. By mid-1863 purpose-built ships based on the Clyde steamer model were entering the trade. The new runners incorporated additional features intended to reduce their chance of capture and make them even more effective. Telescoping smokestacks, hinged masts, camouflage paint schemes, and underwater steam blow-off pipes were used to diminish the likelihood of their being seen or heard, while improvements in steam machinery and longer length-to-beam ratios (as much as 10 to 1) significantly increased speed. Advanced construction techniques, including the use of steel hulls, increased cargo capacity and yet maintained the shallow draft needed for work in Southern waters. Although most of the purpose-built vessels were sidewheelers, some twin-screw types were also used and proved effective blockade-runners. By late in the war ships were being built that could carry as many as 1,500 bales of cotton on a 9ft draft at speeds approaching 15kts.[18]

The Confederate Government's policy regarding blockade-running was initially one of non-intervention. With the exception of backing an embargo that temporarily controlled cotton exports in an attempt secure European support, President Davis preferred to rely on the private sector to manage the Confederacy's imports and exports. In late 1862, when more profitable goods for the civilian sector began to take precedence over much needed but less lucrative military supplies, the Ordnance Department purchased several blockade-runners of its own. Other Government agencies entered into contracts with private companies in order to ensure a steady supply of supplies, though exorbitant rates were often charged for cargo space. With ever increasing demands for war material, the Government finally took steps to more closely regulate blockade-running. In 1864 Congress passed laws controlling, among other things, the import and export of specific items and requiring private operators to reserve a predetermined amount of cargo space for government use. At the same time, the Government decided to establish its own line of blockade-runners to be operated by the War Department. As a result, at least fouteeen steamers were placed under construction in Britain but only a few were completed by the war's close.

The Confederate Navy's involvement in blockade-running closely mirrored that of the central Government. Like the War Department and its attendant bureaux, the Navy preferred to reply on private enterprise for the export of cotton to provide needed funds, and the import of supplies to supplement local production. From the beginning the Navy never continuously operated a fleet of blockade-runners, preferring instead to acquire vessels on an *ad hoc* basis to fulfill specific requirements that could not be met by the private runners. Yet despite its sporadic participation in blockade-running, the Navy generously allowed its officers to captain ships belonging to state Governments, private firms and other national departments. John J Guthrie, John N Maffitt and John Wilkinson were among numerous naval officers who proved to be effective blockade-runner commanders while working outside the Navy Department.

Although sparse and often contradictory records make a precise determination difficult, the Confederate Navy operated at least nine blockade-runners during the war. The schooner *Camilla* might be considered the Navy's first such vessel. Originally the famous racing yacht *America*, *Camilla* was purchased jointly by the Navy, State and War Departments in the spring of 1861 to transport Government purchasing agents from Savannah to England. Thereafter, *Camilla*'s activities – which possibly included blockade-running – are shrouded in mystery until her March 1862 capture near Jacksonville, Florida. There is no question about the steamer *Fingal*'s activities for she delivered one of the most valuable cargoes brought into the Confederacy. Purchased abroad in September 1861 by naval agent James D Bulloch for joint Army–Navy use, *Fingal* was a 178ft x 25ft x 18ft single-screw, iron-hulled ship that had been built earlier in the year on the River Clyde by J & G Thomson. Under the personal supervision of Bulloch and Army agent Edward C Anderson, *Fingal* ran the blockade into Savannah in November 1861 with an exceptionally large and valuable load

of munitions and supplies for the Navy and War Departments. When an outward run was thwarted by vigilant Union blockaders, *Fingal* was turned over to the Tift brothers and converted into the ironclad *Atlanta*.

Efforts to unravel the covert operations of the Navy's second blockade-runner, *Theodora*, are complicated by a series of changes in ownership, name and mission. Built in Greenpoint, New York, in 1851 as the 177ft x 27ft 6in x 11ft 2in sidewheel Charleston–Fernandina packet *Gordon*, the vessel first operated in the early months of the war as a successful privateer. Because of her speed and shoal draft, the Confederate Government chartered *Gordon* in early October 1861 to carry State Department commissioners John Slidell and James M Mason to Cuba for trans-shipment to Europe. Concurrently, *Gordon*'s name was changed to *Theodora*, probably in an attempt to confuse Union spies. After her return from a successful mission, Captain Duncan N Ingraham bought *Theodora* for joint use of the Navy and War Departments. Although the records are murky, the Navy apparently had responsibility for operating *Theodora*, while all operating costs (including the initial purchase price) were reimbursed by the War Department. *Theodora* made at least four successful trips through the blockade while under dual Army–Navy control. This alliance apparently existed until March or April 1862 when the vessel was sold to John Fraser and Company. As *Nassau* she was captured a short time later trying to run the blockade into Wilmington.[19]

The acquisition of the Department's next two runners occurred when naval funds abroad were nearly depleted by the extensive building and purchasing programmes initiated by Bulloch, North and others during the first two years of the war. To finance these and future overseas procurements Mallory ordered two fast warships, CSS *Stono* and CSS *Oconee*, converted for the purpose of running cotton out of the Confederacy. Neither vessel proved capable of fulfilling this important mission. *Stono* had been built as the wooden, single-screw, steamer *Isaac Smith* in 1861 at Brooklyn, New York. Measuring 171ft 6in x 31ft 4in x 9ft, she was acquired for Federal service in 1861 during the rapid build-up of the Navy. In January 1863 she was captured in the Stono River, South Carolina, near Charleston, after being disabled by Confederate shore batteries. Renamed *Stono*, she served around Charleston Harbor until her transition to a blockade-runner on Mallory's orders. Her service as such was both brief and disappointing. Running out of Charleston on the night of June 5 with a load of cotton, *Stono* was wrecked on the breakwater near Fort Moultrie and was incapable of continuing the voyage. *Oconee* faired

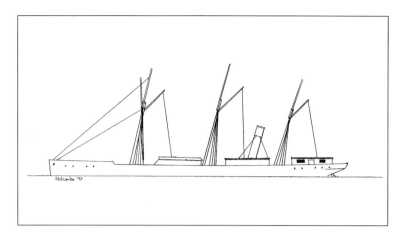

CSS *Coquette*. The Navy's most productive blockade-runner. (Robert Holcombe)

little better. Built in 1856 in New York as the 169ft 6in x 30 x 8ft 6in sidewheel Charleston–Florida packet *Everglade*, she was taken into the Georgia Navy in early 1861 and renamed *Savannah*. Soon afterwards she was transferred to the Confederacy, serving as the Savannah squadron's flagship for the next two years. In late April 1863 her name was changed to *Oconee* and she was prepared for blockade-running. After considerable delay she escaped to sea in mid-August with a cargo of cotton. Lightly built for coastal packet service, *Oconee* was unsuited for carrying heavy loads on the open ocean and on August 18, in heavy seas, she broke up. Miraculously, her crew survived, though several were captured by Union blockaders.

Simultaneously with his efforts to secure vessels at home to transport cotton out of the Confederacy, Mallory was pressing Bulloch to purchase a fast steamer in Britain. Mallory's immediate goal was to import a pair of English-built marine steam engines for a warship building in the South, but the vessel would continue to be used by the Navy as a regularly operated blockade-runner following the successful delivery of the machinery. Hampered by insufficient funds, Bulloch was finally able to purchase the steamer *Coquette* in early October 1863. Recently built on the Clyde, *Coquette* was a sleek, twin-screw, iron-hulled vessel with dimensions of 228ft x 25ft x 12ft 2in. Her rated speed was a quick 15kts, though she managed only a little better than 13 during trials. Following even more delays, including engine problems which forced her to return to Bermuda for repairs, *Coquette* finally ran the machinery into Wilmington in early March 1864. Although continually plagued by bad luck – she once damaged a propeller

running into Wilmington, then collided with a British warship in Bermuda – *Coquette* managed another five profitable trips through the blockade for the Navy before boiler problems forced her sale in July.

CSS *Helen* continued the Navy's hard-luck affair with blockade-runners but with end results far more tragic than before. Built as the sidewheel *Juno* on the Clyde in 1860, she had been seized, then purchased, by the Navy after running the blockade into Charleston in July 1863. Renamed *Helen*, she operated around Charleston Harbor as a gunboat before being chosen to run the blockade with cotton on Navy account. Loaded with 220 bales, *Helen* left Charleston in stormy weather on March 9, 1864. The following day, leaking and overloaded with slowly swelling water-logged cotton, *Helen* broke in two and sank. Of a crew of thirty, only two survived.

The Navy blockade-runner *Laurel* was initially purchased by Bulloch for the purpose of supplying the newly acquired cruiser *Shenandoah* in neutral waters near Funchal, Madeira. Once this task was accomplished in late October 1864, *Laurel* was ordered to proceed to Nassau and load with supplies, then slip through the blockade into a Southern port. A Clyde-built, iron screw steamer measuring 207ft x 27ft x 10ft, *Laurel* was ill-suited for late-war blockade running; her top speed was only 11.5kts and she drew an excessive 11ft of water when carrying only 500 bales of cotton. Consequently, after reaching Charleston on December 1, 1864, *Laurel* was transferred to the Treasury Department and renamed *Confederate States*. Despite her deficiencies, she made at least one other successful trip through the blockade before the war ended.

After the cruiser *Olustee*'s return to Wilmington from a productive second raid along the northeast coast of the United States, the Navy ordered her to be disarmed and retrofitted for blockade-running. As the 220ft x 24ft x 14ft *Atalanta*, a twin screw iron steamer built in 1863 at the Thames yard of John and William Dudgeon, she had been a fast and successful private runner before her purchase by the Confederate Navy in mid-1864. Under her newest guise as *Chameleon*, she was to make a quick run to Bermuda then return with provisions for Robert E Lee's near-starving army in Virginia. Captained by Lieut John Wilkinson, *Chameleon* left the Cape Fear River for Bermuda on the night of December 26 as Federal forces were engaged in their unsuccessful first assault on Fort Fisher. When *Chameleon* returned with her load of provisions nearly a month later, Wilkinson found Fort Fisher in Union hands and the port of Wilmington closed. Following a failed attempt to deliver his cargo to Charleston, Wilkinson sailed

Chameleon for Liverpool in late March 1865 and turned her over to Bulloch for disposal.

Approximately one half of the blockade-runners placed under construction by the Confederate Government in 1864 entered service before the South's last Atlantic port was closed. Of these, only the steel-hulled sidewheeler *Owl* reached Navy hands. The product of Liverpool shipbuilders Jones, Quiggen and Company, *Owl* represented the latest in blockade-runner design. Measuring 230ft x 26ft x 10ft 11in and painted a pale reddish colour, she was capable of carrying 800 cotton bales on a 7ft 6in draft at 13kts. Because the Government was unable to pay for the runners, arrangements were made for two private firms to cover their construction costs. Once completed the companies were to retain control of the vessels until the purchase prices were reimbursed through shipping incentives, then they would be turned over to the War Department. But when *Owl* arrived in Wilmington in late summer 1864 she was mistakenly seized by the Navy Department, briefly causing strained relations with the British. Once the misunderstanding was rectified, the Navy purchased *Owl* outright and turned her over to Cmdr John Maffitt, seasoned veteran of numerous trips through the blockade. Maffitt safely departed Wilmington during the first attack on Fort Fisher in December, but only narrowly escaped capture a month later when he entered the Cape Fear River only hours after the fort's fall. Thwarted also in an attempt to enter Charleston, Maffitt shifted his base of operations to Havana, intending to deliver supplies into Galveston, Texas, the Confederacy's last major port. From Cuba *Owl* made one of the last successful runs in and out Galveston harbor before the final collapse of the Confederacy. At the war's end Maffitt took *Owl* back to Britain, arriving in Liverpool in mid-July 1865.[20]

Torpedo craft

The development of effective torpedo craft in the Confederacy resulted from the perfection of a workable spar torpedo system. The weapon consisted of an explosive charge attached to a long, hinged shaft mounted on the bow of a vessel. Containing from 50 to 150lb of powder, the explosive section was usually equipped with multiple pressure-sensitive fuzes. Detonation occurred when the spar was lowered underwater and rammed into another ship's hull. Robert Fulton had conceived the general plan of pole-mounted underwater explosive devices as early as 1810, but little

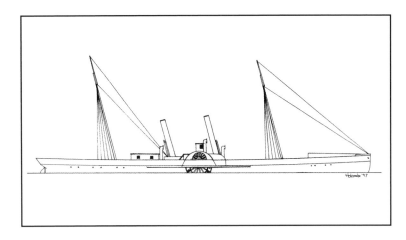

CSS *Owl.* Under Lt John N Maffitt, *Owl* was one of the last ships to successfully run the blockade before the end of the war. (Robert Holcombe)

was done to develop the idea into practical form. The outbreak of the Civil War revived interest in the spar torpedo and several plans were formulated for its use. None were put into effect until March 13, 1863, when Confederate Army engineer Captain Francis D Lee successfully demonstrated the potential of the weapon by destroying a hulk in Charleston harbor using a spar torpedo mounted in a fragile 20ft row boat. Less than a week later Lee's hastily-converted 'canoe', with a Navy crew of seven commanded by Lieut William T Glassell, made a daring attack on the USS *Powhatan* off Charleston. The attack was aborted when one of the crewmen panicked as the torpedo was about to be rammed home, throwing the boat off course. The Navy was so favourably impressed with Lee's makeshift craft that a dozen-plus row boats were converted to carry spar torpedoes, and a Special Service Detachment of sailors from Charleston and Wilmington was formed to operate them. Several operations were planned for these vessels but none were carried through. Due to the light construction of the boats, as well as the limitations imposed on their use by oared propulsion, the special unit was disbanded by the following September. In the meantime, Captain Lee had received permission to construct a steam-powered torpedo ram based on plans earlier submitted to General P G T Beauregard. Technically not a naval vessel, the Navy co-operated in its construction by furnishing an unfinished Maury gunboat hull and other supplies. Lee radically altered the incomplete hull and produced a vessel with an unarmoured wooden casemate that closely resembled a stock Confederate ironclad, only smaller. The ram's principal weapon was a movable, multi-pronged spar carrying three torpedoes. Later referred to as *Torch*, Lee's torpedo ram carried out an attack on the USS *New Ironsides* off Charleston on the morning of August 21, but failed when her engine stopped just under the ironclad's guns. After a narrow escape, *Torch* made no further attempt on the Union blockade fleet, apparently because of unreliable, worn-out machinery.[21]

The arrival of the powerful broadside ironclad USS *New Ironsides* off Charleston in January 1863 caused considerable consternation among the city's populace. To inspire creative methods of dealing with the big Union man-of-war, a reward of $100,000 was offered to anyone who could sink her. Responding at least in part to this bounty, a group of prominent Charlestonians calling themselves the Southern Torpedo Company constructed a small torpedo boat named *David* at Stoney Landing, about 30 miles up the Cooper River from Charleston. Bearing a strong resemblance to a cigar, this unusual craft had an 18ft long cylindrical center section with conical fore and aft ends. She was 48ft 6in loa x 5ft in diameter and powered by a small double-cylinder industrial steam engine turning a single propeller. Amidships a large open hatch gave four crewmen entry into a cramped interior, while on the forward end a fixed Lee spar torpedo was attached. Although closely resembling a submarine – and in fact often mistaken for one – *David* was strictly a surface craft, heavily ballasted so that little more than her hatch combing and smoke pipe appeared above water. With Lieut Glassell in command and a Navy crew aboard, *David* successfully exploded her torpedo against *New Ironsides* on the evening of October 5, 1863, but failed to sink her. The cause was attributed to the torpedo being too near the surface of the water, a fault later rectified with a modified movable spar. Two more *Davids* were commenced by the Southern Torpedo Company

Torpedo Boat *David* as she looked on October 5, 1863 when she torpedoed USS *New Ironsides*. (Robert Holcombe)

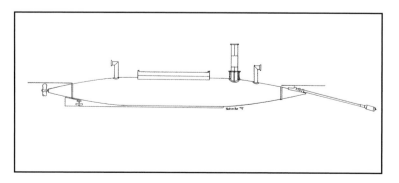

at Stoney Landing while the Navy and apparently the Army started two others at Charleston. These second-generation 'Davids' were slightly enlarged versions of the original, with lengths of about 50ft and diameters varying from 5ft 6in to 6ft. At least two were completed and operated in concert with *David* in the Charleston vicinity. In addition, a 100ft x 8ft torpedo ram version was laid down at Stoney Landing but was incomplete when destroyed by Federal troops near the end of the war. At least five 'Davids' were started in Savannah with one intended for shipment by rail to Mobile. Two more were begun by the Army in Wilmington but were accidentally destroyed by fire before completion, while another was building near Houston, Texas, late in the war.[22]

Torpedo boats built at Richmond were more conventional in design than the 'Davids', with higher freeboards and launch-type hulls. The first built, *Squib*, apparently joined the James River Squadron in early 1864. Although accounts differ, *Squib* was probably about 30ft in length and 6ft in beam, and drew 3ft of water. She carried a small, double-cylinder engine amidships with boiler, stack and engineer's position aft. A single screw propelled the boat. Forward of the engine was the steering wheel and a winch for raising and lowering the spar torpedo. Although constructed of wood, *Squib*'s steam machinery and forward hatch were protected from small arms fire by boiler plate. On the night of 9 April, with a crew of five commanded by Lieut Cmdg Hunter Davidson, *Squib* damaged but failed to sink the USS *Minnesota* off Newport News, Virginia. She was afterwards sent by rail to Wilmington and operated in the Cape Fear River until the fall of the city. Three torpedo boats similar to *Squib* but larger joined the squadron later in 1864. Named *Hornet*, *Scorpion* and *Wasp*, these vessels were 46ft loa x 6ft 3in x 3ft 9in. Serving primarily as picket boats and tenders to the larger warships of the squadron, all three saw extensive service on the James River in the closing months of the war. A torpedo boat of an unknown design was commenced at Wilmington but destroyed in the same fire that consumed the two Army 'Davids'. In early January 1864 Acting Constructor R P Meads was sent from Richmond to Texas to produce one or more 'iron clad torpedo boats' of an otherwise unknown description. Shortages of labour and materials prevented the construction of the vessels.[23]

In the spring of 1864 the Navy Department ordered the construction of twelve torpedo boats at various sites in the South. Four were started at Richmond, two at Columbus, Georgia, and one on the Pee Dee River, South Carolina. The remaining

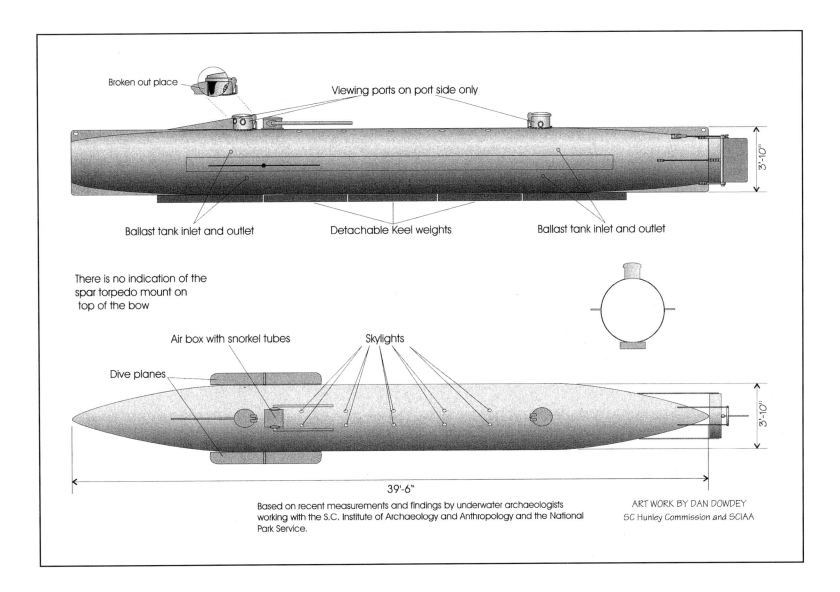

Broken out place

Viewing ports on port side only

Ballast tank inlet and outlet

Detachable Keel weights

Ballast tank inlet and outlet

3'-10"

There is no indication of the
spar torpedo mount on
top of the bow

Air box with snorkel tubes

Skylights

Dive planes

3'-10"

39'-6"

Based on recent measurements and findings by underwater archaeologists
working with the S.C. Institute of Archaeology and Anthropology and the National
Park Service.

ART WORK BY DAN DOWDEY
SC Hunley Commission and SCIAA

CSS *H.L. Hunley*, **based on recent underwater investigations of the wreck off Charleston, SC. (Dan Dowdey, the SC Hunley Commission & SCIAA).**

construction yards are unknown. Designed by Naval Constructor Graves, these boats were apparently of the single-screw launch variety, measuring 50ft x 6ft on a 4ft 6in draft. In addition to a spar torpedo, they were to carry one or two small boat howitzers. Machinery for all twelve was ordered from abroad but CSS *Viper* at Columbus, apparently the only one of the class completed, was furnished with an engine from the adjacent CS Naval Iron Works.[24]

In addition to steam machinery for the Graves boats, the Navy ordered at least twelve complete torpedo vessels from British builders. On instructions from Mallory dated July 18, 1864, Bulloch contracted for six steel boats to be shipped in sections by blockade-runner. The following November Mallory directed

Bulloch to have built six general purpose steam launches which could serve as torpedo or picket boats, as the situation demanded. Although surviving documents suggest that none of the Bulloch-ordered craft reached the Confederacy, a small steam launch later named *General Whiting* arrived in Wilmington by blockade-runner late in 1864. An unusual semi-submersible twin screw torpedo boat conceived by Lieut Joseph Fry was considered for construction but the order with J & W Dudgeon was never confirmed. Measuring 60ft x 12ft x 7ft, Fry's vessel incorporated fast-acting ballast tanks designed to quickly raise or lower her freeboard.[25]

Functional submersible craft had been developed as far back as the seventeeth century but the technological limitations that prevented their becoming practical weapons — notably the perfection of an underwater propulsion system and a method of safely delivering an explosive charge without endangering the submarine — still existed at the beginning of the Civil War. Despite these drawbacks, a surprising number of innovative submarines were built in the Confederacy. Most were the products of private initiative, supported by naval involvement. Two submersibles with which the Navy appears to have been more than casually associated were built at Richmond and Selma, Alabama. At Richmond, a submarine designed by William G Cheeney was commenced at Tredegar Foundry in the fall of 1861. Cheeney's boat was meant to be used with torpedoes developed by Lieut Matthew F Maury but was apparently never put into active service after its launching. In January 1864 the Navy Department contracted with John P Halligen for the construction of a submarine torpedo boat at the Selma Navy Yard. This boat is described as being 'shaped like a trout', with dimensions of 50ft x 6ft x 10ft. On the surface she was powered by a small steam engine, while underwater a six-man crew turned her screw by hand. Intended for use against blockaders off Mobile Bay, Halligen's boat was to be armed with a clockwork torpedo which could be attached to the bottom of a ship. She was successfully launched in the summer of 1864 and turned over to the Army as the CSS *St Patrick* the following January. Several days later she attacked the USS *Octorora* but failed to inflict damage when her torpedo misfired. During this sortie *St Patrick* was used as a surface torpedo boat and was armed with a spar torpedo rather than the intended clockwork device. She received some unspecified injury during the attack and never returned to service.[26]

The CSS *H.L. Hunley* became the first submarine in history to sink an enemy ship in combat when she successfully torpedoed the USS *Housatonic* off Charleston Harbor on the evening of February 17, 1864. The Navy's role in the construction of this exceptional craft was at best minimal, but it did provide operational support and furnished many of the sailors who made up her several crews. *H.L. Hunley* evolved out of two previous attempts by J R McClintock, Baxter Watson, Horace L Hunley and other New Orleans men to create a functional submarine for privateering purposes. The group first built a small 34ft hand-powered submarine named *Pioneer*, which they were forced to scuttle when New Orleans fell. Moving east to Mobile, they built a second submarine variously called *Pioneer II* or *American Diver*. This 36ft boat sank in rough seas near Fort Morgan before an attack on Union blockaders.[27]

Undeterred, Hunley's group next fashioned a submarine from a 25ft boiler in order to save time. By increasing the depth of the boiler and adding tapered bow and stern segments, they produced a submarine which was roomier and more practicable than her predecessors. Measuring approximately 40ft x 4ft x 4ft, the new ves-

sel held a crew of nine, eight of whom operated a crank attached to a single propeller. A speed of about 4mph was achieved with this arrangement. Incorporated into the submarine's design were fore and aft ballast tanks with hand pumps, a rudimentary snorkel system, a mercury depth gauge and a compass. A candle provided light and warned of dwindling oxygen as its flame flickered out. In a successful demonstration of the submarine's potential on July 30, 1863, a coal flat was destroyed using a contact torpedo towed behind the boat as she dived under her intended target. Later the towed system was considered impracticable and replaced by a modified Lee spar torpedo rigged on the bow. A week after the test the still unnamed boat was transported by rail from Mobile to Charleston, where it was believed a greater chance of success existed. Before the vessel could be put into effective use, training accidents claimed the lives of Horace Hunley and most of two crews. Named for Hunley after the second mishap, the boat was handed over to Army Lieut George E Dixon, one of her builders. Dixon trained a new, predominantly Navy crew in the submarine's management and finally achieved success against *Housatonic* several months afterward. When *H.L. Hunley* and her crew failed to return from the mission, it was generally believed that she had destroyed herself along with the Federal warship. In May 1995 a search team financed by the author Clive Cussler located the remarkably well-preserved *H.L. Hunley* some distance from *Houstatonic*'s wreck, confirming at last that she had initially survived the torpedo's blast and sank from unknown causes.

Naval ordnance

The Confederate Navy was more successful in providing its warships with heavy ordnance than any other facet of their construction or equipment. With the exception of the early war period, or in some of the more remote regions of the CSA, the Navy was rarely in need of proper guns for shipboard use. The capture of Gosport Navy Yard in April 1861 fortuitously provided the Confederacy with 1,198 heavy guns, meeting most of the initial needs of both the Navy and Army. This ordnance windfall consisted entirely of muzzle-loading smoothbores, including nearly 1,000 32pdrs and over 50 fine 9in Dahlgren guns. Mallory's desire to rely on advanced technology to offset the enemy's numerical superiority spurred efforts by the Navy to acquire rifled guns to supplement the captured smoothbores. With superior range, accuracy, and penetrating power, Mallory believed that the rifled guns would provide the South with a distinct advantage over the Federal Navy, which was armed almost entirely with smoothbore guns. In the interim many of the 32pdrs seized at Gosport were rifled and reinforced at the breech, but in the fall of 1861 the Navy started producing its own rifled guns. Designed by Lieut John M Brooke for the ironclad *Virginia*, the new gun ultimately became the Navy's standard shipboard weapon. Like the recently introduced Federal Parrott rifle, the first Brookes were distinguished by a single 2in thick, wrought-iron reinforcing band at the breech end. Later Brookes would be double- and even treble-banded for additional strength. The majority were produced in either 6.4 or 7in caliber, but several 8in rifles were also manufactured. Many ironclads, like *Atlanta*, *Savannah* and *Tennessee*, were armed wholly with Brooke rifles, with the 7in guns typically serving as pivot-mounted bow and stern chasers and the 6.4s in broadside. The four-gun ironclad *Richmond* was an exception, carrying 7in Brookes as both broadside and pivot guns. Because some officers believed that the explosive power of the smoothbore shell was more effective than the rifle against wooden vessels, many warships were purposely provided with a diverse armament of rifles and smoothbores. Most of the Navy's wooden gunboats carried mixed batteries, with a rifled cannon usually carried as the forward pivot gun. The ironclad *Virginia II* – the most heavily armed vessel built by the Confederates – carried a mixed battery of an 8in Brooke rifle forward, an 11in Brooke smoothbore aft, and two 7in Brooke rifles in broadside. Double-banded 10in and double- and treble-banded 11in Brooke smoothbores were produced late in the war. These powerful guns were designed exclusively for use against Federal ironclads at moderate ranges. They were most often used aboard ship in combination with rifled cannon. In addition to *Virginia II*, the ironclads *Columbia* and *Fredericksburg* are known to have been equipped with large caliber Brooke smoothbores. For protection against boarding parties, most ironclads carried one or two small howitzers, usually 12pdrs, on their spar deck.[28]

7in Brooke rifle cannon, from the CSS *Jackson*. (WMCWNH)

Confederate warships procured abroad were commonly armed with foreign manufactured cannon. British Armstrong, Blakely, and Whitworth pattern guns were the predominant types used. Like their gunboat counterparts in the Confederacy, the commerce cruisers usually carried armaments consisting of both rifles and smoothbores. The celebrated *Alabama* carried a 7in Blakely rifle as her forward pivot, an 8in smoothbore as her after pivot, and six 32pdr smoothbores in broadside. Conversely, *Florida*'s main armament consisted entirely of Blakely rifles: two 7in guns pivot-mounted on her centerline and six 6in guns in broadside. Heavy foreign guns imported into the Confederacy rarely found their way aboard ship. Exceptions include the ironclads *Huntsville* and *Tuscaloosa*, each of which carried a single 7in Blakely rifle in combination with American ordnance.

The successful adaptation of the Lee spar torpedo system to small craft led to its widespread use on a variety of larger warships. *Chicora* and *Palmetto State* at Charleston were apparently the first ironclads to be fitted with spar torpedoes in the spring of 1863, closely followed by *Atlanta* at Savannah. Later virtually all of the James River squadron vessels were likewise armed. One of the most unusual vessels to carry a spar torpedo was the ex-blockade-runner *Juno* (later *Helen*), which served for a time around Charleston Harbor as a patrol boat. At Mobile, the small tug *Gunnison* mounted a spar torpedo, though apparently none of the major combatants there were so equipped. Late in the war the ironclad *Charleston* was rigged to carry barrel torpedoes which could be rolled off her stern into the path of pursuing ships.

Machinery and propulsion systems

No segment of the Navy's construction programme has come under harsher criticism than steam engineering. The common view that the Confederacy was incapable of producing adequate steam machinery and that its home-built warships were universally underpowered and unreliable is to a certain extent valid, particularly for the early war period. Under Engineer-in-Chief William P Williamson, the engineering office's unenviable reputation resulted in large part from its initial need to rely on secondhand machinery to power the Navy's warships. Taken from smaller, lighter vessels, this machinery usually proved unsuitable for heavier vessels, especially ironclads. Heavy industries capable of fabricating steam engines and boilers existed in the antebellum South, but most had quickly converted to munitions production and none were initially

prepared to construct powerplants for the Navy. It was just this situation in the early months of the war that caused Mallory to convert *Merrimack* into an ironclad rather than attempt the keel-up construction of a warship and all of its component parts. Later the Navy would produce reliable, purpose-built machinery under Williamson's guidance, but its early forced reliance on engines ill-adapted for the purpose produced a tarnished reputation not entirely warranted nor easily contradicted.[29]

Marine steam machinery of the mid-nineteenth century was produced in a wide assortment of designs. Engines of the period were usually characterized by the configurations of their cylinders, valves, driveshaft connections, condensing systems, steam pressures and other factors. All were reciprocating and commonly of the single expansion variety – steam turbines not being perfected until after the war, and multi-cylinder expansion engines only then being introduced abroad. Steam boilers also varied considerably. They could be horizontal or vertical in their placement, and come with an enormous variety of tubes and flues. As a result of this diversity, many forms of engines and boilers found their way into Confederate warships, making it difficult to generalize about their application. Usually one or two engines and from one to six boilers were installed amidships in the vessel's hold, but exceptions were prevalent. *Mississippi* had sixteen boilers providing steam to three engines, while several gunboat classes had their powerplants located in the extreme stern. Tow boat engines, because of their power and suitability for screw propulsion, were frequently placed into Confederate ironclads. *Chicora, North Carolina, Palmetto State* and *Richmond* received tow boat engines, and *Manassas* was converted from the twin-screw towboat *Enoch Train*. Most tow boat engines were vertical, low-pressure (usually less than 50psi) single-cylinder types, though *Manassas* and *Chicora* were equipped with two horizontal engines. Speeds achieved as a result of these conversions ranged from 4 to 7kts. The prevalence of steam paddleboats on the South's many inland rivers resulted in the Navy's widespread use of high pressure (150psi maximum) riverboat engines and boilers as substitute powerplants. The early sidewheel wooden gunboats *Carondelet, Bienville, Gaines* and *Morgan* received secondhand riverboat machinery while two ironclad classes, the sidewheel *Nashville* and centerwheel *Missouri*, were designed to make use of the ubiquitous engines. Efforts to adapt riverboat engines to screw propulsion were generally less successful. Their characteristic long-stroke, slow-moving design, which made them unsuited for turning propellers, required an elaborate gearing system to achieve the higher revolutions needed for efficient screw propulsion. The sin-

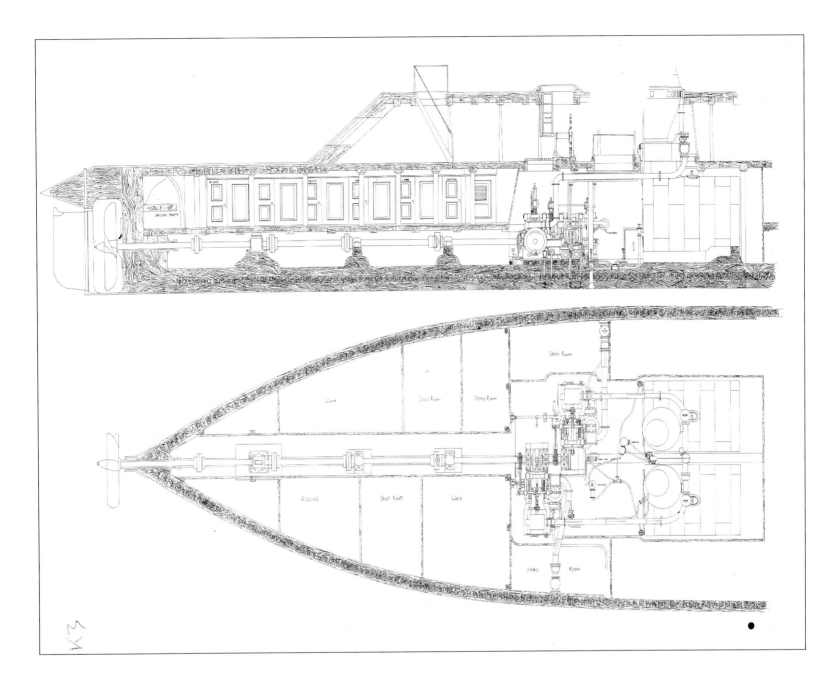

CSS *Savannah's* steam machinery, built at the CS Naval Iron Works, Columbus, Ga. (WMCWNH)

gle-screw ironclad *Tennessee II* worked comparatively well with such an arrangement, achieving a speed of 7kts, but the twin-screw *Tuscaloosa* and *Huntsville* could attain speeds of only 2½ and 3½ kts using similar systems. Unlikely sources of powerplants include a number of small portable sawmill, or 'plantation,' engines acquired for use in *Hampton* and probably other small gunboats, and a pair of captured locomotive engines used in the ironclad *Neuse*. Other captured engines, removed from a Union warship on the Rappahannock River, were intended for a small gunboat building

at Halifax, North Carolina. Evidence indicates that some machinery was recovered from beached blockade-runners for warship use. The twin double-cylinder engines intended for ironclad *Texas* closely match those built by J & W Dudgeon for a series of twin-screw blockade-runners. *Texas's* engines possibly came from the Dudgeon runner *Kate*, which grounded leaving Wilmington in 1863 and was later stripped of her machinery. *Virginia II* reportedly had British-type steam machinery but its provenance is unknown.

Beginning in late 1861 the Navy contracted with private establishments in Georgia, Louisiana, South Carolina, Tennessee and Virginia for the construction of purpose-built marine machinery. These agreements provided machinery for the gunboats

Chattahoochee and *Macon*, the ironclads *Arkansas*, *Louisiana*, *Mississippi*, and probably others.[46] The Navy also acquired machinery from abroad. In addition to the small torpedo boat engines previously mentioned, the blockade-runner *Coquette* delivered in mid-1864 a set of large steam engines manufactured by Fawcett & Preston of Liverpool. These engines were being assembled at the Columbus Naval Iron Works for an unknown warship when the war ended. In 1864 Mallory directed naval agent James D Bulloch to procure two sets of engines and boilers for the double-ended ironclad at Richmond designed by Naval Constructor Graves. The war ended before this machinery could be completed. Two pairs of British engines fell into Federal hands when the blockade-runner *Princess Royal* was captured in 1863. Meant for Charleston ironclads, one set ended up powering the USS *Kansas* instead.

In 1862 the Navy Department moved to establish its own plants for the exclusive production of marine steam machinery. Two private firms, Schockoe Foundry at Richmond, and the Columbus Iron Works Company at Columbus, Georgia, were leased by the steam engineering office and placed under the command of experienced naval engineers. Renamed the CS Naval Iron Works, the Columbus facility became the most important of the two units. By converting existing machinery, or making new engines outright, the Naval Iron Works produced about fifteen sets of engines and boilers for Confederate warships. Ironclads *Tennessee*, *Milledgeville*, *Jackson* and *Columbia* were among those vessels receiving Columbus powerplants. Operating as the Confederate Naval Works, considerably less is known about the output of the Richmond plant. It is believed to have furnished machinery for several of the small gunboats on the James River, as well as ironclads *Fredericksburg*, *Virginia II*, *Albemarle*, *Neuse*, *Raleigh* and others.

Conclusions

By purchase, construction and capture the Confederate Navy was able to place as many as 130 warships of all types into operation. Although overshadowed by technologically superior vessels introduced later, the conventional wooden gunboats acquired by Mallory in 1861 nevertheless provided indispensable service. They constituted the early Navy until more advanced ships could be acquired, then operated in the auxiliary capacity and performed other duties unsuited for the lumbering ironclads. Bulloch and his naval agents were generally successful in acquiring ships that served well their intended role as commerce raiders. There were failures, but *Alabama*, *Florida*, *Shenandoah* and others wreaked havoc on Northern shipping by capturing over 300 merchant ships and causing the transfer of hundreds more to foreign registry. Although the raiders failed to draw substantial numbers of Union warships from the blockade or influence the outcome of the war, their depredations accelerated a decline in the American merchant fleet from which it did not recover until World War I, and disheartened Northern maritime interests while boosting Southern morale.

The Navy's inconsistent involvement in blockade-running was probably detrimental to the Confederacy's war-making abilities. With a surplus of career officers the Navy should have acquired additional ships and become more agressively engaged in the trade. Much the same can be said for the Navy's often ambivalent attitude towards torpedo craft. Although these weapons suffered from technological limitations not solved until after the Civil War, a more vigorous policy for their construction and use could have provided the Navy with an additional serious threat to enemy naval activities. Efforts to equip warships with ordnance and motive power met with mixed results. Ordnance production was one of the Navy's most successful endeavours. Rarely did the Department want for proper shipboard guns after the first year of the war; surplus production even permitted the Navy to supply many of its fine Brooke guns to the Army. The acquisition of satisfactory steam machinery remained a problem for much of the war. It was mid-war before plants were established and reliable engines designed specifically for warships produced. Inevitably the Confederate Navy succumbed to a numerically and industrially superior force. But it is a tribute to Mallory, Bulloch, Porter and many other farsighted naval men that the South was capable of establishing in four short years a modern, technologically advanced navy where none before existed.

Robert Holcombe

Chapter Four
FACILITIES

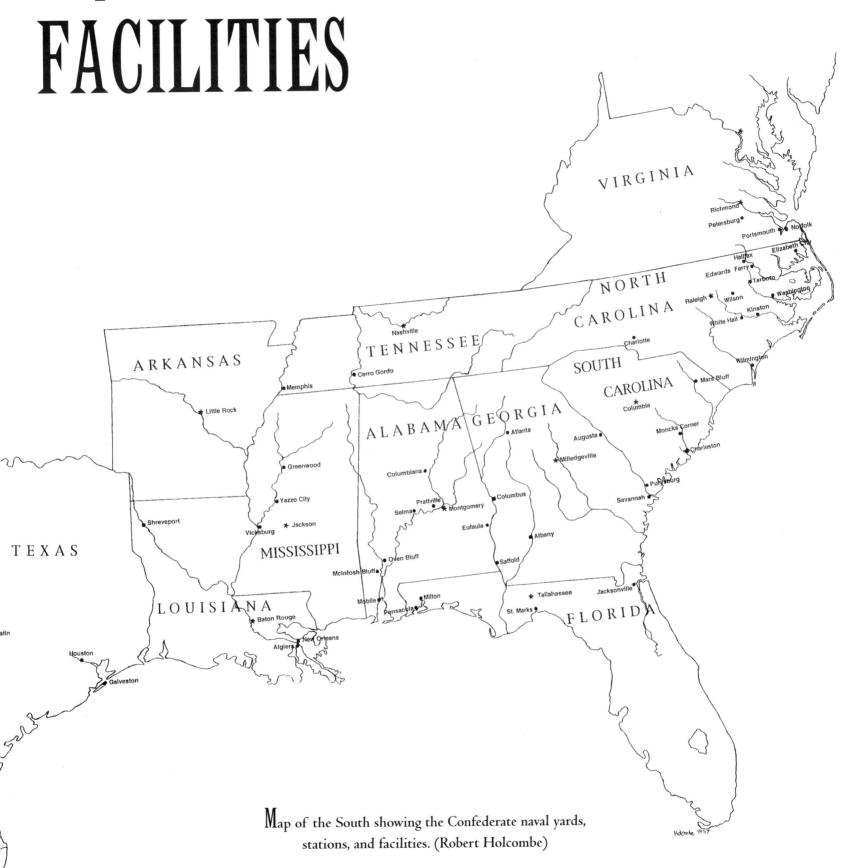

VIRGINIA

Richmond
Petersburg
Portsmouth • Norfolk
Halifax • Elizabeth City
Edwards Ferry
Tarboto
NORTH
Raleigh • Wilson
CAROLINA
Kinston
White Hall • Washington

Nashville
Charlotte
TENNESSEE
Wilmington
SOUTH
Cerro Gordo
CAROLINA
ARKANSAS
Mars Bluff
Memphis
Columbia

Little Rock
Moncks Corner
ALABAMA GEORGIA
Augusta
Charleston
Greenwood
Atlanta
Milledgeville
Columblana
Purysburg
Yazzo City
Prattville
Columbus
Shreveport
Selma • Montgomery
Savannah
Vicksburg • Jackson
Eufaula
TEXAS
Albany
MISSISSIPPI
Safford
McIntosh Bluff
Oven Bluff
Milton
Tallahassee
Jacksonville
Mobile
LOUISIANA
Pensacola
St. Marks
FLORIDA
stin
Baton Rouge
Houston
Algiers • New Orleans
Galveston

Holcombe 1997

Map of the South showing the Confederate naval yards,
stations, and facilities. (Robert Holcombe)

Secretary of the Navy Stephen R Mallory's goal of building a modern navy based on steam and armour required an industrial base that scarcely existed in the new Confederacy. Thinking Southerners like New Orleans publisher J D B DeBow, Georgia foundry owner Mark Cooper, South Carolina planter James H Hammond, and editors of newspapers large and small had for years stressed the need for a diversified Southern economy with a solid industrial base. If the South were to be a nation free and independent, it must replicate the North's self-sustaining economy, they said. 'To *breed*, *raise*, and *manufacture*' was the policy the South must follow, said DeBow, if it were to be a nation.[1]

A well-developed iron industry was critical to industrial development. Southern border states contained iron works of modest size: foundries and rolling mills existed in the upper South from St Louis in the west to Baltimore in the east. In Richmond lay the crown jewel of Southern heavy industry, the Tredegar Iron Works. There were small foundries in cities across the Deep South from New Orleans to Savannah; and heavy railroad manufacturing and repair shops in Atlanta, Nashville and Chattanooga. A survey of antebellum Southern industry might suggest a young and vibrant infrastructure that could blossom into a strong foundation to support an industrialized war.[2]

But in contrast to the North, industrialization had barely touched the South. Pre-war Southern industry suffered intermittent operation, undercapitalization, low productivity and poor market penetration. Pennsylvania turned out over half the iron goods made in the United States. Ohio ranked second, New Jersey third. In the South, manufacturing of all kinds had been declining, not growing, for over a decade.[3] The war would move Southern entrepreneurs and the Confederate Government to develop an industrial base. But compared to the North, they began with nearly nothing.

The Gosport and Warrington Navy Yards: the armoured Navy begins

The Confederate Navy Department's most basic need was for shipyards to build vessels of war. The secession of Virginia and Florida handed the Confederacy two facilities: Gosport Navy Yard at Portsmouth near Norfolk, Virginia, and Warrington Navy Yard at Pensacola, Florida.

The shipyard at Portsmouth had existed since colonial days.

In 1794 it was turned over to the Federal Government, and it became the premier naval repair facility in the United States. The largest and most famous ships of the US Navy would visit Gosport to repair and refit, and the yard became a training ground for artisans in the shipbuilding trade. In 1851 Gosport had five ship-houses, three dry-docks and a boatbuilding slip, as well as mast and rigging and sail houses. It also had ropewalks, smitheries, carpentry shops, and storage for cordage, timber, copper, iron, and other materials required for ship construction and repair.

Through the 1850s the yard continued to expand, with a new sawmill, foundry, boiler shop, ordnance department with test batteries, and another blacksmith shop. A new stone quay with two large lifting cranes was built, and the largest crane in any US navy yard was erected at the wharf in 1858. Railroad tracks connected shops and storehouses with construction areas on the waterfront.

But with the political crisis of 1860, work at Gosport all but ceased. The work force, which had swelled to 1400 in 1858, was cut to 700. Where a few years before great steam frigates were under construction, now there was only a little repair work on a few warships, including the newly-arrived and oft-troubled *Merrimack*.

With Lincoln's election, Southern life was thrown into uncertainty. When Florida seceded, the Warrington Navy Yard at Pensacola surrendered to state forces; and United States naval personnel were withdrawn and many assigned there resigned from the Navy. John L Porter, Warrington's Naval Constructor, was ordered back to Gosport, where he had been born and received his professional training. There, he found: 'Everything...was disorder and confusion. The men were standing around in groups about the Yard and no one could work.'

The populace around Portsmouth had grown hostile; and Gosport's Commandant, Charles S McCauley, was torn between orders to save his ships and supplies, and to avoid committing acts that might antagonize the people and force a conflict. Paralysed with uncertainty, McCauley decided to withdraw from Gosport. At 1pm on the afternoon of April 20, 1861, the Yard's gates were closed; and the destruction of the Yard and the vessels within its waters commenced.[4] Gosport Navy Yard, having served the United States Navy since that service's birth, was abandoned.

While Gosport had been productive and well-appointed, Pensacola's Warrington Navy Yard, begun in 1825, languished for lack of interest and funding. Only when Florida Senator Stephen R Mallory took up its cause did Warrington begin to grow. But just two warships, the 800-ton *Seminole* and the 2,000-ton *Pensacola*, were built there. US naval vessels called there more for resupply than for refit and repair.

When Florida seceded and the yard fell into Confederate hands, a small contingent of US troops occupied nearby Fort Pickens. The Confederacy assigned Captain Victor M Randolph to command the yard, and Warrington began converting merchant vessels for privateering work and blockade-running, and repairing the *Fulton*, an old sidewheeler laid up there. Fort Pickens disrupted this work by lobbing shells into the Yard, and into its suburbs, Warrington and Woolsey. At the end of February 1862, Secretary Mallory would tell the President: 'The Pensacola yard being commanded by the enemy's guns, has been useless as a naval establishment.'[5]

Meanwhile, Gosport under the Confederacy was once again thriving. At first glance, the destruction had seemed devastating. Shipyard clerk William H Peters reported to his new employers, the Virginia State Navy:

It is difficult to estimate the value of property destroyed.... The extensive row of buildings on the north front of the yard, containing large

quantities of manufactured materials...were, with their contents, entirely destroyed. Ship-houses A and B, which were very large wooden structures, the former containing the line-of-battle ship *New York*, on the stocks, were also totally destroyed.

But the materials left undamaged were an incredible cache for the new Confederacy. Paymaster Peters made an inventory of the Yard's remains. He found all the quarters undamaged, and the foundry and its dependent shops, the machine shop, five large storehouses, several workshops, and tons of goods and stores were also spared. Food, clothing, timber, copper, iron, anchors and chains, sails and cordage, guns and carriages and tackle were also there. Armaments included over a thousand heavy cannon, shot and shell and stands of grape, and 333,000lb of gunpowder. Construction and repair equipment, machinery, ships' parts and stores were lightly damaged or completely unhurt. Although the

Warrington Navy Yard, Pensacola, Florida. (Naval Historical Center)

Tredegar Iron Works, Richmond. (Library of Congress)

Yankees had mined the great granite dry dock (built over a period of nine years at a cost of $1m), Lt C F M Spotswood flooded the dock and saved it. Richmond's *Daily Enquirer* boasted that, at Gosport, 'we have material enough to build a Navy of iron-plated ships.' For a day, Captain Robert Pegram of the Virginia State Navy commanded the Yard. He was succeeded by Captain French Forrest, CSN.

As Gosport had grown in the antebellum era, private shipyards and foundries like Graves & Nash and Mahaffey's Iron Works grew up nearby. Mahaffey's had fitted engines and boilers to the USS *Mississippi* and *Powhatan*, and often challenged Gosport for government contracts. The Confederate Navy soon annexed it.

Gosport's first important work for the Confederacy was to refurbish the massive store of naval guns, build gun carriages, and disburse the cannon throughout the Confederate States. But the yard's great mission would be conversion of the burned and scuttled frigate *Merrimack* into the ironclad *Virginia*. The nearby Atlantic Ironworks contracted to supply the *Virginia* project with tools, machine parts, a mechanical punch and drill presses, brass fittings, and nuts and bolts, templates for all the *Virginia's* armour plate, and the grate bars for her spar deck (casemate roof).[6]

A primary need for an ironclad navy was armour plate. Mallory could rely on Richmond's Tredegar Iron Works to produce some armour; but the need was nationwide, as ironclads were soon under construction at Memphis, New Orleans, Savannah, on the Cumberland River and elsewhere. It would take far more than the Tredegar's production to satisfy these requirements.

Thus in May 1861 Captain Duncan Ingraham surveyed iron foundries across the South. He inspected the Tennessee Iron Works in Nashville, Scofield and Markham's Gate City Iron Works in Atlanta, even Daniel Hillman & Co in Kentucky, just 40 miles from Ohio, hoping to find new suppliers of armour. None of these could roll iron plate thick enough (although Scofield and Markham would soon develop the capacity and become the major supplier of armour to the lower Confederacy). For the time being, the Tredegar was the Confederacy's only source of armour.

The *Virginia* project became the test-bed for the components of a new armoured navy. Lieut John Mercer Brooke tested variations of iron armour at a naval battery on Jamestown Island, assisted by the battery's commander, Lt Catesby ap R Jones. They

Captain French Forrest, commandant of the Gosport Navy Yard, Portsmouth, Virginia, during the construction of the ironclad *Virginia*. (Library of Congress)

Commander John M Brooke. (George M Brooke)

found that two layers of 2in iron plate would withstand the heaviest naval guns then in use. This configuration would become the Navy's standard – until powerful new 15in Dahlgrens used against the CSS *Atlanta* required the move to 6in of armour. The order for the *Virginia's* armour (estimated need was a thousand tons) was placed with the Tredegar Iron Works.

The Tredegar already had government contracts to cast cannon, shot and shell, bar and bolt iron, and boiler plate. Yet, it made the *Virginia's* armour plate its top priority. Of the estimated thousand tons required, the foundry rolled 732 tons to order, plus 360,700lb of 2in x 8in bars for the project's general ironworking needs. It was paid $123,015, mostly in Confederate bonds.[7]

Secretary Mallory wanted his Navy armed with rifled cannon and asked Brooke to design a rifled gun for use aboard the ironclad. Thus did Brooke develop the Confederate Navy's standard

piece of ordnance, the Brooke rifle. Smoothbores like the Dahlgren and Columbiad were cast thick around the breech to contain the bursting energy of the powder charge. Robert Parrott in New York and English ordnance-makers Armstrong and Blakeley reinforced the breeches of their rifled guns with iron bands. Brooke chose this approach, substituting a number of narrow iron bands, heated for expansion, then slipped over the breech and allowed to cool and shrink to clasp it tightly. This added strength allowed Brooke's rifles to fire heavier charges. Brooke's guns became famous for their accuracy and punching power.

For the *Virginia*, the Tredegar cast gun barrels to Brooke's specification. They were sent to Norfolk, where Brooke had Gosport's shops build a machine to bend and weld flat iron bars into bands of the correct diameter. The smithery heated the bands, slipped them over the breech, and let them cool and contract. The first 7in Brooke tested threw its 100-pound shell approximately 4½ miles. John Mercer Brooke was satisfied.[8]

While the *Virginia* was being finished and a new ironclad begun, the Gosport facility was expanded to supply all the new Navy's needs. Commandant Forrest even developed a small ordnance laboratory. Initially, it manufactured time fuzes for explosive shell. These fuzes, paper cylinders filled with a combustible powder, were made in 5-, 10-, and 15-second lengths that could be cut to burst shells at any time specified.

At the Gosport laboratory, the combustible was tamped into the fuzes by hand, which made burning uneven. In better equipped laboratories, the process was mechanical, giving a uniform pack, an even burn, and better prospects for a shell bursting at the intended time. Two of Gosport's laboratory workers, E A Jack and James Jordan, designed a fuze tamper. Jack drew up plans, submitted them to Forrest, and was soon on his way to Richmond to present his ideas to the Navy Department. Forrest told him to look in on the Richmond Arsenal and also learn how to make percussion caps. Shortly, Brooke would have the fuze machinery built, and the Gosport laboratory would expand its operations and make percussion caps, bullets, shot, shell and shrapnel.

The Navy expected Gosport to become the major manufacturer of ship engines for the Confederacy. Despite claims of foundries at New Orleans, Mallory admitted that only in Tennessee were there resources enough to build complete steam engines and all their ancillaries. The Department moved Gosport closer to full marine engine production by buying the Tredegar's Nasmyth steam hammer to finish heavy castings like propeller shafts.[9]

On March 24, 1862, Secretary Mallory ordered Captain Sidney Smith Lee to assume command at Gosport, summoning French Forrest to duty in Richmond. Major General George B McClellan's Union Army of the Potomac, having landed in Hampton Roads to begin its Peninsular Campaign against Richmond, threatened the Norfolk area and the safety of Gosport. Secretary Mallory had already given Commandant Lee the first intimation that Gosport may be lost.

> You will begin at once, without attracting special attention or notice to the subject, to pack carefully and get ready for transport all the fine machinery and tools not required for your operations in your workshop.

Through the rains of April, Major General Joseph E Johnston's Confederate Army withdrew slowly up the peninsula toward Richmond, leaving Norfolk protected by a small force under Major General Benjamin Huger. Johnston considered the area expendable.

For the Confederate Navy, loss of Norfolk would be a catastrophe. Under Confederate ownership, Gosport was growing into a complete naval manufacturing complex. Here were to be built ironclads and gunboats. Here were to be made engines and boilers, anchors and ordnance and running rigging, caulk and cordage, appliances and appointments, everything for a ship from her keel to the paneling in the captain's quarters. Gosport, one of the best navy yards in North America, was expected to be the premier shipbuilding and naval manufacturing facility in the Confederacy.

And it was being thrown away, the Army conceding it without a thought. The best the Navy could do was to save as many of the ships being built there – and as much equipment – as possible. That was an enormous task, and Commandant Lee did not appear, in Mallory's opinion, to comprehend it. Mallory seemed unable to direct Smith Lee's attention to the crisis. Despite the Secretary's continued insistence, Lee did not keep him informed of details. The Commandant may have assumed that an officer of his experience could be trusted to make the right decisions, and he may have had little time for dictating daily reports. But Mallory did not have the confidence in him that Lee assumed. 'Norfolk is in serious peril,' Mallory lectured. Lee must do all possible to save ships and stores.

Although Mallory hoped that some miracle might save Norfolk, he continued to plan for Gosport's evacuation. In the first week of May, 1862, workers dismantled, packed, and shipped materials and machinery. Mallory told Lee to have Gosport's

inspector of ordnance, Commander Richard L Page, 'secure immediately a safe place in North Carolina, at Raleigh or elsewhere, for a laboratory, and to transport all the ordnance stores he can save to North Carolina...' Paymaster Peters, now yard storekeeper, was to send off clothing, provisions and other stores as soon as Page found a place.

Mallory told the Commandant to make sure he had a clear understanding with General Huger over the use of the railroads to move yard supplies and equipment to North Carolina and to 'confer with him as to the time for the abandonment and destruction of the public property.' With Richmond threatened by McClellan's relentless advance, Mallory told Lee: 'You will send nothing to Richmond that can be sent to North Carolina'. The Department was calling to Richmond, however, all materials involved in finishing warships which had been begun in Portsmouth. On the night of May 6, the *Patrick Henry* towed the unfinished ironclad *Richmond* and gunboat *Hampton* up the James River. The *Henry's* consort, *Jamestown*, towed a brig filled with the *Richmond's* ordnance stores and another unfinished gunboat.

At Richmond a navy yard was established on the site where, in the 1700s, Robert Rockett had operated a ferry. The ferry owner of old would give the new Confederate Navy Yard its name – Rocketts. A four-story brick building dominated the yard. The site would soon include a wharf, sheds and launchways for the construction of new ironclads, gunboats and torpedo boats; and a companion yard across the river.

When General Huger's force withdrew and joined Johnston's army, Norfolk lay open to capture. On the evening of May 9, Lt William H Parker, awaiting completion of his gunboat *Dixie*, heard firing to the north. Midshipmen went aloft and saw shells bursting over Confederate batteries. Parker hurried ashore to the Commandant's quarters and told Lee that the Yankees were preparing to invade. Lee doubted it, as he had heard nothing from General Huger. Parker left the commandant about 11 pm, with Lee satisfied they were still safe. But at dawn all officers were ordered to begin destruction of the yard. Parker recalled:

> We set fire to the buildings and ships, and tried to blow up the dry dock; in fact destroyed everything we could. I set my vessel on fire with much regret; a few more days and she would have been ready to go to Richmond. We continued the work of destruction until we heard the Federal troops were in Norfolk, and then took our departure in the cars for Weldon....[10]

The Charlotte Navy Yard: the Navy regroups

Many of Gosport's workmen and their families moved to Richmond. Those with shipbuilding skills were assigned to Rocketts Navy Yard. Those with machine and foundry skills were transferred south to Charlotte, North Carolina, the site Commander Page had selected for the Navy's new manufacturing facility. Page chose Charlotte for a new 'navy yard' because it was inland, safe from invasion, and at a junction of several railroads. The Department sent Lt William Murdaugh to Charlotte to find and secure a site. Murdaugh found one: a lot on East Trade Street between the North Carolina Central and the South Carolina Railroads. Its distinguishing feature was a large brick building lying between the two lines of track. On Murdaugh's recommendation, the Navy purchased the lot.[11]

Captain Samuel Barron commanded the site for its first five months. But it was Commander Page who created the heavy manufacturing facility that would become known as the Charlotte

Navy Yard. When Page took command, he established both his headquarters and his living quarters in the old United States Mint on West Trade Street. He had a loading dock built from the brick building to the North Carolina Central's track to unload stores and machinery from Gosport. In came lathes, planers, smiths' and carpenters' tools, molds and flasks and other forge and foundry equipment. The Navy rented warehouses nearby and filled them with stores and materials from Portsmouth.

Gosport was evacuated in May. By July, one of its salvaged cranes was up and helping put Charlotte Navy Yard into opera-

tion. In August a steam hammer saved from Pensacola was set up, and Charlotte was in the heavy forging business.

Charlotte first produced gun carriages, projectiles and laboratory stores (friction primers, time fuzes, hand grenades and signal rockets) and blocks for standing and running rigging. Page's forges made some of the machinery he needed to get into production. He told his bureau chief, Commander George Minor, that his main building needed to be both expanded and strengthened.

Page built a new cupola furnace and two coke ovens for his foundry and made patterns and flasks for castings. He also expanded the smithery, which would house the Nasmyth hammer brought from Gosport. 'This hammer', Commander John M Brooke reported, 'will forge the heaviest shafting used on shipboard or the largest frigate's anchor.' With its steam hammers, Charlotte became the Navy's major supplier of propeller shafts. Among the projects receiving shafts from the Charlotte Navy Yard were ironclads building at Yazoo City (Mississippi), Selma (Alabama), Savannah (Georgia), Charleston (South Carolina), the Roanoke River (North Carolina) and Richmond (Virginia).[12]

At the end of February 1863, Richard Page was transferred to command afloat at Savannah. He was replaced at Charlotte by Captain George N Hollins. But Hollins's tenure was short. On March 15, he was replaced by Page's nephew, Commander Catesby ap R Jones who, just a year before, had commanded the *Virginia* the day she fought the *Monitor*.

Though he was promoted to commander for the affair, Jones's career had not soared since the *Virginia's* destruction. Immensely talented, his skills lay in the same areas as John Mercer Brooke's — ordnance, engineering, and design. At the beginning of the war, Brooke had been ordered to Richmond and had established himself as a key officer in the Navy Department. Until the Department could find a place to use his talents, the hero of the *Virginia* commanded a small gunboat, the *Chattahoochee*, on the river above Apalachicola, Florida.

While Hollins was a pure sailing man, Catesby Jones's pre-war ordnance work with John A Dahlgren gave him a background in design and manufacturing that suited him to running the Charlotte Navy Yard. But Jones was at Charlotte just two months before being assigned to superintend the new national foundry in Selma, Alabama. And Commander Page, having just settled in at

Rocketts Navy Yard in foreground, Graves' Yard across the James River, Richmond. (Library of Congress)

Captain George N Hollins. (Porter, *Naval History of the Civil War*)

Savannah, was ordered back to Charlotte. Until Page could be relieved at Savannah, the Charlotte Yard was under the direction of Chief Engineer Henry A Ramsay.

By late 1863 Page's stock of casting patterns and flasks had grown, increasing his product line. He now turned out engine parts.

The Charlotte Navy Yard, like other manufacturing sites both private and Government owned, suffered shortages of materials. One of the items no longer available in mid-1863 was sheepskin for fuze washers. To replace it, the Yard scrounged scraps of cow leather and drew them through the harness makers' slitting knives. 'It answers as well, if not better, than sheepskin', Page told Commander Brooke.

In early 1864 Commander Page, perhaps frustrated at being an industrialist while others went to war, resigned his naval commission and joined the Army. With the rank of brigadier general, he assumed command of Fort Morgan and all heavy batteries at Mobile Bay.

Captain Sidney Smith Lee was slated to replace Page, but he lobbied successfully for the post of Chief, Bureau of Orders and Detail, and stayed in Richmond. By default, command of the navy yard fell to Chief Engineer Henry Ashton Ramsay, who had come to Charlotte from Gosport after destruction of the *Virginia*, on which he had been chief engineer. He had served the Charlotte Yard as chief of engineering almost from its inception.

Confederate manufacturing facilities all suffered a shortage of manpower. Over 300 Gosport men had come to work at Charlotte, but there were never enough skilled hands. In May 1864, the labour shortage stilled the yard's big steam hammers. Large forgings needed in shipyards all across the Confederacy could not be made. And in those yards, work on ironclads was delayed. In addition, the navy yard's repair work on locomotives came to a stop.

Chief Ramsay worked his meagre force days, nights and Sundays. But production lagged, even on such vital items as gun carriages and wrought-iron projectiles. He told Commander Brooke the Yard needed seven more machinists, eight blacksmiths, eight gun-carriage makers, two blockmakers, a pattern maker, a coppersmith, and two molders before it could function at even a minimum production level.

The Navy Department called on its most successful overseas operative, Commander James D Bulloch, to recruit skilled labour in England to immigrate to the Confederacy. In the fall of 1864, Bulloch contracted with seventeen English foundrymen to immigrate, but none succeeded in getting into the Confederacy. Later in the year, three skilled workmen did make it through on the blockade-runner *Stag*. They were assigned to Charlotte.

Ramsay's production also suffered from poor quality iron supplied by North Carolina and Virginia furnaces. In late 1864 the iron was so bad that the manufacture of many items – including projectiles – ceased. The demand for armour-piercing wrought-iron bolts was heavy from shore batteries at Mobile, Charleston, Wilmington and the James River: and the Charlotte Navy Yard was the only place capable of producing wrought-iron shot.

Charlotte's slender workforce ate well by Confederate standards. Although the Navy's ration was reduced by orders from Richmond to about that allowed the Army, the storehouse at Charlotte held not only bacon and flour, but also the unobtainables – coffee and sugar.

Charlotte's workforce was organized into a naval defense battalion of three companies, with Ramsay holding the rank of major. Although they were occasionally called out to help defend the area against raiders, these interruptions were not nearly as frequent as those of the workmen at Rocketts and the Richmond Ordnance Works.

Ramsay had a small cadre of workmen acting as marines to guard the Yard. Toward the end of the war he received a detail of real marines to take on this duty.

In April of 1865, with the fall of Richmond, Commandant William H Parker and the midshipmen of the Confederates States Naval Academy were charged with moving and guarding the contents of the Confederate Treasury as the government moved south. On April 8, 1865, Parker's command arrived in Charlotte and deposited the gold and silver in the commandant's quarters, the old US Mint.

After provisioning themselves from the Yard's storehouse ('The storekeeper rather objected to it' Parker recalled; 'he wanted requisitions approved by the Secretary of the Navy, etc., but I told him it was no time for red tape....'), the midshipmen departed with the treasure, reinforced with a company from the navy yard. 'These

men were principally from Portsmouth, Virginia,' Parker recalled, 'and they remained with me to the end. A better set of men I never served with.'

The withdrawal continued to Abbeville, South Carolina, where the midshipmen and the navy yard contingent were dismissed. In later years Parker wrote: 'I have a distinct recollection of their marching off in gallant array, with their field music playing Dixie, on their return to Charlotte'.[13]

Manufacturing and supply: engines, armour, shoes and more

The loss of Norfolk, Pensacola and New Orleans forced the Confederacy to establish new facilities (like the Charlotte Navy Yard) at more defensible sites in the interior. Responsibility for this fell on Commander George Minor, Chief of the Bureau of Ordnance and Hydrography, and on his successor, Commander John M Brooke. Minor contracted with private foundries from Virginia to Alabama for pig and bar iron, for hammered and rolled iron and iron plate, and for guns, mortars, shot and shell. Now he began developing the naval works at Selma, Charlotte, Atlanta, Richmond and Petersburg that would supply the Navy's (and much of the Army's) heavy ordnance and munitions. From this policy would also develop navy yards at Rocketts (Richmond), Selma, Shreveport (Louisiana), Yazoo City, Columbus (Georgia) and elsewhere, and other manufacturing sites at Columbia, Augusta, Albany, and Columbus. Some of these subcontracted work to foundries in small towns like Prattville and Eufaula (Alabama).

A supply of powerful steam engines and all the ancillaries — propeller shafts, boilers, steam and inlet pipes, valves, flywheels, gears, links, etc — was vital to the Confederate Navy. Early in the war Mallory told the President that 'the steam engine is as essential to the warship as her battery...' But in the Confederacy, he said:

> The want of workshops of large capacities is severely felt. No marine engines, such as are required for the ordinary class of sloops of war or frigates, have ever been made in any of the Confederate States, nor have workshops capable of producing them existed.... Parts of three such engines only have been made in Virginia, but the heavier portions of them were constructed in Pennsylvania and Maryland, and had we the workshops, the construction of one such engine would require a year.

Chief Engineer H A Ramsay, Charlotte, North Carolina, Navy Yard. (Elizabeth S Steen)

Chief Engineer James H Warner, commandant of the CS Naval Iron Works, Columbus, Georgia. (WMCWNH)

In the summer of 1862, Mallory asked Chief Engineer William P Williamson to report on the possibilities of marine engine production. Williamson's response cited three major problems. First was a scarcity of skilled workmen. Most Southern machinists, foundrymen and blacksmiths were in the Army. Those still in civilian life were already contracted to the Government making ordnance at exorbitant wages ($6 – $10 per day). Wages were so high, Williamson said, that 'the amount of work done has decreased'. The Chief explained that 'exorbitant wages almost invariably produce this effect, the operative not finding it necessary

to work every day'. Mallory, in his report to the President, attributed the scarcity of mechanics

> to the fact that a large portion of those employed in the Confederacy were Northern men or foreigners, who have, in consequence of the war, left the country, while our own mechanics are generally in the Army.

The Army was repeatedly called on to detail skilled soldiers to Government manufacturing facilities, Mallory said, 'and yet not half the number required can be obtained.'

A second difficulty was the scarcity of materials, of which Williamson listed 'iron, steel, tin, sheet copper, india-rubber packing, etc., and the various mountings and equipments, which have heretofore been obtained from the North.'

The third and more basic difficulty was the lack of machinery, tools, and facilities. Manufacturing facilities had deceased dramatically with the loss of Norfolk, Nashville and New Orleans; and until Charlotte came on line, there was no place in the Confederacy to do heavy wrought-iron work.[14] Gosport, with its well developed physical plant and its background in marine engine repair, might have given Mallory's new Navy a chance to be competitive with the US squadrons in power and speed. Its loss was a crippling blow.

The Navy expected Commander Page's Yard at Charlotte to provide marine engines. But that duty would fall to Shockoe Foundry in Richmond and an iron works in Columbus, Georgia, at the head of navigation on the Chattahoochee River. Columbus was a Deep South industrial and distribution center that thrived on river traffic. Its industrial district boasted not only cotton mills, but iron and brass foundries and machine shops specialising in steam engine and boiler repair, and in the manufacture of small steam engines for local industry. William R Brown's Columbus Iron Works contracted to make field pieces for the Confederate Army, but it was the shop's boiler business that drew Chief Engineer James H Warner's attention early in the war. Warner leased the works in the spring of 1862, and they became the Confederate Naval Iron Works.[15]

Under Chief Warner, the works would build marine machinery – boilers, valves, Stephenson links, flywheels and gearsets, and entire engines – for vessels all over the eastern Confederacy. And technical crews from the works would accompany machinery to install it in ironclads at Wilmington, Charleston, Savannah, Mobile, Selma, on Alabama's Tombigbee River, and at other shipbuilding facilities in the Deep South.

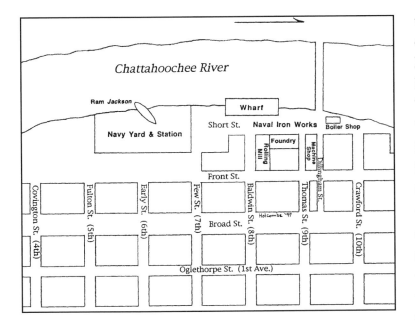

Chattahoochee River

Ram Jackson

Wharf

Navy Yard & Station

Short St.   Naval Iron Works   Boiler Shop

Foundry

Rolling
Mill   Machine
Shop

Front St.   Dillingham St.

Covington St. (4th)   Fulton St. (5th)   Early St. (6th)   Few St. (7th)   Baldwin St. (8th)   Thomas St. (9th)   Crawford St. (10th)

Broad St.   Holcombe '97

Oglethorpe St. (1st Ave.)

CS Naval Iron Works and Navy Yard, Columbus, Georgia.
(Robert Holcombe)

The Confederate Naval Iron Works consisted of several brick buildings and wooden sheds on Short Street, just behind the city steamboat wharf, straddling the Muscogee Railroad. The foundry contained a small rolling mill, with a blast engine and three furnaces, that formed iron into rough bars and plates. Warner expanded the pattern shop to make forms to cast engine parts, valves and fittings. He acquired a steam hammer from Mobile to forge links, shafts and piston rods; and bought metal-working equiment – lathes, planers, drill presses – for the machine shop. A large boiler factory, copper and carpentry shops, and a smithery with twenty forges completed the works. They ran twenty-four hours a day.

The Naval Iron Works rebuilt engines salvaged from steamboats, and built new and complete engines. One of these engines, for the ironclad *Savannah* in Savannah, caused Warner considerable embarrassment. The engine broke down on the ship's trial run, stranding the vessel almost within sight of Union troops at Fort Pulaski. She was towed back to Savannah, an ignominious end to her maiden voyage. Chief Engineer J W Tynan found that a rivet had been left lying loose in a steam line. The steam drove it into the cylinder; and it jammed the piston, damaging piston, rod, cylinder and head. Warner cast a new cylinder, head, piston (with follower and rings) and straightened the rod; and Tynan had the engine together and the *Savannah* operable within two weeks.

Warner contracted with other Columbus foundries, as well as with foundries in Eufaula and Prattville, Alabama, for production of ancillary steam machinery, and continued to expand the Naval Iron Works' physical plant throughout the war. He endeavoured to build a larger rolling mill at the works, hoping to match the Tredegar at Richmond, Gate City at Atlanta and the Selma Iron Works in producing iron armour. He contracted with famed bridge builder Horace King, an ex-slave, who provided both lumber and labour gangs to the Naval Iron Works and the nearby Columbus Navy Yard, to put up the mill. King's crew dug a flywheel pit and laid foundations in a long brick building on the south side of the railroad, and installed equipment that Warner made or acquired. The mill's engine was large – a 30in cylinder with a 42½in piston stroke. The flywheel, 22ft in diameter, weighed 28 tons. It was nearly ready for operation when Major General James H Wilson's army, sweeping southeastward through Alabama, captured Columbus on April 16, 1865, just two weeks after he laid waste to the extensive naval works at Selma.

The Columbus Naval Iron Works attempted to cover the Confederacy's needs in steam engine and boiler manufacture, installation, engineering consulting, and mechanical work. But it was never able to satisfy the Navy's demand for engines: throughout the war, blockade-runners continued to bring in English-made engines. But its production improved and expanded over the course of the war. When Columbus was captured in April 1865, the Iron Works was ready to ship two new engines for an ironclad building in Wilmington and had two more ready for assembly. It also had castings and forgings complete for a pair of engines destined for an ironclad in Charleston, and had nearly finished a pair of engines for an ironclad building on Alabama's Tombigbee River.[16] The loss of Gosport had set back marine engine manufacturing too far for the Confederacy to recover in three years, but Warner's Columbus Naval Iron Works was closing the gap.

While ships required heavy industrial items, sailors required shoes, uniforms and food. Nelson Tift, after prodigious efforts in building the ironclads *Mississippi* and *Atlanta*, returned to Albany, the south Georgia town he had founded in the 1850s. There he developed stockyards, a slaughterhouse and a meat packing plant; set up a steam-powered gristmill in the tollhouse of his Flint River bridge, and built bakeries. From shipbuilder, he became purveyor of foodstuffs to the Navy. His production remained small, supplying primarily the Savannah Squadron. The squadron's paymaster, W W J Kelly, was responsible for the works.

In the summer of 1863, Navy agent William F Howell was sent to Augusta to develop a supply network to collect wheat,

Engines of the CSS *Chattahoochee*, produced at the CS Naval Iron Works, Columbus, Georgia. (WMCWNH)

fruits and vegetables from Georgia, Alabama and the Carolinas. He dried and processed the fruit and vegetables, had wheat ground at private mills and bread baked in Augusta, Columbus and Montgomery, bought large stocks of salt and beef, and contracted to buy hogs (600 by mid-fall, 1863), which he butchered, cured and packed. Howell learned to barter molasses, flour and textile goods for bacon, beef, and pork. As all articles became more dear and inflation ran rampant, he found barter more and more effective. His bureau chief, Paymaster John DeBree, told the Secretary that 'in many districts where not a pound of bacon or wheat can be bought at any price...the sight of a pound of yarn, or a Yard of cloth will produce an effect almost magical.' Howell contracted with South Carolina's Graniteville Mill to supply him yarn and cloth, but his goods were seized by the Army's Quartermaster General. The Army offered to sell the Navy shirts and drawers at cost, but Howell wanted the cloth – jeans, woollens and osnaburgs – to barter for food.

Both Howell at Augusta and Tift at Albany tried to get stills in operation, and both found themselves circumscribed by state laws. Ultimately, Howell would prevail, and successfully supply the Navy both whiskey and vinegar.

DeBree came to appreciate Howell's abilities, praising his 'clear-headed suggestions' as the chain of agencies he established

throughout the southeastern Confederacy provided more and more of the Navy's provisions.

As the Confederate Army appropriated the output of all Southern textile mills, it forced the Navy to compete with speculators at blockade auctions for clothing and shoes. The loss of access to the Confederate West in the summer of 1863 accentuated the problem. Thus DeBree's Bureau of Provisions and Clothing opened sewing and cutting operations in Savannah, Mobile and Richmond, using whatever cloth came to hand (Paymaster Thomas R Ware at Mobile found his best source to be Havana, via the blockade.) Squadron commanders and heads of station complained about the amount, quality and uniformity of clothing issued, which promoted Bureau Chief DeBree to tell Mallory:

> I can not but think that a knowledge of one-half the difficulties encountered would stop at once carpings and fault findings by officers who have been accustomed to have their requisitions promptly met by a fully prepared bureau. The fact of the men not being uniformed is of secondary importance to their being clothed, and the fortunes of war having cut off the only supply on which we could depend rendered the use of the only means at hand absolutely necessary.

Shoes were scarce too. 'All that could be bought have proven worthless and last but little time,' DeBree said, 'while the demands of the Army have been greater than their supply.' Paymaster Ware made canvas shoes at Mobile, and in the winter of 1863 – 64 Howell at Augusta began making leather shoes. He acquired a

Nelson Tift's Flint River bridge house in Albany, Georgia., which served as a slaughter house, bakery, and barrel factory for the Navy. (Robert Holcombe)

British cutting machine that mass-produced both uppers and soles, which substantially eased the Navy's shoe problem.[17]

Aboard ship, and in naval batteries ashore, a myriad of items were necessary to work naval guns, from cordage and blocks to gunpowder, primers and fuzes, elevating screws, sights, and carriages. Small naval works across the Confederacy supplied these. In 1862 the Navy established a rope works at Petersburg, Virginia, that supplied cordage to the Army, and to private coal mines, railroads and canal companies. Sales to private industry allowed the works to supply the Navy free of cost and still turn a substantial profit.[18]

The Navy's gunpowder mill was also at Petersburg. But in the summer of 1862 Chief Engineer T Alphonse Jackson dismantled it and moved it to Columbia, South Carolina for safety. Civilian chemist P Beaudery Garesché had overall responsibility for the works. Chief Jackson expanded the facilities and refined the incorporating (mixing) mills to produce different grades of powder for small arms, boat howitzers, and the large caliber smoothbores and rifles that were the Navy's stock-in-trade.

By the spring of 1864, Jackson had a foundry operating as an adjunct to the powder mill, building railroad cars and repairing locomotives. During parts of 1863 and 1864, he was detached to Lt David McCorkle's ordnance works at Atlanta, overseeing band production for the breeches of Brooke cannon being cast at Selma. But Garesché's powder works at Columbia would be his primary duty station until their destruction when General William T Sherman captured Columbia.

Lieut David McCorkle's Atlanta Ordnance Works had originated in New Orleans under the direction of Lieut Beverley Kennon, who shocked the Navy Department in 1861 by contracting with New Orleans iron foundries for almost a million dollars in ordnance. The contracts were a disaster: the foundries delivered miscast, mismade ordnance full of flaws. Most of the first cast weapons were condemned, and the contracts were not fulfilled. Kennon, disgraced, was replaced at New Orleans by Lieut John R Eggleston.[19]

Under Eggleston's management, the New Orleans Naval Ordnance Works made gun primers and shell fuzes. When he was assigned to duty afloat, Lieut McCorkle replaced him. During Captain David Farragut's attack on New Orleans, McCorkle stayed at his post, gathering and shipping out ordnance stores until Union troops reached Canal Street.

McCorkle shipped machinery and stores to Atlanta and hastily reopened his operation in the first buildings he could rent. Commander A B Fairfax toured the works shortly after McCorkle resumed operations. 'Neatness and order reign in the establishment and the work done is good and economical,' Fairfax reported.

McCorkle rented several plots of land on the Georgia railroad, built workshops, and moved his operation. He was soon casting solid shot and shell, building gun carriages, and manufacturing fuzes and friction primers for Admiral Franklin Buchanan's Mobile Squadron. He also produced shot and shell for the Army of Tennessee's field artillery.

Artillery projectiles developed by the Navy for use in its Brooke rifles. (WMCWNH)

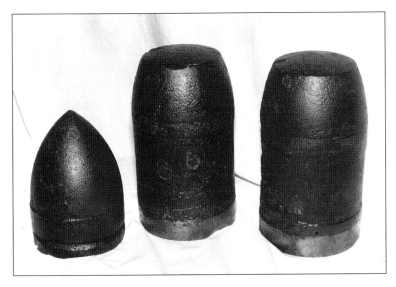

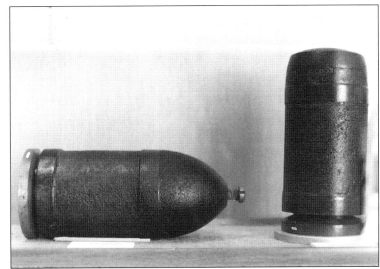

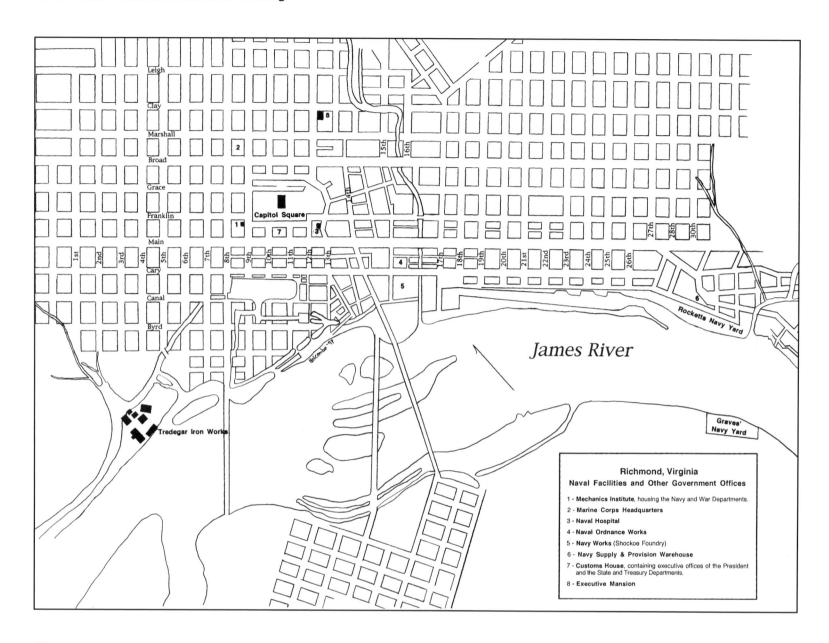

Richmond, Virginia
Naval Facilities and Other Government Offices

1 - **Mechanics Institute**, housing the Navy and War Departments.

2 - **Marine Corps Headquarters**

3 - **Naval Hospital**

4 - **Naval Ordnance Works**

5 - **Navy Works** (Shockoe Foundry)

6 - **Navy Supply & Provision Warehouse**

7 - **Customs House**, containing executive offices of the President and the State and Treasury Departments.

8 - **Executive Mansion**

Naval facilities in Richmond. (Robert Holcombe)

Throughout 1863 McCorkle's works grew and he asked that his leased plots be purchased to provide some permanence and security, and for funds to build quarters on the grounds. At that time, he and his assistants were renting rooms in town.

He expanded his product line. Elevating screws for Brooke guns from the Selma Naval Gun Foundry and brass percussion fuzes became major lines, and his supply responsibility grew to include the squadrons at Charleston and Savannah.

In August 1863 Scofield and Markham appealed to McCorkle for help with the Fulton County militia, which had charged thirteen of the rolling mill's men with desertion for failing to report for drill. McCorkle wrote to state Adjutant and Inspector General

H C Wayne, naming the men threatened with arrest, and quoting the Act of Congress that exempted them.[20] As a result Scofield and Markham had no more problems with the militia.

In Richmond, Lieut Robert Minor established the Richmond Ordnance Works, which finished Brooke rifles cast at the Tredegar Iron Works. It received bored barrel blanks from the Tredegar, rifled and banded them, added accouterments, and sent them into service. The Richmond works also made gun carriages, finished projectiles cast at Lynchburg and the Tredegar (filling them with powder and affixing sabots and fuzes), and made fuzes, primers, and cartridges. Minor also oversaw Shockoe Foundry's manufacture of engines for the James River Squadron.

In October 1863, Minor won assignment to an expedition to free Confederate prisoners held on Johnson's Island in Lake Erie. Lt Alexander M DeBree replaced him and ran the works until his return. DeBree had been an assistant inspector of ordnance, posted to the Tredegar, responsible for the quality of gun metal used by the ironworks to cast the Navy's guns. He and his civilian assistant, Elliott Lacy, tested the tensile strength and density of a sample of metal used in each gun.

In the Naval Gun Foundry at Selma, Commander Catesby Jones zealously tested high-grade north Alabama iron and refused to use any but the best in his production. But the Naval Gun Foundry was under Jones's command. DeBree, an adjunct to the privately-owned Tredegar Iron Works, was sometimes overwhelmed trying to sort through pigs and blooms of indifferent quality while the Tredegar's foundry foreman pushed him to release iron for production. Heavy demand for finished ordnance and the Tredegar's frantic production pace pressed heavily on DeBree, and occasionally a defective piece got by. One, a 7in Brooke mounted on the *Atlanta*, was condemned in Savannah in July 1863.

As at other Confederate naval installations, the detailed employees of the Richmond Ordnance Works were enrolled and drilled as a naval battalion. During the summer of 1864, much of their time was spent under arms in the field, which crippled production at the works. A few civilian mechanics struggled to keep ammunition going to the naval squadrons and coastal batteries of the eastern Confederacy.

At Charleston, Lt Nicholas Van Zandt headed a small ordnance depot, turning out gun carriages, projectiles, and fuzes. With the variety of coast artillery around Charleston harbor – old US guns, new Confederate pieces, and exotic British patterns – Van Zandt was well positioned to observe the handling, and the effects, of a variety of weapons. Thus Charleston, in Van Zandt's eyes, became the Confederate Navy's *de facto* test facility for heavy ordnance.

In Atlanta, McCorkle continued to improve his works. He built a coke oven, put up a steam hammer, improved his machine shop, and acquired a still from the old US Mint in Dahlonega. He made 85° proof alcohol, purer than that obtainable anywhere else, and supplied the Selma Naval Gun Foundry as well as his own works.

But in June 1864, progress stopped. With Sherman's approach, McCorkle needed a safer site. He chose Augusta, home of the Confederate Army's massive gunpowder factory and an extensive arsenal. He wrote to Catesby Jones:

I have been advised by Gen'l Johnston to move all stores and machin-

ery. I am moving the boilers and engines today. All the lathes, planers, steam hammer &c already shipped. It makes me very sad to break up here. Every house, every piece of timber has gone up and been laid under my own eye.... I have just finished a fine stable and enclosed a neighboring lot for the mules to feed and exercise. I have just finished three lathes for fuzes and the place commenced to look up.

Two weeks later he told Jones:

I have all surplus stores packed-ready for a move. I hope Joseph [Johnston] will give me time to save everything. If it were not for the panic it would create I would move most of the stores now.[21]

By mid-August McCorkle was in Augusta. He leased land and put up temporary buildings to house his foundry, gun carriage shop and other facilities, hoping he would soon be back in production. Until then, his responsibilities to Charleston, Savannah and Mobile would have to be assumed by Charlotte, Richmond and Selma.[22]

After McCorkle's move from New Orleans to Atlanta, production had resumed quickly. But in 1864 the Confederacy was a changed nation. The railroads were almost worn out, and supplies of everything, from firebricks to roofing nails to paper, were exhausted. Despite McCorkle's best efforts, by late November 1864 his refugee works were still not in operation.[23]

The loss of Atlanta also meant the loss of the lower South's armour production. The Gate City Rolling Mill was on the Georgia Railroad near Oakland Cemetery. During the siege of Atlanta, the Army of Tennessee's ammunition train was parked on that line, near the foundry. When the Confederate Army abandoned Atlanta, seven locomotives and eighty-one freight cars full of ammunition were blown up in front of the mill.

Five hours were occupied in this work of demolition, which also included the rolling mill....Every building for a quarter of a mile around was either torn to pieces or perforated with hundreds of holes by shell fragments.

Scofield and Markham had managed to get away with some of their machinery. As Sherman closed in, they dismantled and moved what they could to Columbia. But operations never resumed and Mallory told President Davis: 'The stoppage of this mill has been a serious drawback to the progress of naval construction, the hulls of several vessels being in readiness to receive their armour.'[24]

The naval gun foundry: triumph in the wilderness

Throughout the war, the Confederate Government sought to both stimulate private industry and create government-owned industrial plants. In September of 1862, Secretary Mallory asked for an appropriation of $2m to help private contractors develop iron and coal resources to fulfill contracts already made with the Navy. Seven of these contracts were with Virginia iron producers; only one each was with furnaces in North Carolina, Tennessee, and Alabama.

But it was in Alabama that the Navy would develop its greatest industrial plant. A national foundry to serve both the Army and Navy was high on the Government's needs list. Both services surveyed private iron works in the Deep South, seeking a plant for the government to buy and develop. The preference was for Mark Cooper's Etowah Iron Works in Cartersville, Georgia. But the Confederate Government wanted Alabama businessman Colin McRae to act as its financial agent in Europe; and McRae demanded the Government buy his Alabama Manufacturing Company in Selma, Alabama, before he would agree to go overseas.

Thus a site for a national foundry was secured. But unlike the Etowah Iron Works, the Selma facility was not operational. With government contracts for both rolled iron and heavy ordnance, Colin McRae told Colonel Josiah Gorgas in July 1862:

> I shall spare no effort to get the works here underway as speedily as possible.... I am driving the rolling mill and foundry on together, though by contract I was to commence making cannon on the 1st of September and rolled iron on the 1st of December.

McRae searched the eastern Confederacy for workmen, and complained about the impossibility of getting skilled men from the Army, sounding the mournful refrain of Southern industrialists both government and private — the Army would not detail skilled soldiers to build the tools of war.

When McRae left for Europe in 1863, his non-functioning foundry became the Army's responsibility. Sixteen months had gone into efforts to make the facility operational, and not a gun had been cast nor a plate of iron rolled. Major N R Chambliss took up the challenge and struggled with strikes and desertion by skilled workers, badly made machinery, unfinished facilities, and slow deliveries of coal and iron from nearby mines.

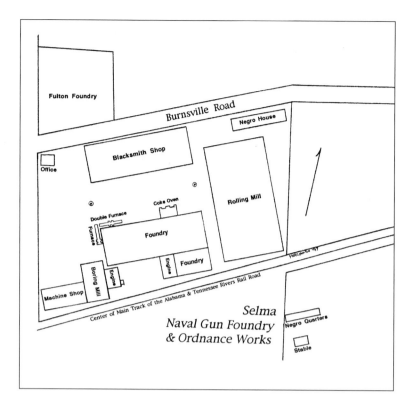

Selma Naval Gun Foundry and Ordnance Works. (Robert Holcombe, from an original in the National Archives)

Then the Army backed out of the agreement, surrendering all control to the Navy, but asking to be supplied by the foundry as compensation for its part in the purchase. The Navy transferred Commander Catesby ap R Jones from Charlotte, with orders to get the works into production as quickly as possible. Jones arrived in Selma at the end of May 1863.

Catesby Jones saw heavy ordnance — Brooke rifles — as the Confederacy's primary need. Once gun production was established, he could turn his full attention to completing the rolling mill.

Getting Selma into production was critical. Enemy activity in Virginia disrupted the flow of pig iron to the Tredegar; then the foundry was swept by a devastating fire, putting it out of production for over five months.

Jones called his work the Naval Gun Foundry. He threw himself into efforts to get it operational. By November he had finished the foundry's walls and braced and strengthened its roof, rebuilt and repositioned a gun pit crane, rebuilt the gun pit and rerouted a spring that had forced its way into the pit, begun the foundation for a cupola furnace, repaired and braced several furnaces, and built shelters over them. He built an elevated railroad and a special car to carry guns to and from the foundry. He rebuilt the machine shop and the boring mill and scoured the Confederacy for boring bits and reamers, and laid another stretch of track to move heavy barrel blanks from the gun pit to the boring mill. A smithery was erected with furnaces and twenty forges for banding guns.

Gosport had built a machine for bending the Brooke guns' iron bands. Jones tracked it down, sitting idle at the Augusta arsenal. It would prove to be a prize acquisition.

Commander George Minor had endorsed the quality of north Alabama iron, but no one had cast guns with it and its characteristics were unknown. Jones needed to experiment. 'To do this with heavy guns would be most satisfactory', he told Brooke, 'but there would be much time lost besides being expensive.' He would cast several 6pdrs to study the quality of the metal and experiment with casting techniques. He had experimented with them before, and thus had a baseline on the characteristics of other gun metals for comparison.

Jones wanted consistent quality in his iron. He could not get it, he feared, buying pigs from different furnaces. He recommended that, if one furnace's output proved superior in quality to the others, the Government buy that works so he could control its production. Jones found that the Bibb Iron Works turned out consistently high quality iron. In July 1863 the Bibb works was put up for sale, and the Commander asked Major William Richardson Hunt of the Niter and Mining Bureau to buy it.

Jones sought to insure the quality of his personnel through the same methods Robert E Lee used to develop his Army of Northern Virginia – get rid of those who could not perform at a level of excellence and replace them with those who could. Despite a dearth of skilled labour, he released the master machinist, master carpenter, and molding shop foreman he had inherited from Colin McRae. Master Julian Fairfax, CSN, was told his assistant superintendent's position no longer existed under Jones's new table of organization. Lt Charles C Simms, who had served on the *Virginia*, replaced him with the title of executive officer.[25]

Like all good sailors, Jones truly wanted service afloat. He lobbied his old commander from the *Virginia*, Franklin Buchanan, for a position in Old Buck's squadron at Mobile. His friends, like Robert Minor at Richmond, tormented him with innocent comments like: 'No one has yet been ordered to the *Virginia* [II] here....If you were not on more important duty, I am inclined to believe that you would have command of her'.[26] But the Navy had found Jones's niche at Selma. The Naval Gun Foundry – and its

promised rolling mill – were too important to allow him to escape to sea duty.

When the Army relinquished control of the foundry, Colonel J L White of the Selma Arsenal sought to claim most of its workmen, but Jones fended him off. In the following months Jones and White battled for workers, Jones diplomatically, the Colonel with a truculent bad grace. He had his reasons: like all wartime manufacturers, he was having trouble obtaining workmen, and he did not want competition for labour in his own neighbourhood. But when White sent the provost marshal to arrest one of Jones's workers, Commander Jones made friends with the provost and kept the workman.

He was on good terms with most Army officers (most of the foundry's early production would be for the Army), and professionals like Colonel George W Rains at Augusta were most helpful. But White would prove a bitter, recalcitrant foe for the duration of the war.

While Jones struggled to get the foundry's gun casting operational, his furnaces and forges produced large-caliber shot and shell for the Army. Both Vicksburg and Port Hudson were supplied from the Naval Gun Foundry for their prolonged, thundering duels with the fleets of David Farragut and David Porter. The foundry also cast machine parts for arsenals, including Selma's. Jones used these requisitions as occasions to lobby Colonel White for help in procuring workmen for the foundry. After all, Jones told the Colonel, if he had the manpower, he could turn out even more work for the Army.

White took no notice. Jones, dejected, wrote to Brooke:

> There appears but little desire to reciprocate on the part of the Army, as represented by the arsenal here. They might often be of great service to us, but when they furnish articles it is with so much apparent reluctance that I never ask for anything if I can avoid it.

Selma Arsenal even refused to supply him lanyards and friction primers to test his 6pdrs. McCorkle sent them from Atlanta.

Jones thought his work for the Army should loosen the strings that bound skilled workmen in the Army's ranks. The Confederate Government had made provision for transferring soldiers with skills from front line regiments to workshops. But there was a catch: the law required an applicant, like Jones, to identify a prospective workman by name and unit, and request that man's detail from field duty to the foundry. Then, both the war department and the requested man's unit commander had to approve the transfer. Few field commanders were willing to voluntarily deplete their units. And as the war ground on and casualties and desertions thinned the ranks, there was even less willingness to give up riflemen to factory work.

Jones kept up a campaign of complaint, suggestion and salesmanship to increase his work force. He wrote to the Army – arsenals and fortifications he supplied, unit commanders, conscript officers – citing the ordnance and ammunition he was sending the Army and suggesting that he could do even more if he just had the manpower. Whenever he was unable to fill a requisition – for mortars, small ordnance, shot and shell, or cast machine parts – he never failed to mention that only the shortage of manpower prevented him from complying with the request. He complained to Brooke as Chief, Bureau of Ordnance and Hydrography; he complained directly to Mallory; and to Mallory's counterpart, the Secretary of War; he complained to his brother officers. In late

Commander Catesby ap R Jones. (Naval Historical Center)

1864 President Jefferson Davis, on a morale-building tour of the Confederacy, visited the Naval Gun Foundry. Walking round the works with the President, Commander Jones relentlessly lobbied for more skilled workers. The President could only shake his head and say: we're doing the best we can. When Jones applied for ten marines – molders, carpenters, machinists, a blacksmith and a boilermaker – from Buchanan's squadron at Mobile, even his old mentor refused him. Jones, angered and exasperated, wrote Commander Brooke: 'I can understand the difficulty of obtaining details from the Army, but when the matter is within our own control I do not see why there should be any trouble'.

In early September 1863, the War Department tantalized Jones with the promise of a contingent of skilled workers already detailed and soon to be sent. Six weeks later, one man arrived and went on sick call. 'It almost appears useless to ask to have men detailed...' Jones said.

Jones could not even keep all the labour force he had. Some detailed soldiers deserted, and civilian workers were forced by inflation to leave the foundry for higher paying jobs in private facilities. In the summer, sickness decimated the work force. Indeed in 1863 the severity of the summer's sickly season almost overwhelmed him. The foundry's hospital filled to overflowing, and foundry and navy yard workers filled the city hospital.

The sickly season incapacitated black workers just as it did white. And there were other problems with slave labour, among them owners who let the Navy train their slaves as ironworkers, then withdrew them from the naval foundry to rent them to private foundries at higher wages. The only remedy, in Jones's opinion, was for the Government to own the slaves.

With even his manual labour force dwindling, work on the rolling mill lagged. In every corner of the Confederacy, ironclads languished, unfinished, awaiting armour. The Confederate Navy's ironclad programme ran in slow motion, due in part to a lack of labour, and even more due to the dearth of armour plate. Catesby Jones's works should have been the remedy. He knew it, and he was humiliated by his inability to help. He told Brooke:

> We are building iron clads whilst we have not iron to cover those now afloat, and if I had the mechanics I have applied for the mill would have been in operation before this.

Jones gave to the rolling mill as much attention as possible. He sent mill foreman T S Alvis on a tour of other rolling mills, bought templates from Etowah Iron Works, had a draftsman make drawings of equipment at the Shelby Iron Works, and on occasion

A rare 11in Brooke smoothbore, manufactured at the Selma Naval Gun Foundry. (WMCWNH)

pulled his workmen from other jobs to work on the rolling mill's foundations and structure. But such a luxury was rare. At times, not two days' work were devoted to the rolling mill in two months. In offcial correspondence, Jones told Brooke that the rolling mill project should be abandoned. But privately he admitted that these recommendations should not be taken seriously: they were made for Mallory's eyes in an effort to make the mill a departmental priority.

When the neighbouring Shelby Iron Works offered to buy the rolling mill, the Confederate Government, the Navy Department, and Brooke's bureau all responded with alacrity. Shelby President Horace Ware arrived at Jones's office with a letter authorising Jones to transfer ownership of the rolling mill to Shelby, if Jones felt it advisable. Reluctantly, Jones agreed, and sent the Secretary a lengthy report, explaining his reasons for giving up the project. He was against privatising any Government works: but in this case, he must assent. For, 'with the means placed at my disposal, it could not have been completed within a year'.

Commander Jones struck a good bargain with Mr Ware, who agreed to finish, staff and run the mill where it sat – at the Naval Gun Foundry. He promised to have it operational within three months (it would take nine months, in fact), and agreed to supply the Navy with 60 tons per week in armour plate, boiler plate or gun bands during the mill's first month in operation, with the quota increasing monthly until, within five months, it would be providing the Navy with 120 tons per week.

In his report to the Secretary on the conclusion of the deal, Jones could not resist a parting shot:

I may be permitted in concluding to express my regret that my applications for mechanics have not been granted. Had they been, the mill would have been in operation and enough iron rolled for all the vessels in this part of the Confederacy. We should also have had more guns in service.[27]

In early 1864, the Naval Gun Foundry was producing Brooke cannon. Jones's first successful 7in Brooke rifle went to Mobile for the ironclad *Tennessee*. He told Admiral Buchanan: 'I do not know how I could express my confidence in the gun than by saying that if I had to fight the ship I should place it where I thought it would be most fired.'

Hidden behind the scenes of the Naval Gun Foundry's long struggle to get into production was an agonising trail of mishaps, frustrations, and aggravations. Jones redesigned and rebuilt the entire gun casting operation, from furnaces to testing system. Such basic details as the length, depth and radius of rifling; correct dimensions of finished gun barrels; and procedures for heating the gun bands were not provided by the Tredegar or Commander Brooke. Jones had to find them ... or guess. Equipment promised – like the banding machine and a trunnion lathe – took months to arrive, or was never sent at all. Suppliers of fuel and iron, even of foundation stone and timber, were frequently late with deliveries, and they often sent substandard and mis-made materials. Equipment failed and malfunctioned: furnaces ruptured during casting, contaminating 20,00lb of gun iron at a time. Early on, getting a gun out of the cooling pit was a life-threatening adventure requiring days of struggle and frustration.[28]

Jones expected to produce Brooke rifles in two calibers – 6.4in and 7in. But his first 6.4in, cast in December 1863, was over-bored. Rather than waste the gun, he suggested reboring it as an 8in smoothbore. Commander Brooke liked the idea: 8in shell guns on Marsilly carriages would be excellent in broadside. Brooke followed his approval of the 8in smoothbore with drawings for two more Brooke smoothbores, a 10in and an 11in. By the time Ware had the rolling mill in operation (late November 1864), Jones would be sending 10- and 11in guns to Charleston and Mobile.

Within a year's operation, the Naval Gun Foundry met the emergency needs of both coastal defense and fleet service and was stockpiling Brooke rifles and smoothbores, awaiting requisitions from Charleston, Savannah, Mobile and elsewhere. Jones now expanded his line, tooling up to produce 20- and 30pdr Parrott rifles, mortars, and 12pdr field guns for the Army. Over the course of its existence the Naval Gun Foundry made 102 Brooke guns, 20 mortars, and several 20- and 30pdr Parrott rifles. The last gun shipped from Selma was a variation, an 11in Brooke rifle sent to Fort Huger, above Mobile, on March 17, 1865.

On April 2, 1865, the Confederate Government evacuated Richmond. Lt Minor's ordnance works, the navy yard at Rocketts, Shockoe Foundry and the Tredegar Iron Works were all abandoned or destroyed. That same day, Major General James H Wilson's army entered Selma, forcing destruction of the Naval Gun Foundry and rolling mill, and the Army's great ordnance complex.[29] From Selma, Wilson continued southeastward through Alabama to the Chattahoochee River and Columbus, Georgia, where he destroyed Chief Warner's Naval Iron Works. With that, the last of the Confederate Navy's great manufacturing facilties and the hard-earned industrial mobilization of an agricultural nation passed into history.

Dr Maurice Melton

Chapter Five
SHIPBUILDING

Studies of ante-bellum industry count over 140 private shipyards in Dixie (the South) in the 1850s, suggesting a thriving Southern marine industry. But the statistics are misleading. Of permanent yards launching vessels onto the seas of commerce, the South had but a few. And of the ten US naval yards that built and repaired warships, the South had only two – Gosport Navy Yard at Portsmouth, Virginia and Warrington Navy Yard at Pensacola, Florida.

Most Southern 'shipyards' were spots on a river bank where an entrepreneur cleared a place and built his own boat. Then, with boat and builder launched into the carrying trade, the woods grew back to the river's edge and the shipyard disappeared. Ante-bellum Southern shipbuilding was more a means to enter the shipping business than a ship *building* business. Although it possessed a lion's share of the nation's seacoast and navigable rivers, the pre-war South built no more than 20 per cent of its ships. In fact, like other Southern manufacturing, shipbuilding declined significantly in the decade before the war.

The seceding states quickly established navies, buying commercial steamboats and arming them. But they were not warships. Commodore Josiah Tattnall, who commanded the Georgia and South Carolina squadrons of these makeshifts, told a visiting British journalist: 'Long before the South has a fleet to cope with the North, my bones will be whitening in the grave.' When Tattnall tried to defend Port Royal, South Carolina, in November 1861, Captain Samuel F DuPont's invasion fleet pummelled the rebel riverboats and pushed them off the field of battle. What the South needed were real warships like DuPont's, designed and built to carry guns and fight.[1]

Gunboats and ironclads: the early efforts

The Confederacy hoped to both buy warships from England and France, and stimulate a Southern shipbuilding industry. The Navy planned to build a hundred or more light-draft, heavily armed vessels to defend the South's ports and rivers. But from the outset, Secretary of the Navy Stephen R Mallory sought to emulate the technologically sophisticated French and British. Rather than trying to compete with the United States Navy in wooden frigates, he wanted ironclads.

So did the people of the Confederacy. From the moment of the new nation's creation, citizens flooded the Navy Department with offers to build ironclad vessels to defend Southern waters and break Mr Lincoln's blockade. Among the applicants was a Florida acquaintance of Mallory's, Asa F Tift. Asa and his brother Nelson, a Georgia entrepreneur, submitted a model of an armoured ship that featured flat surfaces and angles in place of the elegant sweeps and curves of traditional seagoing vessels. Such a ship could be built by house carpenters, the Tifts said, with the participation of highly skilled ship's carpenters kept to a minimum. The brothers offered to build such vessels as Navy Department agents, working 'without pecuniary compensation from the Government...or any other reward than that which every citizen must feel who can, in any way, contribute to the defense of our country'.

Searching for builders, Tift approached Savannah, Georgia,

Asa Tift. (Monroe County May Hill Russell Library, Florida)

Nelson Tift. (C B Pritchett, Jr)

foundry owner Alvin Miller and his neighbour, shipbuilder Henry Willink, Jr. Both expressed interest in doing business with the Navy, but no interest in building the Tifts' armoured monster. Miller told Tift he could build an engine for one of Mallory's wooden gunboats; and Willink, at the shipyard, could construct the boat. Tift suggested that they talk to Mallory in Richmond.[2]

Henry F Willink, Jr was a second-generation Savannah shipbuilder. As a child he endured just three years of formal schooling before going to work in his father's shipyard. After seven years with his father, he secured a position in the famous William H Webb shipyard in New York, studying ship design and construction there for nine years. He returned to Savannah in 1851 to take over his father's business. In 1861 he was 36 years old and the acknowledged local master of the trade.

Willink called on Mallory in Richmond, and on November 2, 1861, contracted to build two wooden gunboats — hulls, rigging, spars, sails and outfits — for the sum of $36,000 each. The gunboats' plans were drawn by Naval Constructor John L Porter.

Willink would be paid in $6,000 increments: the first payment due when the stem, sternpost and keel of either ship were laid. The second payment would be made when the frame was complete; the third when she was planked; the fourth when the deck was framed; the fifth when the deck was laid, planed off and finished; and the final installment 'when either vessel shall be completed in every respect according to the specifications...' Such installment payments became standard in Confederate Navy construction contracts.

Willink's contract called for delivery of the first ship, to be named *Macon*, by February 20, 1862. But war fever depleted

Henry F Willink, Jr. (Georgia Historical Society, Savannah, Georgia)

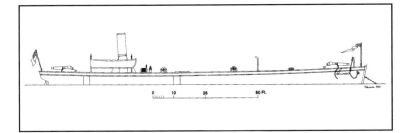

CSS *Macon*, as built. (Robert Holcombe)

Willink's work force and disrupted normal sources of supply, impeding progress. Not until early December did he meet the requirements for his first payment – a keel laid and a stem and sternpost raised. Not until late January was her hull framed. In February, as her intended completion date passed, she was planked, and in March her deck was framed.[3]

By this time, a wooden gunboat named the *Morgan* had already been launched in Mobile, Alabama, and another, the *Gaines*, was nearing completion. Henry D Bassett and William Oates had contracted to build them in September 1861 when labour and materials were more plentiful.

But as soon as these ships were completed, Bassett and Oates lost their carpenters and mechanics to the Army.[4] This was a portent of problems to come for all Confederate shipbuilders, whether contractors like Bassett and Oates or Henry Willink, Navy Department agents like the brothers Tift, or Confederate naval officers commanding new Government shipyards.

Predating Henry Willink's contract, too, was an agreement between Lt Augustus McLaughlin, CSN, at Columbus, Georgia, and David S Johnston, authorizing Johnston to build a gunboat at a steamboat landing called Saffold (Mrs Johnston's family plantation), 175 miles below Columbus on the Chattahoochee River. Johnston was to be paid $47,500 for the vessel in six installments. She was to be a three-masted ocean-going gunboat with two engines driving twin screws. She was to be finished in four months, and would be named the *Chattahoochee*.

Born in Madison, in middle Georgia, Johnston was an attorney who married into a planter family deep in the southwest corner of the state. He was an entrepreneur at heart, an energetic man with big ideas. He had never seen a boat built, but he thought he could build one.[5]

But Johnston had trouble finding workers. His plantation's slaves could supply manual labour, but he needed skilled workmen

David S Johnston, builder of the *Chattahoochee*. (Albert W Weems, Jr.)

with shipbuilding experience. Without them, work fell seriously behind schedule...even more so than at Savannah.

Still, both Johnston at Saffold and Willink in Savannah looked forward to larger Government contracts. Willink and Alvin Miller developed a plan for an ironclad. Late in 1861 they built a model and sent it to Richmond. In mid-January, 1862 the Secretary responded: 'If you are disposed to enter upon the construction of a vessel of this description, and can complete her within a reasonable [time], I will be very glad to confer with either or both of you as early as practicable.'

A second trip to Richmond brought Willink a contract for two ironclads – not on the model he had sent, but of a new design by John L Porter, the first example of which the Confederate Navy was already building at Gosport.

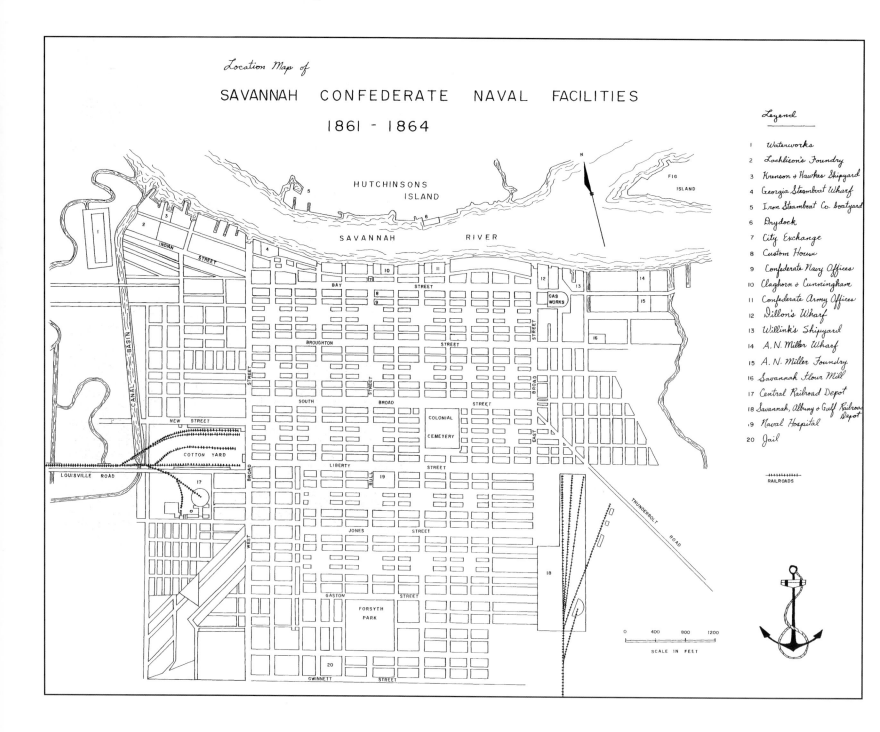

Location Map of

SAVANNAH CONFEDERATE NAVAL FACILITIES
1861 - 1864

Legend

1. Waterworks
2. Lochlison's Foundry
3. Kranson & Hawkes Shipyard
4. Georgia Steamboat Wharf
5. Iron Steamboat Co. boatyard
6. Drydock
7. City Exchange
8. Custom House
9. Confederate Navy Offices
10. Claghorn & Cunningham
11. Confederate Army Offices
12. Dillon's Wharf
13. Willink's Shipyard
14. A. N. Miller Wharf
15. A. N. Miller Foundry
16. Savannah Flour Mill
17. Central Railroad Depot
18. Savannah, Albany & Gulf Railroad Depot
19. Naval Hospital
20. Jail

RAILROADS

HUTCHINSONS ISLAND

FIG ISLAND

SAVANNAH RIVER

N

0   400   800   1200
SCALE IN FEET

Naval facilities, Savannah, Georgia. (Samuel Lawson)

Mallory asked Willink how long he would take to complete the ironclads. Willink replied that six months would be reasonable under ordinary circumstances; but given the scarcity of labour, he could not bind himself to that. Mallory replied that the ships must be finished in four months, not six. Willink thought it impossible, but promised to do his best, and the deal was done.[6] Mallory released Willink from his obligation to build the second

wooden gunboat. Ironclads, not wooden ships, were what the Confederacy needed, and Mallory's attention – and his department's construction projects – became devoted almost exclusively to armoured ships. Gunboat contracts were cancelled in favour of ironclad projects (unless, like Willink's first gunboat – and Johnston's – they were too far advanced to be scrapped). The *Macon* became a part-time project as Willink made the ironclads his yard's top priority.

The *Chattahoochee's* projected completion date, February 17, 1862, passed with Johnston's gunboat even further behind than

Willink's. Work was impeded, not only by a scarcity of labour, but by the river. Winter rains caused it to flood, covering the building site. At times the torrent rose high enough to cover the boat frame. Johnston feared that the whole structure — frame, keel, and the blocks and timbers they sat on — would be swept away. But they stood firm.

In early March, Johnston advertised in the Columbus *Daily Sun* for 'Twenty ships' carpenters, joiners, caulkers, and hands accustomed to ship and steamboat work', promising that 'anyone in the Army can be furloughed to work there'.

Johnston now had contracts for several gunboats and saw himself as a successful shipbuilder with a growing business. He advertised his building site as 'THE C.S. NAVY YARD...AT SAFFOLD, EARLY COUNTY, GEORGIA'. Although he was a civilian contractor, he was building for the Confederate Navy, and the distinction between civilian site and naval facility escaped him.

The Saffold site was unhealthy, and illness interfered with construction. In October, 1862, only two of thirty-eight workers were healthy enough to be on the job. By the end of November the work crew had increased to a hundred, but forty to fifty of them were too ill to work.

With construction behind schedule, Lt McLaughlin withheld Johnston's payments until March 25, 1862, then made a payment representing the first three installments, plus part of another, totalling $21,333.33.

Contemporaries attributed part of the delay to Johnston's interest in becoming a full-time shipbuilder. He spent money, time and effort enlarging his shipyard, they said, building new facilities and buying equipment. River gossip said the *Chattahoochee* money went on this expansion. But with independent wealth, Johnston (locally known as 'the Colonel') was not dependent on Government payments to finance his business.

He also spent time frolicking in Columbus. A naval officer wrote to his fiancee, a Saffold-area girl: '...the *gallant Colonel* lost $800 playing faro on his last trip to Columbus; got exceedingly drunk and did many other things not very profitable to his reputation or his finances'.

More delays were caused by the need to revise and remanufacture engine parts sent from Columbus. Chief Engineer James H Warner, CSN, designed the gunboat's engines and built them at the Columbus Iron Works, which the Navy leased in September 1862. The *Chattahoochee's* engineer, John Horry Dent, Jr remarked:

'Seems everything they send down have to have some alterations'. Nor was it easy to get machinery in a timely manner. The engineer complained: 'We could complete the engines very soon if we had the work down from Columbus. They seem to take their time up there'.

McLaughlin asked trusted rivermen to report on Johnston's activity...or lack of it, and began making frequent visits himself.

A Advertisement for shipyard workers. (WMCWNH)

ONE HUNDRED HANDS WANTED,
AT THE
CONFEDERATE
STATES NAVY YARD!
LOCATED ON THE
CHATTAHOOCHEE RIVER!
AT
Saffold, Early Co., Georgia.
To Build Gun Boats!

SHIP Carpenters, Joiners, Caulkers, Mechanics of every kind, Blacksmiths, Hewers and Laborers, both white men & negroes, can find employment at the Confederate States Navy Yard. As several Gun Boats are now in progress of construction and under contract, the hands may expect steady employment and good wages.

All the hands employed at the Navy Yard are exempt from Military duty, and not subject to a draft.

Any person now in the service, who desires a situation at the Navy Yard, can obtain a Furlough to work there, by application to D. S. Johnston. Saffold, Early county, Ga.

The Confederate States Navy Yard is situated on the Chattahoochee River, at Saffold, Early county, Ga., and is accessible by Steamboats making regular trips from Columbus, Ga., via Eufaula, Ala., and Fort Gains, Ga.

D. S. JOHNSTON.
Saffold, Ga., Mar. 5, 1862.   20-tf

A model of the CSS *Chattahoochee*. (WMCWNH)

On August 12, he made what would be the final lump-sum payment to Johnston. Thereafter, the Navy Department, through McLaughlin, paid only the contractor's expenses – labour, materials, tool rental.

McLaughlin, in fact, took over the job of finishing the ship. He ordered materials – copper, rubber packing, and over a ton of iron for Chief Warner to forge the ship's propeller shafts and coupling boxes. He ordered a caboose (galley) – galley stove, stovepipe, boilers with cocks for the stove, oven pans, mess gear – as well as three water closets from the Columbus firm of D B Thompson.

In late summer, McLaughlin ordered furnishings – tables, chairs, hammocks, a looking glass – as well as interior carpentry, two steering wheels (one brass-mounted), and steam pipe to connect engines, boilers, and the galley. River steamers ferried both skilled workmen (at wages of $3 to $5 per day) and materials from Columbus to Saffold.

McLaughlin built a sail room, with ten sail-maker's benches, and a rigging loft at Saffold. Sailmakers Charles Godwin of Columbus and James Dempsey of Apalachicola moved there, working 40 to 60 days (at $4.25 per day) with canvas and cordage supplied by Columbus cotton mills.

In July 1862, Commander Catesby ap R Jones arrived to command the ship and take over McLaughlin's duties. At Jones's direction, workmen relocated the galley, altered mast placement and design, and built sail and rigging rooms in the cramped area below deck. By September 14, one of the gunboat's masts had been

stepped and another was ready. By October 3, all were in place and being secured by standing rigging.

As Commander Jones got to know David Johnston, his opinion of the contractor fell. He wrote to a brother officer that 'the longer he [Johnston] lives, the greater rascal he becomes'.

In late November, the Navy Department revoked Johnston's contract and directed that the *Chattahoochee* be finished at a new navy yard McLaughlin was building in Columbus. Workmen, tools and materials were moved to Columbus, and David Johnston was out of the boat-building business. His gunboat, scheduled for completion by February 17, 1862, finally went into commission January 1, 1863.[7]

New Orleans

In September 1861, while Bassett and Oates were signing their Mobile gunboat contracts and Willink and Miller were considering doing business with Richmond, Asa and Nelson Tift went to New Orleans to build their ironclad, the *Mississippi*. New Orleans had drawn another entrepreneur, E C Murray, a Kentuckian with over twenty years' experience building riverboats. Murray sent the Navy Department a plan for an ironclad, and Mallory contracted with him to build a vessel, to be called the *Louisiana*, for $196,000. Murray would be paid in six installments of $24,500 each, with a final payment of $49,000. Delivery date was set for January 25,

CSS *Louisiana*. (Robert Holcombe)

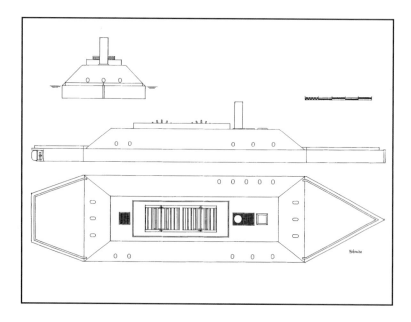

1862, with a bonus/penalty clause: $98 would be awarded the builder for each day prior to deadline the ship was completed, or a $98 penalty imposed for each day over. Delays caused by materials shortages or transportation problems would not invoke the penalty. Price increases in iron beyond $60 per ton would be covered by the Navy Department.

Murray established a yard in Jefferson City, above New Orleans, on a plot loaned by Laurent Millandon. The *Louisiana* would be a paddle-wheel steamer, with small propellers to aid in steering. To avoid battle damage, the two wheels were mounted inboard, in line astern, one running in the wake of the other. An engineer predicted that the engines, taken from the riverboat *Ingomar*, would never turn the second wheel.

John L Porter drew working plans for the Tifts' *Mississippi*. In his opinion, it would take them nine months to build the vessel...if they ever started.

The Tifts still intended to subcontract the ship and engine to qualified builders. They asked Leeds & Co., New Orleans' largest foundry, about the engines, and found them unenthusiastic. The job would require at least four months, Leeds said. The brothers turned to the Patterson Iron Works, who agreed to both manufacture and install the engines within 90 days for $45,000 (plus a $5,000 bonus if they made their projected date).

The Tifts approached three New Orleans shipyards about building the hull. John Hughes & Co declined the job, but offered to rent the brothers space, a sawmill, and workers. Hyde & Mackay offered to build the hull for $125,000 but refused to be bound to a completion date. Harram & Co would build it for $147,000, but likewise refused to promise a completion date.

In the end, the Tifts decided to build the entire ship themselves on a four-acre plot adjoining E C Murray's, also loaned by Mr Millandon. They rented an office for $10 per month and bought a sawmill for $3,200.

The Tifts bought their timber in the lower Mississippi Valley, mostly around Ponchatoula, Louisiana and Summit, Mississippi. E C Murray had contracted with a Florida timber merchant. When the blockade cut him off, he bought from sources on Lake Pontchartrain, and on the New Orleans and Jackson Railroad.

The Tifts hired John Brough, an assistant engineer working for the Navy, to advise on and install the *Mississippi's* engines. They soon replaced him with E M Ivens, a local agent of Richmond's Tredegar Iron Works. Ivens became engineer in charge, reporting to Chief Engineer James H Warner at Columbus, Georgia. Ivens saw that the *Mississippi's* planned engines were too small. The Tifts

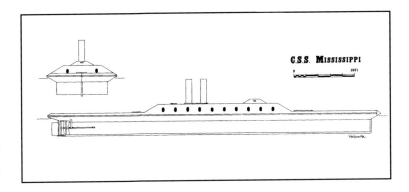

CSS *Mississippi*. (Robert Holcombe)

doubled her furnace and boiler capacity (increasing her length by 20ft), and estimated that they would have 1,500 horsepower turning three propellers. The Patterson Iron Works charged $65,000, for the additional furnaces and boilers, which Chief Warner felt reasonable.

But Patterson's did not have the men to do the work. As Nelson Tift said: 'There was a great deficiency of mechanics of all kinds, especially in the machine shops. There was a good deal of Government work on hand at all the shops in New Orleans, and they were all pressed for hands'. The Tifts, searching for qualified machinists, got only one propeller molder sent from Richmond. But the Navy Department sent Naval Constructor Joseph Pierce with twenty ship carpenters. Their government pay scale contributed to a strike by New Orleans shipyard workers, who demanded a dollar a day increase in wages. For six days local yards were silent, except the Tifts', where Pierce's Richmond artisans continued to work, and Murray's, where workers were promised the increase if it became effective. A hostile contingent of workers soon forced these men to lay down their tools and join the strike. Finally, with negotiations at an impasse, Murray and the Tifts agreed to meet the strikers' demands in their yards. Other yards followed suit, and construction resumed.

Workers at both Murray's and the Tifts' yards were enrolled in local militia companies, and company commanders demanded that workmen take time off to drill. When the builders got exemptions for their workers, unit commanders sent the provost marshal with arrest warrants for the missing militiamen, and the shipbuilders had to battle to keep them.

The Tifts contracted to have the *Mississippi's* armour rolled by Scofield and Markham in Atlanta. Initially, the mill declined: they did not have the rollers to make 2in iron plate. But Nelson Tift met with them in Atlanta, and his order of 1,000 tons of armour plate (and an additional 80 tons of nuts and bolts) induced the mill to modify its rollers and enter the armour plate business.

Murray contracted for the supply of armour with the Cumberland Iron Works in northern Tennessee. But Federal forces took the Cumberland River valley, and for two weeks Murray's workers sat idle, waiting for armour that would never come. In desperation, he bought 500 tons of T rails from the Vicksburg & Shreveport Railroad – a poor substitute for rolled armour plate.[8]

New Orleans could have become the Confederacy's western shipbuilding center. Cosmopolitan and internationally connected, the city thrived on both upriver steamboat trade and ocean-going commerce, so marine building and repair facilities were numerous. Seven foundries in the city claimed to manufacture marine engines. And across the river at Algiers were shipyards and drydocks.

But the costs at New Orleans were stunning. Where Henry Willink built gunboats for $36,000 each in Savannah, at New Orleans John Hughes was paid $76,000 for the *Bienville*, and $80,000 to convert the *Livingston*. Even then, neither was an adequate warship.

Too many in New Orleans saw the war as an opportunity. Sharp operators sold the Navy a broken-down tugboat appraised at $5,000, for $30,000. Called the *Yankee*, she was recommissioned the *Jackson*. Captain Lawrence Rousseau was lured into ship contracts that escalated into enormous cost over-runs, and his successor, Captain George N Hollins, paid nearly a quarter million dollars for a half-dozen sternwheelers too fragile to carry ordnance.

The competition for labour and supplies among the Confederates was intense. The Navy had yards converting two merchantmen into the gunboat *McRae* and the commerce raider *Sumter*, and the Army had yards converting two of New Orleans' dry docks into the floating batteries *Memphis* and *New Orleans*. Naval agents like the Tifts and Murray, building gunboats and ironclads from the keel up, were voracious users of marine labour and services. The state of Louisiana had yards turning riverboats into the gunboats *Governor Moore* and *General Quitman*, and privateers like James McClintock and Baxter Watson were building warcraft as bizarre as the submarine *Pioneer*.

The explosion of business allowed shipyards and foundries to turn out substandard work at exorbitant prices. The lure of public money threw the river community into a climate of greed; and the Confederacy gained incredibly little, at enormous expense, from a marine industry that seemed so promising. A student of the situa-

tion wrote that 'swindlers, speculators, and profiteers on the New Orleans river front cooked the South's goose while stealing the golden eggs'.

Yet there was New Orleans' Committee of Public Safety, and a few private citizens like Laurent Millandon, who seemed highly motivated patriots. The Committee aided both the Tifts and Murray in defending their workmen against militia commanders, helped Murray to acquire his railroad iron armour, pushed local foundries to turn out work for the ironclads; and when it found that the builders could not get work done because the Navy Department was not paying its bills, raised $250,000 and offered the Tifts 'money without limit'.[9]

The Tifts worked systematically on their *Mississippi*, building the vessel from the keel up. Unlike private builders in Memphis, Savannah, and elsewhere, they were able to acquire workmen. Over two hundred men laboured on the ship. The brothers reported to Mallory: 'We are progressing very well with our structure....We fasten, calk, paint and finish perfectly as we advance'.

But waiting for engines, propeller shafts, armour and guns slowed them down. The ship's three propeller shafts should be of wrought iron. But no iron works in the Confederacy, not even the famed Tredegar in Richmond, could make the 50ft center shaft for the main propeller. Thus began a search for an adequate shaft in some existing ship. In late January, two that could be spliced were found in the wrecked steamer *Glen Cove* in the James River near Richmond. Under prodding from Secretary Mallory, the Tredegar agreed to pull them from the wreck and rework them. 'In past times articles of this kind were procured from the North', groused Tredegar foreman John Tanner.

Without a heavy steam hammer (which had been sold to the Navy and moved to Gosport Navy Yard), the shafts had to be welded and spliced by hand. 'We had 50 men working at it at a time', Tanner said, 'whereas, if we had a suitable hammer, we would not require more than 10 at a time'. Mallory came by almost every day, including Sundays, to check on the shaft's progress. When it was ready in late March, a special railroad car had to be built to transport it to New Orleans.

The ship's quarter shafts were contracted with Ward & Co of Nashville, which first promised to put up a new air furnace and hammer to make them, then declined. The Tifts next approached Leeds & Co, already occupied in making shafts for John Shirley's *Arkansas* and *Tennessee*, building at Memphis. The brothers contacted Clarke & Co, who were using a substantial advance on other Government contracts to put up a steam hammer and additional furnaces. For payment in advance, Clarke agreed to forge the two quarter shafts, and Leeds would finish them on their lathes.

In the spring of 1862, as Captain David Farragut's invasion fleet worked into the lower Mississippi River, Mallory feared that the Murray and Tift vessels would not be ready to meet the Yankees. He telegraphed the Tifts: 'Work night and day to get your ship done, without regard to expense', and: 'Strain every nerve to finish ship. Expend money to encourage mechanics if essential to speed completion'. And: 'Cannot you hire night gangs for triple wages?'

Mallory told Commander John K Mitchell, replacing George Hollins as commander afloat, to 'stimulate' the builders to finish the ships. Mitchell was authorized to take over the *Louisiana* and complete her if he felt Murray was not doing everything possible to finish her. But Mitchell saw no way to speed the process.

Mallory assigned Commander Arthur Sinclair to captain the *Mississippi*, and sent him to hurry the Tifts. He, too, found no way to rush the ship's completion.

On April 19, 1862, the *Louisiana* was towed downriver to help defend Fort Jackson and Fort St. Philip against David Farragut's fleet. Her engines, though operable, could not move her. She would fight as a floating battery.

The next day the *Mississippi* was launched. For months the Tifts had stubbornly refused, in the face of pressure from both Mallory and the Committee of Public Safety, to launch her. Putting her in the water before her propeller shafts were installed would only increase the time needed to finish her, they protested, and Commander Sinclair agreed. Her center shaft and propeller had now, finally, been installed, along with her two quarter shafts. But *their* propellers were still on the wharf at New Orleans. The brothers built a dock to install them, and began fitting armour as it arrived from Atlanta. Nelson Tift had ordered it cut to size, so each plate had its place in either an inner or an outer course.

She still did not have her guns. The Tifts asked repeatedly: 'When shall we get them?' The guns would never come. And the last of the *Mississippi's* armour was on a train from Atlanta the day she burned as David Farragut's fleet took New Orleans.[10]

Gosport

The vessel that would command the attention of the Confederate nation and the world was built in Virginia. The capture of Gosport Navy Yard at Portsmouth, near Norfolk, with the wreck of the frigate *Merrimack*, gave Secretary Mallory an opportunity to build an ironclad to protect the Virginia coast, break the blockade and, he hoped, raid New York. Gosport was one of the finest shipyards in North America, well stocked with both the essentials and the ancillaries for building and repairing warships. Here, some of the best talent in the Confederate Navy began creating the ironclad *Virginia* out of the frigate *Merrimack*.

When Secretary Mallory called for plans for an armoured ship, Lt John Mercer Brooke and Naval Constructor John L Porter both submitted similar designs. Although Brooke received credit, Porter never gave up the belief that the ship's design was his. On the recommendation of Brooke, Porter, and Chief Engineer William P Williamson, the *Merrimack's* hull and machinery were used as the platform for the *Virginia*. Work began under Porter's direction even before Congress appropriated money for it. Nearly all of Gosport Navy Yard was involved in the project. Fifteen hundred workmen poured over the ship, working in shifts day and night, including Sundays. Free blacks and slaves were employed as well as white artisans, and women made mattresses, boat cushions, and curtains.

Newspaper reporters from around the world visited Gosport to report on the *Virginia* project, forcing Commandant French Forrest to institute security measures and restrict access. Security tightened further as the Confederates began to suspect spies in Norfolk of sending out notes in bottles tossed into the Elizabeth River.

When the project started, Lt Brooke had a general plan, but with no construction details finalized. These evolved as the conversion progressed. For Naval Constructor Porter, building to Brooke's ever-changing design made the job a nightmare. Every revision upset the construction plan and put the project further behind. Some changes, like a revision in the armour plating, affected major attributes like the ship's draft and her true waterline. While Porter tried to cope with this situation, Brooke and others in the Navy Department, as well as congressmen, newspaper editors, and people in the street lambasted the constructor for not getting the vessel finished. She was to have been completed by November 1861. But 1862 dawned with the ship far from finished.

Porter had served at Pensacola's Warrington Navy Yard in the 1850s and was involved in building the sloop of war *Seminole*. The ship's construction was flawed, and Porter was charged with neglect of duty. He was acquitted, but embittered. Now, as he labored night and day on the Confederacy's premier ironclad

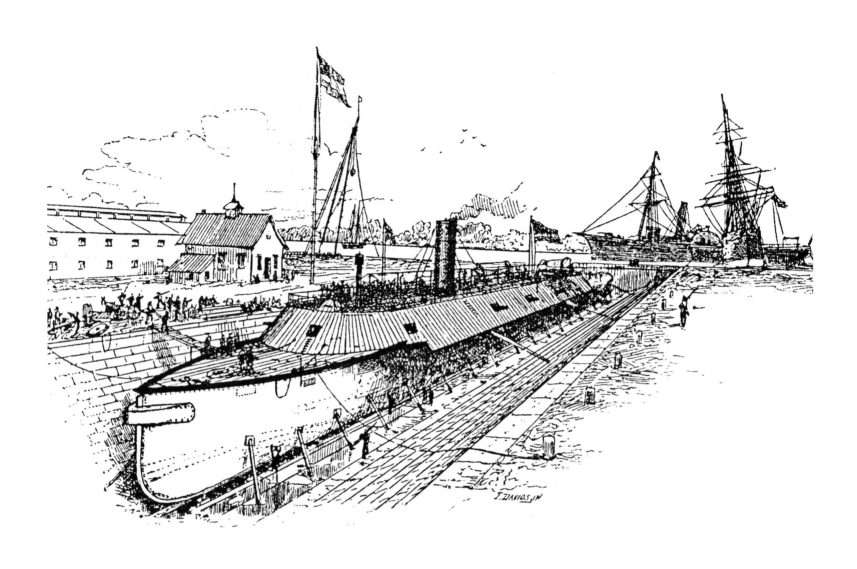

Virginia under conversion at the Gosport Navy Yard, Portsmouth, Virginia. (*Battles & Leaders*)

under the criticism of the Richmond press, the knowledgeable mariners of Norfolk, and John Mercer Brooke, virtually every man he encountered, whether naval officer or civilian, assured him that his project would be a failure. 'Hundreds – I may say thousands – asserted she would never float', he recalled. Porter heard it all from the pundits. The weight of her armour would turn her upside down; she would never answer her helm; the firing of the guns in the casemate would deafen her crew; they would suffocate inside that iron casing. The negatives fell endlessly on Porter's ears.

Commander Charles McIntosh often dropped by to watch the ship's construction. As he left for New Orleans and command of the *Louisiana*, he told his friend, Chief Engineer Henry A Ramsay: 'Good-by Ramsay. I shall never see you again. She will prove your

coffin'.[11] Indeed, McIntosh would never see Ramsay again. He would die of wounds received aboard the *Louisiana*, while Ramsay and the *Virginia* went on to fame and glory.

At the same time, other vessels were contracted with Portsmouth's independent shipyards, like Page and Allen, and Graves and Nash. Page and Allen had opened in 1851. The yard built revenue cutters for the US Government, and sought, but never won, contracts to build frigates.

The Confederate Navy Department actively pursued both these yards. Graves and Nash subcontracted two small gunboats (112ft length with a 20ft beam) to the neighbouring Atlantic Iron Works for $12,000 each, and contracted to build two larger gunboats themselves. One, the *Dixie*, was promised to Lt William H Parker, commanding the *Beaufort* in the James River Squadron.[12]

Once the *Virginia* was launched, Gosport began construction of a new ironclad, the *Richmond*. Smaller and more refined, she was built from the keel up to a design drawn by John L Porter. 'One such vessel would be worth a fleet of wooden vessels', said Mallory.

The yard laid down two small gunboats, the *Nansemond* and the *Hampton*. But with the *Virginia's* success in destroying the wooden frigates *Cumberland* and *Congress*, and her epic battle against the ironclad *Monitor*, Mallory was firmly committed to ironclads. In urging the building of more ironclads and fewer gunboats, he found himself riding, not leading, a wave of entrepreneurs and patriots from all over the Confederacy who petitioned him for contracts to build armoured ships.

Mallory was deeply concerned with completing the *Richmond* to defend Gosport. With General George B McClellan's Army of the Potomac pushing against Confederate defenses on the Peninsula, the Confederate Army seemed ready to give up Norfolk. Gosport might have to rely solely on the Navy to keep the enemy at bay, and Mallory wanted a maximum effort to complete the ships on the stocks. He told Gosport's new commandant, Sidney Smith Lee, that the *Richmond* was essential to Gosport's defense, 'and the work upon her must not cease night or day'.

That became a point of contention. Porter felt that an around-the-clock work schedule would be counterproductive, creating discord among his workers. And if they were induced to work at night, the work would have to be done by lantern and candle: and open flame was dangerous around the shipyard.

Lee agreed with Porter, and Mallory could not sway them. Time and again he issued orders for night work, but got no response. 'You do not inform me', he complained to Lee, 'whether night gangs of men are at work on the *Richmond* or not.....Men and money must be employed without limit to complete her'.[13]

When General Joseph E Johnston abandoned the Norfolk area, the *Richmond* was launched and towed up the James River to a new navy yard established at Richmond. There, the ironclads *Fredericksburg*, *Virginia II* and *Texas* would be built over the course of the war, as Norfolk, and all its shipbuilding industry, were lost.

Along with the fall of New Orleans, the loss of Norfolk and its well-developed shipbuilding apparatus was a crushing blow to the Confederate Navy. Makeshift yards like Gilbert Elliott's North Carolina corn field, Lt Isaac Brown's Yazoo River cotton wharf, and Captain Ebenezer Farrand's Alabama river banks could never hope to replace the sophisticated facilities in Portsmouth and New Orleans.

The Arkansas

Where shipbuilding had struggled in the ante-bellum South, the war brought forth a flood of men seeking contracts for gunboats and ironclads. The Navy Department contracted with John T Shirley to build the *Arkansas* and *Tennessee* at Memphis; with Charleston foundry owner James Eason, who laid the keel of the *Chicora* behind the city post office; and with young Gilbert Elliott, who built the *Albemarle* in a cornfield on the Roanoke River; while in Savannah Henry Willink was laying the keel of the *Savannah*.[14]

John Shirley used congressmen and generals to help him win his Memphis contract. Signed in October 1861, the agreement called for two ironclads to be delivered in just two months – by December 24, 1861. Shirley laid their keels at Fort Pickering, a landing below the city. He rebuilt two sawmills and ordered oak for framing and pine for planking and, because his contract required progress before receiving his first payment, he spent $34,000 of his own money getting the project in motion.

Shirley advertised for ship carpenters in St. Louis, New Orleans, and Mobile, later expanding his search to Charleston, Richmond and Baltimore. He tried to requisition carpenters from the Army but found that Major General Leonidas Polk would not detail workmen from his command, even though he had recommended Shirley and his ships to Confederate congressmen. Secretary Mallory wrote, personally requesting Polk's help. Shirley asked for men by name and by unit, but got only six or eight, where he needed a hundred. 'He [Polk] persistently refused to detail any more', Shirley complained.

The builder found railroad iron for armour in Memphis and in Arkansas, but bolts and spikes were scarce. The Cumberland Iron Works rolled an order for him, but Lt Isaac Brown seized it for ships he was building in Nashville. So Shirley scrounged bolts and spikes in small lots wherever he could find them. He built a drill press and began drilling mounting holes – six per rail – in his 'armour'. With evidence of Shirley's good work Stephen Mallory, hungry to have ironclads afloat and tearing into Union fleets, began advancing money beyond the contract's requirements. But without an adequate work force, progress was slow. Sometimes Shirley had as many as 120 men at work; other times, no more than twenty.

Christmas – Shirley's completion date – passed with the *Arkansas* half finished, the *Tennessee* barely begun. In March Lieutenant Henry K Stevens, executive officer, wrote to his wife:

'Our work goes on very slowly, and it seems impossible to get it done faster'. The quality of the work was poor, he said: the ship was a 'humbug'.

After the first battle of Manassas, Major General P G T Beauregard was transferred to Tennessee. He considered the Navy an integral part of his defense and offered Shirley all the skilled workmen in his ranks, if the builder would supply their names and units. Perhaps exasperated at trying to deal with the Army, Shirley ignored the offer.[15]

Through early 1862, Federal forces pushed south, forcing the Confederates out of their defensive line anchored on Columbus, Kentucky. Then, they invaded northern and middle Tennessee. On April 7, Island No. 10 in the Mississippi fell, leaving only Fort Pillow defending Memphis. Mallory telegraphed Commander Charles H McBlair, the *Arkansas*'s new captain: 'Get your boat to New Orleans and complete her as soon as possible, if she is in danger at Memphis'. But Shirley could see completion ahead. The vessel's woodwork was nearly finished, and machinery and boilers were being installed. On April 24 he told Beauregard that the *Arkansas* would be ready within fifteen days; the *Tennessee*, two weeks after that.

But the next day, word reached Memphis that New Orleans had fallen. Now, McBlair felt compelled to act. He hurriedly launched the *Arkansas*. The steamer *Capitol* took her in tow, togeth-

CSS *Albemarle* under construction at Edward's Ferry, NC. (*Battles & Leaders*)

er with a barge carrying armour, stores, and engines purchased for the *Tennessee*, and set off down the Mississippi River. The frame of the *Tennessee*, with most of her planking planed and lying in the yard, was burned on the stocks. Her armour was waiting across the river in Arkansas. Fortunately for Shirley, he had not yet paid for it.

McBlair had decided on Yazoo City, on the Yazoo River above Vicksburg, as a refuge. When word arrived that Farragut's fleet had advanced to Baton Rouge, Louisiana, McBlair took the vessel further up the rain-swollen river to Greenwood, Mississippi. During the voyage, the barge with the *Arkansas*'s armour sank.[16]

Where John Shirley had been energetic, Commander McBlair was lethargic. The *Arkansas* lay moored at Greenwood for nearly a month – guns, stores and machine parts cluttering her deck – with no visible progress. Major General Earl Van Dorn at Vicksburg complained, as did Beauregard, forcing Mallory to act. On May 29, 1862, Lieutenant Isaac N Brown appeared at Greenwood with orders to relieve McBlair of command. Mallory wanted the energetic Lt Brown to complete the *Arkansas* and do something significant with her.[17] McBlair was resistant. 'I came near shooting him', Brown recalled, to get him out of the way. Called to Richmond, McBlair complained of the insolence Brown, the junior officer, had shown him.

Lt Brown found the *Arkansas* 'a mere hull, without armor; the engines were apart; guns without carriages were lying about the deck; a portion of the railroad iron intended as armor was at the bottom of the river...'[18]

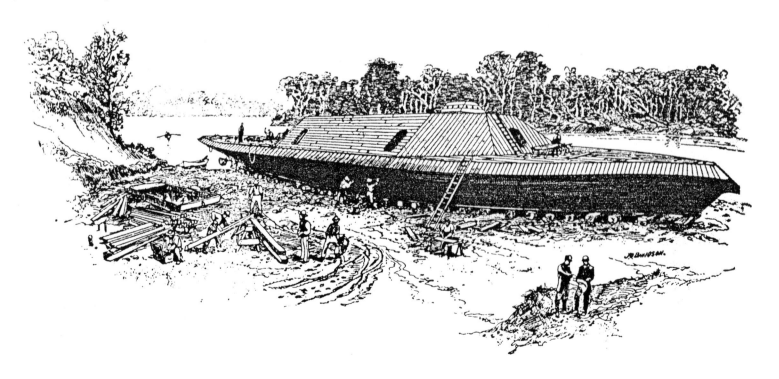

Brown stripped armament from two refugee gunboats, the *General Polk* and the *Livingston*, to round out the *Arkansas*'s battery. He collected ordnance stores from the Army at Vicksburg and from Lt David McCorkle's naval ordnance laboratory at Atlanta. Only four gun carriages had come from Memphis. Brown found carpenters in Canton, Mississippi who agreed to make carriages, and he sent Lt Stevens to oversee their construction. In two weeks Stevens reappeared, with four ox teams hauling the gun carriages on wagons.[19]

After five weeks at Yazoo City the *Arkansas*, nearing completion, moved downriver to Liverpool Landing. Within three more weeks, she would be out in the Mississippi, tearing through the fleets of David Farragut, David Porter and Alfred Ellet.

The western Navy Yards

Isaac Brown's efforts to finish the *Arkansas* had created a navy yard at Yazoo City, with shipways, machine shops, carpenter and blacksmith shops, and saw and planing mills. Less than two weeks after the *Arkansas*'s sortie into the Mississippi River, the gunboat *Mobile* was brought to the yard for conversion to an ironclad. The yard had become a permanent fixture that might help create a counter-offensive on the Mississippi.

On September 16, 1862, Secretary Mallory authorized Navy Department agents Thomas Weldon and John McFarland to build a John L Porter-designed sidewheel ironclad at Yazoo City. The contract price was $300,000.

When ships were threatened and time critical, the Secretary urged builders to spare no expense to complete their vessels. But in initial agreements, he encouraged thrift and economy. His memorandum directed Weldon and McFarland to proceed 'as if you were building for yourselves and had to pay the money out of your own pockets'.

Within a week of the Department's agreement with Weldon and McFarland, Isaac N Brown was ordered back to Yazoo City. He was now a commander, promoted for the *Arkansas*'s gallant battles around Vicksburg. He had authority to oversee Weldon and McFarland's project, and stimulate the building of other ships at the Yazoo City Navy Yard. A few weeks before, Commander Eben Farrand had been similarly ordered to take over shipbuilding activities at Selma, Alabama.

Henry D Bassett, the *Morgan*'s builder, had contracted on May 1, 1862 to build two ironclads at Selma to defend Mobile.

Gilbert Elliott, builder of the *Albemarle*. (Robert G Elliott)

Brown's new officers discovered that he 'is not afraid of responsibility and there is nothing of the Red Tape about him...' He moved the *Arkansas* back downriver to Yazoo City, where there had been some steamboat repair business before the war.

Isaac Brown made the *Arkansas* a community effort. He met with plantation owners, asking for overseers, hands, and blacksmith forges. He recruited over two hundred workmen from local army units, and impressed civilian mechanics and blacksmiths into service at his new navy yard.

Brown quartered his work force aboard the *Capitol*. He divided it into shifts and kept work going twenty-four hours a day, seven days a week. Lanterns and pine knots illuminated the construction site at night.

Although called floating batteries, they were to have engines, ordered from Chief Engineer Warner at Columbus. The first vessel, the *Tuscaloosa*, was scheduled to be completed in just two months. The other, the *Huntsville*, was to be finished 30 days later.

Bassett cleared a site on the riverbank above Selma, built some sheds, contracted for timber and iron, and began recruiting workmen. Keels were quickly laid, but work was slow, held up by shortages and delays in materials. On the *Tuscaloosa*'s completion date, July 1, Bassett regretfully informed Mallory that he was only three-fifths finished.

Naval Constructor Joseph Pierce inspected the project and reported that the greatest problem was non-delivery of engines and boilers from Columbus. Chief Warner had orders for machinery from yards all over the lower Confederacy. He was far behind. Work on the *Tuscaloosa*'s engines had not even begun, he said, because iron ordered from furnaces near Selma had not arrived in Columbus.

Thus another project had passed its completion date. It was this persistent tardiness on the part of civilian contractors and agents – Shirley and the *Arkansas*, the Tifts and the *Mississippi*, Murray and the *Louisiana*, Johnston and the *Chattahoochee*, Willink and the *Macon* and *Savannah*, and others – that induced Mallory to order Commanders Brown and Farrand to oversee construction at Yazoo City and Selma.[20]

Under Eben Farrand's direction, the Selma yard laid the keel for another ironclad, which would take the name of the vessel destroyed at Memphis – the *Tennessee*.

John Shirley himself was now at Selma with a partner named DeHaven, building a sidewheel ironclad. Again, Shirley was doomed to disappointment, for the ship was damaged in launching and sold to reimburse the Government for its advances.[21]

While the eastern shipyards – Rocketts, Elliott's, James Eason's and F M Jones's at Charleston, Willink's and others – built screw-propelled ironclads to the *Richmond* design, builders in the interior often used riverboat concepts. At Columbus, Selma, Yazoo City and Shreveport, builders laid down paddlewheel vessels like Murray's *Louisiana*, or like the sidewheel *Nashville*, built at Montgomery for the Mobile Squadron.

Lt Jonathan H Carter, ordered to build 'one or more ironclad vessels of War' on the Red River, contracted with the firm of Moore and Smoker in Shreveport, Louisiana, on November 1, 1862 to build two ironclads, the first to be completed within six months. She would be river style, carrying a 22ft diameter wheel

within the after part of the casemate. Her keel was laid in December.

Hoping to concentrate the builders' efforts and get one ship completed, the Department suspended the builders' contract for the second vessel. Carter protested: he felt that both could be ready for launching by the river's traditional June rise. But the Department was firm.[22]

By the fall of 1862, Secretary Mallory's ironclad building programme looked successful. In the east, the *Richmond* was soon completed and a new ironclad, the *Fredericksburg*, was underway at Rocketts in Richmond. Gilbert Elliott signed contracts for two ironclads in North Carolina, and at Kinston and Wilmington three others were laid down. The *Chicora* and *Palmetto State* were

Captain Ebenezer Farrand. (Alabama Department of Archives & History, Montgomery, Alabama)

commissioned and the *Charleston* was begun at Charleston. Henry Willink's *Savannah* was coming along and a new Savannah firm, Krenson & Hawkes, would soon begin the *Milledgeville*. In the Deep South, the ironclad *Jackson* would be laid down at Columbus, Georgia, the sidewheeler *Nashville* was under construction at Montgomery, Farrand's Selma yard was building four ironclads, Isaac Brown at Yazoo City had one under conversion and one under construction, and Lt Carter's first ship was taking shape at Shreveport. Private contractors and the Navy were responding to the war's needs with enthusiasm.

But the Confederacy's industrial infrastructure could not keep pace. All of these projects relied on either Scofield and Markham's Gate City rolling mill in Atlanta or the Tredegar Iron Works in Richmond for armour, and on the Confederate Naval Iron Works at Columbus or the Shockoe Foundry in Richmond for engines and boilers. The need to supply so many projects overloaded these vital industries. When Henry Willink asked Scofield and Markham to bend armour plate to fit the *Savannah's* casemate corners, he was told they were too pressed with orders to do customized work. Willink must take care of his own fitting.

At least, Willink was getting his orders filled. His early start put him high on Atlanta's priority list. And at Columbus, Chief Warner built Willink's engines and boilers, and sent to Savannah a crew to prepare the ship's engine beds and boiler stays, and install the machinery when it arrived. When engines and armour were available, shipbuilders completed their ironclads. And in late summer of 1863, the *Savannah* was commissioned.[23]

At Selma, Henry Bassett induced the Shelby Iron Company in nearby Columbiana to schedule 25 tons of iron for Columbus so Chief Warner could build the *Tuscaloosa's* engines. But once the iron was ready to go, two-thirds of it was held up for lack of transportation. Warner, exasperated, reworked engines pulled from the river steamer *Chewala*. He sent them to Selma in December, and they were installed by the first of January.[24]

At Yazoo City, Weldon and McFarland lacked even such common items as nails. The only thing plentiful was green timber. A cache of nails hoarded by the state was discovered at Meridian. The Yazoo builders obtained them and began hammering together a hull. They caulked it with cotton, a common practice now when even oakum was in short supply.

At Shreveport, Moore and Smoker were building to the same specifications of need — green timber caulked with cotton. While John Smoker scoured Jackson and Vicksburg for nails, anchors, chains, and odd lots of iron, Lt Carter searched from Virginia to Texas for mechanics, machinery and accouterments. He tried to get ships' carpenters detailed from the Army. He requested help from naval commanders in Jackson, Selma, Mobile and Richmond, and discovered how fierce was the competition for skilled craftsmen.

By necessity he learned to play the game. When Army officers promised him sixteen carpenters from their commands at Port Hudson, word got out; and both Eben Farrand and Isaac Brown tried to poach his covey. Brown got Governor Pettus of Mississippi to plead his case. But Carter sent Moore and Smoker racing to Port Hudson to defend his interests. Their personal intervention, and Carter's appeals to the integrity of Port Hudson's commander, won the day for Shreveport.

Lt Carter wanted to name his new ironclad *Caddo* after a local Indian tribe and the parish in which she was being built. But the Department chose to name her *Missouri*.

Carter bought a riverboat's engines and boilers for $65,000, and the Department sent an engineer to refurbish them. By the end of February, the hull was planked and caulked, and her upper deck was in frame. At the end of March, her engines and boilers were lowered into the hold; and in mid April, just two weeks after her scheduled completion date, she was launched...but far from finished.

Meanwhile, Eben Farrand and Isaac Brown were competing for armour. Both placed orders with Scofield and Markham. But Atlanta's production was committed to ironclads in Georgia, and both came away empty-handed. Brown placed orders with the Shelby Iron Works at Columbiana, contracting in late September for 400 tons of 2in iron plate to be delivered by December 1, 1862.

But there were problems. Shelby's rolling mill could not produce 2in plate, although the company's president thought machinery could be installed in time to meet the Yazoo contract. There was also a previous comittment to deliver 'the entire proceeds of the work' to the War Department. Shelby officials were called to Richmond to explain themselves, and gave such a good enough account that their contract to supply Commander Brown's armour was approved.

But by the delivery date (December 1), Shelby still could not roll armour plate. Not until March 1863 would they be in production. Then, Commander Farrand, nearby at Selma, succeeded in pirating Brown's iron plate to armour his own ships. Brown sent an agent to Columbiana to try to negotiate his yard back into the picture. When that failed, he embarked on a fruitless search for railroad iron for armour. By the middle of April, he realized that armour would not be forthcoming for months; certainly not before the dry season locked his vessels in the Yazoo River. Even Isaac Brown could not overcome the realities of supply and demand.

At Shreveport, Lt Carter never so much as hoped for armour plate, but resigned himself to using railroad rails. For Carter,

labour remained the problem. He began detailing soldiers he found on furlough, then informing their commanders once they were safely under his control.

At the Yazoo Navy Yard, the loss of the armour order was only one of Brown's problems. Receding water caused the river bank to give way, careening the vessel he was building on to its side. Then, in May, Federal warships began probing the river. By May 20 they were at Haynes Bluff, just 50 miles from the yard. Within a few days they closed the distance; and Yazoo Navy Yard and its incomplete vessels went up in smoke. All Isaac Brown's efforts since the *Arkansas* came to naught.[25]

Destruction of Krenson & Hawkes Yard, Savannah, on the Confederate evacuation of the city, December 1864. (*Leslie's Illustrated*)

At Shreveport, Carter's next problem was armament. Guns and carriages would not pass through the gun ports, so they must be aboard before the casemate was closed. The Navy Department sent three cannon in early February, only to have them commandeered by the Army at Grand Gulf. Attempts to borrow heavy ordnance from the Army proved fruitless, thanks in part to Carter's brother naval officers. Lt Charles M Fauntleroy had objected strenuously to being assigned to Shreveport. Once there, he roundly cursed the *Missouri* to all who would listen. Assigned as the Navy's liaison to the Army, his duty was to obtain Army co-operation in completing and using the vessel. Instead, he preju-

diced Lt Gen E Kirby Smith against her to the point that the general refused to allow guns to be loaned to the Navy. Fauntleroy also poisoned the minds of the ship's officers and the local citizenry, prompting Carter to tell Mallory: 'Had Lt Fauntleroy not come to this place the "Missouri" would now have her crew and four guns on board and be ready for service'.

Carter tried to commandeer guns from the captured *Harriet Lane*, but the Army beat him to it. He then tried the captured ironclad *Indianola* and came away with two prizes – a 9in and an 11in Dahlgren shell gun. He built carriages of railroad iron and mounted the guns in the *Missouri's* bow. An old 32pdr completed the battery.

Carter's problems seemed endless. The paddlewheel's shaft and couplings needed repair, a design error required that her rudder box be rebuilt, and she leaked heavily. The loss of Vicksburg and Port Hudson made the *Missouri* less vital, even to Carter. His station commander and all his officers wanted to vacate Shreveport. General Smith would render no help, and Carter himself admitted that the ironclad's officers and men could be better employed elsewhere.

The *Missouri* made her first trial run in June, 1863 and did 6 knots instead of the builders' promised 10. But Carter's difficulties continued and kept the vessel out of service until January 1, 1865.[26]

After launching the ironclads at Selma, Eben Farrand closed the Selma Navy Yard and followed his ships to Mobile, where he established a new yard with Joseph Pierce, William Hope, Sidney Porter and Henry Bassett as constructors. He had nearly 300 workmen to finish, repair and maintain his ships.

Farrand also developed satellite yards up the Tombigbee River, sending Acting Naval Constructor William Hope to McIntosh Bluff in the spring of 1864. There, with sixteen ship carpenters and a contingent of joiners, fasteners, blacksmiths, and laborers, Hope began building four *Alabama* class cruisers.

Three ironclads' hulls were struggling along at Oven Bluff, a swampy site 60 miles above Mobile where Farrand had opened a yard in the summer of 1862. One of the ships laid down there was a large sidewheeler, the others 150ft propeller-driven vessels. Sickness, and the usual shortages – workers, armour, and engines – retarded their construction even more than was usual in the Confederacy. They were launched and towed to Mobile, but never finished.[27]

The Columbus, Georgia, Navy Yard

In Columbus, Georgia, Lt Augustus McLaughlin built an ironclad to defend the Chattahoochee River. In the Navy Yard he founded to finish the *Chattahoochee*, he had a slip dug in the riverbank, angled 30 degrees downriver so the new vessel could be launched without running ashore on the Alabama bank. Like the *Louisiana* and *Missouri*, she would be propelled by a paddle wheel housed in the after part of her casemate. The plans were drawn by Chief Naval Constructor John L Porter.

McLaughlin requested command of the vessel – and proposed the name *Muscogee* for the local Indian confederacy. The department would choose to name her *Jackson* instead, after the capital city of Mississippi.

The woodwork of the vessel's casemate and flatbottomed hull went quickly, and by the end of 1863, McLaughlin was waiting for high water to launch her. But the flood he awaited came so suddenly that yard workmen were taken by surprise, and they could not drive the blocks out of the launchways. McLaughlin tied on a steamboat and tried to pull her off. As the river continued to rise, the bow floated, but the stern stuck fast. When the river began falling, workmen cleared away mud and debris and attempted to drive out the blocks. But the river fell rapidly – more than a foot an hour – and the attempted launch failed.

On February 6, 1864 McLaughlin journeyed to Richmond for an interview with Secretary Mallory. The Secretary reminded him that his vessel must not draw more than 6ft of water. Recalling that he had measured 5ft 9¼in of water under the ironclad's stern during the recent freshet, that it had not floated the vessel, and that at the time the ship was without armour, engines and boilers, ordnance, munitions, coal and stores, McLaughlin was certain her draft would easily exceed 7ft. Drastic alterations would be necessary. McLaughlin suggested lengthening her by 30 feet to increase her buoyancy, and changing her motive power from paddle wheel to two screw propellers. Mallory directed John L Porter to survey the vessel and render an opinion. Porter journeyed to Columbus and inspected the ship on February 25, and agreed with McLaughlin. He ordered the wheel removed and its well closed, the vessel lengthened 37 feet to increase buoyancy, and the casemate shortened 54 feet to decrease weight. The changes would inevitably set the vessel's launching back months.

Porter's new drawings arrived on March 13, and the yard set to work rebuilding the ironclad. The after casemate was torn apart, the wheel housing dismantled, and the wheel removed. On

A model of the CSS *Jackson*. (WMCWNH)

April 23, her new machinery was installed. The forward part of the casemate was then torn down, and the whole shield rebuilt, 54 feet shorter than the original. The carpenters found it difficult work, as the casemate had been solidly built.[28]

Meanwhile, McLaughlin began a new construction project, a torpedo boat. Private Southern investment groups had been experimenting with submersible and surface torpedo craft since the beginning of the war. When the submarine *H L Hunley* successfully destroyed a blockader, interest increased.

In Charleston, South Carolina, boat-builder Theodore Stoney, Dr St Julian Ravenal, and several friends formed The Southern Torpedo Company and engaged David Ebaugh to build a torpedo boat. They envisioned a man-powered boat like the *Hunley*, but non-submersible. Ebaugh recommended a steam engine. To Ravenal's objection that the engine would be too big and make too much noise, Ebaugh replied 'that a steam engine could be put in his *hat*', and the exhaust could be muffled. In fact, the North Eastern Rail Road had a small steam engine that should do quite nicely.

Ebaugh laid out a full-size pattern of the boat under a niter shed at Stoney's Landing on the Cooper River. He described the boat as

> 5 feet in diameter and 48½ feet long, 18 feet of the middle of the boat was same size tapering to a point at each end. The ends was made [sic] of large pine logs turned off with a grove [sic] to receive the ends of the planking, the timbers was [sic] made of 1½ inch oak doubled and riveted together, they were placed about 15 inches apart, the planking was the whole length 1½ inches thick hollowed on the inside to fit the timbers and rounded on the outside, the planking was riveted to the timbers,...corked [caulked] and launched.

While Ebaugh built the hull, the North Eastern's master machinist, John Chalk, retrieved the steam engine from storage and modified it to drive the boat. Ebaugh floated the vessel down to Charleston harbor where, at the railroad wharf, a crane lifted it from the water to a flatcar, and it rolled into the railroad shops for fitting of boiler and engine.

Ravenal, Stoney, shipbuilder Marion Jones and his partner Captain John Furguson inspected the boat. They were disappointed. She looked like a cigar, and they were certain she would capsize in the water. Jones asked Ravenal to give him the little vessel's machinery and let him build a torpedo boat. But Ebaugh refused to give up the steam engine. He ballasted the boat with scrap iron, completed a successful trial run, and turned her over to the Navy, which reimbursed him $1,500 he had invested in her construction. The Navy used old boiler tubes to make a spar to push a torpedo ahead of her. Called the *David*, she would successfully attack the ironclad *New Ironsides* and put her out of action for a year.

The *Hunley* and *David* proved the feasibility of torpedoes as offensive weapons; and a new class of small attack vessel, the 'David', went into production. Ebaugh contracted to build two (plus a small steam ram powered by Scottish engines), and Furguson and Jones began two more 'Davids' at Charleston. A derivative called the *Squib* was built at Rocketts in Richmond. When she successfully attacked the USS *Minnesota*, four more were laid down there. John P Halligan built the trout-shaped *St. Patrick* at the old navy yard in Selma; two were begun at Wilmington; the Army Engineering Department began several at Savannah and one at Mobile; and Lt Carter laid one down at Shreveport.

McLaughlin was told that Mallory intended to have two torpedo boats built at Columbus. It was a propitious time, as McLaughlin had been able to increase his force of carpenters. He pushed Acting Naval Constructor William A Graves for drawings of the boats. When they arrived, carpenters began cutting and shaping frames and planking. No drawings of engines or boilers were sent, but Chief Warner had small boat boilers and engines on hand and sent off drawings of a set to Chief Williamson for approval. McLaughlin expected to have the torpedo boat, which would be named *Viper*, completed within six weeks.

Work went quickly, then hit a snag. The Naval Iron Works had no small bar iron for bolts and spikes. McLaughlin requisitioned it from Major William Richardson Hunt at Selma, but Hunt did not receive the letter. All the *Viper's* frames and planking were cut and her machinery was ready, but without bolts and spikes, work stopped. McLaughlin wrote Hunt again. While wait-

ing for iron, he visited Charleston to study torpedoes and the method of attaching them to boats on long spars.[29]

While the *Viper's* hull lay in pieces, labour trouble struck. McLaughlin's lone blacksmith, Patrick Rudy, on detail from the Army, took two weeks' sick leave, then refused to return to work, claiming British citizenship and demanding civilian wages. His claim was approved until McLaughlin pointed out that he had served a year in a Florida regiment and 13 months on detail in the Navy yard, without claiming British nationality. McLaughlin turned Rudy over to the conscript officer at Macon 'for continued neglect of duty', and asked that Rudy be held several days in the conscript camp. 'I believe that when he finds his claims of British Protection of no avail and has had a few days Experience in the Conscript Camp he will be quite ready to come back to work here,' McLaughlin explained. But when Rudy bowed to the inevitable and

Lt Augustus McLaughlin. (WMCWNH)

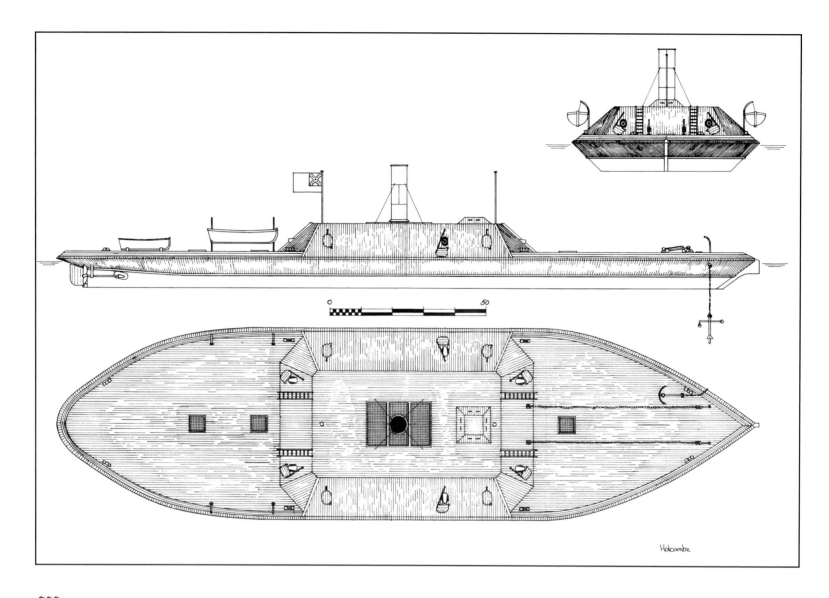

Holcombe

CSS *Jackson*, built at Columbus, Georgia, 1863-5. (WMCWNH)

agreed to return to Columbus, the camp commander sent him without an escort; and he disappeared. His getaway led to an epidemic of British citizenship claims among yard workers.[30]

With the Navy department under criticism for failing to break the blockade; for not successfully defending Norfolk, Pensacola, New Orleans, Memphis and the Mississippi River; and for destroying vessel after vessel to prevent their capture, Mallory was under fire — and perturbed at the lack of success at sites like Columbus. The *Chattahoochee* was out of action following a boiler explosion, a small boat expedition against Apalachicola had failed, the *Viper* was still in pieces, and the ironclad *Jackson* was a disaster. The secretary's communications showed his frustration at McLaughlin's lack of accomplishments, and the lieutenant protested in his own defense:

I am aware of your anxiety to get this vessel completed. No one can feel more disappointed than myself at the length of time she has been on the Stocks — and though the progress has done as you say, no credit to the Service, I respectfully submit that it has not been through any fault of mine.

Without mentioning Porter's name, he laid the blame at the feet of the naval constructor who had designed her.

McLaughlin and the ironclad project were taking criticism locally from the Columbus *Daily Sun* and from someone who identified himself as 'Farmer' in the *Early County News*. 'Farmer' called McLaughlin a speculator intent on his own enrichment, and lauded David Johnston who, 'had he been given the contract on the present unfinished folly, it would long since have proved a terror to the enemy and the pride of our country'. In subsequent letters, 'Farmer' continued to laud David Johnston, while condemning Lt McLaughlin for incompetence and corruption. The Confederacy should follow Napoleon's example, said 'Farmer', and shoot incompetents like McLaughlin.

In the summer, with Sherman invading Atlanta, Columbus' detailed shipyard workers began drilling with small arms. On November 19, the shipyard company was sent to defend Savannah, leaving work on the *Jackson* and *Viper* to a skeleton crew of civilian carpenters. The yard's detailed labour force would be gone until January 6, 1865. While they were in the field, on December 22, 1864, the ram *Jackson* was finally launched.

On March 23, 1865, workmen moved a submersible workroom beneath the *Jackson* and began shipping her starboard propeller. Within two days, both propellers were in place. Sight boxes and locks for her Brooke rifles and shell and armour-piercing bolts arrived from Selma. A pilot named Austin was detailed from the 2nd Florida Cavalry.

On March 31, 1865, the torpedo boat *Viper* was launched. But the enemy was advancing. By April 15, General James H Wilson's army, which had destroyed the Army and Navy manufacturing centers at Selma, was within 12 miles of Columbus. The next day, Easter Sunday, the battle for Columbus raged through the afternoon and evening. Neither the *Chattahoochee* nor the *Jackson* were yet operable. They would be destroyed without seeing combat.[31]

Lt McLaughlin's greatest problem in completing the *Jackson* had been the miscalculation of the vessel's draft. But McLaughlin's ironclad, his gunboat *Chattahoochee*, and the other ironclads, gunboats and torpedo boats laid down in the Confederacy – both those completed and carried into action like the *Virginia, Arkansas, Albemarle* and *Palmetto State*, and those never completed like the *Mississippi, Milledgeville, Texas* and *Columbia* – all suffered from the same deficiencies. Lack of seasoned timber led virtually every Confederate builder to use fresh-cut, unseasoned wood that warped and checked; and home-built Confederate hulls leaked excessively.[32] And every vessel had its construction schedule retarded by shortages of skilled and unskilled workmen, and shortages of machinery and accoutrements – engines, boilers, shafts and propellers, armour, iron fastenings, guns and carriages.

The young Confederacy developed an exceptionally active industrial base, particularly in naval construction. But the enthusiasm of the Navy Department, its officers, and the country's entrepreneurs was never enough to develop combat parity in any theatre of the war. The early loss of the major shipbuilding centers – New Orleans and Norfolk – together with those that gave promise – like Pensacola, Jacksonville, Memphis – were irreparable blows. And Southern-style shipyards – hastily cleared lots in backwater towns, in corn fields, at plantation wharfs – could not compete with the industrial might of the United States.

Dr Maurice Melton

Chapter Six
THE OFFICERS

Southerners in the pre-war Navy

On the eve of the Civil War, there was, for many, a thin line between patriotism and treason. What was the most significant loyalty? Was it loyalty to nation, region, state, kinship, or ideology? For some the decision was rather obvious, especially those from the deep South. Lieutenant John McIntosh Kell of Georgia, home on leave from the Pensacola Navy Yard, attended the state's secession convention on January 19, 1861 and observed Georgia's withdrawal from the Union. Within the hour, he wrote his letter of resignation from the US Navy. He later wrote: 'If not the very first, I was among the first to take this step'.[1] Kell meant the first from Georgia, for Southern officers tended to resign when their states seceded, and therefore officers had been resigning since South Carolina, the first state to secede, left the Union on December 20, 1860.

During February 1861, resigning officers were allowed to depart without stigma. This was chiefly because the outgoing administration of President James Buchanan took the view that the US Constitution did not give him the power to prevent secession. Buchanan's Secretary of the Navy, Isaac Toucey, accepted resignations and did not threaten to arrest officers departing to their states. Toucey replied to Commander Raphael Semmes, an Alabamian at that time serving with the Lighthouse Board in Washington, immediately upon receiving Semmes' resignation: 'Your resignation as a commander in the Navy of the United States, tendered in your letter of this date, is hereby accepted'.[2] Thus the Federal Government formally released the resigning

officers from their service contracts and any oath taken as part of the contract. There was no legal requirement to state a reason for resignation, and acceptance was at that time the equivalent of an honorable discharge. However, the subsequent Lincoln Administration and its Secretary of the Navy, Gideon Welles, believed the states could be coerced and therefore that resigning officers were 'deserters'.

Americans who chose the Southern cause were less reprehensible to Northerners than Southern sympathizers who remained in the North. Amid mass meetings, club membership purgings, the firing of professors, and ministers pouring hellfire on the heads of the disloyal, came the loyalty oath.[3] Naval officers, among others, who refused to take it immediately found themselves under suspicion. For Southern officers looking to their own interest, it was easy to take the oath. The Northern side offered positions of rank and pay not readily available in the South.

Naval officers in the border states often engaged in agonizing decisions. Lieutenant John Taylor Wood, an instructor at the Naval Academy in Annapolis in 1861, was born in Minnesota Territory of a Rhode Island father and Louisiana mother. His parents remained loyal to the Union and his younger brother went south. His wife was from Maryland. The Woods wanted to remain neutral. On April 21 he resigned his commission in the Navy because he did not want to transfer to Newport, Rhode Island with the Naval Academy, and remained on his small farm in Maryland. For weeks there was no word from Washington, and then he found that he had been dismissed as of April 2, 1861. Thus, Wood's prejudicial release was given the additional odium

John Taylor Wood in old Navy uniform. (*Battles and Leaders*)

grandson of Zachary 'Old Rough and Ready' Taylor sorely vexed the Union Navy as the South's greatest coastal raider.

A factor that received much attention in the North, and probably weighed heavily with Welles, was whether a resigning naval officer had attended the US Naval Academy. To have been educated by 'charity' and then resign in a crisis was at least ungrateful in Northern eyes. Welles also took the cue from Lincoln as a result of conversations with the President (but apparently not a direct order) to purge the service of men with suspected loyalties. Not lost on Welles too was the censure by the US House of Representatives of the lenient policy of former Secretary Toucey by a vote of 95 to 62 on March 2, 1861. Then, after the Confederate bombardment of Fort Sumter on April 12, the pressure of war caused a hardening of public sentiment in the North, and Lincoln strengthened his decision-making role.

There were about 1,550 US naval officers on the eve of war and about a quarter of them resigned. Roughly the same number of Southerners remained with the Union.[5] A list of the resigned officers, grouped by rank and including some numerical data, is included in the appendix of this book. Without them the Confederacy would have been devoid of naval officers with experience at sea.

One of the most striking anecdotes regarding the deeply divided loyalties among naval officers in Washington, as well as the impact of Fort Sumter, was set down by Lieutenant David Dixon Porter, who, although under suspicion at the time, remained with the Union.

> A short time before Fort Sumter was fired upon, the Commandant of the Washington Navy Yard (Captain Franklin Buchanan) gave a large party at his headquarters on the occasion of the marriage of his daughter, to which the President and his cabinet were invited. A number of disloyal officers were present, and the house was everywhere festooned with the American flag, even to the bridal bed; yet just after Sumter was fired on, the Commandant, including his new son-in-law (Lt Julius E Meiere, USMC), resigned their commissions and left the Washington Navy Yard to take care of itself.[6]

of dismissal prior to the onset of war at Fort Sumter.

At his farm near Annapolis, Wood realised the storm must soon break in earnest. When the first real battle took place on July 21 at Bull Run, he welcomed the apparent Southern victory. Lower Maryland was in turmoil, and Wood purchased a revolver and constantly moved his family (wife Lola and small son, Zach) to avoid arrest. On September 3 he started south with his family from near Baltimore. The Woods reached the Potomac River, found a small boat, and crossed in a storm that lashed the water over the gunwales. The soaked refugees finally landed on the Virginia side of the river near George Washington's birthplace. They then headed for Richmond, where Wood's uncle, Jefferson Davis, was President of the Confederacy. Dismissing him from the Navy (not corrected by the Navy Department until 1931) had been Secretary Welles' mistake, for it seems to have been the chief factor in Wood's decision to go South[4]. A flamboyant fighter, this

The establishment of an officer corps

Southern naval officers had little to do with precipitating the war, as most were non-political and many had probably never voted. These men obviously suffered more from their resignations than

US Navy officers posing with members of the Japanese Treaty Commission at the Washington Navy Yard, May 15, 1860. A year later several of these officers would be in the Confederate Navy. Those going South include: standing (2nd from left) Lt Henry H Lewis; (5th from left) Lt Charles C Sims; (6th from left) Commander William McBlair; (7th from right) Captain Franklin Buchanan; (4th from right) Lt William L Maury; and (2nd from right) Marine Purser Richard T Allison. (Naval Historical Division)

fellow Southerners who remained with the North, but also more than Southern army officers who resigned. Because of the Southern emphasis on the Army and neglect of the Navy, Southern army officers rose to high rank; young army lieutenants attained promotions and national reputations. But Confederate naval officers, because of the small navy, found it difficult to advance in rank. Those in command of US vessels at the onset of war sailed them into Northern ports and relinquished their ships before joining their states. It was a point of honour with them, but it left the South without a single first-rate fighting ship. Men who had commanded large warships in the US Navy, now were in charge of river steamers, converted merchantmen, canal boats, tugs, and makeshift ironclads.[7]

Lieutenant John Newland Maffitt, who believed that free government is based on the consent of the governed, relinquished command of his ship, the USS *Crusader*, in New York, resigned and made his way to the 'cradle of the Confederacy',

Southern independence would come without war, and was unconvinced when Maffitt described war preparations in the North. In addition, Davis thought that Southern officers should have brought their ships with them, and undoubtedly knew that Maffitt had defiantly refused to relinquish the *Crusader* when threatened by a Confederate takeover earlier at Mobile.[9]

One of Confederate Secretary of the Navy Stephen R Mallory's first problems was what to do with the hundreds of former naval officers that applied to the Government for commissions. Since, in March 1861, the Navy consisted of twelve small ships, the problem of supply and demand was acute, especially since they wanted ranks at least as high as that they had held in the old Navy. Adding to this problem was a number of civilians who wanted posts such as surgeons or paymasters, many armed with written entreaties from Confederate congressmen. As a bow to morale, Mallory allowed the same rank the officers had in the old Navy, and adhered to, at least early in the war, his practice of appointing no civilians if resigned officers were available for the position.[10]

Although many Southern states had established provisional navies, consisting of various small craft, that were turned over to the Confederate Government, for over a year there were far more naval officers than positions available afloat. Many of them sought service with the Army or commanded shore batteries while still in the Navy. All of them eventually found duty of some kind, and Mallory commissioned additional officers. A Southern naval academy was established to train more junior officers. The maximum number of naval officers on duty at any one time (April 1864) was 727.[11]

To provide for the officers who had resigned from the US Navy, Congress on April 21, 1862 established the following slots: 4 admirals, 10 captains, 31 commanders, 100 first lieutenants, 25 second lieutenants, 20 masters, 12 paymasters, 40 assistant paymasters, 22 surgeons, 15 passed assistant surgeons, 30 assistant surgeons, 1 engineer-in-chief, and 12 engineers. To pave the way for the deserving, all the admirals, 4 of the captains, 5 of the commanders, 22 of the first lieutenants, and 5 of the second lieutenants would be promoted 'solely for gallant or meritorious conduct during the war'.[12] Promotion based on merit rather than seniority appealed to younger officers such as Lieutenant Wood, who, even in the old Navy had complained about 'moss backs'. Clearly, the South's naval effort could not be sustained by arthritic old men. That summer, Wood wrote from Drewry's Bluff:

Montgomery, Alabama. There he was disappointed with the scant attention paid to creating a navy. He wrote: 'The government instantly seemed to be at sea, without rudder, compass, or charts by which to steer upon the bewildering ocean of absolute necessity'. The Navy's lack of importance to the Confederate Government at the beginning of the war is reflected in the aggregate appropriations for each department early in March 1861. Of fourteen separate entries, the only one that received less money than the Navy was the Executive Mansion – $17,300 for the Navy and $5,000 for the building.[8]

'Naval sons of the South', like Maffitt, had left the Federal service at great personal and professional sacrifice. Now, in an interview with President Jefferson Davis, Maffitt was stunned to hear that the South did not need a navy. Davis believed that

16 Mch 1861
all Confirmed

To the President
of the Congress of the Confederate States.

I nominate Ebenezer Farrand of Florida, late a Commander in the Navy of the United States, to be a Commander in the Navy of the Confederate States.

Thomas W Brent of Florida, late a Commander in the Navy of the United States, to be a Commander in the Navy of the Confederate States

Raphael Semmes of Alabama, late a Commander in the Navy of the United States, to be a Commander in the Navy of the Confederate States.

Henry J Hartstene of South Carolina, late a Commander in the Navy of the United States, to be a Commander in the Navy of the Confederate States.

Jefferson Davis

President Jefferson Davis's 1861 nomination of Thomas W Brent, Ebenezer Farrand, Raphael Semmes, and Henry J Hartstene as commanders in the Confederate Navy. (WMCWNH)

The promotions have produced quite a stir in naval circles. A party consisting of Commodore Forrest, Sinclair, Farrand, Pegram, and others are endeavouring to have the law repealed and a stop put to further advancement except by the old system of stagnation. I am sorry for this, for I believe that promotion as a reward for distinguished services in battle will be the making of our service. You may take it out of the hands of politicians – for this appears to be the main objection – and make the advancement subject to a board of naval officers, three of the oldest officers, or one from each grade selected by the officers

themselves. Put as many checks as you please on the law to prevent smuggling, but still promote for fighting; otherwise the Navy never can be kicked into vitality. Admiral Buchanan's promotion laid Commodore Forrest up for some days. He was not visible at the office.[13]

Wood himself was promoted to first lieutenant in September 1862, chiefly as a result of his service as commander of the aft pivot gun on the CSS *Virginia* during the famous battle with the USS *Monitor* the previous spring at Hampton Roads. Wood considered battle essential for morale within, and public support of the naval program. He was in the forefront of the agitation for an even stronger emphasis on merit over seniority for promotion because too many 'old infirm drones' were retarding the service. Wood at war's end was a captain, which means he was promoted two times. The primary reason for this was that he was attracted to undertakings which helped ensure that the Southern Navy would be 'kicked into vitality.'[14]

Yet, in spite of heroic action by many, advancement was difficult. Prior to 1862, the highest rank in the old Navy had been captain, corresponding to colonel in the Army. While most of the resigned officers entered Confederate service with the same rank as they had in the old Navy, most of them came out of the war with perhaps one step in rank. There were only two admirals in the Confederate Navy – Franklin Buchanan for meritorious service while in command of the CSS *Virginia* during the first day of the Battle of Hampton Roads, and later Raphael Semmes for his exploits while in command of the CSS *Alabama*.[15]

Training

Of the midshipmen at the US Naval Academy in 1861, nearly 40 per cent resigned. In some cases, their fathers submitted resignations for them, and in others the superintendent at Annapolis sent a list of resignations to Secretary of the Navy Welles. Those who had completed their studies (called passed midshipmen – now teaching at Annapolis) were treated less favourably; all the fifteen passed midshipmen who resigned were dismissed except three, whose resignations were accepted.

It was over two years before the Confederate Government established a training school for future officers. Accordingly, the midshipmen were at first stationed throughout the South and studied as regular navy duties permitted, in the manner of the US

Navy prior to the establishment of the Academy at Annapolis. Following legislation by the Confederate Government, Secretary Mallory in June 1863 directed Lieutenant William H Parker, who had graduated at the head of his class at Annapolis, where he was also an assistant professor of mathematics, to begin the work of establishing a Southern naval academy. For lack of a better place, the academy was placed under the Office of Ordnance and Hydrography. It was decided that the academy would be a working warship, the CSS *Patrick Henry*. The vessel was converted at the shipyard at Rocketts Landing on the James River at the

Confederate capital at Richmond to provide a school and dormitory on board. This included two small 'recitation rooms' located between the paddle boxes on deck, a mess hall, rifled and smooth-bore guns, sails as well as steam power, and an armed launch. Inadequate billets on the ship caused some of the midshipmen to be housed in cabins on the hilltop bastion downriver at Drewry's Bluff, or in other warships.[16]

Modelled on the US Naval Academy, the school began in August 1863. Approximately fifty acting midshipmen were appointed by Confederate Congressmen from their districts and by President Davis from the Confederacy at large. The boys were required to be between fourteen and eighteen years old, and had to pass physical and mental entrance examinations and be of good moral character. Many had resigned from Annapolis. The South's

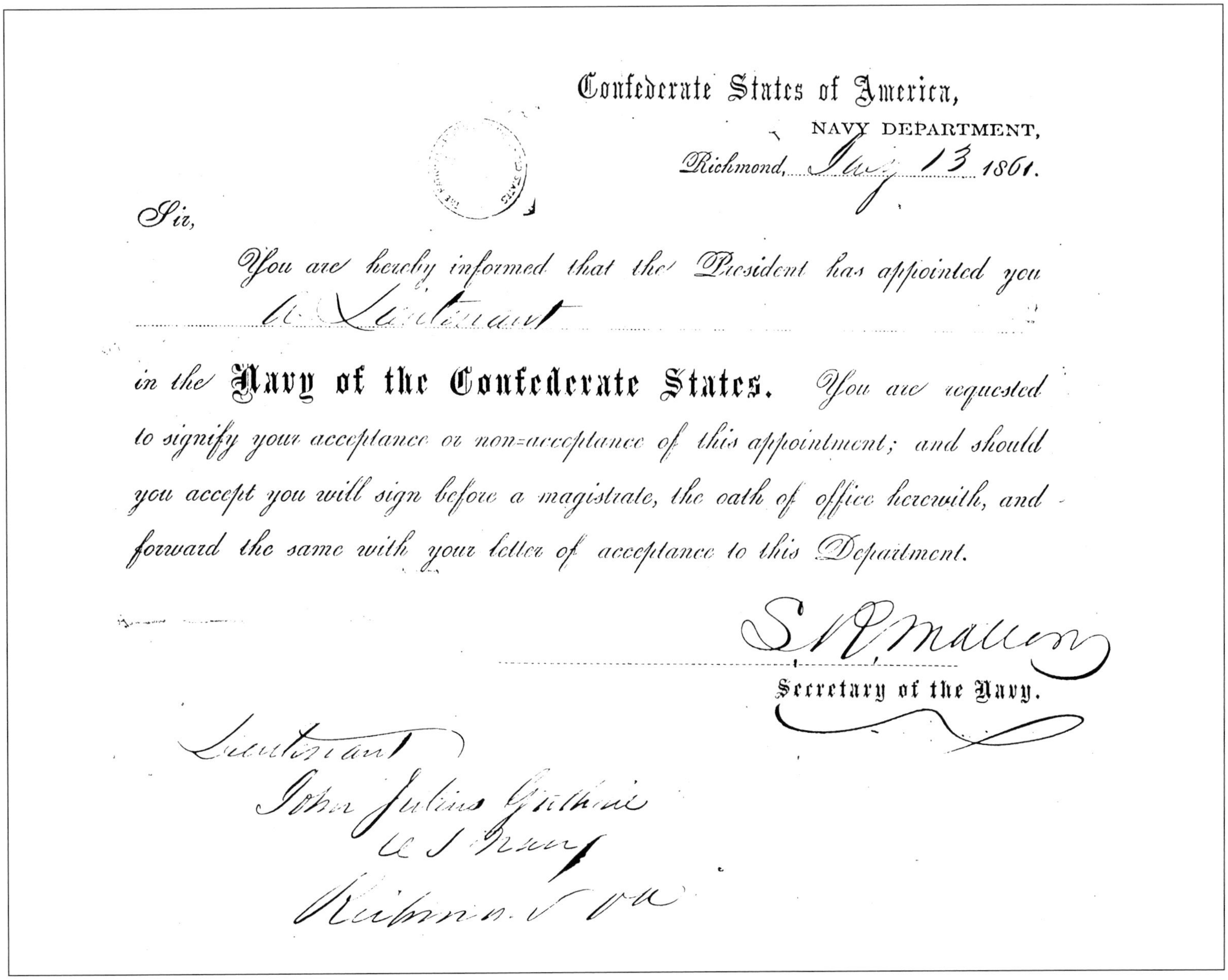

Officer's commission of Lt John Julius Guthrie. (National Archives)

Confederate States of America,
NAVY DEPARTMENT,
Richmond, _July 13_ 1861.

Sir,

You are hereby informed that the President has appointed you

a Lieutenant

in the **Navy of the Confederate States.** You are requested to signify your acceptance or non-acceptance of this appointment; and should you accept you will sign before a magistrate, the oath of office herewith, and forward the same with your letter of acceptance to this Department.

S R Mallory
Secretary of the Navy.

Lieutenant
John Julius Guthrie
C S Navy
Richmond Va

Lt William H Parker. Parker was superintendent of the naval school from its inception until the close of the war. (Scharf, *Confederate States Navy*)

distinguished families were represented in the student body.[17]

The *Patrick Henry* was a suitable war college. Anchored in front of Drewry's Bluff (Richmond's main defense on the James seven miles below the city) the vessel was to be sunk in the channel between the obstructions in the river if Federal ironclads attempted to run the land batteries. The midshipmen could often see and hear the constant movement of Union and Confederate troops on the banks of the river, where the confronting armies clashed in skirmishes and exchanged artillery fire. In addition, the school ship also served as a receiving ship for prisoner exchange under flags of truce on vessels plying between Drewry's Bluff and the Federal stronghold down river at Harrison's Landing.[18]

Amid blasts of opposing cannons at Drewry's Bluff, the school's instructors, half of them naval officers and the other half civilian experts, taught the midshipmen seamanship (one of Superintendent Parker's textbooks, *Elements of Seamanship*, was used by both sides during the war) astronomy, navigation, English, mathematics, physics, history, a foreign language, drawing and

drafting, infantry tactics and ethics[19]. Graduating after the four year course, a midshipman appeared before a 'board of visitors' – senior officers not associated with the school – and sat proficiency and aptitude examinations which led to selection as an officer. By November 1864, fifty-nine from the school had become passed midshipmen, approximately half of whom had resigned from Annapolis. Forty were scheduled to graduate the following December, making almost a hundred graduates. These figures were

Regulations of the schoolship *Patrick Henry* provided instructions for the organization and daily routine of the midshipmen, as well as guidance for the school's instructors and other officers. (National Archives)

REGULATIONS

OF THE

C. S. SCHOOL-SHIP, PATRICK HENRY.

CHAPTER I.

ORGANIZATION.

1. The C. S. School-Ship, Patrick Henry, shall be under the supervision of the officer in charge of the office of Ordnance and Hydrography, and he shall personally inspect the vessel at least once a year.

2. A commandant, of rank not lower than that of a lieutenant, will have the immediate government and command of the school-ship, and will be held responsible for its discipline and good management. All communications to the Navy Department on subjects connected with, or relating to the ship, are to be made, or forwarded by the commandant to the officer in charge of the office of Ordnance and Hydrography.

3. An executive officer shall also be attached to the ship, whose rank shall not be below that of 2d lieutenant. He shall be the executive officer of the school-ship, and also in charge of either the department of seamanship, gunnery, or navigation.

4. There shall be attached to the ship two officers, of rank not lower than that of master, who, in addition to the duties of the ship, shall have charge, each, of one of the departments of seamanship, gunnery, or navigation.

5. No officer of the navy shall exercise military command on board the school-ship unless subordinate to the commandant, excepting the officer of the navy who may at the time be in charge of the office of Ordnance and Hydrography.

6. There shall be attached to the school-ship, a surgeon or assistant surgeon, paymaster or assistant paymaster, master, secretary, and such warrant and petty officers, and other persons of inferior ratings, as may be authorized by the Secretary of the Navy.

7. There shall also be attached to the ship the following professors, viz:
   One Professor of Mathematics.
   One Professor of English Studies.
   One Professor of Modern Languages.

8. The relative rank and precedence of the members of the academic staff to be determined by the date of commission or appointment.

somewhat in keeping with future expectations, because by 1864 there were 106 slots each year authorized by the Congress for the Naval Academy, about half of whom were expected to graduate.

In April 1865, as Richmond was evacuated in the face of advancing Union troops, Mallory ordered the destruction of the James River Squadron. Superintendent Parker and the midshipmen were charged with guarding the Government specie and private coin from Richmond banks during the trip south. This was a test of their character, and they performed well. Every report of that journey paid tribute to the staunch behaviour of these young men. On May 2, 1865 the school was disbanded at Abbeville, South Carolina. The school, the South, and the Navy had cause to be proud of the midshipmen.[20] While these young men were thwarted in their naval careers (after the war none were allowed in the US Navy), the Confederate Naval Academy produced men who later became Congressmen, Senators, successful lawyers, judges, physicians, civil engineers, bankers and businessmen.

Command and the senority system

Before the war Secretary Mallory had been chairman of the US Senate Naval Affairs Committee and had sponsored the Naval Retiring Board, which had placed officers on an indefinite furlough (leave) list. If such furloughs were upheld, this amounted to forced retirement from the Navy. To the embarrassment of Mallory, after becoming Secretary of the Navy, many of the Southern officers at Montgomery had been cashiered by his board

Photograph of Midshipmen Samuel P Blanc (far right) and army friends, taken in Richmond while he was assigned to the schoolship *Patrick Henry*. (Charles V Peery)

CSS *Patrick Henry*. (Scharf, *Confederate States Navy*)

during the past five years. Among those at Montgomery, for example, was Lieutenant Maffitt, who had been placed on the retirement list in 1855. He had felt disgraced, and was unwilling to become 'an idle and degraded pensioner of the government' — naval officers were unused to the concept of retirement. Maffitt had fought back at a Court of Inquiry in 1857 and won the right to remain on the active list. His subsequent remarkable career, in both navies, proved that he should not have been on the list.

When Mallory met Maffitt in Montgomery, the Secretary was so uncomfortable and defensive that Maffitt later told a friend that, 'he had been received by the Secretary of the Navy as if he

[Maffitt] had designs upon him'. The result of the meeting does no credit to Mallory. Maffitt left the encounter without an offer to serve in the Confederate Navy, and it was only through the intervention of such Southern notables as Benjamin Hill and Robert Toombs that he did receive a commission as a lieutenant in the Confederate Navy.[21]

Questions on Practical Seamanship served as a textbook for young midshipmen serving on the schoolship *Patrick Henry*. It was written by the school's commandant, Lt William H Parker. (National Archives)

QUESTIONS ON PRACTICAL

SEAMANSHIP;

TOGETHER WITH

HARBOR ROUTINE AND EVOLUTIONS;

PREPARED FOR THE MIDSHIPMEN OF THE C S. NAVY,

BY

WM. H. PARKER,

COMMANDING C. S. SCHOOL-SHIP PATRICK HENRY.

RICHMOND:
MACFARLANE AND FERGUSSON, PRINTERS.
1863.

Important orders from the Navy Department usually contained Secretary Mallory's signature, otherwise orders included the phrase 'by command of the Secretary of the Navy'. The Office of Orders and Detail prepared the orders. Until March 1863 the chain of command for operations was from the Navy Department to area commanders; for example, the naval commander for the defense of Georgia and South Carolina. The area commander could command his warships in person, but for certain operations he might designate a subordinate, who was usually the ranking officer of one of the vessels participating in the operation. Beginning in March 1863, the station commander was removed from the operational chain of command. The Secretary designated commanders of naval forces afloat and listed the ships attached to the command, usually referred to as a squadron. The squadron commander held the temporary rank of flag officer.

For secret orders, Mallory utilized a dictionary code. First, both ends of the command system had to use copies of the same dictionary. In a double column page format, the first column was designated A, and the second B. For example, a coded word might be expressed 323, B, 15. The first number referred to the page, the letter to the column, and the second number to the number of words from the top of the column.[22]

In May 1863, the Confederate Government gave Mallory authority to expand his concept of promotion based on meritorious service. This time, however, the law did not involve promoting junior officers over senior ones, or forcing the older ones into retirement. Instead, the act of Congress created a new 'provisional' Navy while retaining the old 'regular' Navy. All enlisted men were immediately transferred to the provisional Navy, while officers would be individually transferred by presidential appointment. By June 1864, the younger and more energetic officers had been transferred to the provisional navy, usually with a step in rank. This termination of the seniority system worked fairly well. The older, higher ranking officers who could have continued to command with ability squadrons of ships but were unsuited for the small Confederate Navy, became bureau chiefs in Richmond and commanders of the Navy's industrial facilities. Officers too ill for active duty were also retained in the regular Navy. Those in the regular Navy could not serve afloat and made up a kind of retired list. But these officers escaped the humiliation of being forced out of the service, or superseded on the same list by their juniors.

The double classification system did cause some problems as the war progressed. The division of officers on two lists, with duties confined strictly to certain spheres, did not allow for some

Left to himself, Mallory issued orders that were sometimes too strict, such as ordering Flag Officer George N Hollins upstream with all naval vessels from New Orleans. Other orders were so vague some commanders did not know what was expected of them, such as those issued to Captain Josiah Tattnall of the flagship CSS *Virginia*. Orders of a general nature, full of options, worked best for the commanders of the commerce destroyers, such as the CSS *Alabama* and CSS *Florida*, who were too far afield for coordination.[24]

Regulations for the Confederate Navy were largely based on those of the pre-war US Navy. (National Archives)

ORDNANCE INSTRUCTIONS

FOR THE

CONFEDERATE STATES NAVY

RELATING TO THE

PREPARATION OF VESSELS OF WAR FOR BATTLE,

TO THE

DUTIES OF OFFICERS AND OTHERS WHEN AT QUARTERS,

TO

ORDNANCE AND ORDNANCE STORES,

AND TO

GUNNERY.

THIRD EDITION.

Published by Order of the Navy Department.

LONDON:
SAUNDERS, OTLEY, & CO., 66 BROOK STREET, W
1864.

Title page from the *Ordnance Manual*, which was printed in London. (WMCWNH)

REGULATIONS

FOR THE

NAVY OF THE CONFEDERATE STATES.

862.

NAVY DEPARTMENT. }
RICHMOND, April 20th, 1862. }

The following Regulations for the Navy of the Confederate States are published, by direction of the President, for the government of all concerned. They will accordingly be strictly obeyed, and nothing contrary to them will be enjoined or permitted in any portion of the naval forces of the Confederate States by the officers thereof.

S. R. MALLORY,
Secretary of the Navy

RICHMOND:
MACFARLANE & FERGUSSON, PRINTERS.
1862.

needed flexibility. In some instances, the dual arrangement negated the prompt assignment of officers to new positions. Most troublesome, as more commands afloat became available, was the assignment of much-needed officers to sea duty from the regular Navy.[23]

Mallory's command decisions are controversial. President Davis did not intervene in the affairs of the Navy Department.

Junior officers of the
CSS *Alabama*. (WMCWNH)

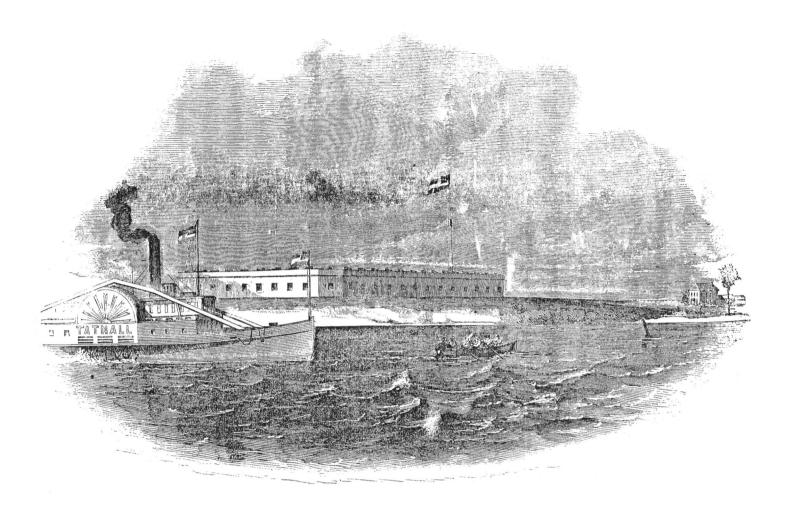

CSS *Savannah* (erroneously named *Tattnall* in this illustration) was the flagship of the Georgia Navy in the early months of the war before purchase by the Confederate Navy. (*Harper's Weekly*)

Ship and station administration

The Confederate Navy's guide for shipboard organization was the US Navy's *Ordnance Instructions*. The quarterdeck was a fighting ship's command post. It was usually located on the stern of a ship's upper deck, but was in any event the part of a naval vessel set aside by the captain for ceremonial and official use. When the men were called to stations the captain stood in overall command on the quarterdeck near the wheel or compass.

The executive officer assumed a position near the captain and took charge of manoeuvring the vessel. Sometimes called the first lieutenant, he was expected to be familiar with the duties of everyone on the ship. The executive officer was also expected to develop a thorough knowledge of his ship and how it handled. 'All the drudgery of the ship is his', noted Lieutenant Kell of the CSS *Alabama*, 'the demand upon his temper and his abilities is enormous'. The position called for wisdom, good judgment, and professional skill. He had to represent the captain's wishes, and yet avoid any blunder the captain was capable of making himself. The executive officer at times stood between officers and other officers, officers and men, and the captain and the entire ship's company. In addition, he was sometimes expected to be the captain's confidante.

The master, also on the quarterdeck, assisted in matters of seamanship and navigation. He had duties similar to that of captain in the merchant marine, who in the absence of the owner of the ship, had final authority at sea. But on a fighting ship, the master was part of the naval chain of command.

Two or more midshipmen delivered the captain's orders to positions out of earshot of the quarterdeck and also acted as signal officers. Varicoloured flags were used for daytime signals with different combinations having different meanings that were read from a signal book provided to each ship. At night, coloured lights were arranged above, beside, or below each other as desired for a particular message. The Navy also used whistles and flares.

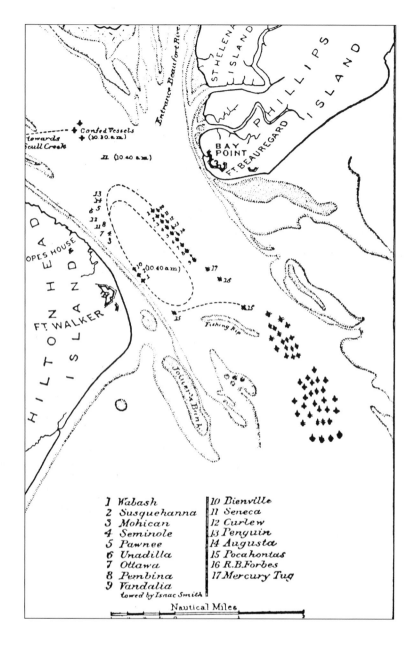

ity over the other. There was potential for trouble because the station commander provided personnel, stores, and repairs to the flag officer afloat, yet the new arrangement for station administration seems to have functioned smoothly — a testament to the finer qualities of Confederate naval officers.

A commander afloat (flag officer) had a staff that often varied in size, but would include the captain of the flagship (flag captain) who was also chief-of-staff and deputy commander. A flag lieutenant was ordnance officer. He prepared orders and recommended enemy targets for each ship. The flag officer's aides, two or more midshipmen or master's mates, delivered orders to the flag captain or by signal or boat to other ships. The aides sometimes went ashore to scout the movement of enemy ships. The flag officer's staff could also contain a surgeon who worked with the

Commander John N Maffitt commanded a variety of ships in Confederate service, including the gunboat *Savannah*, cruiser *Florida*, ironclad *Albemarle*, and blockade-runner *Owl*. (Scharf, *Confederate States Navy*)

Map of the Battle of Port Royal, November 7, 1861
(*Battles & Leaders*)

The station commander's staff consisted of a lieutenant who doubled as ordnance officer, an aide, a surgeon, a paymaster, and an engineer. Naval activities ashore under the charge of the station commander included ordnance works, receiving ships, storekeeper, hospitals, and marine detachments. He had control over ship construction on his station, with the authority to confiscate an unfinished ship from constructors and complete or destroy the vessel.

There seems to have been little conflict between the commander of a station and the commander of forces afloat after the separation of the two commands. Personal and professional adjustments had to be made since neither commander had author-

On the windswept deck of the blockade-runner *Lilián*, Maffit is to the left on paddlebox evaluating a threat on the horizon. (*Illustrated London News*)

flagship's medical team, and an engineer who advised on engineering problems. The flag officer had responsibility for naval shore batteries in his area as well as his ships. He shifted men back and forth between the ships and batteries, and coordinated the two forces during battle[25].

On at least one occasion during the war, there was a serious disagreement between a flag officer and his flag captain. Lieutenant Maffitt reported for duty to Savannah on May 9, 1861 where the station commander, Captain Josiah Tattnall, was assembling a tiny fleet to defend the waters off South Carolina and Georgia. Maffitt took command of the CSS *Savannah*. The 406-ton paddlewheel steamer (formerly the *Everglade*, a passenger boat that plied the inland route between Savannah, Georgia and Jacksonville, Florida,) was Tattnall's flagship. Maffitt termed the vessel an 'absurd abortion of a man-of-war'. With Tattnall as flag officer and Maffitt as flag captain on the *Savannah*, the 'mosquito' fleet steamed to Port Royal Sound to defend two forts against the advance of a large Union naval task force intent on capturing the fine South Carolina harbor. On November 6 Tattnall went ashore to confer with the Army commander at Fort Beauregard, and Maffitt steamed out and engaged the enemy at long range, receiving damage to the *Savannah*. An 11-inch shell fired by the USS *Seneca* struck near the wheelhouse on the 'miserable little cockleshell' of a flagship and carried away bulkheads and stanchions. A hole was also punched at the flagship's waterline, but Maffitt suffered no casualties.

Maffitt's aggressiveness brought disapproval from Tattnall. The flag officer suspended Maffitt from command of the *Savannah*. Tattnall contended that the order he gave when he left the ship was to remain at anchor, but Maffitt wrote: 'I did not so understand him, but on the contrary, understood him to direct that no soundings by the enemy should be permitted'. Back in Savannah, the two commanders reconciled, but Maffitt soon requested and Tattnall approved Maffitt's transfer to General Robert E Lee's staff as naval aide. Maffitt later distinguished himself as a blockade runner and commander of the CSS *Florida*.[26]

A naval officer detailed to army duty either retained his naval rank or obtained a temporary army rank. He had the same authority as army officers in the position and did not report to the Navy. The assignment of a naval vessel to army command was more complicated. The naval officer commanding such a ship was under the authority of the Army commander and deployed his vessel accordingly. Almost always, the transfer of a ship to Army command represented the desire of the Army and not the Navy. In river and harbor warfare, movement is restricted and the Army was in the better position for command, although experienced naval

Lt Isaac C Holcombe, in regulation uniform. (Charles V Peery)

officers found it difficult to serve under young army officers ashore. Where there were large bodies of water, the reverse command situation was called for because the water governed both army and naval operations. This system of command was used in the sounds of North Carolina and probably should have been devised for Charleston, Mobile, and New Orleans.[27]

Uniforms

In 1861, the office of Adjutant and Inspector General issued regulations for service uniforms. Most officers were to wear a long double-breasted gray coat with two rows of navy buttons down the upper front. Trousers were to be gray or white and loose enough at the bottom to fit over boots or shoes. Caps were to be gray, about four inches in height, with a patent leather visor. Buttons (small, medium and large), shoulder straps, cap emblems and gold strips around the lower sleeves distinguished one rank from another. The most noticeable insignia, especially at a distance, was the strips of gold lace around the sleeves. The top strip was looped. A flag officer had four strips; three designated a captain; two a commander; and one a lieutenant.[28] [For more details see appendix on uniform and dress at the end of this book.]

In reality, many officers wore their blue uniforms from the old Navy. Had better conditions for clothing existed in the Confederacy, gray uniforms would not have been popular with most naval officers. As one former Southern officer, James R R Morris Morgan, wrote in his memoirs: 'Who had ever heard of a gray sailor, no matter what nationality he served?' Seldom was an effort made to enforce the dress code so that on all the stations and ships officers wore blue, gray, and sometimes black uniforms. However, Admiral Buchanan of the Mobile Station ordered the official gray uniform to be worn while on duty. Buchanan was indignant when an officer who had never had a uniform reported for duty in a *black* coat. One officer, who had formerly admired Buchanan, wrote:

> A week or more since the remnant of the crew of the Arkansas arrived here, Admiral Buchanan...[informed] the officers that he had no use for them, as they had no uniforms!...I have heard it said that with some ladies a sleek coat...with brass buttons has a wonderful effect, but I was not prepared to believe that with a man who claimed to be a warrior of age (there is no doubt of that)...from this, I deduce that a fashionable tailor can do more to make a good officer in the estimation of old Buchanan than the great creating Prince of Heaven.[29]

Uniform coat of Commander Catesby ap R Jones.
(WMCWNH)

Pay and living conditions

An admiral in the Confederate Navy received compensation equivalent to a full general in the Southern Army, $6,000 a year except that a general commanding an army received $1,200 more. Hyphenated generals in field commands also drew slightly more than an admiral at $6,600 (while there were many Confederate generals there were but two admirals in the South.) However, naval compensation improved dramatically for other ranks. The next rank below admiral was captain (equivalent to colonel in the Army), who drew as much as $5,000 if he commanded a squadron, compared to half that for a colonel. An Army major drew just under $2,000 per annum while a naval commander was paid almost a third more. This comparative trend continued through the lower ranks of officers, but with less difference. For example, a naval second lieutenant on sea duty made $1,200 per annum, the same as a first lieutenant in the Army. Ironically, the Confederate naval pay system listed increases for five-year increments in a nation that existed for only four years.

Pay Table for Naval Officers[30]
(1863)

Amounts are given for sea duty only; lesser amounts were paid for non-sea duty.

Rank	Annual Pay $
Admiral	6,000
Captain	
Squadron Commander	5,000
other sea duty	4,200
Commander	2,825
Lieutenants Commanding (at sea)	2,550
First Lieutenant	1,500
Second Lieutenant	1,200
Fleet Surgeon	3,300
Surgeons	2,200
Passed Assistant Surgeon	1,700
Assistant Surgeon	1,250
Paymaster	2,000
Assistant Paymaster	1,200
Master	1,000
Passed Midshipman	900
Midshipman	550
Boatswain, Gunner, Carpenter, Sailmaker	1,000

For the following, no distinction was made between sea duty and non-sea duty.

Chief Engineer	1,800
First Assistant Engineer	1,250
Second Assistant Engineer	1,000
Third Assistant Engineer	750
Naval Storekeeper	1,700
Naval Constructor	2,600
Secretary to Squadron Commanders	
when Commander-in-chief	1,000
not Commander-in-chief	900

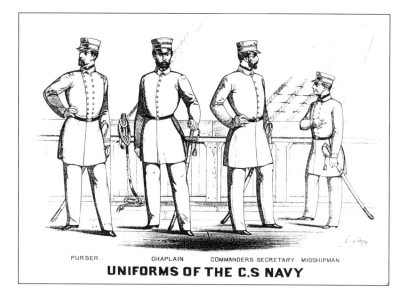

PURSER   CHAPLAIN   COMMANDERS SECRETARY MIDSHIPMAN
UNIFORMS OF THE C.S NAVY

COMMANDER   PASSED-MIDSHIPMAN.CHIEF-ENGINEER   MASTER
UNIFORMS OF THE C.S. NAVY

FLAG OFFICER   CAPTAIN   LIEUTENANT   SURGEON
UNIFORMS OF THE C.S NAVY

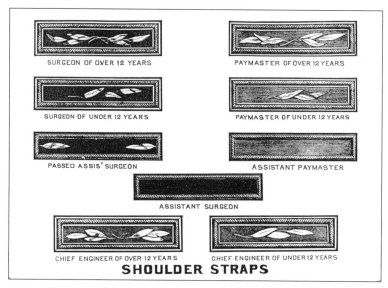

SURGEON OF OVER 12 YEARS   PAYMASTER OF OVER 12 YEARS

SURGEON OF UNDER 12 YEARS   PAYMASTER OF UNDER 12 YEARS

PASSED ASSIS† SURGEON   ASSISTANT PAYMASTER

ASSISTANT SURGEON

CHIEF ENGINEER OF OVER 12 YEARS   CHIEF ENGINEER OF UNDER 12 YEARS
SHOULDER STRAPS

The uniform regulations published in 1861 provided for the colour, cut, trim and insignia of the naval officer's uniform. (WMCWNH)

Given the South's inflation rate, the pay table became less and less meaningful during the war. Some officers coped because they were connected to affluent families, and almost all seemed to have followed the custom of socialising with prominent families wherever they were stationed. Naval officers were held in high regard, and women loved to visit the ships. For everyday existence, however, most officers probably relied on the naval service. Lieutenant George W Gift of the Mobile Station explained: 'On my liberty days I go on shore to half past nine and find some friends and acquaintances with whom I consume the time until 2pm I then return on board to dinner (and by the way we live very well) and remain until after quarters at 4 and then go ashore until tea time'.

Living conditions were mostly pleasant for the officers at the Mobile Station, in spite of Buchanan's penchant for regulations. He was probably the best station commander, and was universally admired for his courage and aggressiveness. The city's population was 25,000 and it was one of the most cosmopolitan cities of the South. Officers could take advantage of downtown attractions, such as oyster houses, wine shops, gambling and drinking places. The squadron's wooden vessels rotated every two weeks to a month guarding the entrances to Mobile Bay and when in harbor anchored near a hotel. Typically they served four watches – two days on duty and two days off.

The war did not dampen the social activities of the city, which were a tonic for the normal duty of waiting – a monotony com-

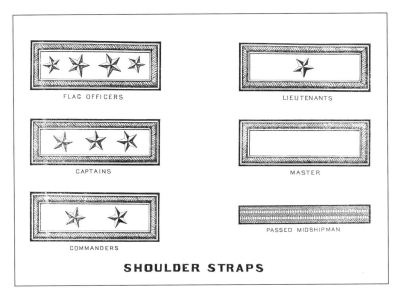

SHOULDER STRAPS

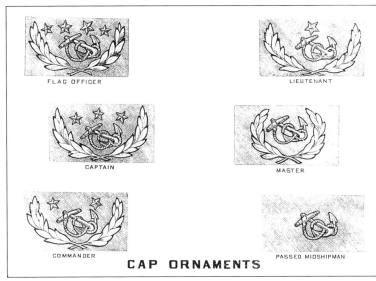

CAP ORNAMENTS

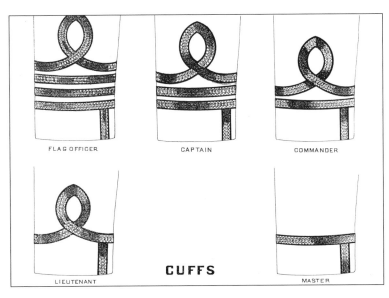

CUFFS

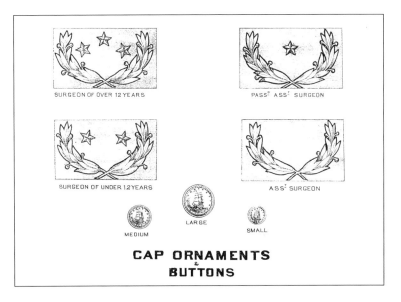

CAP ORNAMENTS & BUTTONS

mon in all wars. The officers repaid their visits to families ashore by holding balls and dinner aboard ship and taking moonlight cruises on the bay. Buchanan favoured and sometimes participated in such affairs. A journalist described one boat excursion: 'A very good band of music from one of the regiments of the garrison played, and dancing was soon got up in the splendid saloon....Admiral Buchanan, who was looking on, joined in this, and naturally by doing so created a great deal of confusion and merriment, at which he was in high glee'.[31]

For the midshipmen of the James River Squadron, the day was more structured. Midshipman J Thomas Scharf explained:

If the routine of a day was not broken by a summons to man the guns on shore, or do scouting, or take part in boat expeditions, it was full of hard work on board. The morning gun was fired at seven o'clock,

and at eight a breakfast of hard-tack and a decoction of sweet potatoes or beans that masqueraded as coffee was served. Sick call, studies and recitations occupied the hours until two o'clock, and then a dinner of salt-junk, perhaps a mess of vegetables, and the inevitable cornmeal that became a staple article of diet when wheat-flour climbed toward $1,200 per barrel in Confederate currency. School exercises and dress parade took up the remainder of the afternoon, and the day ended with tattoo at 9:30, and taps at ten o'clock."[32]

Routine aboard ship was organized and regular, and therefore officers knew what to expect each day and could plan for free time and attempt to defeat boredom. They read books and newspapers, spun tales and wrote letters home. On the CSS *Chattahoochee*, on the river of the same name at Columbus, Georgia, there was only one mail call a week. The vessel was not likely to see action, which

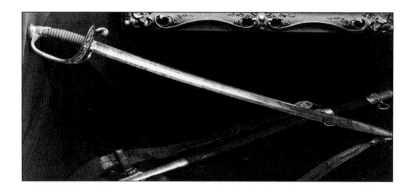

Model 1852 regulation US Navy officer's sword, carried by Chief Engineer James H Warner during his Confederate service. (WMCWNH)

caused complaints of no chance for promotion and of unfulfilled dreams of glory. However, they apparently ate from 'as elegant a table as one would wish'. While the ship was under construction, the officers lived ashore in temporary quarters, as they often did in other ports when not at sea. Perhaps the most anticipated activity was visiting nearby plantations and joining the social life. When the officers moved on board the vessel, the local ladies returned visits, and 'enjoyed strawberries and a pound cake and cream tea'.[33]

On the high seas, officers at times encountered spartan conditions. On the commerce destroyer CSS *Shenandoah*, the gunpowder was at first stored in the officers' quarters, and the officers cheerfully worked with the men fitting out the ship because the vessel

Confederate naval officer's 'dolphin head' sword, manufactured by Robert Mole, Birmingham, England, under commission from the CS Navy Department. (WMCWNH)

was short-handed. They bunked on the open decks and shared the crew's toilet facilities (deck wash buckets). The gunpowder was finally stored in a small room directly under the commander's cabin — carefully guarded against accident. When the officers gained access to their cabins — there were seven for ten officers — the furnishings of each consisted of a wash stand and a bunk. The ship's commander, Lieutenant James Waddell, who was long accustomed to comfortable quarters, expressed outrage at the furn- ishings of his apartment.

> 'What a cabin!' he railed...'Look at it! Look at that broken old plush-bottomed arm chair — my only piece of furniture! Smell of that carpet on the floor, stinking of dogs or something worse! No berth, no bureau, no lockers for my clothing, no washstand, no pitcher, no basin! Did ever a man-of-war's captain have such an apartment as this before? I'd like some of my shipmates in the old Navy to see this', and he laughed mirthlessly.
>
> But the commander was game. After this outburst he endured his privations without further murmuring. While the work of fitting the ship was at its peak, with useful labour for every hand to do, he would limp forward and take the wheel himself so that another able-bodied seaman might be released for the emergency work.[34]

While the *Shenandoah* was a converted merchantman, the *Florida* was built originally as a Confederate cruiser, much like a British gunboat in size and configuration. Lieutenant Maffitt, the commander of the successful first cruise of the *Florida*, found that the exposure of the deck and the incessant wakefulness necessary to his command adversely affected his health. During the raid he had given up his stateroom to females (if among the prisoners) taken on the high seas and slept on the deck. When he sailed the *Florida* into Brest, France in August 1863, an international set of visitors came aboard. Maffitt came to the top of the companionway to receive them and invite them to his cabin. Among the group was a correspondent for the London *Times*, who wrote: 'his plainly furnished little room looked as business-like as a merchant's office. The round table in the center was strewn with books and innumerable manuscripts, and on the shelves were formidable looking rows of account books, charts, etc. I may observe of the cabin, as of every other part of the *Florida*, that none of it appears to have been built for ornament — all for use!' Maffitt, pointing to the mass of charts, files, papers and account books, concluded 'you see I've no sinecure of it'.[35]

Engineers, surgeons, paymasters

In the field of engineering, there was less carryover from the US Navy than in other areas because engineering was a comparatively new field and its status was not well defined. Basically, engineers designed, acquired, installed, operated and maintained engines both ashore and at sea. On April 21, 1862 the Confederate Government established the Office of Engineer-in-Chief, which became directly responsible to the Navy Department. Only one man held the position – Chief Engineer William P Williamson. There was only one commissioned officer rank, that of chief engineer, and three warrant officer ranks – first, second and third assistant engineer. An examination was required before promotion to chief engineer. Mallory appointed assistant engineers, or they could receive acting appointments from certain officers subject to Mallory's approval.

Some engineers were appointed from civilian life, and enlisted men were often appointed to the junior ranks. An experienced fireman, barely literate, could become a third assistant engineer. In the early part of the war, engineering officers served in a branch of their own, but later chief engineers began to serve in ordnance works. Chief engineers were attached to the staffs of major commands and at least one was sent abroad to procure engines. They also served on trial boards for new or rebuilt ships and on examining boards for the promotion of other engineers. Some were in charge of engineering departments aboard ships. Chief engineers remained in the engine room of a ship during battle, while their officers and men rotated in and out of the engine room.

The Office of Engineer-in-Chief had two main functions. It produced engineering designs for new vessels or alterations to old ones, and helped develop new designs. The Office developed no operation instructions, safety regulations, engineering data, or training programmes, and many of the designs it issued were defective – the latter sometimes the mistakes of naval architects and draftsmen. There were few engineering officers in the old Navy from the South compared to the other officers, and the proportion of engineers from civilian life was at least ten to one in favour of the North. As the war progressed, the Confederate Navy's engineering improvisations were increasingly made by less and less experienced engineers.

The Chief Surgeon of the Navy was Surgeon-in-Charge W A W Spotswood, who headed the Office of Medicine and Surgery from 1861 to 1865. He was responsible for purchasing medicine and medical supplies and other medical department duties as assigned by the Navy Department. Spotswood also supervised hospitals, surgeons, and the health of naval personnel. In 1864, the Office of Medicine and Surgery issued *Instructions for the Guidance of the Medical Officers of the Navy*, which contained information on such things as diet and hospital routine.

Medical officers consisted of surgeons, passed assistant surgeons, assistant surgeons, and, after December 1861, assistant surgeons for the war. All the surgeons and most of the assistant surgeons were from the old Navy. Medical officers served on staffs, at naval hospitals and stations, at recruiting stations, in the field with marines, and aboard ship. Their battle stations aboard

The *Instructions for The Guidence of Medical Officers* directed naval surgeons in the proper medical practices ashore and afloat. (National Archives)

INSTRUCTIONS

FOR

THE GUIDANCE

OF

THE MEDICAL OFFICERS

OF THE

NAVY OF THE CONFEDERATE STATES.

RICHMOND:
MACFARLANE & FERGUSSON, PRINTERS.
1864.

ship were usually in the wardroom, where they stood ready with instruments, bandages, and drugs. They defended the spirit ration aboard ship as a medical measure.

Medical journals, kept by surgeons, were upon request submitted to the Office of Medicine and Surgery. Anchorage in swamp areas resulted in outbreaks of malaria and yellow fever. Officers who were chronically ill were sent home and required to report at intervals to the Navy Department. Medical officers treated sailors on sick call and sent them back, removed them from duty or sent them to a hospital – located at Norfolk, Richmond, Wilmington, Charleston, Savannah, Mobile and Pensacola. Medical officers also made practical recommendations for improvements in their patients' health.

A substantial cache of Union medicines was captured with the fall of the Norfolk Navy Yard, while others were concocted in Chief Surgeon Spotswood's office in Richmond. Attached to the office was Purveyor Robert Lecky (1863–5), a chemist and apothecary. Spotswood was proud of the mixing of such items as sulphuric acid, opiates, and iodine by Lecky and his two assistants. In addition, a few drugs were imported through the blockade. As a result, the Navy, unlike the Army, had a substantial amount of medicines. Evidence also suggests that patients, including Union prisoners, were given the best care available in a blockaded country. Hospitals were given special food allowances. In the naval hospital at Savannah, for example, patients ate better food than those whose meals were consumed in the surgeon's mess. Surgeons always encouraged fresh fruits and vegetables, especially in ports.

Fiscal agents of the Navy were referred to as paymasters. They were members of the Office of Provisions and Clothing. In charge of the bureau was Paymaster John DeBree, (1861–4) and then Paymaster James A Semple (1864–5). Both had seen US Navy service. DeBree was old and increasingly dependent upon Semple (son-in-law of former President John Tyler), who was admired and competent, and who had control over the Confederate treasure before some of it disappeared in April 1865.

All the original paymasters had been pursers in the old Navy, and were assigned to major stations and staffs. They sometimes had assistants, none of whom had prior naval service. In order for a civilian to be commissioned an assistant paymaster, the applicant had to be twenty-one years old, prove he could keep a ship's books, present letters of character reference, and pass an examination before a board of paymasters. Promotion was by seniority, and both ranks had to be bonded. A paymaster ranked with lieutenant. A third grade was clerk to a paymaster, an appointed, not a commissioned, officer. He ranked with a midshipman and had to be eighteen years old. The clerk was appointed by and dismissed by the captain on recommendation of the paymaster.

Paymasters requisitioned, safeguarded, and paid out money to naval personnel, and, where there were no naval agent or storekeeper, they paid naval contractors. They procured, stored, maintained, accounted for, and issued food, clothing, and 'small stores' – jackknives, needles, tobacco, spices, and other items of personal use. Paymasters resisted the daily spirit ration (under control of the master) for financial reasons. The paymaster's funds were retained in an iron strongbox and they had other containers for books and accounts. The battle station of paymasters was in their offices where they were available to open storerooms for repairs.[36]

'Of course he's not a sailor – he's just a sea-going clerk.' This comment about a paymaster was from Lieutenant Waddell, the commander of the *Shenandoah*, as he went over his list of officers.[37] Yet much credit is due the initiative and ingenuity of navy paymasters, for in spite of severe shortages, they were successful in furnishing provisions and stores.[38]

Confederate naval officers scored some notable successes during the war. Probably the most outstanding was the destruction of Federal commerce on the high seas, a Southern equivalent of the Union land march through Georgia and the Carolinas. The flamboyant cutting-out expeditions against the Federals in home waters set an example for action within the Navy and provided a needed boost to naval and civilian morale. Several officers made significant contributions in naval procurement abroad and toward advanced naval technology at home. Despite some misgivings about resigning from the US Navy, they were as a group fiercely loyal to the Confederate Navy. Buchanan, for example, had attempted without success to withdraw his resignation, yet the Confederacy's senior admiral constantly desired action during the war and was wounded twice.[39] The South's naval officers did well notwithstanding tremendous handicaps and odds.

Dr Royce Shingleton

Chapter Seven

SEAMEN, LANDSMEN, FIREMEN AND COAL HEAVERS

Recruitment

The recruits 'are certainly a very different class of men from those I selected', wrote Lieutenant John Taylor Wood of the men sent from General John B Magruder's command at Yorktown for transfer to the CSS *Virginia*. Wood, a grandson of Zachary Taylor and naval aide to Jefferson Davis (Wood's uncle), had identified a major recruitment problem for the Navy – misfits sent by lesser Army officers. Wood complained: 'I find that but two of the men selected by myself were sent; the others are men that I did not see, nor even visit their encampment.'[1] The cause of this dilemma was a dearth of trained seamen in the South. The region had an abundance of naval brass, but there had been hardly any enlisted men from the South in the US Navy or the Northern merchant marine and scant Southern maritime commerce from which to draw sailors.

While most of the Confederate Navy's enlisted personnel came from the Army, recruiting stations, called naval rendezvous, were set up in the traditional way in seaport cities. Each rendezvous usually had a sea officer, surgeon, and two or three junior officers. They advertized in newspapers and with posters. Rendezvous were established in Richmond, Norfolk, Raleigh, Savannah, Macon, Mobile and New Orleans. A potential recruit could be as young as fourteen, but those below twenty-one had to have parental consent. The recruiters used (if available) printed forms called shipping articles to record basic information on the applicant, who was also examined by the medical officer. Because Southerners paid little attention to the Navy, early in 1862 a

bounty of fifty dollars was offered to any recruit enlisting for three years or the duration. Men transferred from Army camps were treated the same as those recruited by a naval rendezvous.

The enlistment ratings were seaman, ordinary seaman, coal heaver, fireman second class, landsman and boy. The highest rating for the common sailor was petty officer, but applicants were not accepted above the rank of seaman. If the recruit was a former petty officer, his previous experience was recorded but he had to work his way up once on station. The rate of seaman required the

Recruitment notice in the *Savannah Evening Mail*, May-June 1861. (National Archives)

WANTED,

FOR THE NAVY OF THE CONFEDERATE STATES,

200 ABLE-BODIED SEAMEN

Ordinary Seamen and Landsmen.

RATES OF PAY.

Seamen (per month)	$18
Ordinary Seamen (per month)	14
Landsmen do	12

Four cents per day allowed in addition, for Grog

D. MANIGAULT MORRIS, C. S. Navy.

Confederate sailor on shore duty at Manassas Junction, 1861.
(*Harper's Weekly*)

The youngest applicants, those between ages fourteen and seventeen, shipped as boys.[2]

Free blacks could serve provided the local squadron commander or the Navy Department approved, and slaves served with their masters' approval. It was stipulated that no unit could number in excess of five per cent black. Figures on blacks are lacking, but there are occasional references to them by participants, and it is certain that some of them served in such capacities as coal heavers, officers' stewards, and also as skilled tidewater pilots. The most famous and mercurial black to serve the Confederate Navy was Moses Dallas. From Duval County, Florida he initially entered the US Navy as a pilot in 1863 and that year deserted to the Confederate Navy. Dallas earned praise and high pay for his effectiveness as a pilot of the Savannah Squadron. On the night of June 2-3, 1864 he was officially listed as killed in a Confederate attack that captured the USS *Water Witch* at the mouth of the Ogeechee River. The Confederate Navy paid for his funeral. Three months later, however, Dallas turned up in the 128th US Colored Infantry. After the war, Moses Dallas returned to Duval County. If there were two men by the same name, they also hailed from the same place.

On April 16, 1862 the first draft law passed by the Confederate Congress provided that trained seamen in the Army could apply for transfer to the Navy. On October 2, 1862 another act permitted men who were subject to the military draft to enlist in the Navy. The Army resisted losing men because of their own manpower shortage, but calls upon the Army were necessary. On May 1, 1863 a stronger law provided that the Navy Department could demand seamen or ordinary seamen from the Army who desired transfer. In spite of these laws, reluctant Army commanders allowed only a small trickle of men to the Navy. The largest single transfer took place on March 22, 1864 to compensate for the recent (February 17, 1864) general military conscription law when 960 (of the 1,200 ordered) were shifted from the Army to the Navy. By this time, some fine sailors came from the Army because of the law that allowed the Navy Department to request specific transfers. Yet the South's short supply of sailors caused the Navy to take an increasing number of landsmen from the Army to bring its ranks to a bare minimum.

It was much easier to obtain crews for the high seas cruisers; many of these men were recruited in foreign ports. The chief obstacle was the British Foreign Enlistment Act – neutrality legislation that prohibited recruitment by belligerents within the empire. There were enough enticements for service on the

applicant to have at least two years' experience at sea, and those shipped as ordinary seaman must have had at least a year of sea service. In addition to the recruit with sea experience, enrolling officers also eagerly sought a landsman if he had a needed trade.

commerce destroyers, however, to cause evasion of the law, such as men leaving port as 'passengers' and formally joining the crew once on the high seas. Vessels fitted out to cruise against commerce also held out to the men the excitement of adventure and the expectation of prize money. These men would be paid in gold and they were unlikely to see combat.

Cruisers, such as the CSS *Florida,* that at some point were in a Confederate port had many Southerners in their crews, unlike those that were never in a Southern port, such as the CSS *Alabama,* which had Southern officers and foreign crews. Lieutenant John Newland Maffitt, commander of the *Florida,* ran the blockade into Mobile in spectacular fashion to obtain a crew and equipment. With difficulty he assembled a crew of some one hundred men, many of them from among the soldiers of Fort Morgan and foreigners from the merchant service. Maffitt wrote that they came on board 'in driblets – many rated as seamen who in the old service would merely pass as very ordinary, ordinary seamen.'[3] The commando officer, John Taylor Wood (see below), had begun to hand-pick his men. As commander of the CSS *Tallahassee* (the avenger of the *Alabama*), Wood sailed from Wilmington in August 1864 with a select crew of 120 officers and men from the James River Squadron. The *Alabama* had a multinational crew. Captain Raphael Semmes noted that his command consisted of English, Dutch, Irish, French, Italian and Spanish sailors. These vessels were also notable for gathering recruits from among the prisoners taken on board from prizes. Many crewmen came aboard the CSS *Shenandoah* in an unusual manner to avoid the enlistment prohibition. The commander, Lieutenant James I Waddell, accepted forty-five stowaways after clearing Melbourne, Australia. Fourteen mysteriously appeared from the hollow bowsprit (where they almost suffocated), twenty more from dry water tanks, and the remainder from the lower hold. When assembled before Waddell, the old sea dogs claimed to be natives of the Confederacy, although they were mostly Englishmen, Scotsmen and Irish. Later at sea, Waddell enlisted a few Hawaiians from among prisoners.

The Confederate Navy's total enlisted strength probably did not exceed 4,500 men during the war (compared with 51,500 sailors in the US Navy) and at no time did the Confederate Navy number over perhaps 4,000 enlisted men. Counting officers, the Confederate Navy numbered about 5,000, so that the Federals outnumbered the Confederates approximately ten to one in naval manpower.

Of the estimated 5,000 officers and men to serve in the Confederate Navy, it is estimated that at least 845 (16.9 per cent)

Unidentified Confederate sailor. Identified photographs of Confederate sailors are extremely rare. (WMCWNH)

were of Irish birth or origin. This figure is borne out by John Kennington, who studied the muster rolls of 100 men transferred from the Army of Tennessee at Dalton, Georgia to the Savannah Squadron on March 3, 1864, and found that 16.6 per cent were of Irish birth, descent, or nationality. The Kennington study also gives the other origins of these transfers. The results are revealing in different ratings: seaman, 25 per cent English; ordinary seaman, 29.6 per cent Irish; landsman, a tie between Kentucky and Louisiana with 18.2 per cent each from those states.[4]

Training

In the Confederate Navy, personnel matters were handled in the Office of Orders and Detail. Recruits were usually sent in small groups to a receiving ship at a naval station. The receiving ships were old vessels used as naval 'boot' camps – barracks and training ships before their regular assignments. They were ready in full commission and fully rigged for training purposes. The receiving ships were the CSS *United States* at Norfolk, the CSS *Arctic* at Wilmington, the CSS *Indian Chief* at Charleston, the CSS *Sampson* at Savannah, the CSS *Dalman* at Mobile, and the CSS *St. Philip* at New Orleans. The descriptive list with name, place of rendezvous, period of enlistment, age, place of birth, complexion, height, colour, rating, trade, marks and scars, special qualifications, and record of service as a petty officer, accompanied each man. The

paymaster forwarded copies of the descriptive list to the Navy Department.

On the receiving ship the recruit received the rudiments of seamanship. Along with a set of clothing, he was given what training the ship could offer, including drill on large and small guns, working sails and pulling boats. Astute men also learned something of discipline and a knowledge of naval lore and customs from the small cadre of officers and petty officers who served as

instructors. Most of the training occurred later, when the men reached their permanent assignments. Recruits were eager to leave the receiving ship because they were not given liberty without approval of the station commander.

When a ship's captain needed replacements, he sent a request through his squadron commander, who forwarded consolidated requests to the commanding officer of the station. He in turn ordered recruits from the receiving ship, if available, otherwise he requested the Office of Orders and Detail to order replacements from a station having sailors. To crew a new ship, the station commander specified the number of men of each rating he wanted. The Office of Orders and Detail corrected and approved the list before ordering the station commander to assign the men from his receiving ship. Commanding officers of ships were usually prohibited from hand-picking their men, but frequently requested men familiar to them from past service. In turn, men could request a specific assignment or commanding officer.

There was one advantage and one disadvantage in training the sailors. Most of the ships were steam-driven so that learning to work sails was not critical. This was especially true of the river and harbor craft of the home squadrons (the crews of high seas cruisers, which used a combination of steam and sail, were often foreigners who had experience with guns and sails). On the other hand, the Navy had a habit of shifting sailors from one command to another as needed. Threats of Union attack along coasts and rivers caused transfers from port to port. The practice continued until the war's end despite commanders' repeated protests. Soldiers who transferred from one command to another usually carried along their equipment; but ships' guns varied greatly as did their engines. Hence reassigned sailors often had to be retrained.

The Confederate adaptation of the US Navy's *Ordnance Instructions* was the training guide book on the South's warships. Each recruit was assigned to one of five combat divisions. Each officer and petty office was in charge of a specific area or task when ready for battle at general quarters, and trained the crew daily in assigned duties. The great object was to prepare the crew to work together for battle.

The master's division kept the ship underway, which including steering and (if needed) rigging. The boatswain, quartermasters, the captains of the afterguard and forecastle, and the ship's cook belonged to this division. They stowed hammocks and battened hatches (to prevent leakage), distributed small arms, filled fire buckets, furnished drinking water to all stations, dropped the boats astern, took soundings, readied grapnels, put in place a spare tiller and compass and secured chronometers and navigation instruments from battle damage. Most of the men around the ship's commanding officer on the quarterdeck belonged to this division, including the helmsman.

Confederate naval battery at Manassas Junction, 1861. (*Harper's Weekly*)

The engineer's division consisted of the engineers, firemen and coal heavers. They operated the ship's engines and repaired any damage. The chief engineer took personal command in the engine room, while his assistants and crew operated on watches, with four to six men on each boiler and engine. Heat was a problem here, especially in summer. With temperatures rising to 150°F, a five-minute rotation of men took place during battle. Off-duty sailors went into fire-fighting or repair parties, or augmented gun crews. Conversly, men could be drafted from some of the other divisions to augment the engineer's division, if needed. The executive officer (first lieutenant or 'luff') had the authority to shift men from one assignment to another on board the ship.

The surgeon's division set up the surgery in a place designated by the ship's commander; usually it was located in the wardroom. The surgeon and his assistants prepared to receive the wounded with medical instruments, bandages and drugs. The surgeon also issued tourniquets to the gun quarters for emergency use.

Gun divisions, each with one heavy pivot gun or as many as six smaller guns, were in charge of a lieutenant and his midshipman assistants. Most of the emphasis aboard ship was put on drilling with the guns in the home squadrons (less so by the cruiser captains), and occasionally seamen practised with live ammunition. An individual gun crew was overseen by a sailor with the rank of petty officer and title of first gun captain. A crew varied from eleven on a smooth-bore 32pdr to twenty-seven for a large pivot rifle. At battle stations, the gun crews spread sand on the deck to improve traction and absorb blood, placed supply boxes nearby that contained waist belts with leather fittings, and equipment for the guns. When all was ready the captain of the ship gave the order to cast loose the guns. The heavy guns had to be manhandled forward by rope and tackle after every recoil. Gun divisions also supplied men for boarding parties, which included all the petty officers and most of the best seamen. Other gunners were detailed as pikemen to repel boarders and, equipped with buckets, as firefighters. Gunners also might be designated to help the carpenter's mates man the pumps.

The powder division, commanded by a lieutenant along with the gunner and his mates, was closely associated with the gun divisions. At general quarters, the powder crew covered magazine openings with wet canvas screens and before entering the magazines divested themselves of metal objects and donned all-cotton smocks, pants and shoes. The division officer sent orders from the deck designating projectiles and charges. The gunner remained in the main magazine and the mates took position in the smaller

powder and shot rooms. Immature powder boys, who carried powder from the magazine openings to the guns, made this work even more dangerous. In case of fire, the gunner and his mates flooded the ammunition rooms. In addition to supplying ammunition and supplies to each gun, the powder division also aided the carpen-

Confederate sailor. (*Battles & Leaders*)

ter's crew in repairing hull damage, helped to move the wounded, and supplied men for boarding parties.

A drum beat signalled general quarters. If the gunners were to cast loose their guns, a single roll of the drum followed the beat; if magazines were to be opened two rolls followed the beat. A rattle called away boarders, and a gong sounded for pikemen. A ringing bell was the fire alarm. At each signal, the boatswain and his mates gave verbal orders throughout the ship, while the master-at-arms and ship's corporals patrolled for shirkers on the lower decks.

A vivid description of a crew readied for engagement has been recorded by a participant. The setting is aboard the CSS *Arkansas*, where the crew had levelled their guns with a spirit-level in order to fire directly without elevation as they prepared to face, among others, the USS *Carondelet* on the Yazoo River in July 1862.

Confederate battle rattle. The rattle was used to call designated sailors to the spar deck prior to boarding an enemy ship. Used in conjunction with the gong, it was the call for all hands to repel boarders. (WMCWNH)

> As it is now daylight, let me describe the scene on a man-of-war's deck, cleared for action, or at least that man-of-war, on that occasion. Many of the men had stripped off their shirts and were bare to the waists, with handkerchiefs bound round their heads, and some of the officers had removed their coats and stood in their undershirts. The decks had been thoroughly sanded to prevent slipping after the blood should become plentiful. Tourniquets were served out to division officers by the surgeons, with directions for use. The division tubs were filled with water to drink; fire buckets were in place; cutlasses and pistols strapped on; rifles loaded and bayonets fixed; spare breechings for the guns, and other implements made ready. The magazines and shell-rooms forward and aft were open, and the men inspected in their places. Before getting under way, coffee (or an apology therefor) had been served to the crew, and daylight found us a grim, determined set of fellows, grouped about our guns, anxiously waiting to get sight of the enemy.[5]

'Serve vent and sponge' was the prescribed first order for firing a ship's gun. The first gun captain, standing near the breech, gave this and other orders for loading, aiming and firing under the direction of division officers or the ship's captain. The second gun captain, positioned near the breech on the opposite side, stepped forward and placed a thumbstall over the vent to seal it while two crewmen called sponger and loader rammed a dampened wool sponge on a rod through the muzzle to clean the barrel.

The gun captain then ordered 'charge with cartridge'. The powder man then handed the loader a cartridge in the form of a woollen bag filled with powder: red for short range, white for medium range, and blue for long range. (The pass boxes carried by the powder men corresponded to the colour of the cartridge.) The

sponger and loader rammed the charge through the muzzle to the proper depth at the breech. The depth was determined by paint on the rammer for each type of cartridge, and by the gun captain who inserted his primary wire into the vent to touch the charge. The rammer was removed when he said 'home'.

'Charge with shot' was the next order. Two shot men now approached the muzzle, one from either side, and inserted the shot or shell. The sponger and loader pushed the projectile to a painted line on the rammer and said 'home'. The gun captain then uttered 'run out', whereupon two port tackle men, distanced on each side of the muzzle, opened the gun port shutters. Two side tackle men, distanced on either side of the breech, pulled their lines to roll the gun forward to deck chocks, and tied off temporarily with a half hitch. If needed, the next command was 'point'. Two handpike men positioned outside the gun captain at the breech stood ready to shift the gun carriage right or left until the order 'well' came from the gun captain. 'Prime' then rang out, and the second captain moved to the breech and pushed his primary wire through the vent and punched a hole in the powder bag. The first captain then inserted a primer into the vent and stretched the lanyard rearward for a better sight angle over the barrel. 'Ready', ordered the gun captain, holding a clinched fist above his head as a signal that all was ready. The side tackle men pulled away their half hitches, two train tackle men, standing well to the rear of the piece, pulled their lines taunt. The sponger and loader looked away from the muzzle. All the gun crew, except the first captain, covered their ears.

'Fire' was the order that almost everything else in the Navy was designed to accomplish. The gun captain gave the order and pulled the lanyard. Upon firing, the piece recoiled to the length predetermined by the length of the tackle lines. Firing continued approximately every five minutes, except when the enemy was near, then the division officer would order 'quick fire,' in which case the charge and projectile were rammed home in one motion. Finally came the command 'secure.' This ended the action and the gun was cleaned and implements returned to storage. The gunner and his mates then coated the barrel with tallow.[6]

SKELETON WATCH BILL

FOR A SCREW STEAMER OF THE THIRD CLASS, ARMED WITH TWO XI-Inch GUNS AND FOUR 32-Pdrs. OF 57-Cwt. EACH.

STATIONS	CAPTAINS	COXSWAINS	SEAMEN	ORDINARY SEAMEN	LANDSMEN	BOYS	OTHER PETTY OFFICERS TO KEEP WATCH	PETTY OFFICERS, IDLERS	FIREMEN	COALHEAVERS	TOTAL
Forecastlemen	1	1	5	4	1	...	...	...	...	...	12
Foremastmen.............	...	...	...	2	...	...	...	...	...	...	2
Foretopmen	1	1	4	4	2	...	...	...	...	...	12
Mainmastmen	...	...	2	...	...	...	...	...	...	...	2
Maintopmen	1	1	5	4	1	...	...	...	...	...	12
After Guard	2	...	...	6	10	...	...	...	...	...	18
Messenger & Sideboys	...	...	...	...	...	4	...	...	...	...	4
Petty Officers	...	...	...	...	...	...	11	9	...	...	20
Firemen	...	...	...	...	...	...	...	...	14	...	14
Coalheavers	...	...	...	...	...	...	...	...	...	14	14
Total of each grade	5	3	16	20	14	4	11	9	14	14	110

ENGINE WATCH BILL.

To be similar, in every respect, to those already mentioned, reducing the number of Firemen and Coalheavers so as to correspond with the above allowance.

Conditions of service

Unlike the Civil War soldier, the sailor fought a comparatively safe conflict. The seaman's view of battle action was often limited to what he could see through a gunport. The enemy was frequently a dot on the horizon. Confederate seamen served mainly on river and harbor craft that had some kind of protection, such as iron, or iron-reinforced wood, or even cotton bales. Fighting was methodical. He repeated the functions of his battle station. Unless struck directly by the enemy, the main problem for the crewman was choking smoke and deafening noise. But at close range, an accurate shot from a large smoothbore, or 'bolt' from a rifled cannon, might penetrate any but the heaviest armour. Flying splinters of wood and iron then became missiles of destruction, while a shot that hit the boilers could scald men in the interior of the ship.

When trouble came it could be terrible, as the following scene on the CSS *Tennessee* described by the duty surgeon attests.

> For an hour and a half the monitors pounded us with solid shot, fired with a charge of sixty pounds of powder from their eleven-inch guns, determined to crush in the shield of the *Tennessee*, as thirty pounds of powder was the regulation amount. In the midst of this continuous pounding, the port-shutter of one of our guns was jammed by a shot, so that it could neither open nor shut, making it impossible to work the piece. The admiral [Franklin Buchanan] then sent for some of the firemen from below, to drive the bolt outward. Four men came up, and two of them holding the bolt back, the others struck it with sledgehammers. While they were thus standing there, suddenly there was a dull sounding impact, and at the same instant the men whose backs were against the shield were split in pieces. I saw their limbs and chests, severed and mangled, scattered about the deck, their hearts lying near their bodies. All of the gun's crew and the admiral were covered from head to foot with blood, flesh and viscera. I thought at first that the admiral was mortally wounded. The fragments and members of the dead men were shoveled up, put in buckets and hammocks and struck below.[7]

Good men who wanted more than the infrequent naval battle action might find excitement as part of a cutting-out expedition. This was essentially a commando raid in the sense that it acquired in the Second World War against an enemy ship. Many of these

A skeleton watch bill for a gunboat crew from Regulations for the Confederate Navy. (National Archives)

raids took place during the war, and it is doubtful, considering the routine of naval life, that such raids adversely affected the man-power needs of the Navy. Commander John Taylor Wood, believing the Navy was too inactive, became the South's leading coastal raider, and the men chosen for temporary assignment under him knew they were destined for bold action – or what the seamen termed 'nervous work'.

Wood's raid in February 1864 against Union-held New Bern, North Carolina was the most notable of the war. Designed as a naval support element of an unsuccessful land assault by Confederate land forces to retake the port town, the naval portion of this expedition was successful in capturing and destroying the gunboat USS *Underwriter* in the estuary at New Bern near Pamlico Sound. Hand-picked crews, fully armed, equipped and provisioned, reported from Richmond, Wilmington and Charleston for special service duty at Kinston, the point of rendezvous up the Neuse River from New Bern. The strike force, of some 285 officers and men, including at least twenty-five marines, descended the Neuse in boats. Until this time the seamen had been told neither the object nor destination of their mission, and they now knew the mission would involve hand-to-hand fighting and they would capture the enemy or be destroyed.

Pouring sheets of rain drenched the raiders as they drew near their target in the night-time attack. An alert watchman aboard the *Underwriter* hailed the approaching boats. The rattle was sprung to alert the crew; the ship would have to be boarded with the crew armed and at quarters. Since further caution was useless, the oarsmen sent the boats forward at top speed. The Federals opened on the raiders with destructive rifle fire. Wood's coxswain, a brawny Virginian, met a fate both sudden and heroic. With the tiller between his knees and a pistol in each hand as he urged the men on, he fell dead on the oarsmen with a ball in his forehead. The bowmen threw the grappling hooks and the oarsmen made the climb with the flashes of small arms in their faces. As each came up, he selected and rushed his man amid wild yells of impassioned voices. Soon the deck was slippery with rain and blood. Fighting became general across the deck and within a few minutes the raiders forced the enemy down the companionways and into the ward room, steerage and coal bunker. The 325-ton gunboat was now a prize.

The Confederates learned that steam was low and the fires banked on the *Underwriter* so they could not get under way as a cruiser as planned. Worse still, Federal shore batteries now opened on the vessel, turning the prize into a trap. Wood set the ship

Night attack on USS *Underwriter*. (*The Confederate Soldier in the Civil War*)

ablaze and escaped with twenty-six prisoners. He lost five killed, fifteen wounded and four missing. The boarding cutters bore the marks of heavy fire; the wooden plugs inserted averaged fourteen to each boat, evidence of one of the most arduous cutting-out expeditions in history.[8]

Another potential danger for seamen was the failure of the ship's power plant. Engines were often improvised from whatever parts could be obtained from other ships. (Engines were also placed in pre-designed ships instead of starting with the engine and then designing the hull, steering controls, guns, armour, living quarters and storage spaces in conformity to the power plant.) This practice often resulted in inadequate engines that, along with poorly-trained engineers, led to the overtaxing of the plant during battle. A resulting engine breakdown could leave the ship at the mercy of the enemy.

Another power plant malfunction, which could be costly in human lives, was the boiler explosion. On May 27, 1863 the war's worse engineering malfunction took place on the gunboat CSS *Chattahoochee* near Blountstown, Florida, some fifty miles below Columbus, Georgia. An order to raise steam initiated an argument in the engine room over the amount of water in the boiler. The fireman on watch had allowed his boiler, which was red hot, to become empty. The voices attracted the pilot, William B Bilbro, who should have stayed away, and the chief engineer, Henry Fagan, who had just descended the engine room ladder as Bilbro admitted water to the boiler.[9] Steam flashed to great pressure inside the boiler and it exploded. Scalded men ran about the deck in great pain. Then a gunner warned of the danger from the powder magazine which was only three feet from the boiler. This sent many crewmen over the sides where three drowned. A total of eighteen were killed by scalding or drowning. Lieutenant George W Gift Wrote: 'The ship has sunk to her decks, her large supply of ammunition is all lost. I shall get her guns out as soon as possible'.[10]

Engineering was a great weakness in the Confederate Navy. Deficiencies in training cost the Confederacy more ships than any other cause except grounding. The South had furnished few engineers in the pre-war Navy, especially among the rank and file. Enlisted ranks were fireman first class, fireman second class, and coal heaver. They usually had no particular skills but were paid more than deck hands because of the dangerous and unattractive nature of their duties. Those who entered the Navy as firemen usually had some experience with steamboats, locomotives or sawmills. Otherwise, firemen came from the landsmen aboard ship who had previously volunteered for duty as coal heavers. Divided into watches, firemen managed fires with different fuels: anthracite and bituminous coal, various kinds of wood, and 'quick heat' additives such as pine and pork extracts. They were expected to be familiar with tools to maintain and repair machinery except for broken cylinders, valves, or shafts which were usually replaced by the naval works at Columbus or Charlotte.

Living conditions for seamen received scant attention in ship design. Life aboard the ironclads was especially harsh. There was little opportunity for exercise and the men became soft and subject to pulmonary diseases. Over twenty per cent of the men at a given time were usually sick. The berth areas were poorly ventilated (there is no evidence that blowers were ever fitted), and hands choked on noxious gas from the boilers. Dampness, heat, and cold were retained by tons of iron that enclosed the vessel. They were leaky as well and in winter ice covered the decks. By mid-war, crews began to eat and sleep in warehouses or tents ashore, or in another ship such as a tender or receiving ship.

On the ironclad *Tennessee* in Mobile Bay in August 1864, Surgeon Daniel B Conrad noted that the crew had been uncomfortable for many rainy weeks waiting for battle. The wet, hot atmosphere brought on 'that oppressiveness which precedes a tornado'. It was impossible to eat below because of the heat and humidity. 'Intense thirst universally prevailed.' The men took their hardtack and coffee standing, soon 'creeping out of the ports on the after deck to get a little fresh air'. It was impossible to sleep inside and, with the decks wet at night, the crew became 'desper-

ate'. Everyone looked forward to the impending action which, regardless of the outcome, would provide 'a positive feeling of relief'.[11]

Men on the ironclads not only experienced poor living conditions, but received less pay than crewmen on the commerce destroyers. Crewmen in the home squadrons also suffered the ravages of inflation within their structural pay scale. A sailor's pay account, administered through the Office of Provision and Clothing, contained his enlistment date, term, promotions, payments to him, any advances, and any credit for abstaining from the spirit ration. (A few cents a day credit if he did not take his half-pint.) Commanders could withhold up to three months' pay if they suspected desertion, and a sailor's pay was withheld if he owed the Government. There was an allotment system and naval agents provided tickets for travel but if a sailor died only the Secretary of the Navy or fleet commander could sanction the funeral at Government expense.

Personal effects and clothing were sent home only if the deceased was free of debt to the government, otherwise the items were sold at auction. If a sailor was disabled in battle, he could receive half pay (full pay after February 17, 1864 if able to qualify for limited duty in the Invalid Corps). When a sailor's term of enlistment ended, he could re-enlist and receive three months' bonus.

Pay for enlisted personnel generally followed the scale of the US Navy. The monthly pay scale for Confederate sailors listed below is from the *CS Navy Register, 1863* [12] (the South had no large fighting ships such as frigates).

	$
Yeomen	
In ships-of-the-line	49
In frigates	44
In sloops	34
In smaller vessels	28
Armorers	
In ships-of-the-line	34
In frigates	29
In sloops	24
Mates	
Master's (not warranted)	29
Boatswain's	29
Gunner's	29
Carpenter's	29
Sailmaker's	24
Armourer's	24

Masters-at-Arms	29
Ship's Corporals	24
Coxswains	28
Quartermasters	28
Quarter Gunners	24
Captains	
Of forecastle	28
Of tops	24
Of afterguard	24
Of hold	24
Coopers	24
Painters	24
Stewards	24
Ship's	34
Officer's	24
Surgeon's	28
Cooks	
Ship's	28
Officer's	24
Masters of the Band	24
Musicians	
First Class	19
Second Class	16
Seamen	22
Ordinary Seamen	18
Landsmen	16
Boys	12, 13 & 14
Firemen	
First class	34
Second class	29
Coal-Heavers	22

Pay was insufficient, in inflated greenbacks, and often in arrears. Robert Watson, one of the 100 men transferred directly from the Army of Tennessee on March 3, 1864, shipped as an ordinary seaman on board the ironclad CSS *Savannah*. Watson, one of the more literate sailors, performed various writing chores aboard ship, including writing letters for his shipmates, and kept a diary. Watson confirmed that, as ordinary seaman, his pay was eighteen dollars a month but he must have drawn advances because when the crew was paid on May 10, 1864 he recorded in his diary: 'I got no money and don't expect to get any for the next six months for it takes all my wages to pay for my soap and tobacco. Soap is $7.30 per bar and tobacco is $3.00 per lb.' He contin-

ued that 'some of the men have been on board over a year and this is the first time they have drawn any money and none of them drew over $30.00 Some did not draw a cent.'[13]

Petty officers

The two main categories within the enlisted ranks were petty officers and seamen (those below petty officer were generally called seamen regardless of their pay grade). The petty officer rating was temporary and easily lost. Promotion came from within to fill the needs of the ship. Although no one transferred as a petty officer, commanders received descriptive lists of men who could be promoted. Only master's mates, boatswain's mates, gunner's mates, coxswains, quartermasters, quarter gunners, and captains of tops and holds succeeded to command positions. Another distinction among petty officers was a priority system according to their duties.

The following list of petty officers is arranged in descending order of rank.[14]

Master's Mate - Concerned with seamanship, basically an officer candidate.

Master-at-arms - In charge of prisoners and ship discipline.

Yeoman - Responsible for the storage and issue of ship's provisions.

Surgeon's Steward - Assisted the medical officer and was expected to have some knowledge of pharmacy.

Ship's Corporal - Assisted the master-at-arms.

Armourer - Maintained small arms aboard ship.

Cooper - Made and repaired containers such as barrels and casks.

Ship's Cook - Prepared meals for the crew.

Boatswain's Mate - Handled deck rigging.

Gunner's Mate - Kept the guns and ammunition.

Carpenter's Mate - Made wood repairs on the ship and checked for leakage.

Sailmaker's Mate - In charge of the ship's canvas.

Coxswain to the Squadron Commander - Responsible for the flag officer's boat.

Quartermaster - Assistant to master's mate; steered the ship.

Quarter Gunner - Assistant to gunner's mate.

Coxswain - In charge of a boat.

Captains of Tops and Holds - Responsible for rigging or storerooms in certain parts of the ship.

Fireman First Class - Expected to have the ability to run engines without the engineer.

Painter - Mixed and issued paint.

Steward to Squadron Commander - Served meals, cleaned cabin, maintained uniforms.

Armourer's Mate - Assistant to armourer.

Cabin Steward - Served ship's commander.

Wardroom Steward - Served the officers.

Cabin Cook - Prepared meals for the commanding officer.

Wardroom Cook - Prepared meals for lesser officers.

Insignia for petty officers to be worn on their uniforms were authorized by the Confederate Government's office of Adjutant and Inspector General. Regulations prescribed a foul anchor (not more than 3in in length) embroidered in black silk on the sleeve of their gray jackets above the elbow and in front. In summer, a blue foul anchor was to be worn on the sleeve of their white frocks. Boatswain's mates, gunner's mates, carpenter's mates, sail-maker's mates, ship's stewards and ship's cook were to wear the insignia on their right sleeve and most of the others on the left sleeve.[15] Few, if any, petty officers seem to have actually worn the insignia because neither known photographs nor records reveal any symbol of rank. This may be due to the frequent turnover in the Confederate Navy or the small crews on Confederate vessels.

Uniforms and equipage

Confederate tars had adequate clothing most of the time. Paymasters of the Office of Provisions and Clothing initially clothed the few hundred navy men in blue from stores captured in 1861 at Norfolk and Pensacola. When Congress authorized expansion to 3,000 men late in 1861, Secretary Mallory sent naval agents to Europe to purchase uniforms and still the emphasis was on the traditional navy blue.[16] Men on the cruisers were better dressed because of easier access to uniforms abroad. An Englishman who shipped on the cruiser CSS *Nashville* in 1861 described his first uniform: 'I wore a blue woollen shirt open at the neck, a black silk handkerchief, with ample flowing ends, tied loosely around the neck; blue trousers made very tight at the knee and twenty-two inches in circumference at the bottom, and on my head a flat cloth cap ornamented with long black ribbons.' In his sea-chest, the sailor had a pea jacket, sea boots, and underclothes.[17]

'Jack Tar' was to receive clothing upon entry into the Navy and after that a clothing allowance for replacement of garments.

Confederate sailor's cap. (WMCWNH)

Regulation issued by the Office of Adjutant and Inspector General in 1861 called for winter uniforms of gray cloth jackets and trousers (or gray woollen frocks with white duck cuffs and collars), and black hats. In summer, white frocks and trousers and black or white hats were to be worn. The collars and cuffs were to be lined with blue cotton cloth. In all seasons, the neckerchiefs (silk) and shoes (or boots in very cold weather) were to be black. Thick gray caps could usually be worn at sea, except at muster.[18]

By 1863 the Navy Department had printed a circular that gave the cost and quantity of clothing to be issued.[19]

Each year	Article	Cost ($ per item)
1	Round jacket	10.40
2	Cloth trousers	5.94
3	Canvas duck trousers	1.82
3	Barnsley sheeting frocks	1.85
3	Flannel overshirts	3.03
3	Flannel undershirts	1.79
2	Flannel drawers	1.72
4	Pair of shoes	2.90
4	Pair of socks	0.95
2	Caps	1.51
2	Silk handkerchiefs	1.65

Every three years

1	Pea jacket	15.07
2	Blankets	3.11

A few items, such as mattresses, that the Navy was unable to issue at the time have been omitted from this list, and it is doubtful whether those listed here were issued with regularity across the Confederacy. Nor could the promised clothing allowance to maintain a sailor's sea bag be relied on, for Seaman Watson wrote that 'we are not allowed any clothing money but have to pay for everything we draw out of our wages'. While Watson seems to have been fairly well supplied (he mentioned drawing articles of clothing on different occasions, and donning a white uniform on a warm day by order of the commander), he also noted: 'Made myself a cap during the day.'[20] Sailors had long made clothing from scraps of old sail or other material. In the Confederacy it became a necessity more than a custom.

Naval agents in the Confederacy bought cloth on the open market and subsequently oversaw the manufacture of uniforms at Richmond, Savannah, and Mobile. The styles varied and by the end of 1862 some gray uniforms could be seen in the enlisted ranks; but since blue never disappeared, the end result was a variety of colours and patterns. Sailors also added civilian clothing to their uniforms, so that they resembled merchant seamen more than naval personnel.

The most serious clothing problem was lack of shoes. Footgear was now more necessary than on sailing vessels because men could hardly stand watch barefoot on steam vessels and ironclads. Uninsulated decks next to engine rooms became very hot. Ironclads in particular were a problem in winter, when a layer of ice or sleet sometimes covered the upper deck. The Navy's only shoe factory at Graniteville, South Carolina was taken over by the Army, and naval agents bought most of the shoes from England. As the problem continued, the Office of Provision and Clothing sent a pattern for useful canvas shoes (developed in 1863 by Paymaster Thomas R Ware of the Mobile Squadron) to each squadron in the hope that the makeshift footware could be locally produced.

The Navy had a routine for checking a seaman's clothing supply. The men laid their gear on the deck for inspection by the division lieutenant, who was responsible for counting each article per man and forwarding a list of deficiencies to the commanding officer. The commander could in turn order an issue of available clothing against each man's pay. Although accompanied by com-

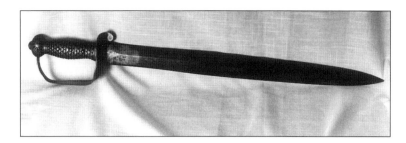

Model 1841 US Navy cutlass. A type often used by Confederate sailors and copied by several Southern manufacturers. (WMCWNH)

mendable efforts, the problem of inadequate naval clothing was apparently never solved. During the fall of 1864, crewmen of the James River Squadron stood watch on ironclads without shoes, peacoats or even blankets for warmth. Yet the seamen inside the Confederacy, while not as well clad as those serving on the high seas, were nonetheless better clothed than Southern soldiers.

Another advantage sailors had over soldiers was that seamen had no assigned hand-held weapons to maintain and carry. If the sailor did see battle, he was usually assigned to working the guns or operating the ship in ship-to-ship action. The armourer would disperse weapons in battle situations that might result in close fighting, but during the war such action was almost entirely confined to action ashore by parties carrying small arms in night patrols or cutting-out expeditions. Men were trained for boarding and defense against boarders in ship-to-ship fighting, but such action almost never took place during the Civil War.

(*Top*) A Confederate-made cutlass based on the US Model 1841, but with a wooden grip instead of the latter's distinctive brass grip and D-guard. (*Bottom*) A British cutlass captured on the privateer *Beauregard*. (WMCWNH)

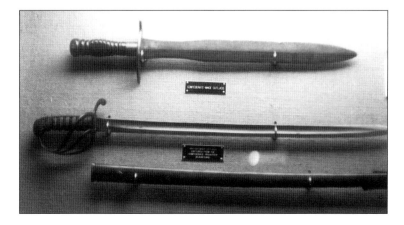

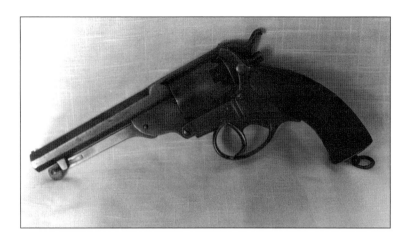

The Kerr .44 cal., five-chambered revolver, manufactured by London Armoury Company, London, England, was imported in quantity for use by the Confederate Navy. (WMCWNH)

Many of the small arms used by Confederate tars were captured Northern makes imported from England, or copies of them manufactured in the South. The model used depended greatly on where the sailor was stationed and even on his assigned ship, since there was a wide variety of models issued. A popular long arm was the Maynard (or Perry) carbine. It was fired by a conventional percussion cap, and when the trigger guard was lowered, the breech tipped upward for loading with a semi-fixed brass cartridge. It weighed about 6lb and was of .52 caliber. The other standard shoulder arm was the British Enfield rifle. Its relatively short barrel and serviceability made this general infantry weapon of the South popular among sailors. It was of .547 caliber and fired a bullet similar to the minié and could accommodate either a cutlass or sabre bayonet. This muzzle loader weighed about 9lb and was very accurate at 800 yards and fairly accurate at 1,100 yards.

The most common handgun in the Navy was probably the Colt pattern revolver. (The original Confederate naval pistol, a single-shot muzzle loader, proved too expensive to produce.) The model 1851 US Navy Colt, a .36 caliber weighing just over 2½lb, was the prototype of most revolvers made in the Confederacy. The Remington (or Whitney) or at least a Southern made copy, also saw service. This revolver was a .44 caliber that weighed nearly 3lb. The LeMat revolver made in France by the French-born Confederate J A F LeMat, was a .44 caliber nine-shot weapon that included a shotgun charge under the barrel. Other foreign-made

revolvers used by Confederate tars included the English Kerr, the English Deane and Adams, and the French-Belgium Lafeaucheaux.

The cutlass usually issued to Confederate vessels was a copy of the 1841 US Navy cutlass. This 1861 Confederate Navy cutlass was 27in long with a grip and curved hand guard of brass. There were several variants of this model, including one that was distinguished by its curved steel guard and handle of wood. A very different model had an 18½in double-edged blade and an 'S'-shaped guard. Imported models included the Courtney and Tennant pattern that was based on the English cavalry sabre; it was 20in long with a wide guard below the thumb position and double edged. Also widely used was the Enfield cutlass-bayonet, which was identical to British Navy issue and resembled the 1862 US Navy cutlass. This Enfield model was 33in long and had a slightly curved blade.[21]

Boarding pikes, used for defense against boarders, were fast becoming obsolete during the war because of the use of revolving pistols and rifles with bayonets. While rarely used, some of these weapons were nonetheless found on board Confederate vessels. Over two thousand pole arms were captured when Norfolk fell, and some were manufactured in the South. The standard length became 12ft; the blades were usually 8in long and either flat or triangular. The naval pike, unlike its land service counterpart, had a rounded butt that was not covered with iron.

The sailor's belt held carrying cases for ammunition consisting of a rifle cartridge box, a pistol cartridge box and a cap box. Made of black leather, few of these accouterments survive to the present day, and are difficult to identify as to origin. Confederates captured some of this equipment from the Norfolk, Pensacola and New Orleans shipyards. The rifle cartridge box was 7¼in by 5¾in and could hold forty rounds. The pistol box, 5in x 2½in, held sixty rounds. The cap box, 2½in by 2¼in, contained a vent pick. All three pouches were US Navy patterns. Haversacks (large canvas bags) were used to carry additional ammunition. The two most common revolver holsters were the Colt and Remington patterns, which would easily accommodate most revolvers. Both were open at the bottom and were made of black leather. The Remington pattern was nearly 8in long, while the Colt was a shorter 5½in long. Cutlass and bayonet scabbards were made of black leather or canvas and tipped with a brass or leather ferrule. The Confederate sailor had to be adaptable to master the many types and patterns that made up his battle equipment.

Dr Royce Shingleton

Chapter Eight
THE MARINES

The Act of March 16, 1861, 'To provide for the organization of the Navy,' created a Corps of Confederate States Marines in the image of the parent. Section 9 of this legislation clearly stated that 'All laws of the United States heretofore enacted for the government of the officers, seamen, and marines of the Navy of the United States, that are not inconsistent with the provisions of this act, are hereby adopted and applied to the officers, seamen, and marines of the Navy of the Confederate States.'[1] With the laws of the old service came the regulations established for the United States Marine Corps in 1852.

The 1852 rules and regulations for Marines afloat and ashore defined the role of the Corps during a period of transition. While aboard ship, Marines still provided security, in effect acting as ship's police, acted as orderlies to the commanding officer and performed ceremonial functions; their duties in battle had undergone significant changes. Marine sharpshooters who formerly practiced their deadly craft from the fighting tops of full-rigged men-of-war were no longer necessary in the mid nineteenth century steam-driven navy. Coupled with the advent of the steam engine as the major source of propulsion on the sea, the rifled gun came into vogue. Possessing effective ranges far outdistancing those of smoothbore cannon, the rifled gun rendered muzzle-to-muzzle fighting obsolete. The ability to batter an enemy without closing with him made marksmen performing their specialities from lofty perches unnecessary. Expelled from the tops by the advance of technology, Marines found new duties on the gun deck, formerly the exclusive province of the bluejackets. During the decade that preceded the Civil War, Marines were trained to man both primary and secondary batteries. Ultimately, their skills at the guns equalled those of their naval counterparts. In a letter written by 2nd Lt Ruffin Thomson in early 1864, the role played by Confederate States Marines was succinctly stated: 'The Marines are drilled in Artillery as well as Infantry tactics & in truth in their proper sphere they are simply *Naval Artillerists*,' while retaining 'their rifles, which are useful in enforcing subordination & repelling boarders . . . .'[2]

Ashore, the duties of Marines attached to the naval stations remained unchanged. Subject to the orders of the naval officer in command of an installation, the primary responsibility of Marines was to provide security for it. Further, at the direction of the President in times of civil unrest, Marines, as a nineteenth-century version of a rapid-reaction force, could be, and were called upon to snuff out any threat to public order. In the years immediately preceding the outbreak of the Civil War, US Marines were twice called upon in this capacity: on June 1, 1857, crushing an attempt by hired thugs known as 'Plug-Uglies' to disrupt elections being held in Washington, DC, and on October 17, 1859, putting down the insurrection precipitated by the abolitionist John Brown at Harpers Ferry, Virginia.

The role the Marine Corps was intended to play in the naval establishment of the Confederate States was, in consequence of the Provisional Congress appropriating the laws and regulations governing the US Marine Corps, identical. The structure, however, was somewhat different.

The Confederate States Marine Corps was initially designed as a six-company battalion commanded by a major. The staff

Colonel Lloyd J Beall, Commandant, CS Marine Corps. (Scharf, *Confederate States Navy*)

consisted of a quartermaster, a paymaster, an adjutant, a sergeant-major and a quartermaster-sergeant. Each of the six companies was to be commanded by a captain, assisted by one first and one second lieutenant. The enlisted component of the companies was four sergeants, four corporals, two musicians and one hundred men.[3] When events of the next several weeks demonstrated that the Confederacy would have to resort to force of arms to assert its independence, the numbers of the Corps were deemed insufficient to meet the exigencies of wartime service. Consequently, the battalion was increased to regimental strength.

An amendatory act, dated May 20, 1861, provided that the staff would consist of a colonel, a lieutenant colonel, a quartermaster with the rank of major, a paymaster with the rank of major, an adjutant with the rank of major, a sergeant major and a quartermaster sergeant. The line embodied a major, ten captains, ten first lieutenants, and twenty second lieutenants. The rank and file, in ten companies, were forty sergeants, forty corporals, two musicians, ten drummers, ten fifers and 840 privates.[4]

Officers of the Confederate States Marine Corps

The Staff

Colonel, Commandant

Lloyd James Beall (1808–87). Maryland. USMA, 1830. Second lieutenant, 1st US Infantry, 1830–36. First lieutenant and captain, 2nd US Dragoons, 1836–44. Major and paymaster, US Army, 1844–61. Resigned, April 22, 1861. Appointed colonel and commandant, May 23, 1861.

Lieutenant Colonel

Henry Ball Tyler, Sr (1800–79). Virginia. USMA, 1818–20. Non-graduate. Second lieutenant, USMC, May 23, 1823. First lieutenant, April 1, 1830. Captain, March 12, 1845. Adjutant and inspector with the rank of major, July 18, 1857. Dismissed, May 4, 1861. Lieutenant colonel, CSMC, June 18, 1861.

Adjutant and Inspector with the rank of major

Israel Greene (1824–1909). Wisconsin. Second lieutenant, USMC, March 3, 1847. First lieutenant, July 19, 1855. Dismissed, May 18, 1861. Captain, Provisional Army of Virginia, May 25, 1861. Resigned, June 1861. Captain, CSMC, June 19, 1861. Major, adjutant and inspector, August 24, 1861.

Paymaster with the rank of major

Richard Taylor Allison (1823–1909). Maryland. Paymaster, USN, 1849–61. Dismissed, May 6, 1861. Major and paymaster, CSMC, May 10, 1861.

Quartermaster with the rank of major

Samuel Zaccharios Gonzalez (1817–1907). Florida. Naval storekeeper, 1854–61. Resigned, January 1861. Major and quartermaster, CSMC, April 3, 1861. Resigned September 13, 1861.

Algernon Sidney Taylor (1817–99). Virginia. Second lieutenant, 5th US Infantry, August 1, 1838. Transferred to USMC, February 21, 1839. First lieutenant March 3, 1847. Brevet captain, March 27, 1847. Captain July 17, 1857. Dismissed, May 6, 1861. Lieutenant colonel, Provisional Army of Virginia, May 8,

1861. Resigned, December 1861. Captain, CSMC, December 3, 1861. Major and quartermaster, December 4, 1861.

The Line

Major
George Hunter Terrett (1807–75). Virginia. Second lieutenant, US Marines, April 1, 1830. First lieutenant, July 1, 1834, and captain, March 16, 1847. Brevet major, September 13, 1847. Dismissed, May 6, 1861. Colonel, Provisional Army of Virginia, May 8, 1961. Resigned August 22, 1861. Major, CSMC, June 20, 1861. Lieutenant colonel, PACS, May 23, 1864.

Captains
Reuben Tripplett Thom (1823?–73). Alabama. First lieutenant Company G, 1st Regiment, Alabama Volunteers, June 16, 1846 to May 28, 1847. Second lieutenant, 13th US Infantry, August 3, 1847. Mustered out, July 15, 1848. Captain, 1st Artillery, Alabama Regular Army February 5, 1861. Resigned, March 1861. Captain, CSMC, March 25, 1861.

Andrew Jackson Hays (c. 1825–96). Alabama. Second lieutenant, USMC, December 4, 1847. First lieutenant, July 17, 1857. Resigned, March 1, 1861. Captain, CSMC, March 29, 1861. Lieutenant colonel, PACS, May 6, 1862.

George Holmes (1825–75). Florida. Second lieutenant, Company C, Florida Battalion, June 28, 1847. Captain, March 8, 1848. Mustered out, July 8, 1848. Second lieutenant, USMC, March 8, 1849. First lieutenant, April 5, 1858. Resigned, February 28, 1861. Captain, CSMC, March 29, 1861.

Alfred Crippen Van Benthuysen (1836–71.) Louisiana. Reportedly served as a mercenary during the Crimean War, in China and in the wars for Italian unification. Captain, CSMC, March 30, 1861.

Jacob Read (1825–64). Georgia. Second lieutenant, USMC, March 3, 1847. First lieutenant, August 19, 1855. Resigned, February 27, 1861. Captain, Company D, 1st Regiment, Georgia Regular Army, March 5, 1861. Captain, CSMC, May 21, 1861. Dismissed from the Army and Marine Corps by sentence of court-martial, February 1 1863.

John Douglas Simms, Jr (1822–81). Virginia. Second lieutenant, USMC, October 7, 1841. First lieutenant, September 14, 1847. Brevet captain, September 13, 1847. Captain, May 7, 1861. Dismissed, July 8, 1861. Captain, CSMC, July 15, 1861.

Jabez Cushman Rich (1812–65) Virginia. Second lieutenant, USMC, June 13, 1834. First lieutenant, February 24, 1839. Captain, November 27, 1853. Dismissed, May 22, 1861. Captain, Virginia Marine Corps, April 20, 1861. Dismissed, July 23, 1861 Captain, CSMC, October 26, 1861. Dropped, October 10, 1862.

Julius Ernest Meiere (1833–1905). District of Columbia. Second lieutenant, USMC, April 16, 1855. First lieutenant, March 1, 1861. Dismissed, May 6, 1861. First lieutenant, CSMC, May 8, 1861. Captain, December 5, 1861.

George Pendleton Turner (1837–1905). Virginia. Second lieutenant, USMC, September 27, 1856. First lieutenant, June 8, 1861. Dismissed, June 25, 1861. Second lieutenant, Virginia Marine Corps, May 2, 1861. First lieutenant, CSMC, July 2, 1861. Captain, December 5, 1861. Dismissed, December 11, 1862.

Robert Tansill (1812–90). Virginia. Private, USMC, March 16, 1833. Corporal, June 14, 1833. Sergeant, January 1, 1834. Re-enlisted, 1836 and 1840. Discharged, November 3, 1840. Second lieutenant, USMC, November 3, 1840. First lieutenant, March 19, 1847. Brevet captain, November 17, 1847. Captain, November 29, 1858. Dismissed, August 24, 1861. Captain, CSMC, January 22, 1862. Resigned, February 15, 1862. Captain of infantry, CSA, February 15, 1862. Colonel, Virginia volunteers, February 14, 1862. Commanding 2nd Virginia Artillery, February 14–May 23, May 1862. Colonel, PACS, May 27, 1863.

John Rogers Fenwick Tattnall (1829–1907). Georgia. Second lieutenant, USMC, November 3, 1847. First lieutenant, February 22, 1857. Dismissed, November 22, 1861. Captain, CSMC, January 22, 1862. Colonel, PACS, April 17, 1862. Commanding 29th Alabama Infantry Regiment, April 26–November 24, 1862.

Thomas Smith Wilson (1837–1900). Missouri. Second lieutenant, USMC, December 13, 1857. First lieutenant, May 25, 1861. Dismissed, August 24, 1861. First lieutenant, CSMC, January 24, 1862. Captain, October 10, 1862.

Calvin Lawrence Sayre (1832–94). Alabama. Second lieutenant, USMC, June 3, 1858. Resigned, February 14, 1861. First lieutenant, CSMC, March 29, 1861. Major, PACS, August 28, 1862. Captain, CS Marine Corps, December 11, 1862.

Becket Kempe Howell (1840–82). Louisiana. Second lieutenant, USMC, August 1, 1860. Resigned, March 1, 1861. First lieutenant, CSMC, March 29, 1861. Captain, February 1, 1863.

First lieutenants

Henry Laurens Ingraham (c. 1837–78). South Carolina. USNA, 1852–54. Non-graduate. Second lieutenant, USMC, July 1, 1858. Resigned, March 8, 1861. First lieutenant, CSMC, March 29, 1861. Resigned, November 22, 1861. First lieutenant of artillery, CSA, November 16, 1861. Captain, PACS, October 7, 1862.

Richard Henry Henderson (1831–80). District of Columbia. First lieutenant, CSMC, April 16, 1861.

Adam Neill Baker (1835–62). Florida. Second lieutenant, USMC, September 12, 1853. First lieutenant, August 1, 1860. Dismissed, May 22, 1861. First lieutenant, Virginia Marine Corps, April 20, 1861. First lieutenant, CSMC, June 6, 1861. Deserted, November 13, 1861. Dropped, October 10, 1862. Private, Company I, 15th Massachusetts Infantry, July 30, 1862. Killed in action at the Battle of Antietem, September 17, 1862.

Henry Ball Tyler, Jr (1829–96). Virginia. Second lieutenant, USMC, January 2, 1855. First lieutenant, October 23, 1860. Dismissed, June 21, 1861. First lieutenant, CSMC, August 20, 1861. Dismissed, December 10, 1861.

David Greenway Raney (1838–1903). Florida. Corporal, 1st Florida Infantry, April 4, 1861. Discharged, May 3, 1861. Second lieutenant, CSMC, April 22, 1861. First lieutenant, December 10, 1861.

James Robert Young Fendall (1838–67). Mississippi. Private, Company H, 18th Mississippi Infantry, May 20, 1861. Discharged, October 2, 1861. Second lieutenant, CSMC, July 3, 1861. First lieutenant, December 10, 1861.

Wilbur Fiske Johnson (1841–74). Georgia. Mate, US Coast

Survey, November 26, 1860. Declined. Private in Company D, 2nd Battalion, Georgia Infantry, April 20, 1861. Discharged, July 11, 1861. Second lieutenant, CSMC, June 29, 1861. First lieutenant, December 5, 1861. Resigned, July 4, 1862. First lieutenant of artillery, CSA, July 5, 1862.

Thomas Peyton Gwynn (1836–1919). Virginia. Private, Company G, 6th Virginia Infantry. Discharged, October 4, 1861. Second lieutenant, CSMC, September 20, 1861. First lieutenant, February 15, 1862.

James Thurston (1840–1911). South Carolina. Private, Company A, 2nd South Carolina Cavalry, June 26, 1861. Discharged, November 1, 1861. Second lieutenant, CSMC, September 20, 1861. First Lieutenant, July 4,1862.

Francis Hawkes Cameron (1838–1900). North Carolina. Acting master's mate, US Coast Survey, 1859–61. Second lieutenant, CSMC, September 20, 1861. First lieutenant, October 10, 1862.

James Francis Claiborne (1833–67). Louisiana. Private, Company B, 1st Special (Rightor's) Battalion, Louisiana Infantry, April 15, 1861. Discharged, November 2, 1861. Second lieutenant, CSMC, October 28, 1861. First lieutenant, October 10, 1862. Dimissed, January 14, 1863.

Fergus McRee (1839–83). Missouri. Second lieutenant, 1st Missouri Artillery, 1861. Second lieutenant, CSMC, October 9, 1861. First lieutenant, October 10, 1862.

David Bradford (c. 1832–1903). Mississippi. Private, Company I, 10th Mississippi Infantry, May 7, 1861. Discharged, November 22, 1861. Second lieutenant, CSMC, November 22, 1861. First lieutenant, December 11, 1862.

Nathaniel E Venable (1836–1893). Texas. USMA, 1852–54. Non-graduate. First sergeant, Company I, 23rd Virginia Infantry, September 23, 1861. Private, Company D, 25th Battalion, Virginia Infantry, September 1, 1862. Discharged, October 21, 1862. Second lieutenant, CSMC, October 24, 1862. First lieutenant, January 11, 1863.

Henry Lea Graves (1842–92). Georgia. Private, Company D, 2nd Battalion, Georgia Infantry, August 7, 1861. Discharged, January

22, 1862. Re-enlisted. Discharged October 24, 1862. Second lieutenant, CSMC, October 24, 1862. First lieutenant, February I, 1863.

Edward Cantey Stockton (1835–80). South Carolina. USNA, 1849. Passed midshipman, June 12, 1855. Master, September 16, 1855. Lieutenant, February 7, 1857. Dismissed, June 30, 1858. Second lieutenant, South Carolina Navy, January 1861. Second lieutenant, CSMC, July 1861. Appointment terminated, September 30, 1861. Captain, Company G, 21st South Carolina Infantry, January 13, 1862. Resigned, April 15, 1862. Master, CSN, March 6, 1862. Lieutenant, February 26, 1863. First lieutenant, PNCS, January 6, 1864.

John Douglas Fowler (1831–62). Alabama. Private, Company D, 4th Alabama Infantry, April 25, 1861. Discharged, October 13, 1861. Second lieutenant, CSMC, October 26, 1861. Died, August 31, 1862.

Robert McGready Ramsay (1832–90). Tennessee. Private, Company L, 1st Georgia Regiment, Georgia Regular Army, April 20, 1861. Discharged, October 26, 1861. Second lieutenant, CSMC, October 28, 1861. Dismissed, July 9, 1862. Scout, Army of Tennessee, 1862–4. Private, Company E, 12th Battalion, Tennessee Cavalry, March 1, 1864.

Henry Melville Doak (1841–1928). Tennessee. Private, Company E, 19th Tennessee Infantry, June 11, 1861. Regimental sergeant-major, June 11, 1861. Discharged, July 7, 1862. Second lieutenant, CSMC, November 12, 1862.

Albert Seaton Berry (1836–1908). Kentucky. Private, Company A, 13th Kentucky Cavalry, March 24, 1862. Discharged, February 14, 1863. Second lieutenant, CSMC, February 15, 1863.

Edward Fenwick Neufville (1841–90). Georgia. Private, Georgia Hussars, June 1861. Private, Chatham Artillery, 1st Georgia Volunteers, January 2, 1862. Discharged, April 3, 1863. Second lieutenant, CSMC, February 23, 1863.

John Steele Van de Graaff (1834–88). Texas. Private, Company E, 1st Texas Infantry, August 1, 1861. Discharged, March 17, 1863. Second lieutenant, CSMC, March 17, 1863. Resigned, September 11, 1863. Major, Texas State Troops, October 1863.

Daniel Gonzalez Brent (1842–1918). Florida. Private, Company K, 1st Florida Infantry, May 31, 1861. Discharged, March 31, 1863. Second lieutenant, CSMC, March 30, 1863.

James Campbell Murdoch (1840–89). Maryland. Private, Company M, 1st Virginia Cavalry, June 14, 1861. Mustered out, June 1862. Private, Company A, 1st Maryland Cavalry. Discharged, April 1863. Second lieutenant, CSMC, April 8, 1863.

Samuel Muir Roberts (1838–91). Louisiana. Private, Company B, 1st Special (Rightor's) Battalion, Louisiana Infantry, April 15, 1861. Transferred to Company D, 1st Virginia Artillery, 'Richmond Howitzers,' March 8, 1862. Discharged, April 8, 1863. Second lieutenant, CSMC, April 8, 1863.

John Lawrence Rapier (1842–1905). Louisiana. Private, 1st Company, Louisiana Foot Rifles, April 22, 1861. Sergeant-major, Coppen's Battalion, Louisiana Zouaves, July 1862. First lieutenant, September 1862. Resigned, July 11, 1863. Second lieutenant, CSMC, July 11, 1863.

Lloyd Beall Stephenson (1838–1913). Virginia. Second lieutenant, Company F, 8th Virginia Infantry, 1861–April 1862. Sergeant-major, 35th Battalion, Virginia Cavalry, 1862–February 11, 1864. Second lieutenant, CSMC, February 11, 1864.

Ruffin Thomson (1841–88). Mississippi. Private, Company H, 18th Mississippi Infantry, June 4, 1861. Discharged, January 15, 1864. Second lieutenant, CSMC, February 11, 1864.

Thomas St George Pratt (1836–95). Maryland. Private, Company A, 2nd Battalion, Maryland Infantry, October 8, 1862. Discharged, February 11, 1864. Second lieutenant, CSMC, February 11, 1864.

Henry Harrison McCune (1840–77). Missouri. Private, Company A, 2nd Missouri Infantry, December 8, 1861. Captain and assistant quartermaster, January 16, 1862. Resigned, July 7, 1862. Second lieutenant, CSMC, March 14, 1864.

Edward Crenshaw (1842–1911). Alabama. Second lieutenant, Company F, 17th Alabama Infantry, September 9, 1861. Captain, Company B, 9th Battalion/58th Regiment, Alabama Infantry,

President of the Confederate States of America

TO ALL WHO SHALL SEE THESE PRESENTS,

GREETING

Know Ye that reposing special Trust and Confidence in the Patriotism, Valour, Fidelity and Abilities of
I do appoint him
in the Marine Corps of the **CONFEDERATE STATES**
to rank as such from the   day of   18   He is therefore carefully and diligently to discharge the Duties of   by doing and performing all Manner of Things thereto belonging
And I do strictly charge and require all Officers, Seamen and Marines under his Command to be obedient to his Orders as   And he is to observe and follow such Orders and Directions from time to time as he shall receive from me or the future **PRESIDENT** of the Confederate States of America or his Superior Officer set over him according to the Rules and Discipline of the Marine Corps

BY THE PRESIDENT   Given under my Hand at   this
day of   in the Year of our Lord One Thousand Eight
Hundred and

Secretary of the Navy

Registered 1st

March 2, 1863. Resigned, April 25, 1864. Second lieutenant, CSMC, May 3, 1864.

Everard Townes Eggleston (1841–85). Texas. Private, Company B, 1st Special (Rightor's) Battalion, Louisiana Infantry, April 15, 1861. Private, Fenner's Battery, Louisiana Artillery, May 16, 1862. Second lieutenant, CSMC, May 8, 1864.

John DeBerniere Roberts (1843–80). South Carolina. Private, Company G, Hampton's Legion, July 15, 1861. Sergeant, February 28, 1863. Discharged, June 2, 1864. Second lieutenant, CSMC, June 7, 1864.

Eugene Robinett Smith (1843–1929). Tennessee. Private, Company C, 2nd Tennessee Infantry, April 10, 1861. Second lieutenant, Company B, 25th Tennessee Infantry, May 11, 1863. Captain, May 12, 1863. Resigned, September 13, 1864. Second lieutenant, CSMC, September 13, 1864.

John Albert Pearson, Jr (1845–65). Arkansas. Private, 3rd Arkansas Infantry, May 21, 1861. Private, 3rd Louisiana Infantry, March 1862. Discharged, July 15, 1862. Aide de camp to Brig Gen Frank C Armstrong, July 1862–September 1864. Second lieutenant, CSMC, October 8, 1864.

The rank and file: recruiting service

The process of recruiting in the Confederate States Marine Corps also differed from that of the Old Corps. The major recruiting effort of the US Marine Corps centered on the Recruiting Rendezvous. Once enlisted by a recruiting officer, new recruits were sent to Marine Barracks, Washington for instruction. After a period of training, new Marines were dispersed from Washington as circumstances required. Later in the war, the CS Marine recruiting practices followed a somewhat similar practice, but in the early days of the Confederate service, captains were responsible for recruiting their own companies. Recruiting duties were immediately undertaken by Captains Reuben T Thom, George Holmes, and Alfred C Van Benthuysen after they had received their appoint-

CS Marine Officer's commission blank. (Andrew H Parker)

ments, the first at Montgomery, with the latter two at New Orleans. The term of enlistment was four years, and a bounty of ten dollars was offered as an inducement. Captain Thom began recruiting on March 25, 1861, the day he was appointed. Among the first enlisted was Jacob Scholls, a veteran of four years in the Regular Army, and twelve in the Marine Corps, ten of them as a non-commissioned officer. Thom, untutored in the ways of the Marine Corps, recognized Scholls's experience as a most desirable commodity. He immediately promoted him to the rank of sergeant.

As the number of officers increased, and the role of the Corps expanded, Marine recruiting offices were opened in other cities. Captain Andrew J Hays, after recruiting in New Orleans on behalf of his fellow company commanders between May 17 and June 8, 1861, was ordered to Memphis, Tennessee to begin enlisting Marines for his own company. Captain Thom continued recruiting his company at Mobile, Alabama until September 14 when he was relieved by 1st Lt George P Turner. Captain John D Simms was sent to Nashville, Tennessee to begin recruiting his company on July 17, but before he could enlist a single man, was recalled to Richmond.

Recruits were obliged to undergo a physical examination before being enlisted as Marines. If no medical officer of the Navy was available, the services of a private physician were contracted. In the fall of 1861, such services came dearly. Lieutenant Turner paid a Mobile doctor $100 per month for examining recruits. In addition to the expense of medical attention, twenty-five cents had to be paid for each oath of enlistment sworn before a justice of the peace.

Although the companies commanded by Captains Thom and Van Benthuysen were filled, and that by Holmes nearly so during the spring and summer of 1861, subsequent recruiting efforts of the Corps were not successful. The four-year term of enlistment, the comparatively small bounty, and the reputation for Marine discipline seemed to conspire to send prospective recruits into the ranks of the volunteer forces. Even when the term of enlistment was reduced to three years, the bounty raised to fifty dollars (April 1862), and a premium of $2 paid to persons for each qualified recruit they brought to the Corps, recruiting failed to be stimulated. The largest number of Marines under arms at any time was 571 at October 31, 1864.[5]

At the start of the war, enlisted Marines were paid on a par with troops of the Army. On a monthly basis, first sergeants received $21, sergeants $17, corporals $13, musicians $12, and privates $11. A pay raise of $4 per month was granted to the enlisted men by the Congress on October 10, 1862, and another on January 19, 1865, increasing monthly pay by $3. The pay of Marine officers, on the other hand, remained constant throughout the war. The Commandant received $195 per month, Lieutenant Colonel Tyler $170; the adjutant, paymaster, and quartermaster $162; Major Terrett $150; the captains $130; the first lieutenants $90; and the second lieutenants $80. Additionally, officers received $9 per month for every five years of service. Pre-war military service in the armed forces of the United States was counted.

Service of Confederate States Marines ashore and afloat

Pensacola, Florida was the focal point of Marine Corps activity during the first year of the war. The facilities on the mainland had been seized by state forces of Florida and Alabama in January 1861, but control of the harbor lay with Santa Rosa Island and Fort Pickens, whose guns commanded access to and from Pensacola. It was expected that Confederates would seize Fort Pickens as soon as sufficient troops were on hand to undertake the task. To that end, Marines being recruited at New Orleans and Montgomery were designated early on for duty at Pensacola. On April 3, 1861, 1st Lt Henry L Ingraham arrived at the Warrington Navy Yard, apparently to secure a suitable bivouac for those to follow. On April 8, he returned, bringing with him a squad of Marines. These few, Ingraham told a reporter for the *Montgomery Daily Mail*, were but the first of a large Corps that was being recruited and *en route* to Pensacola.[6]

Seventy Marines, led by their commanding officer, Captain A C Van Benthuysen, arrived at the Navy Yard on April 26. They were put to duty at a heavy battery defending the wharf. More reported from Montgomery. On May 12, 150 Marines left New Orleans under the charge of 1st Lt Becket K Howell. By the summer of 1861, over 300 Marines were stationed at Pensacola forming a battalion of three companies attached to the 3rd Brigade, Army of Pensacola: Captain Holmes's Company A; Captain Van Benthuysen's Company B, and Captain Thom's Company C.[7] On July 26, Lt Col Henry B Tyler, reported for duty and assumed command of the battalion.

For the next several weeks, Marines refined their skills at the great guns, patrolled the waters of Pensacola Bay as Harbor Police

with Lt Henry L Ingraham commanding, performed duty aboard the steamer CSS *Time* as a regularly assigned Guard commanded by 2nd Lt David G Raney, and walked post as sentinels at the Warrington Navy Yard. Two detachments, twenty men from Company A under the command of Lt Howell, and another twenty from Company B led by Lt Richard H Henderson, were sent away to form the Marine Guards of the intended commerce raiders CSS *Sumter* and *Alabama*.[8] As summer droned on, nothing remotely approaching belligerency touched the Marine Battalion. This would all change in mid September.

On the night of September 13–14, 1861, a raiding party consisting of sailors and US Marines from USS *Colorado* swept into Pensacola Harbor under the cover of darkness. The boat operation had a dual purpose. The first objective was to burn the privateer *Judah*, a schooner fitting out at the wharf. The second was to disable the heavy gun that defended the Navy Yard docks. Both missions were carried out successfully. Federal sailors and Marines came swarming over the sides of the schooner. After a sharp fire fight in which three CS Marines were wounded, the crew of the privateer was driven from the ship. Burning tar balls, fuel oil, and other combustibles finished the work. In a matter of minutes, *Judah* was aflame. The second landing party stormed ashore, shot down the CS Marine sentry at the battery, and spiked the gun, carrying off the tompion as a trophy.

A retaliatory raid carried was launched by Confederate forces during the night of October 8–9. An assault force of about 1,000 men, including a contingent of CS Marines, was collected and ferried across Pensacola Bay aboard CSS *Neaffie* and the steamer *Ewing*. The troops landed just after 2am, and headed straight for the Federal camps outside the walls of Fort Pickens. Although an aroused sentry fired a warning shot at the approaching rebels, the 6th New York Zouaves were caught by surprise. Their camp was overrun and put to the torch. The commanding officer of the expedition, Brig Gen Richard H Anderson, quite satisfied that the mischief caused by the earlier raid had been paid back, ordered his force back to their boats. During the ensuing withdrawal, Confederate troops dealt with harassing fire all the way back to the beach. While the troops re-embarked, 1st Lt Calvin Sayre, CSMC, joined the rear guard, and was severely injured by a gunshot wound to the thigh. Pvt William Huddleston was knocked down by a round shot from the fort. Marine Huddleston was trundled into one of the boats, but Lieutenant Sayre was left on the beach in the confusion, and fell into the hands of the enemy.[9]

Over the course of the next six weeks, the only event within the Marine Battalion that departed from the daily routine of guard duty and drill was the desertion of 1st Lt Adam N Baker. On November 13, Lieutenant Baker commandeered a small boat and fled to Fort Pickens. He was quickly sent aboard USS *Mississippi* where he was interrogated at length by Captain Thomas O Selfridge, USN. Baker was completely co-operative and gave Selfridge 'much useful information in regard to the plans of the enemy'.[10]

The information divulged by Baker no doubt played a role in the ensuing bombardment of the military installations at Pensacola by Fort Pickens and the Federal warships on station off shore. At 10am on November 22, the Confederate defenses at Fort McRee, Fort Barancas and the Warrington Navy Yard came under a heavy fire from Pickens, USS *Richmond* and USS *Niagara*. Captain Van Benthuysen's Marines sprang to their gun, but after firing only two shots, were ordered to stand down. The shots from the Marine battery drew the attention of Federal gunners, and their return fire put the steamers CSS *Time* and *Nelms* in peril. The Marines retired to their bombproof, spending the rest of the day out of action.

During the night, the two steamers were withdrawn from the wharf, and on the morning of the 23rd, Van Benthuysen's Marines had the opportunity to prove their mettle. The cannonade resumed at 10.30am, and over the course of the next eighteen hours, the Marine battery fired twenty shots, all but five taking effect on Fort Pickens. The contest, little more than forty hours of target practice since neither side made any offensive move against the other's positions, sputtered out at 4am, November 24. The Marine gunners fired the first and last shots of the second day's duel.[11]

The two-day artillery exchange of November 22–24 marked the zenith of military affairs at Pensacola. The pressure of Federal forces on other points in the Confederacy brought about a siphoning off of troops. The Marine Battalion was among the first to be affected. On September 18, the need for Marines at the Georgia and South Carolina Naval Station caused Captain Holmes's Company A to be ordered to duty at Savannah. Orders dated November 26 sent Captain Thom's Company C to the Navy Yard at Norfolk, Virginia for duty aboard the ironclad CSS *Virginia* and other vessels of the James River Squadron. Captain Van Benthuysen's Company B departed Pensacola on February 13, 1862 for duty at the Mobile Naval Station. Pensacola was ultimately abandoned by the Confederates on May 10, 1862.

The Marines detached for service aboard CSS *Sumter* arrived at New Orleans on May 24, 1861. *Sumter*, under the command of Cdr Raphael Semmes, CSN, eluded Federal blockaders off the mouth of the Mississippi River and began her career as a commerce raider. Two of her Marine Guard went aboard the captured brig *Cuba* as part of a prize crew on July 4, 1861. During the remainder of *Sumter's* cruise, Marines kept watch over prisoners taken from unlucky merchantmen that crossed Commander Semmes's path. Marine Lieutenant Howell had little difficulty with his Guard while at sea, but once *Sumter* touched port at Cadiz, troubles began. A number of Marines took advantage of being in port and slipped away from the ship; some turning themselves in at the United States Consulate. When Semmes laid *Sumter* up at Gibraltar on January 18, 1862, more went over the side.

CSS *Sumter*, her hull ridden with barnacles and her boilers worn out, was ultimately abandoned at Gibraltar. A token force was left aboard, including a Marine Guard in the charge of Sgt George Stephenson. On October 15, 1862, Acting Masters' Mate Joseph Hester killed *Sumter's* commanding officer, Midshipman Williams Andrews, and was taken into custody by British authorities. Stephenson, as the ranking, although non-commissioned, officer, suddenly found himself in command of the ship. Thus Sgt Stephenson held the distinction of being the only Marine, Federal or Confederate, to be in charge of a ship of war during the Civil War.[12]

The Marines destined for CSS *McRae* left Pensacola on June 27, 1861, but service on the Atlantic was not in their future. Increased surveillance by blockaders prevented *McRae* from following *Sumter* to sea. When it became apparent that the ship would be confined to duty on the Mississippi, 1st Lt Richard H Henderson was ordered back to Pensacola, and the Marine Guard left in the charge of Sgt John Morgan.

McRae's Marine Guard, along with fifty-five Marine recruits then at New Orleans under the command of Captain Reuben Thom, took part in the occupation of Ship Island on July 6, 1861. On July 9, the Confederate forces on Ship Island engaged in an artillery duel with USS *Massachusetts*. The Confederate guns outranged those aboard *Massachusetts*, and the Federal warship was compelled to withdraw. Lt Alexander F Warley, the senior naval officer of the expedition, praised the efforts of Captain Thom and the Marines saying, 'Where work was to be done, there was the captain to be found and his men working as I never saw raw recruits work before.'[13]

The Marines aboard *McRae* subsequently saw battle action during the operations at the head of the Passes, October 12, 1861, around Island No from March 4 to April 7, 1862, and at the Battle of Forts Jackson and St. Philip, April 24, 1862. In the latter engagement, she fought a number of Union warships at close quarters. In the process, *McRae* was severely damaged and compelled to withdraw from the fight after suffering heavy casualties. Of the twenty Marines who were initially assigned to her in June 1861, only nine were taken prisoner after the battle.

The Marines of Captain Holmes's Company A served aboard the 'Mosquito Fleet' stationed at Savannah, Georgia and Charleston, South Carolina. This squadron, commanded by Captain Josiah Tattnall, CSN, was made up of converted sidewheelers, tugs, and other vessels barely worthy of the term 'warship.' Nevertheless, these vessels were all the Confederacy had to challenge the Federal armada that arrived off Port Royal, South Carolina in early November 1861.

The Confederate defenses at Port Royal consisted of Fort Walker on Hilton Head Island, and, on the opposite side of the sound, Fort Beauregard on Bay Point. Tattnall's squadron patrolled the waters between the two forts. Marines from Company A were attached as follows:

CSS *Savannah*, Marine Guard commanded by Capt George Holmes

CSS *Sampson*, Marine Guard commanded by 2nd Lt David G. Raney

CSS *Resolute*, Marine Guard commanded by 2nd Lt James Thurston

CSS *Huntress*, Marine Guard commanded by 2nd Lt Francis Hawkes Cameron

On November 4 and 5 gunboats from the Federal fleet cruised into Port Royal Sound and were greeted by shellfire from the forts and Tattnall's vessels. Little damage was done to either side, but the intent of the intruders, to gauge the ranges of the rebel guns, was satisfied. The main attack, scheduled for November 6, was delayed by foul weather. However, the next morning brought ideal conditions for battle.

At 9am, November 7, the Federal squadron got under way. Commanding the squadron was Captain Francis S DuPont, USN, a sailor for nearly fifty years with a mind in tune with new tactics in naval warfare. His plan of attack was to steam between the two forts in an elliptical course, firing at the Confederates as his guns registered, but never giving the shore batteries the opportunity to return fire at stationary targets. The plan worked masterfully, Although DuPont's warships suffered moderate damage, the two forts were devastated.

Of greater concern to DuPont was the potential of the long-range rifled guns mounted on Tattnall's gunboats. As the Federal

ships reached the turning point in their course, Tattnall's flotilla darted into the fray. The harassing fire from the Confederate vessels was so disruptive that DuPont dispatched USS *Susquehanna* and *Minnesota* to deal with them. At the approach of the heavy warships, Tattnall wisely made for safer waters, steaming for the protection of Skull Creek at the rear of Hilton Head Island. Although the Confederate ships were out of harm's way, their crews were not out of the fight.

To this point in the battle, the Marines had had little opportunity to prove their mettle. Now they would get their chance, or so it seemed. Tattnall, sensing that the gunners at Fort Walker were at the end of their endurance, sent Captain Holmes and the Marines of the Flagship *Savannah* ashore at Seabrook's Landing with orders to reinforce the hard-pressed garrison. The Marines from *Sampson* and sailors from the flotilla loaded up with naval ammunition, and, with Tattnall at their head, set out shortly thereafter.[14]

As Holmes and his Marines neared Fort Walker, the sounds of the great battle diminished. The Marines were halted and Holmes went forward to assess the situation. During his absence, a flight of demoralized refugees from Fort Walker swept by the Marines. The fort had been abandoned. The Marines, nevertheless, held their post and when the second group from the Confederate squadron came up, Captain Tattnall found them waiting for Holmes to return. The naval commander quickly determined that all his force could do was to round up the survivors of Fort Walker's garrison and bring them off to Savannah. Placing Marine Lieutenant Raney in charge of the rear guard, the Confederate force retired.

Shortly after Fort Walker had been abandoned, Fort Beauregard followed suit. In less than six hours, the United States Navy crushed the defenses of Port Royal. More importantly, the victory would provide a base from which Union naval forces could maintain a continuous blockade of the southern coast of the Confederacy.

The Marines serving aboard the tiny Georgia and South Carolina squadron saw action again when Tattnall attempted to draw Federal gunboats into battle near Fort Pulaski on November 26, and again on January 29, 1862. However, the Confederate force was unable to prevent DuPont's gunboats from landing men and guns at advanced positions from which Fort Pulaski would be attacked. These Federal forces ultimately bombarded the fort into submission on April 11, 1862.

In the aftermath of Fort Pulaski's capitulation, Confederate

States Naval Secretary Stephen R Mallory determined that the services of the Marines attached to the Georgia and South Carolina Station would be of more value in the defenses of the James River near Richmond. Accordingly, on May 22, 1862, Company A left Savannah for new duties at Drewry's Bluff, the new base camp of the Confederate States Marines.

Captain Reuben T Thom's Company C arrived at Norfolk, Virginia on December 7, 1861. Guards were promptly sent aboard CSS *Jamestown;* twenty Marines under the command of 2nd Lt James R Y Fendall, and twenty-four commanded by 1st Lt Richard H Henderson went aboard CSS *Patrick Henry.* When CSS *Virginia* went into commission on February 17, 1862, Captain Thom commanded her Guard of fifty-four Marines. A small detachment was left aboard the receiving ship *Confederate States* under 2nd Lt Thomas P Gwynn.

The Battle of Hampton Roads, on March 8–9, 1862, found the Marines aboard all three warships actively involved in the fighting. Marines aboard *Virginia* served one gun, possibly two, during the fighting. The after-action report written by *Virginia's* commanding officer, Captain Franklin Buchanan stated, 'The Marine Corps was well represented by Captain Thom, whose tranquil mien gave evidence that the hottest fire was no novelty to him.' Lt Joseph N Barney, CSN, commanding *Jamestown,* commended Lieutenant Fendall and his Marines, saying, 'In the Action of the 8th & 9th of March, the coolness, rapidity and precision with which your gun was handled was noticed by me as well as a matter of remark with the officers of the ship.' The Marine Guard aboard *Patrick Henry* and Lt Henderson received similar praise from her commander, Cdr John R Tucker, CSN, who 'took pleasure in stating that during the Naval Engagement in Hampton Roads of the 8th & 9th March last, . . . you performed your duty to our entire satisfaction.'[15]

Two months after the historic Battle at Hampton Roads, the CS Navy was compelled to abandon its base at Norfolk and fall back to Richmond. In the process, CSS *Virginia* was blown up on May 11, when her deep draft prevented her from navigating the James River. Her crew and Marines arrived safely at Richmond the next day, and were immediately sent to the fortifications at Drewry's Bluff, the last defensive work that separated the Confederate Capital from the US Navy. CSS *Jamestown* and *Patrick Henry* steamed upriver and, upon reaching the bluff, had their heavy guns removed and emplaced in the works. *Jamestown* was then scuttled as an obstruction. While the crews of the three warships manned the guns on Drewry's Bluff, the Marines were sent into

rifle pits dug along the banks of the James to act as sharpshooters. Their numbers were strengthened by the timely arrival of Captain Van Benthuysen's Company B from Norfolk.

On May 15, 1862, a Federal squadron consisting of the armour-plated USS *Galena,* USS *Monitor,* and the wooden gunboats *Aroostook* and *Port Royal* attempted to batter its way past the Drewry's Bluff defenses. It was unsuccessful. In addition to the pounding the Federal warships received from the Confederate guns at Drewry's Bluff, the rifle fire from the Marine sharpshooters took a toll. Among the casualties inflicted by the Marines was Lt Cdr George U Morris, commanding USS *Port Royal,* wounded in the leg.

Captain Simms's after-action report gave a glowing account of the part his Marines played in the battle:

Drewry's Bluff Battery
May 16th 1862

Colonel,

I have the honor to make to you the following report. On the 15th inst. the enemy's gunboats having made their appearance near the battery at Drury's [*sic*] Bluff, I stationed my command on the bluffs some two hundred yards from them to act as sharpshooters. We immediately opened fire upon them, killing three of the crew of the Galena certainly, and no doubt many more. The fire of the enemy was materially silenced at intervals by the fire of our troops.

It gives me much pleasure to call your attention to the coolness of the officers and men under the severe fire of the enemy. The companies composing my battalion were commanded by Captains Van Benthuysen and Meiere.

Very respectfully,
Jno. D. Simms
Capt. CS Marines
Commdg.

Colonel Lloyd J. Beall
Commdt. CS M. C.
Richmond, Va.[16]

Following the battle, a permanent base for the Marines called Camp Beall was established at Drewry's Bluff. The Marines provided the labour and throughout the summer and fall of 1862 were hard at work constructing quarters. Marines from Drewry's Bluff formed guards for the Navy Yards at Richmond and Manchester (commonly called the Navy Yard opposite Rocketts). Guards were also provided for the reconstituted James River Squadron as new ironclads were commissioned: CSS *Richmond,*

Officer's quarters at Drewry's Bluff. (Connecticut State Library)

December 1862, CSS *Virginia II*, March 1864, and CSS *Fredericksburg*, June 1864.[17] Smaller detachments served aboard the storeship CSS *Gallego* and the gunboat CSS *Drewry*.

The Marine Battalion, in addition to its duties in the Richmond area, also provided contingents for special service. When an attack on Charleston, South Carolina appeared to be imminent, the CS Navy Department responded with uncommon countermeasures. A plan to cripple and capture the Federal iron-clads by boarding was drawn up by Naval Secretary Mallory with Marines designated to play a major role in the operation. Under orders dated February 19, 1863, Marine Companies A, B, and C left Drewry's Bluff under the command of Captain John D Simms, reporting at Charleston three days later.

Training for the operation began at once, with detachments from the Army and Navy joining the Marines. Units consisting of from ten to twenty men were formed from each detachment, and trained for specific tasks. One assault group consisted of two Army contingents and one Marine unit. The latter consisted of thirteen Marines, and was led by Captain Thomas S Wilson, CSMC. Rendering the engine of the target inoperable was the task assigned to the Marines. The plan called for them to board the monitor under cover of darkness. A scaling ladder would be raised against the smokestack. One Marine's job was to mount the ladder and drop bottles of sulphur and gunpowder down the stack. Then, wet blankets handed to the Marine by his comrades below, would be thrown down. This combination would choke and stall the

engine, with toxic fumes spreading below the deck of the monitor. To ensure the smoke remained inside the victim, other Marines were assigned to batter down the smokestack and seal the exposed vent with an iron plate.

While the Marines were working on the smokestack, the two Army units worked on the turret, pilot house, ventilators and

hatches. The turret would be jammed by iron wedges battered into the base. Hatches would be nailed shut. More sulphur and gunpowder were sent below by way of the pilot house and ventilators, with blankets and tarpaulins then sealing them off. A sail thrown over the turret and tied down would give those trapped below decks the choice of surrender or death by asphyxiation.[18]

On April 6, 1863, the long-awaited attack on Charleston began. A fleet of eight monitors and one ironclad under the command of Rear Adm Samuel F DuPont anchored off the harbor and waited for clearing weather conditions. At 3pm, the next day, the assault got under way. The advantage was immediately on the side of the defenders. Confederate engineers had marked the channels with range marker buoys, and, as the monitors made their approach, were showered with a hail of accurate artillery fire from Charleston's defenses.

The special boarding force of Marines, soldiers and sailors stood ready to attack any Federal warship that broke through the outer defenses, but the opportunity to test its skills never materialized. The attackers, after suffering heavy damage, a total of 346 hits were counted on DuPont's vessels, prudently withdrew. When it became clear that the assault would not be renewed, the boarding operation stood down. The Marine Battalion was recalled to Drewry's Bluff on April 22.

The Marine presence at Charleston was restored later that summer. On August 2, 1863, 2nd Lt Henry M Doak, CSMC, left Drewry's Bluff with a detachment of twenty-five enlisted Marines. Upon reporting to duty, Doak and his Marines were sent aboard the ironclad CSS *Charleston*. Over the course of the next five weeks, *Charleston's* Marine Guard clashed with Federal troops three times. On the day that the Marines arrived in Charleston, they took part in a raid on an unfinished battery erected by the Federals on Vincent's Creek. On the night of August 4, a mixed force of Marines, sailors and infantry from the 25th South Carolina surprised a detachment from the 100th New York Volunteers, capturing one officer and ten enlisted men. Shortly thereafter, *Charleston* caught a flotilla of small boats carrying Northern troops on the same waterway. Marines instantly deployed on the roof of the ironclad's shield, and delivered accurate volleys into the swarm of troop-laden craft. Loads of grape and canister from *Charleston's* heavy guns, wreaked havoc among the exposed enemy.[19]

Doak and his Marines, this time taken into battle aboard CSS *Chicora*, took part in the repulse of a Federal boat attack on Fort Sumter during the night of September 8/9, 1863. Having intercepted the signals of the enemy, the Confederate defenders were well-prepared to meet the attack. As soon as the enemy boats reached Fort Sumter, they were exposed to the glare of a calcium light and were caught in a crossfire. The guns of Fort Moultrie fired from the north, those of Fort Johnson from the south, while the rifles, grenades, flaming tar balls and brickbats from the infantry stationed inside the work fell upon the hapless Federals. During the clash, Doak's Marines poured musketry into the attackers from *Chicora's* deck. The attackers pulled away in wild panic. In their wake, over a hundred of their number were left behind, including some two dozen United States Marines, killed, wounded or captured.[20]

Lieutenant Doak was relieved of command of the Guard aboard CSS *Charleston* by 2nd Lt Albert S Berry in October 1863. When the ironclad CSS *Columbia* was commissioned at Charleston, 2nd Lt Eugene R Smith took her Guard aboard on January 1, 1865.

During 1862, two additional Marine Posts were established. The first, Company D at Mobile, was commanded by Captain Julius E Meiere under orders dated September 20, 1862. Assigned to Company D as subalterns were: 1st Lt David G Raney (November 1, 1862), 1st Lt James R Y Fendall (July 8, 1862), and 2nd Lt John L Rapier (December 28, 1863). Operating independently of Company D, but stationed at Mobile was Captain Reuben T Thom, who opened a recruiting rendezvous in the city on May 6, 1862. Marines from Company D formed the Guards for the gunboats CSS *Gaines* and *Morgan*, the ironclads *Baltic*, *Tennessee* and *Nashville*, and provided security for the Mobile Naval Station.

The second, Company E, commanded by Captain John R F Tattnall was organized at Savannah in early November 1862. The first contingent of Marines, intended as the Guard for the ironclad CSS *Atlanta*, was sent to the Savannah Naval Station from Mobile on November 6, under the command of 1st Lt James Thurston. 2nd Lt Henry L Graves joined the post on February 2, 1863. Subsequent postings to Company E included 2nd Lt Edward F Neufville (March 1863), 2nd Lt Daniel G Brent (May 1863), 2nd Lt Henry M. Doak (October 1863–March 1864), and 2nd Lt Thomas St G Pratt (March 1, 1864). Guards from Company E, in addition to the one assigned to CSS *Atlanta*, rotated duty between the ironclad CSS *Savannah* and the Savannah Naval Station.

On June 15, 1863, Cdr William H Webb, CSN, took CSS *Atlanta* from her berth at the Savannah Navy Yard and headed her toward Wassaw Sound. Webb's intentions were to take the two Federal monitors guarding the approaches to Savannah, USS *Weehawken* and *Nahant*, by surprise. After defeating them, Webb planned to shell the huge US Navy supply base at Port Royal and then make a cruise to Fernandina, Florida. His audacious plan came to grief when, on the morning of June 17, *Atlanta* ran hard aground on a sand bar off the tip of Cabbage Island. The two monitors, seeing *Atlanta's* predicament, steamed to a position beyond the traverse of her guns and, at point-blank range, opened fire. The first shot struck *Atlanta's* iron shield with such force that it knocked Lieutenant Thurston and his Marine gun crew to the deck. Five more direct hits caused Webb to strike his colours. The action took less than fifteen minutes.

The ship's company of the captured ironclad were taken prisoner and sent to Port Royal and then to Fort Monroe. The majority of the prisoners were paroled in late June and early July, but the officers, including Marine Lieutenant Thurston, were sent to Fort Warren in Boston Harbor, where they would languish until paroled on October 18, 1864.

In an effort to keep Federal naval blockading forces off balance, the Confederates launched several successful boarding expeditions during the war. Marines participated in two of these operations. In the early morning darkness of February 2, 1864, a cutting out expedition led by Cdr John Taylor Wood, CSN, struck USS *Underwriter*. Twenty-five CS Marines led by Capt Thomas S Wilson took part in the operation which found the Federal gunboat lying at anchor in the Neuse River off New Bern, North Carolina. Detected by the lookout aboard *Underwriter* only moments before the Confederates swarmed over the sides of the ship, her crew was overwhelmed in a brief but violent hand-to-hand struggle. Five attackers, including one Marine were killed in the fighting. Four Marines were numbered among the eleven wounded.

It had been Commander Wood's intention to turn the captured ship on her squadron, but when he found that her boilers were cold, the torch was applied to the prize. His disappointment in not taking his capture into battle did not prevent Wood from allotting praise to the Marines of his expedition. Writing to Colonel Beall, Wood stated:

Sir:

It gives me pleasure to report to you the fine bearing and soldierly conduct of Captain Wilson and his men whilst absent on special duty. Though their duties were more arduous than those of the others, they were always prompt and ready for the performance of all they were called upon to do. As a body they would be a credit to any organization, and I will be glad to be associated with them on duty at any time.[21]

The second expedition was launched from Savannah on the afternoon of May 31, 1864. Seven boats containing a total of fifteen officers and 117 sailors and Marines from the Savannah Squadron slipped down river and tied up at Battery Beaulieu on the Vernon River above Ossabaw Sound. After waiting two days for a Federal ship to come within striking distance, an attack

against the gunboat USS *Water Witch* got under way at 8pm, June 2. Seven boats in two columns silently made their way into the Sound.

Water Witch was lying at anchor about three miles from the mouth of Little Ogeechee River. The two columns of boats slipped up to the ship, one on each side. When about thirty yards away, a voice hailed them through the darkness. Lt Thomas P Pelot, commander of the expedition shouted, 'Rebels! Rebels! Board her!' With that the attacking craft surged forward, and, led by Lieutenant Pelot, the rebels boarders scrambled from their boats to the bulwarks of *Water Witch*.

Although the Confederates caught the ship by surprise, they soon lost their advantage when they became hung up in anti-boarding nets strung above her sides. As the boarders hacked their way through the nets, the ship's crew had time to mount a defense. Small arms fire took a toll among the attackers, but they soon managed to cut the netting down and gained the deck. The Confederates rushed the defenders and a bloody melée followed. Pelot was killed but his men subdued the crew of *Water Witch* in less than ten minutes. A fine sidewheel gunboat had been added to the CS Navy.[22]

The Marines that were involved in the capture of *Water Witch* appear to have been the Guards attached to the ironclads CSS *Savannah* and *Georgia*. Pvt Thomas Veitch of *Georgia's* Guard was brought to the attention of the Navy Department by Flag Officer William W Hunter, commander of the Savannah Squadron, as one of those who 'markedly distinguished themselves' during the fighting.[23]

Another cutting out operation, planned by Rear Adm Franklin Buchanan at Mobile, was scheduled for the night of January 26, 1863. CSS *Crescent* and the steamer *Junior* were to carry the boarders. The target of the operation was USS *Kennebec*, patrolling the Swash Channel south of Fort Morgan. Included in the expedition were Marines from Company D, Captain J E Meiere commanding those sent aboard *Crescent* and those aboard *Junior* by 1st Lt David G Raney.

The expedition got under way on the afternoon of the 26th, and by nightfall was in position to make the attack. However, the blockade runner *Alice (Matagorda)* chose that same night to make her run from Mobile Bay, and grounded in the Swash Channel. Her plight drew the attention of *Kennebec*, and, with the blockader alive with activity, the element of surprise was lost. Admiral Buchanan, who accompanied the expedition aboard *Crescent*, had no choice but to cancel the operation.[24]

Marines served aboard the ironclad CSS *Raleigh* when she drove off Federal blockaders patrolling the waters near New Inlet, North Carolina, on May 6/7, 1864. The much-travelled 2nd Lt Henry M Doak commanded *Raleigh*'s Guard and had charge of one of her starboard guns during the engagement. Despite her prowess in battle, the ironclad's reign as mistress of New Inlet was brief. While returning to her berth at Smithville, the ironclad had just passed Fort Fisher when she ran hard and permanently aground on a sand bar. As the tide receded, the weight of *Raleigh*'s iron shield ultimately broke her back.

The Marine Battalion at Drewry's Bluff was called into action in May 1864 when Federal troops under the command of Maj Gen Benjamin F Butler, USV, moved toward Richmond. With the Army of Northern Virginia fully occupied battling the Army of the Potomac in the Wilderness, few troops were available to counter the threat posed by Butler's men. The ninety Marines at Drewry's Bluff and sixty more guarding the two Navy Yards at Richmond were pressed into service as reinforcements to the thin gray line that hoped to blunt Butler's offensive.

Among the Army troops that were moved to the south side of the James was the 21st South Carolina Infantry. As they passed into the trenches beyond Drewry's Bluff, the South Carolinians were posted next to the Marine Battalion. One of their number, Pvt Henry K DuBose, wrote of his first impression of the Confederate States Marines:

> Along the railway between Petersburg and Richmond the command was marched to Drewry's Bluff. We formed in a line of breastworks, a detachment of marines on our left. These marines were from the gunboats in the James River. The writer, on the left of Company B, came into elbow touch with this pattern of soldiery, as they stood at attention, like statues in their close fitting fighting jackets, erect with their pieces at carry. . . . They did present the appearance of holiday soldiers on parade well groomed and fed, they did not appear as if they would prove very reliable in case of an attack . . . .[25]

As the enemy approached Drewry's Bluff, Marines were thrown forward as skirmishers under the command of 1st Lt Francis H Cameron. After a day of sparring with the rebels, Butler launched his main attack against the Drewry's Bluff line of defense on May 13. The 3rd New Hampshire and 55th Pennsylvania, at heavy cost, wrested control of the first line of trenches from the Confederates, but Butler declined to press his advantage. The fighting petered out on the 16th, and the Federals subsequently withdrew to positions on Bermuda Hundred.

During the course of the battle, Maj George H Terrett, CSMC, the man who broke through the Mexican defenses at the San Cosme Gate outside Mexico City with a handful of Marines in 1847, was with his battalion in the trenches. With him were Mexican War veterans Captain George Holmes, commanding Company A, and Captain John D. Simms, commanding Company B. Leading Company C was Captain Thomas S Wilson, whose recent experience in cutting out USS *Underwriter* proved that he was no parade ground soldier. The role of the Marine Battalion during the Battle of Drewry's Bluff remains a mystery. No records, official or otherwise, are known to exist. However, a clear indication that fighting in the sector held by the Marines had been heavy was that the thirty-three members of Company C expended over 2,000 rounds of ammunition during the course of the battle.[26]

The summer of 1864 saw the Marines involved in what might have been the most daring escapade of the war. In late June, Gen Robert E Lee informed Jefferson Davis that, based upon information he possessed, there was a reasonable chance that the Confederate prisoners held at Point Lookout, Maryland, might be liberated. Since Point Lookout was sited at the tip of the peninsula formed by the Potomac River and Chesapeake Bay, Lee initially thought the rescue in terms of a naval operation. Ships carrying Marines would slip through the blockade, steam north, and again penetrate the cordon of Federal warships. An amphibious landing would be made at Point Lookout. To ensure the success of the operation, he later expanded his speculation to include an Army contingent arriving by way of an overland route.

Davis approved the operation on July 2, setting things in motion. Lee forwarded the particulars of the plan the next day. If successful, Lee modestly thought that the operation might tip the scales of war in Virginia to his favour. At the very least, the news that several thousand rebels were loose in the countryside above Washington would be enough to throw official Washington into apoplexy. In brief, the plan consisted of a land–sea assault on the garrison guarding Point Lookout, organizing the liberated prisoners into armed military formations, and marching them to the point of maximum strategic advantage.

The component parts of the operation were immediately organized. On July 3, a courier was sent to apprise Lt Gen Jubal A Early of his part in the scheme of things. Early's Corps of the Army of the Potomac, after enjoying a string of victories in the Shenandoah Valley, was marching across the panhandle of Maryland. Lee had gambled that fortune would favour Early's troops, and bring them to the gates of the Federal capital. The stakes were that the Army of the Potomac would be compelled to send troops to defend Washington. In turn, Lee's options *vis-à-vis* the weakened Army of the Potomac would be expanded. Now he had another card to play.

Sometime between July 7 and 8, Early was informed that the entire operation depended on his battlefield successes. In order that the two arms of the operation closed around the target simultaneously, Early had to continue his advance on Washington, pin his Federal opponents to the Washington defenses, and send a brigade of his cavalry to ride around Baltimore and on to Point Lookout. All this had to be done in order for the cavalry to arrive at the prison camp by July 12 at the latest.[27]

The Marine Battalion at Drewry's Bluff received orders to report to Wilmington, North Carolina on July 2. Some ninety Marines, the entire force of the battalion, was on the move by midnight. Led by Captains Holmes and Wilson, the battalion included 2nd Lts Everard T Eggleston, John DeB Roberts and Edward Crenshaw. Picking up 2nd Lt Henry H McCune and about forty Marines from the Navy yards at Richmond, the battalion, joined by a contingent of seamen from the James River Squadron, left the capital early in the morning of July 3. Despite having to detour around stretches of track torn up by Federal raiders, the force arrived at Wilmington on the 6th.[28]

The Marines and sailors were sent aboard two blockade-runners commandeered for the expedition, *Florrie* and *Let-Her-Be*. Joining the Marine Battalion at Wilmington were 1st Lt Richard H Henderson and 2nd Lt Lloyd B Stephenson. By the evening of July 9, all was in readiness. Army officers to organize the prisoners were aboard. Arms and accouterments to kit out the Point Lookout prisoners for field service had been stowed below decks. The two ships weighed anchor and prepared to run the blockade.

At sunset, July 10, the ships got under way, and headed for sea. Just as they passed Fort Fisher, a signal came from the fort. A telegram from President Davis had been received, advising that the mission be aborted. Breaches in security had compromised the operation, and to proceed would accomplish nothing. The ships returned to Wilmington.[29]

Although the Point Lookout expedition never came to fruition, part of Lee's intentions were realized. The menace to Washington and the presence of rebel cavalry above Baltimore had the desired effect on the Federal War Department. Two corps were detached from the Army of the Potomac and moved into the capital's defenses.

When the Marine Battalion was ordered back to Drewry's Bluff on July 20, a part of it was retained at Wilmington for service aboard CSS *Tallahassee*, a commerce raider then fitting out for sea. Lt Crenshaw and a Guard of twenty-five Marines went aboard the cruiser on July 30. *Tallahassee* escaped to sea on August 6, and during a cruise that lasted nineteen days and took the Confederate raider as far north as Halifax, Nova Scotia, took thirty-three prizes. Crenshaw and his Marines served with boarding parties and had charge of prisoners taken from the ill-fated merchant vessels. Empty coal bunkers compelled the ship to return to port, and, after successfully eluding the blockaders off Cape Fear, she docked at Wilmington on August 26.

Tallahassee undertook another raid several weeks later. After having her name changed to *Olustee*, the ship penetrated the blockade again on October 29. This time, however, the passage was more difficult. Federal blockaders managed to fire several shots at the ship as she slipped through, a number of them taking effect. This damage caused the cruise to be cut short, and, after taking six prizes, she returned safely to Wilmington on November 7. 2nd Lt Doak commanded the Marine Guard on this second venture.

The day before *Olustee* ran the blockade, another commerce raider successfully passed through the Federal naval cordon at Cape Fear. CSS *Chickamauga* carried a Guard of nine enlisted Marines commanded by 1st Lt David Bradford. *Chickamauga* prowled the shipping lanes as far north as Long Island Sound before heading to St Georges, Bermuda to replenish her dwindling supply of provisions and coal. While at St Georges, sixty-five of the ship's company, including six Marines, went absent without leave. Authorities at St Georges refused to allow the Confederate officers to arrest the absentees. As a result, the undermanned warship was compelled to return. *Chickamauga* took seven prizes during her brief cruise, returning safely to Wilmington on November 19.

Following the capture of New Orleans in April 1862, Rear Adm David G Farragut, USN, listed Mobile Bay as his first priority. The lack of sufficient land forces to co-operate in taking the outer forts prevented Farragut from realizing his goal until the summer of 1864. The two-year breathing space gave the Confederates at Mobile time in which to complete the ironclad CSS *Tennessee* and add her to the defenses of the Bay.

When Farragut's squadron moved into attack position on August 2, the Confederates mounted a desperate attempt to reinforce the garrisons of the two forts guarding the entrance to Mobile Bay. About twenty-five Marines, the Guard from CSS *Baltic* and nearly every available man from the barracks, was hurriedly dispatched to Fort Gaines on Dauphin Island. Capt J E Meiere, with 1st Lt James R Y Fendall and 2nd Lt John L Rapier, arrived at Gaines with this small force on the morning of August 4. The Marines were promptly sent to the skirmish line opposing Federal troops approaching the fort from the west. The morning of August 5 found the Federals advancing in strength. Firing broke out and in the ensuing exchange, Orderly Sergeant Martin Lewis was killed and another Marine wounded. Then, as though by mutual consent, the shooting ceased as both sides turned their attention to the battle being fought in Mobile Bay.[30]

Opposing the Federal squadron at Mobile Bay were the Flagship CSS *Tennessee*, and the gunboats *Morgan*, *Gaines* and *Selma*. All but *Selma* carried a Marine Guard. 1st Lt David G. Raney commanded thirty-five Marines aboard the Flagship, and served one of her broadside guns. Orderly Sergeant John M Bennett had charge of fourteen Marines aboard *Morgan*, while sixteen others were attached to *Gaines* under Orderly Sergeant Rollin Pumphrey.

In the engagement that followed the successful passage of the Federal squadron into Mobile Bay, *Selma* was captured, *Gaines*, heavily damaged, was beached under the guns of Fort Morgan, and *Morgan* driven out of the action. *Tennessee* managed to inflict heavy damage on numerous enemy warships but, in the end, with gun ports jammed, rudder chains and stack shot away, the Squadron commander, Rear Adm Franklin Buchanan wounded in action, was forced to strike her colours. Lieutenant Raney's Marines fought gallantly throughout the three-hour battle, his gun firing the last shot from the ironclad.[31]

After eliminating the naval threat to his operation, Farragut turned his attention to Fort Gaines. A two-day bombardment delivered by monitors at close range convinced Col Charles D Anderson, commanding Fort Gaines, to surrender. Before doing so, Colonel Anderson circulated a paper among his officers, requesting their acquiescence to his decision. Captain Meiere added his signature to the document, but Lieutenants Fendall and Rapier refused. Fort Gaines struck her colours on August 8, and her garrison, including the three Marine officer and twenty-five enlisted men, was taken prisoner.[32]

During the last days of Maj Gen William T Sherman's 'March to the Sea,' the Marines of Company E, were marched several miles west of Savannah to support a battery near King's Bridge on the Ogeechee River. The Marines, commanded by 1st Lt Henry L Graves and 2nd Lt Edward F Neufville, remained in the defenses from December 8 to 20, 1864. During this period, constant small arms and artillery fire passed between the opposing forces, but no

attempt by the Federals was made to storm the position. Ultimately heavy pressure from the north of the city decided the issue. Unable to hold the city against overwhelming odds, Lt Gen William Hardee, PACS, made preparations to evacuate Savannah. Orders came to the Marines on December 20 to fall back. Joined by comrades from the barracks and Savannah River Squadron, the Marines of Company E fell in with several thousand soldiers and crossed a pontoon bridge over the Savannah River into South Carolina. After arriving at Charleston some of the Marines from Company E, namely the Guards that served aboard CSS *Savannah* and *Georgia*, were sent as reinforcements to Fort Fisher under command of 2nd Lt Thomas StG Pratt. The remainder stayed with Capt John R F Tattnall, who, in addition to his responsibilities as commander of Company E, took over those associated with the Marines attached to the Charleston Station.[33]

Confederate States Marines served with distinction during the Battles of Fort Fisher, December 24–25, 1864, and January 13–15, 1865. A Marine detachment had been serving at Battery Buchanan, a five-gun earthwork situated a few hundred yards to the rear of Fort Fisher, since the Navy had assumed control of the place in early November 1864. Between twenty-five and thirty enlisted Marines served at Battery Buchanan under the command of 2nd Lt John DeB Roberts, and later, 2nd Lt James C Murdoch. No Marines were attached to the garrison of Fort Fisher.

At 1pm, December 24, 1864, the opening salvoes of a day-long artillery duel were fired by the Federal fleet against Fort Fisher. Captain A C Van Benthuysen and the Marines of the Wilmington Station were rushed as reinforcements to Battery Buchanan, arriving too late in the day to take part in any of the fighting. Following a failed attempt to blow up the fort during the night with an old hulk filled with 200 tons of gunpowder, the US Navy resumed the contest at 10am, Christmas Day. Toward sunset, an urgent message was received from the fort stating that Union troops had landed and were advancing. Two-thirds of Battery Buchanan's compliment, including the Marines, was sent to the fort. Led by Captain Van Benthuysen, the Marines reached their posts in time to assist in driving the 112th and 142nd New York Regiments from their advanced positions. Their efforts would bring praise from Maj Gen William H Whiting. The unexpected resistance from the fort, coupled with information that a division of Confederate troops was preparing to attack the men on the beach, prompted General Butler to withdraw his troops and bring an end to the expedition.

When another expedition returned to Fort Fisher on January

12, Marines were once again sent into the fort as reinforcements. About a hundred Marines joined the garrison; the Wilmington detachment with 2nd Lts Henry M Doak and John DeB Roberts and led by Captain Van Benthuysen, 2nd Lt James C Murdoch and the Marines from Battery Buchanan, 2nd Lt Thomas St G Pratt and Marines from the now defunct Savannah Naval Station, and 1st Lt David Bradford with the remnant of the Guard attached to CSS *Chickamauga.*

The second attempt to capture Fort Fisher began on January 13, 1865. A methodical naval bombardment opened on the fort at 8am, and continued without interruption for the next fifty-five hours. Union troops landed on the 13th, and, over the course of the next two days, established themselves in forward positions, waiting for the fleet to reduce the fort. Marines were initially assigned to one of the heavy guns on the land face of the fort, but when that was dismounted by the bombardment, a number of them took over a mortar battery. Others went into the bombproofs to await the assault of the enemy infantry. Two, Sgt Philip Smith and Pvt Arthur Muldoon, were assigned to Colonel Lamb as orderlies.

During the morning of January 15, Lieutenant Doak was in charge of the mortars. After sending one shell into a trench filled with Union soldiers, Doak was severely wounded by a direct hit on his battery by a shell from the fleet. Eight Marines in his crew were either killed or wounded in the explosion. Those unhurt quickly carried Doak and the other wounded to the shelter of a bombproof dug into the earthen wall of the fort.[34]

Around 2pm, Private Muldoon reported a large column of US Marines and sailors moving along the beach toward the fort. Sensing that the column would try to break through the palisade fence at the angle of the fort, Colonel Lamb quickly sent troops to the point of danger. Just after 3pm, a blast from the steam whistles of the fleet signalled the naval column to the attack. Private Muldoon shouted, 'Colonel, the enemy are about to charge!' Lamb ordered his troops to their posts. The assault was made with great valour but in the face of a determined resistance. Confederate soldiers, sailors and Marines lined the parapet at the angle, firing as fast as muskets could be loaded and aimed. The column was shot to pieces and repulsed. Of the 1,200 sailors and 400 US Marines that began the attack, 393 were reported as killed, wounded or missing in action.[35]

While the attention of the Confederates was focused on the naval column, Federal troops gained a foothold near the first traverse of the land face. They would not be driven out. The fighting raged from traverse to traverse. General Whiting went down, severely wounded. Colonel Lamb fell, shot through the hips. Marine Captain Van Benthuysen took a wound to the head. After a stubborn resistance lasting nearly six hours, those Confederates still on their feet finally yielded Fort Fisher. Captain Van Benthuysen gathered the surviving Marines and, taking up General Whiting and Colonel Lamb, joined in a desperate dash to Battery Buchanan, firm in the hope of escaping upriver in a steamer. But there was no steamer. The last of the naval force at Battery Buchanan had commandeered the boats, leaving the Marines and soldiers with no alternative but to surrender.

Of the six Marine officers who took part in the fighting, four were wounded in action: Captain Van Benthuysen, severe gunshot wound to the head, Lieutenant Bradford, contusion to the left hip by a shell fragment, Lieutenant Doak, wounded in the face, head and legs by shell fragments, and Lieutenant Pratt, gunshot wound to the right foot. At least seven enlisted Marines made good their escape in the confusion and subsequently returned to duty. Sixty-six were made prisoner, ten of them wounded, three mortally. Between twenty-five and thirty were unaccounted for. Due to the nature of the fighting at Fort Fisher it is likely that most, if not all, of them, were killed in action.

During the last, desperate days of the Confederacy, a plan to slip through enemy lines and destroy the supply base of the Army of the Potomac at City Point was implemented. Naval Lt Charles W Read took charge of a mixed force of soldiers, sailors and Marines, the latter led by 1st Lt James Thurston, on February 3. The expedition was to make it safely to the James River, cut out a Federal gunboat, steam up to City Point, and destroy the stores and facilities there. The expedition was well under way before it was learned that a turncoat had informed the enemy of the mission. Lieutenant Read, faced with the certainty of not being able to fulfill his orders, called off the operation and brought his column back to Drewry's Bluff on February 13.[36]

In the spring of 1865, Drewry's Bluff became a point of concentration for the sailors and Marines from the defunct naval stations of the Atlantic coast. The sailors and Marines who came from Savannah to Charleston in December 1864, found themselves refugees once again when Charleston was evacuated on February 17. Led by Captain John R Tucker, CSN, the mixed force of sailors and Marines made its way north, arriving at Drewry's Bluff in March. Shortly thereafter these men were joined to the Marines of Companies A, B and C. The combined unit was called Tucker's Naval Battalion.

When Richmond was evacuated on April 3, 1865, Tucker's Naval Battalion was swept up in the withdrawal from the Confederate capital. Attached to Maj Gen G W C Lee's Division, Ewell's Corps, the Naval Battalion marched with Lee's Army of Northern Virginia. Ewell's Corps formed the rear guard of the retreating army. On April 6, the pursuing Federal Sixth Corps made contact with Ewell's troops at Sayler's Creek. The Confederates formed line of battle beyond the creek on a small hill.

The Battle of Sayler's Creek ended in defeat for the Confederates but the gallantry of the Naval Battalion was noted by several participants on both sides. The Marines fought hand-to-hand with the 37th Massachusetts, wielding clubbed muskets, firing pistols into each other's faces, and using the bayonet savagely. One wrote, 'Those Marines fought like tigers and against odds of At least ten to one.' Brig Gen Truman Seymour, commanding the 3rd Division, Sixth Corps, stated, 'The Confederate Marine Battalion fought with peculiar obstinacy. . . .' when his troops met unexpected resistance from Tucker's force and were beaten back.[37]

The embattled Confederates could not long hold their advantage. The Federal troops rallied and soon overwhelmed the outnumbered rebels. As the fighting swept up the knoll at Sayler's Creek and beyond, Tucker's Naval Battalion fell back to the cover of a ravine. The battle rushed past and left Tucker and his men unaware of what was happening around them. The rest of Ewell's Corps was surrounded and forced to surrender, but the Marines and sailors remained under arms, ready to continue the fight. Brig Gen Warren Keifer, commanding 2nd Brigade, 3rd Division, Sixth Corps, stumbled upon Tucker's force later in the day, and, after revealing the fate of Ewell's troops to the captain, accepted the surrender of the Naval Battalion. Among those who laid down their arms to Keifer were seven Marine officers and some fifty enlisted men.[38]

Another group of Marines eluded capture at Sayler's Creek and marched on with the remnants of the Army of Northern Virginia. On April 9, 1865, four Marine officers and twenty-one enlisted men were paroled at Appomattox Court House.[39]

Tucker's Naval Battalion was not the only field organization in the final days of the war in Virginia to number Marines in its ranks. A second naval force made up of the seamen and Marines of the James River Squadron took the field on April 3, and left the capital by way of the Danville Railroad. Led by Rear Adm Raphael Semmes, the last commander of the squadron, who now held a temporary commission as a brigadier general, these troops

ultimately found their way to Greensboro, North Carolina, and were included in the surrender terms negotiated by Gen Joseph E Johnston and Maj Gen William T Sherman on April 26, 1865. Also included in the surrender were Captain John R F Tattnall and the remaining Marines from Company E.[40]

As the war drew to a close in Virginia, Marines from the Mobile Station were involved in desperate fighting. A detachment was among the defenders of Fort Blakely during the siege of April 2–9, 1865. One sergeant and nineteen privates were taken prisoner when the fort was overrun. The remainder of Company D, the Marine Guards aboard CSS *Nashville* and *Morgan*, with those from Marine Barracks, Mobile, three officers and twenty-four enlisted men, laid down their arms at Nanna Hubba Bluff on the Tombigbee River on May 10.

The last Marines to give up the struggle were those serving aboard the cruiser CSS *Shenandoah.* These few joined the raider

1st **Lt Becket K Howell wearing the uniform of the US Marine Corps. (Naval Historical Center)**

from the crews of the many prizes sent to the bottom by *Shenandoah,* and enlisted as Marines by her commanding officer, Lt Cdg James I Waddell. When news that the war was over reached Waddell, he steered a course for Europe. On November 6, 1865, Lieutenant Waddell, turned his ship over to British authorities at Liverpool.

The uniforms, arms and equipment of the Confederate States Marine Corps

No regulations pertaining to the uniform and dress of the Confederate States Marine Corps have ever been located. Given the fact that the Corps went through several changes in uniforms, it may be that none were officially stated. However, photographs of Marine officers and existing records from the quartermaster's

2nd Lt Francis H Cameron. (National Archives)

office provide some insight as to what was worn during certain periods of the war.

The first uniform worn by CS Marine officers seems to have been what former officers of the Old Corps brought with them when they threw their lot with the South. Two images taken aboard CSS *Sumter* at New Orleans clearly show 1st Lt Becket K Howell wearing the full dress uniform prescribed by the 1859 regulations of the US Marine Corps.

The January 1862 photograph of 2nd Lt Francis H Cameron shows that significant changes were made. The colour of the uniform remains dark, probably navy blue. The sleeve braid worn by Cameron indicates that the rank markings of the CS Army had

2nd Lt Robert M Ramsay. (B Ramsay Powell)

been partially embraced. However, there is no corresponding collar bar.

The 1862 uniform regulations for the CS Navy changed the colour of uniforms from navy blue to gray. Although the Corps is not mentioned in these uniform regulations, it is apparent that the change also applied to Marines. However, there appears to have been a deliberate effort to retain navy blue in some form as a mark of distinction for the Marine officer.

2nd Lt James Campbell Murdoch. (Museum of the Confederacy)

1st Lt David G Raney. (Margaret Key)

The images of 2nd Lt Robert M Ramsay show a pattern which appears to have been an attempt to incorporate the Army system of indicating organization by the colour of the cuffs and collar. The uniform is obviously gray. While it is impossible to determine the colour of his cuffs, collar and kepi from the images, it is probable that it was dark blue. The collar shows the rank bar of a second lieutenant, but there is no corresponding sleeve braid.

An 1863 image of 1st Lt David G Raney seems to indicate

the adoption of the shoulder knot worn by officers of the US Marine Corps. While the dark cuff was retained, rank is indicated by the shoulder knot and Army-style sleeve braid. The uniform shown in the image of 2nd Lt James C Murdoch follows this style, but lacks the coloured cuff. However, the kepi shown in the Murdoch image appears to have a dark blue crown and band, possibly an attempt to retain the colour associated with the Marine Corps.

The image of Henry L Graves shows him with Army-style sleeve braid and the collar bars of a first lieutenant. Since Graves was not promoted to this grade until February 1864, it would seem that the Corps returned to the system of Army rank markings. However, Graves's uniform coat, now in the collections of the Atlanta Historical Society, obviously underwent significant changes at some point after the photograph was taken. The collar bars remain, although slightly different in design, but the sleeve braid has been removed and shoulder knots added.

The photographs of 2nd Lt Nathaniel E Venable and 2nd Lt Henry M Doak display a uniform that closely resembles the Army pattern. Sleeve braid and collar bars appear in both. The images of 1st Lt David G Raney and 2nd Lt John L Rapier, both taken after their escape from prison in October 1864, also follow this design. The only clue as to the colour of these uniforms appears in a memorandum noting ten yards of gray flannel cloth sold to officers at the Mobile Station in April 1864.[41]

Further complicating the picture of Marine officer uniforms are two references to blue flannel uniforms being worn. In letters written by Lieutenants Graves and Thomson both indicated that these uniforms were intended for warm weather. Since Graves wrote in April 1863 and Thomson in September 1864, it appears that blue flannel uniforms may have been the norm for summer wear.

The first uniforms worn by enlisted Marines were issued to recruits at New Orleans during April and May 1861 and consisted of gray flannel shirts, blue flannel shirts, white shirts (jumpers), white linen pantaloons, and blue cottonade pantaloons Navy caps and military caps of an unspecified style were also issued at Pensacola. On July 10, 1861, Captain Thom turned over what appears to be a supply of the first regular uniform issues to the quartermaster, Major Samuel Z Gonzalez. The list included uniform caps, uniform pantaloons, fatigue jackets, flannel shirts, brogans and white linen pants. No colour or style is indicated.

On May 9, 1861, the Navy Department sent instructions to James D Bulloch, then in England as a special agent, to purchase

for the Marine Corps: 2,000 pairs of pants, 2,000 jackets, 1,000 overcoats and watch coats, 1,000 pairs of shoes, 2,000 flannel shirts, 2,000 pairs of canton flannel drawers, 2,000 pairs of woolen socks, 1,000 blankets, 1,000 fatigue caps, and 1,000 shirts. These items may be what were taken by Captain John D

1st Lt Henry L. Graves. (Atlanta Historical Society)

Uniform worn by Lieutenant Graves. (Atlanta Historical Society)

2nd Lt Nathaniel E Venable. (James Harris)

Simms to Pensacola and Savannah in the fall of 1861 in his capacity as acting quartermaster. On October 4, 1861, he turned over what appeared to be new uniform issues to Captain George Holmes at Savannah. The invoice listed jean pants: five pairs for sergeants, four pairs for corporals, and ninety-one pairs for privates. Also issued were satinette frock coats; five for sergeants, four for corporals and ninety-one for privates. Simms also turned over 100 forage caps, 100 leather stocks, 192 pairs of yarn socks, 62 woollen shirts, 48 blankets, 100 pairs of drawers, 100 pairs of shoes and 100 tweed overcoats.

While no colour for this uniform issue is listed, it is assumed to be dark blue. Since no record of further issues of uniform articles is recorded in the quartermaster record between October 1861 and May 1862, it is probable that the same uniform was worn on the latter date. Frank Vizetelly, a reporter representing the *Illustrated London News*, visited Drewry's Bluff in May 1862, and made a drawing of the CS Marines in their camp. It is evident that Vizetelly intended to show that the Marines were wearing dark uniforms.

The dark blue uniforms soon gave way to gray, as shown by a

2nd Lt Henry M Doak. (Tennessee State Library)

1st Lt David G Greenway. (Dale Snair)

description of Marines attending the funeral of First Sergeant Jacob Scholls on September 2, 1862. In a letter written by Ephriam H Harding, chaplain of the 45th North Carolina Volunteers, the Marines 'were all dressed in white trousers and grey coats.'[42]

The change from blue to gray uniforms is emphasized further by the contents of a March 1863 letter from the Navy Department to Bulloch. Urgently required for the Marine Corps were clothing and shoes for 1,000 men for a year. Notice was drawn to the fact that 'Marine Cloth is gray.' Deserters' notices published in 1863 testify to at least a gray jacket being worn by Marines of the period.

The gray uniform appears to have remained the standard issue of the Corps until January 1864. At that time, Major A S Taylor, Corps Quartermaster, sent 992¾ yards of blue-gray army cloth to the Army Quartermaster's department to be made into uniform coats. A more clearly defined statement regarding the composition and colour of the Marine coat is found on an invoice submitted by the Army quartermaster three months later. In the making and trimming of 485 frock coats, the following materials were used:

2nd Lt John L Rapier. (Adelaide M Trigg, Rapier's granddaughter)

300 yards of canvas, 672 yards of blue jeans, 1,102 yards of cotton sleeves, 15 pounds of black thread and 14 gross 'A' buttons.

The uniform allowance for the enlisted Marine consisted of:

    1 uniform cap

    2 uniform coats

    1 pair epaulettes or counter straps

    8 pair linen overalls

    4 pair woolen overalls

    16 shirts

    2 stocks

    24 pair brogans

    2 blankets

    8 pairs socks

    3 fatigue caps

    4 fatigue jackets

    8 flannel shirts

    1 great coat

    3 pompoms

    2 knapsacks

    6 fatigue overalls

    5 linen jackets

While the uniform issue implies that certain items were available to the enlisted Marine, none of the quarterly returns of clothing, camp and garrison equipage received and issued indicates that they were issued. Pompoms do not appear on any of the returns. Leather stocks, epaulettes and counter straps, although part of the stores for which the company commanders were responsible, are not shown being issued to the enlisted men.

Private William G B Hosch, Company E. (Katherine Hosch Jessup)

Camp of the CS Marines at Drewry's Bluff. (*Illustrated London News*, November 15, 1862)

The only reference to a full dress uniform for enlisted Marines appears on an invoice dated June 8, 1861. On that date, 1st Lt Becket K Howell received twenty full dress uniforms for the Guard of CSS *Sumter* at New Orleans.[43]

The uniform button worn by the Marine Corps has been the subject of much speculation. Examples of buttons with a stippled Roman 'M' have been found in places known to have been sites of Marine Corps activity. All have the back mark of Hammond Turner & Bates of Birmingham, England, the manufacturer of similar buttons issued to branches of the Army: 'I' for infantry, 'C' for cavalry, 'E' for engineers, 'R' for riflemen, and 'A' for artillery. These 'M' buttons have previously been tentatively identified as having been worn by the enlisted men of the Marine Corps. Confirmation that this was the case has been made by a careful examination of the uniform once worn by Pvt Samuel C Curtis, a member of Company C. The uniform coat is fastened by seven of these 'M' buttons.[44] The 'A' buttons referred to above seem to have been issued in lieu of the 'M' button, perhaps when supplies from England were exhausted. Since Marines were thought of as naval artillerists, the 'A' button was likely deemed to have been suitable.

The buttons worn by Marine officers apparently were a discretionary item. An examination of those which appear in the photograph of Marine officer David G Raney reveals the Florida State Seal. Those worn by John L Rapier show the Louisiana State Seal.

Private Allan P Hamm, Company E. (Brooks Hamm)

Nathaniel E Venable's uniform buttons display an anchor motif.

Long arms used by the Marine Corps appear to have been a case of what was available for issue. While the British Enfield-pattern rifle caliber .577 with sword bayonet was the weapon most commonly seen in quarterly returns of ordnance and ordnance stores, it was by no means the standard issue.

The ordnance and ordnance stores return for the third quarter 1861 indicate Company A in possession of eighty-five percussion muskets, type and caliber unspecified. These were replaced by seventy-five Enfield-pattern rifles on November 25, 1861.

On May 16, 1861, Company B received eighty-six percussion muskets, also type and caliber unspecified, from the Army Quartermaster at Pensacola. These were left behind when the company was transferred to Virginia. Ninety-four Enfield-pattern rifles were issued to Captain Van Benthuysen on April 22, 1862.

There are no ordnance returns for Company C at Pensacola, but it must be assumed that weapons similar to those used by Companies A and B were issued. Enfield-pattern rifles were received by Captain Thom on November 28, 1861, just before his company departed the Warrington Navy Yard.

At least three different arms were used by Company D at Mobile. Although a February 1863 recruiting notice promised recruits Enfield rifles, Captain Meiere was compelled to make do with altered M1842 Springfield .69 caliber muskets and .54 caliber Austrian Lorenz rifled muskets.

No ordnance stores for Company E have been located, but a photograph of Pvt Allan P Hamm shows him holding an Austrian Lorenz rifled musket.

On April 27, 1861, Captain Thom turned over the following accouterments to 1st Lt Henry L Ingraham, 'at the Navy Yard near Pensacola for use of CS Marines.' 100 waist belts and plates, 100 cartridge boxes and plates, 100 cartridge box belts and plates, 10 cap pouches and 100 canteen straps. While no description of the belts or plates was noted, it is probable that they were of the same type as those being issued to state volunteer regiments.

Accouterments specifically ordered for use by Marines are described in Navy Department correspondence to James Bulloch, dated September 26 1861: '1,000 waist belts, black leather (such as used in British service), with cartridge box, cap box, and bayonet scabbard, attached by means of slides; 1,000 knapsacks, such as used in British service, with straps to connect to the waist belt.'[45] The image of Private Hamm shows these items in use. Hamm wears a black leather waist belt with the British snake-clasp. Attached to the belt is the Brunswick ball bag, standard issue to British riflemen in 1861.

The sword worn by a non-commissioned officer was attached to a shoulder belt, as opposed to his counterpart in the US Marines who wore his in a frog attached to the waist belt. Edwin Wallace, a product of the Royal Marines and the only Confederate States Marine to be elevated to the post of a sergeant-major of the Corps, had a specially-made sword and belt presented to him on February 22, 1864.[46]

J Thomas Scharf, who, as a young midshipman, took part in the capture of USS *Underwriter* on February 2, 1864, later wrote that the conduct of the Marines during the fight was 'conspicuous'.[47] The same must be said for their varied styles of uniform.

David M Sullivan

Chapter Nine
SHIPBOARD LIFE

The organization of the crew

When a Confederate commerce raider put to sea in a sailing ship with auxiliary steam power, its crew was organized in virtually the same way as in similar ships in the US Navy. Since most Confederate Navy officers had years of previous service in the US Navy, it is not surprising that they would establish regulations, organizations and procedures with which they were most familiar.

The lowest-ranking members of the crew both in terms of age and responsibilities were the boys, who were between the ages of fourteen and seventeen and who delivered powder to the guns. Most of the boys were considered as apprentices, and as such were expected to observe the working of the ship and to pick up useful information that they could apply when they were older.

Men who were under twenty-five and who had no experience but who were strong might find themselves rated as coal heavers and given the task of keeping the engine fires supplied with fuel. Others who were also inexperienced were rated as landsmen and assigned to the deck force where they learned their various duties. Firemen came next and were rated within that rank according to degrees of responsibility. A second-class fireman ranked with a landsman. He was expected to be skilled in the management of fires, boilers and pumps, and to acquire a good general knowledge of the duties and responsibilities of a first-class fireman. A first-class fireman was expected to be familiar with the qualities of all types of coal, and be able to start fires, maintain the proper height and density of water in the boilers, and be familiar with the cocks, valves, stuffing boxes and steam joints. He was also expected to be able to clean and lubricate the engines and pumps. Since the commerce raiders of the Confederate Navy drew their engineers mainly from the British merchant service, it is believed that they had a high level of competence and thus there was no need to make distinctions in the ranks and pay of firemen.

Ranking on the same level as the first-class firemen were those rated as ordinary seamen, who had a high level of proficiency and had usually made two or more cruises. Next highest in rank were the seamen, who were the most experienced and knowledgeable of the enlisted men in shiphandling.[1]

Each crew member was assigned to one of five divisions: the master's division, the engineer's division, the powder division, the gun division and the surgeon's division. Within each division every man received daily training in his duties. These duties sometimes overlapped those of other divisions. In addition, officers rotated men to learn other duties associated with quarter stations in the ship. Thus a man whose regular duties involved spreading, reefing and furling sails would have additional duties serving as an oarsman in the ship's boat, as a member of a boarding party, or at one of the ship's guns. Until a man committed all these assignments and places to memory and performed them out of habit and discipline, he would find it necessary to consult the watch, quarter or station list posted in a prominent place, usually on the binnacle, where every man's place in every situation was noted.[2]

The officer known as the master, who ranked below the lieutenant, was responsible for handling the navigation of the ship, the maintaining of discipline, and the internal arrangements of the vessel. His division consisted of the men who were stationed in the tops of the masts and assigned to duties in the rigging, sails, signals and steerage. Assisting him in these duties were the boatswain, the boatswain's mates, the quartermaster, the captain of the afterguard, the captain of the forecastle and the ship's cook.

The boatswain was a warrant officer who was trained in seamanship and whose duty station was in the forecastle or forward part of the ship. He had charge of the rigging and cordage, the anchor and the ship's boats. He piped the crew to duty with his whistle, which was his symbol of authority. He was usually assisted in his duties by at least one or as many as four mates. Men whose duty station was the forecastle were generally prime seamen. The petty officer who oversaw affairs in that portion of the ship was known as the captain of the forecastle.

Stationed on the masts were petty officers known as the captains of the fore, main and mizzen tops. Working under them were men whose duty it was to set or take in sails and keep the rigging in order.

The quartermaster or helmsman was a petty officer who had charge of the ship's wheel and who responded to orders involving course changes. He had charge of the log, the lead for determining the depth of water under the ship, the ship's flags and signals, lights, compasses, and navigation instruments. Quartermasters were among the most experienced and reliable seamen. The captain's clerk made notes on orders given and actions taken for use in making entries in the ship's log. In some cases a midshipman or two might be standing by ready to deliver the captain's orders to those too far away to hear the executive officer.

The captain of the afterguard was a petty officer under whom the landsmen or less experienced men worked in manning gear on the quarterdeck and poop. Ordinarily they did not go aloft except to loose or furl a mainsail. Landsmen and worn-out seamen were also stationed in the waist, or that portion of the ship between the quarterdeck and the forward part of the ship, where they might be called upon to perform such tasks as serving on a gun crew or helping to set, furl or reef the larger sails.

The cook was a petty officer in charge of the galley who supervised the cooking for all of the crew. Before the dinner hour he brought a sample of what was to be served that day to the officer of the deck for his inspection and approval. Assisting the cook was the ship's steward. A ward room steward served the officers and a cabin steward took care of the commander of the ship. All stewards were petty officers.

A warrant officer whose duties were associated with the spar deck and the domain of the master was the sailmaker, but his divisional assignment was at discretion of the captain. The sailmaker made and mended sails. This involved measuring, cutting and fitting the sails or the repairs. He was assisted by a mate, who was a petty officer, and whose duties included making sails under the direction of the sailmaker and taking care of the sails in the sail room of the ship. The sailmaker also had a gang which helped him with his work.

Another petty officer whose duties were associated with the master's division was the cockswain. It was his job to see that the ship's boats were ready for service on short notice, usually in connection with the boarding of suspected enemy ships. Each boat had a bowman who was to provide and arrange for the provisions in the boat, as well as a cooking vessel, sand, a tinder box, flint and steel, candles, lantern and wood. Each oarsman in the boat had specific duties in addition to pulling an oar. For example, the second oarsman was to provide and stow the fresh water, the boat's anchor, chain or rope, fish hooks and lines, battle axes, and tacks and nails.

The officer in charge of the ship's engine and boilers and their dependent equipment was the engineer and his area of responsibility was known as the engineering division. Assisting him in these operations were the first- and second-class firemen and the coal heavers, whose duties have already been noted. They also repaired any damage suffered by the engine or boilers. These men worked in a very hard environment. With temperatures rising to as high as 150°F, it was necessary to rotate the men in the engine room at brief intervals, especially during a battle. In such circumstances the relief men could be drafted from the masters or the powder division with the permission of the executive officer.

The powder division was in the charge of a lieutenant or a passed midshipman. Under him was a warrant officer known as the gunner, who was responsible for the battery, magazine and ordnance stores. In the performance of these duties he was assisted by his mate and others. Generally the powder division consisted of all those stationed below the gun decks with the exception of the surgeon's division. When a battle was expected, the lieutenant received the keys to the magazine from the captain. Before opening the magazine, the carpenter, who was a warrant officer, and his mates covered all hatches, gratings and air ports. The master-at-arms, who was a petty officer, lit the magazine lanterns and let down wet blankets or canvas that served as fire screens over the magazine hatch. For safety in this dangerous environment the gunner and his mates wore canvas shoes and smock-like clothing in an effort to avoid creating any sparks. Meanwhile the carpenter and his gang removed wardroom bulkheads and other hindrances to the free and rapid movement of ammunition to the guns.

In battle the duty station of the lieutenant in charge of the powder division was on deck watching the action. He sent orders to the gunner in the ship's magazine designating the type of projectile to be used and the amount of powder needed. The gunner and his mate and assistants in the magazine and shell rooms would send up what was needed. Powder men and boys carried bags of black powder and projectiles to the guns as well as any needed supplies. The black powder was packed in wool cloth bags and carried in tin-lined containers known as pass boxes. The carpenter and his mates rigged the pumps and manned guns during a battle. If additional men were needed for the ship's pumps in an emergency they came from those gun crew members who had been designated as pump men.

During a battle the carpenter and his crew made temporary repairs of any damage suffered by the ship. After the battle more permanent repairs were made. At other times the carpenter inspected the masts, spars and hull of the ship to see whether they were in good repair. Any defects in these areas were reported to the commanding officer. One member of the carpenter's crew as usually a cooper, who made any barrels that the ship needed.

The armourer was a petty officer whose duty it was to keep the small arms of the ship in a serviceable condition. The yeoman had charge of the storeroom in which the ordnance stores were kept. He was not to issue nor expend any article in his custody except on the authority of the captain or the executive officer. A petty officer known as the captain of the hold saw to it that all was in order in that part of the ship and supervised the movement and stowage of supplies. Both cargo and supplies had to have their weight distributed so that the seagoing qualities of the ship were best utilized.

A fourth division in the ship was known as the gun division which was under the supervision of a lieutenant with a knowledge of ordnance. The guns on each deck were divided into two or three divisions, depending on the number of lieutenants or other watch officers on board. The goal was to have each division of guns and the persons attached to be commanded by a lieutenant or other watch officer. Gun divisions were then numbered consecutively beginning with those on the forward part of the lowest deck as the first division and continuing to the after division of that deck, and then to the forward division on the next deck above.

Petty officers known as quarter gunners were attached to each gun division to take care of the guns and gun gear. The gear was stored in boxes designated as 'supply' and 'reserve.' When the crew was at quarters for exercises, inspection or battle, he was expected to supply each sailor in his gun division with waist belts with leather accouterments, primer-boxes or other items. During a battle he furnished any needed equipment such as ladles, worms or breechings. Before a battle the quarter gunners obtained fire and buckets of fresh water from the master's division and placed them along the decks for the powder men and boys. Quarter gunners also obtained a fire tub for the used pass boxes. A fire hose was attached to the ship's pumps and made ready for use in case of fire. A quarter gunner or a gunner's mate was also stationed in each of the shell rooms and in the smaller magazine of the ship.

The number of guns assigned to each division depended on the size of the crew and the way the guns were arranged in the ship. Gun crews might vary in size from eleven for a 32pdr smoothbore cannon to twenty-seven for a large caliber pivot gun. In some circumstances, a gun division might be responsible for as many as six smaller guns, with three on each side of the ship. It was expected that gun crews would be fighting on one side of the ship at a time, but if necessary the guns on both sides could be manned at the same time, though at a reduced rate of fire and for a limited period. During an action a gunner's mate or a quarter gunner from the powder division was assigned to a gun division. Men in the gun divisions were also called upon to make minor changes in sail, to be a part of boarding parties, and to help fight fires in the ship, if necessary.

A model of the commerce raider *Georgia*, built in Scotland in 1862-3 as *Japan*. (WMCWNH)

Each gun crew was in the charge of a gun captain, who was usually a boatswain's mate. Confederate ordnance regulations said that gun captains 'should be selected with great care from those in whose skill, coolness, and judgement the greatest reliance can be placed without regard to their rating.' The preferred arrangement was to have each gun crew composed of about one-third petty officers and seamen, one-third ordinary seamen and one-third landsmen and boys. Before any man was permanently assigned to a gun crew, the officers tried to determine his capabilities by questioning him or exercising him at the guns. Members of the gun crew with less experience did not participate in boarding operations, but were armed with pikes and ordered to repel any attempt to board their own ship.

Areas below the spar and gun decks were the sites of the paymaster's office and the spirit room, in which the daily grog rations were stored. The latter room was watched over by the paymaster's clerk in the absence of a marine guard.[3]

A few seagoing Confederate Navy ships carried marines, notably the *Sumter*, the *Shenandoah*, the *Tallahassee* and the *Chickamauga*. The *Sumter* had a twenty-man force under the command of a lieutenant. They did regular shipboard duty, guarded prisoners, and were assigned as members of the prize crew of captured ships. Confederate ordnance instructions suggest that some were used in gun crews and that others might be deployed in the ship according to the dictates of the captain. The marine guard in the *Shenandoah* consisted of sixteen or seventeen men under the command of a sergeant. The size of the marine force in the *Tallahassee* is not known, but it was commanded by a lieutenant. Nine enlisted marines were assigned to the *Chickamauga* under the command of a sergeant, but two of the men were apparently transferred before the ship sailed. Lieutenant Becket K Howell, formerly of the *Sumter*, was the only marine in the *Alabama*. An attempt was made to recruit captured US Marines for service in the *Alabama*, but it was unsuccessful.[4]

A fifth division in a ship was that of the surgeon which was under the direction of that officer. It consisted of the assistant surgeon, if such were aboard, and any persons designated by the captain to assist them. Normally these would include the chaplain and the paymaster. Men from the carpenter's gang were also assigned to help move the wounded. In the Confederate Navy the wardroom was designated as the place for the treatment of the wounded. Before a battle the surgeon was to see that a sufficient number of tourniquets were distributed to the several divisions and to the men in the tops. The surgeon was responsible for seeing that those attached to his division and any others as directed by the captain were instructed in how to use a tourniquet.[5]

In both the Confederate and US Navy, enlisted men were assigned to regular duties in the ship, as well as specific duties in the event of various circumstances. When on watch each division worked the ship and inspected every area to make sure that everything was functioning properly. Any defects were reported by the warrant officers and the master to the captain. Work schedules for the watches were modified to take care of any repairs that were needed or problems that had to be resolved. For major tasks, such as replacing a mast, the entire crew would be employed. Normal duties might range from spreading, reefing or furling the sails, to such additional duties as serving as an oarsman in the ship's boat, as a member of a boarding party, or at one of the ship's guns.[6]

For those who served in the ironclads in Southern rivers, the size of the ship and its mission meant that there was a great deal of difference in the size of its crew and the tempo of daily life. There was no need for men to deal with sails or the details associated with a large ship. In an ironclad the emphasis was on the gun crews and those who worked in the engine room, as well as keeping the ship clean.

In both seagoing vessels and ships assigned to rivers and harbors, the crew was divided into port and starboard watches, and the twenty-four-hour day was divided into seven watch periods. From 4 to 8am was the morning watch; 8am to 12 noon was the forenoon watch; and 12 noon to 4pm was the noon or afternoon watch. The two-hour period from 4 to 6pm was known as the first dog watch. The second dog watch was from 6 to 8pm The evening watch was from 8pm to midnight. From midnight to 4am was the mid or night watch. Without the dog watches the starboard watch would be on duty every night from eight to midnight as well as from four to eight in the morning. The result would be that the members of the starboard watch would have only four hours of sleep, while members of the port watch would have seven hours of rest. Under the dog watch arrangement, every man got four hours of sleep on watch nights and seven hours on other nights. Another alternative was to divide the crew into three watches so that each man would be on duty for four hours and off for eight hours.

Men were stationed at all times in the tops or platforms on the masts above the lower yards. The top men of the starboard

Captain Raphael Semmes (right) and Lt John M Kell aboard the *Alabama*. (Naval Historical Center)

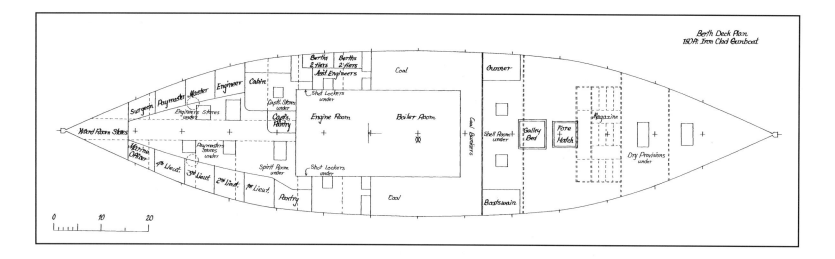

Living quarters on a *Richmond*-class ironclad (Robert Holcombe, from original plans)

and port watches were much exposed to weather and to minimize this they were divided into quarter watches. Under this arrangement the man in the top was relieved every hour by another member of his watch. In the engine room the engineers, firemen and coal heavers were arranged in watches under the direction of the senior engineer of the watch. Men assigned to the engine room were responsible for the engines, boilers and related items, and they were not to be ordered to do other duties except in cases of emergency. When this became necessary, the engineer on duty was to be informed so that he could take any necessary precautions.[7]

The dominant figure in the ship was the commanding officer. He was subject to orders from the Secretary of the Navy and bound by regulations to do things in a prescribed way. When a ship was placed in commission, the commanding officer was to see that officers and crew members were at their stations and learned their duties before the ship went to sea. Commanders were also to see that landsmen and ordinary seamen were taught how to steer, to heave the lead to determine the depth of the water in which the ship was moving, to knit and to splice ropes, to handle and reef sails, to use the sailmaker's palm and needle, and to perform any other duties that were required. Special attention was to be paid to the education of apprentices under the age of twenty-one years so that they would become good seamen and eventually good petty officers. The commanding officer was to choose a competent petty officer or a person of inferior rating who was to instruct the ship's boys in reading, writing and arithmetic.[8]

Many officers in both the Confederate and the US Navy

believed that a familiarity with their subordinates undermined discipline. As a result some, such as Raphael Semmes of the CSS *Alabama*, cultivated an aloof and distant personality. The commander of a ship knew that it was important to cultivate the confidence and trust of all of the crew so that his orders would be carried out without question. The commander was always actively involved in the working of the ship. When something needed to be done, he gave the necessary order to the executive officer, or first lieutenant, who transmitted it orally to the warrant officer whose work gang then on watch was to execute it.[9]

The ship's day

In the Confederate Navy the tempo of daily life at sea was very much the same as that followed in the US Navy. Even the members of the crew who had served in the British merchant service would find many familiar routines in the Confederate Navy. One noticeable difference was that in both the Confederate and the US Navy, there was no talking or singing on deck nor any unnecessary noise that might interfere with the clear transmission of orders. Men who served in the merchant service might expect to hear a sea chantey, and perhaps the sound of a fiddle, when the anchor was raised or other work performed, but in the Navy there was none.

The times set for daily routines were dictated in part by the season of the year, the weather or other immediate needs, the inclinations of the captain and the size of the ship. In situations where the ship was scheduled to take on coal or be cleaned, the day might begin as early as 4am, but in general the hours of rest ended and the shipboard tempo increased with the first light, or about 5am. When the marine bugler sounded reveille, or more often the sound of a drum began the day, the master-at-arms, or one of his corporals, and the boatswain's mate on the current watch would run around the berth deck shouting at the sleeping men and slapping hammocks. As the men awakened to the noise, they responded to orders to rise, to lash up their hammocks and bedding into a tight, round bundle, and to carry it up to the spar or upper deck. There the hammocks were stored in a uniform fashion behind heavy rope nets, called nettings, along the bulwarks. Placing the hammocks in the nettings not only aired them but in the event of a battle, they provided some additional protection from gunfire and splinters as well as a barrier against boarders. Officers who were accustomed to the tempo of life in the peacetime Navy liked to see the men awakened and the delivery of their hammocks completed within seven minutes. Given the number of inexperienced men in the crews of many Confederate warships, it is doubtful that these operations were completed in so brief a time. At least some men would have removed some or all of their outer clothing, and virtually everybody had to slip on shoes. It seems likely that it may have taken ten minutes to get men out of their hammocks and dressed. Even if most of the men delivered their hammocks on deck in an approved length of time, there undoubtedly would have been stragglers and delays before all hammocks and bedding were stored.

The next task was to get out the sand, brooms, holystones and buckets and begin scrubbing and washing down the decks. The berth deck was usually washed with salt water, and the spar or open deck was holystoned by teams of men on their knees working under the direction of a boatswain's mate. When the washing,

rinsing and holystoning operations were finished, the decks were dried by striking them with dry cloths. While some members of the crew were cleaning the decks, others were polishing the brass work. Metal tracks on the deck that made it easy to quickly traverse a cannon were cleaned and burnished. Cannon were cleaned. Sails, rigging, halyards, or ropes for hoisting and rigging sails or yards were checked and maintained, as were the blocks.

When the work of cleaning and maintaining the ship and its equipment were completed, it was time for the men to wash and shave themselves. By 7:30am a crew of a warship was supposed to be washed, combed, dressed in a neat and tidy manner, and lined up for inspection by the master-at-arms.

The boatswain piped breakfast at 8am and each man reported to his own mess. These usually consisted of from eight to twelve men. Sailors who had similar duties, such as members of a gun crew, firemen, coal heavers or topmen would have their own messes. Marines and petty officers messed separately. If there were any boys on board, they were distributed among the messes. Every member of a mess took his turn as the cook or mess orderly. Sometimes a person who was skilled in preparing meals might be hired by his messmates to act as a cook on a permanent basis. It was the cook's job to unlock the mess chest that was assigned to his mess. This contained the cooking utensils, tableware, and the food allotted each week by the ship's cook or by the paymaster. Each member of the mess was responsible for keeping his own mug, knife, fork and spoon. At breakfast each man was supposed to receive one piece of hard, salted beef known as salt junk, and one pint of coffee without milk. After breakfast the dishes were cleaned and returned to the mess chest and the men cleaned their individual cups and utensils.

Once breakfast and the clean up were completed, the men were called to quarters, usually about 9:30am. Guns were inspected to see that they were properly mounted, clean and ready for use.

Living quarters on a *Macon*-class gunboat. (Robert Holcombe, from original plans)

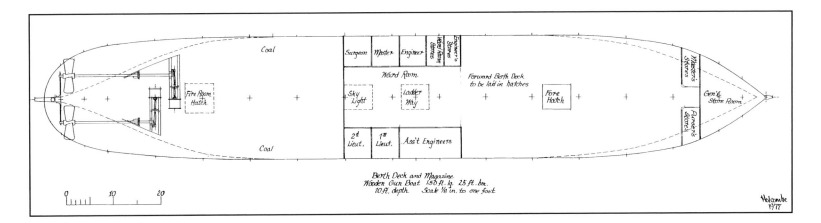

The *Alabama's* sailors practising with cutlasses. (*Century Magazine*)

Rigging and quarters were inspected to see that everything was in order. Men took up their assigned duties and watches. Those with physical complaints went to see the ship's surgeon, who treated them. If they were able to do duty, they took their assigned places. If not, they were placed in the sick bay and treated by the surgeon or an assistant. In smaller ships, where there was no sick bay, a man might be confined to his hammock until his condition improved. When he was not attending to the sick, the surgeon inspected the ship and reported any conditions that in his judgement might impair the health of the crew. Meanwhile members of the crew at their duty stations might pass their time in a relaxed manner. Some might read newspapers or books, write letters or doze. But the sighting of a prize or an enemy warship led to orders being issued that could quickly transform a tranquil scene to one where everyone was poised for action.

The ship's day officially began at noon. It was also the time for the main meal of the day. The fare usually consisted of a piece of beef or pork, vegetables and coffee. The crews of Confederate cruisers usually ate well as a result of the food that they got from captured vessels. In the rest of the Confederate Navy cheese, butter and raisins were supposed to be a part of the daily ration, but they were rarely available. Tea and coffee were available from the blockade runners, but at a great cost. Despite their problems and shortages, Confederate sailors usually ate better than the men in the Army.

After their main meal, crews went to their assigned stations. In commerce raiders, such as the *Alabama*, the captain would pace the quarterdeck, keeping an eye on the weather, the sea and the ship. If the captain wanted to ship to move in a different direction or tack, he would so inform the first lieutenant, or the executive officer of the ship, who, in turn, called out he order to the quartermaster or the man at the ship's wheel. If sails had to be spread, or reefed or furled, the lieutenant gave the order and the men assigned to that duty climbed up the ratlines, and over the yardarm to their designated positions and did what had been ordered. In more tranquil moments, the first lieutenant would pace the spar deck, ordering or suggesting things to be done here or there. It was the duty of the executive officer to examine the ship daily and to determine when it was ready for an inspection by the commanding officer. Every morning and evening he received reports from the master, boatswain, gunner, carpenter and sailmaker about the state of matters under their supervision. The executive officer was expected to inform himself about the capacities of every man in the ship, what stations he had previously filled, and how he could be used to the best advantage to the ship.

Some men were assigned to work under the direction of the boatswain. Others were topmen whose duties included the securing of chafing gear on the yards and rigging. Another topman, seated in a triangle, might be swung around the mast while he lubricated the mast with slush, or the greasy refuse of cooking from the ship's galley. The carpenter's duty on a given day might involve cutting or trimming timber or repairing shot holes or other damage in the ship. The gunner and his mates might be engaged in polishing the guns. The sailmaker was often engaged in repairing sails or awnings as well as making them. The signal quartermaster might take advantage of a warm day to dry or air his collection of flags. Much time was spent in various kinds of drill, including exercising the guns. This was very important because most Confederate sailors had had little or no experience with naval guns. Green hands had to be brought up to a standard of proficiency. When men were lost through desertion, death or transfer, new men had to be trained and integrated into the system. The *Alabama* was fortunate in that about half of its crew were formerly British men-of-war's men.[10] Other ships in the Confederate Navy were not as well off in the level of experience of their crews.

At 4pm the messes ate a light evening meal. The timing of this mess was related to the watch sequence of four hours on and four hours off. Meals took place when the watch was relieved. The time after dinner was traditionally the period of relaxation for all who were not on watch. Some captains used this interval for skylarking, tomfoolery, boxing or other tension-relieving activities.

The intervals between meals were not ideal from a nutritional point of view nor from that of utilizing men at their maximum efficiency. All meals took place within an eight-hour framework, but duties were performed on a twenty-four-hour schedule. Men who had to stand watch at midnight or in the early morning hours were often quite hungry since many hours had elapsed since their main meal. Sometimes these problems were overcome or minimized by the dog watch arrangement (described above).

At 5:30pm the men were again called to their quarters and guns and stations were inspected to see that everything was in order. When this was completed, the boatswain's pipe told the men that hammocks could now be removed from the nettings and prepared for sleeping. For all who were not on watch, this was a tranquil period when men could relax, write or read, listen to an old sailor's yarn or mend their clothing. Cards were prohibited in warships, but checkers (draughts) and dominoes were allowed and were popular. Gambling was also forbidden, but was carried on in a covert fashion. If there was a fiddle or banjo player in the crew, this was the time that he would begin playing and his shipmates might listen or join in song. Sometimes ships produced their own theatrical entertainments.

Those in the crew who wished to smoke had to move to the forward part of the ship. Cigars and pipes were lit by a taper from a whale-oil lamp and afterwards carefully extinguished. Friction matches were strictly forbidden because they exposed ships to the danger of fire. No uncovered light was allowed in any storeroom nor in the hold. Lamps and fuels had to be carefully chosen because of the risk of fire or an explosion.

At 8pm tattoo sounded and the men extinguished lights, fires and smokes, and all not on watch went to their sleeping quarters and prepared to retire. When the sun set at 6pm or later, tattoo was moved to 9pm.[11]

From the letters of Lieutenant George W Clift of the CSS *Chattahoochee* stationed off Saffold, Georgia in January 1863, we get glimpses of daily life on a river gunboat. The crew was awakened at 5am, had their breakfast at 6:30am and began the daily routine. One morning it involved scrubbing the ship fore and aft. When this was completed there was a muster of all hands. Beginning in the morning each gun crew drilled for forty-five minutes. One day the guns were run out, loaded and three broadsides were fired in forty seconds. A drill with a 32pdr cannon mounted forward was completed in thirty-five seconds. To a fellow officer the lieutenant set forth the goal of all the training: 'I am endeavouring to bring thing to *regular* man-of-war style.'[12]

Sailors on duty with the Savannah Squadron had a much less exciting time in the course of defending that port. The ironclad CSS *Georgia* was stationed at Elba Island while the duty station of its sister ship, the ironclad CSS *Savannah*, was at the eastern tip of Fig Island, opposite Fort Jackson. Smaller vessels, such as the gunboat CSS *Isondiga*, and the tenders CSS *Firefly* and CSS *Resolute*, did picket duty off Causton's Bluff and served as transports and supply ships. The steamer CSS *Sampson* served as a receiving ship for newly inducted recruits for a few months in the summer and fall of 1863 before it rejoined the squadron in the defense of Savannah. The squadron was reinforced by the CSS *Macon* in the summer of 1864. In the CSS *Savannah* the daily routines consisted of drills and necessary cleaning and repair activities in the ship. For example, in 1864 Mondays, Wednesdays and Fridays were devoted to small arms drill and to washing clothes. Drilling with the broadside guns occupied some of the morning of Tuesday, Thursday and Friday of each week. General quarters were usually held every Friday morning, followed by the holystoning of the spar deck. The gun deck had to be scraped periodically, and this might take a portion of two mornings. There was a general muster on the first Sunday of every month and all hands were assembled on the spar deck to hear the reading of the Articles of War. Every man removed his cap during this reading. When it was completed the purser called the roll. During the summer the ironclads returned to the city at night and the crews slept ashore. The men of the *Savannah* slept in warehouses. In the cooler months the squadron stayed around Fort Jackson and the men went to town in the *Firefly* or in small boats.[13]

The necessities of life

The officers and men of the Confederate Navy, like seafaring men generally, ate three meals a day, with the main one being at noon. When a ship was in port, the crew were to be issued fresh meat and vegetables for their messes on up to four days of each week unless the surgeon believed that their health required a more frequent issue. At sea the normal daily issue was salted beef or pork supplemented by beans, peas and cheese. In the case of the commerce raiders, food from captured prizes meant that there was a greater variety of food available and little need to rely on the ship's stores. Once when the *Alabama*'s store of ship bread was attacked by weevils and became useless, it seemed that the only solution was to head for the nearest port and to replenish the supply.

Fortunately the ship captured a prize that provided all the bread that was needed. Officers and men varied their diet by catching and eating fresh fish. In foreign ports food that was available locally was purchased for the use of the ship. When the *Alabama* was in southeast Asian waters there was plenty of beef, poultry, vegetables and fruits. In Madagascar the ship took on a number of double humped cattle as well as fresh vegetables and fruit.[14]

In the Confederate Navy the enlisted men were served a daily ration of grog. In the US Navy the ration was one gill of spirits or whiskey mixed with water once a day, and this practice was abolished in 1862. Confederate sailors sometimes received a half pint of wine a day in lieu of whiskey. In the *Alabama*, Captain Raphael Semmes promised his largely British crew that they would receive grog twice a day, at breakfast and at the noon meal. British seamen in the *Alabama* were obviously familiar with the Royal Navy's practice of issuing rum diluted with water as the grog ration. In at least some instances when whiskey was not available the ration was rum mixed with water.

The Confederate Navy regulations stated that the captain was to try to induce his men to relinquish the spirit part of their ration for at least three months and to receive the cost of the ration instead. If Confederate officers tried to follow this regulation, they do not seem to have had any success in changing the habits of the men. One factor that worked against commuting the ration was that those who did so were paid only three cents a day for it. It was not until 1864 that grog compensation was raised to twenty-two cents a day. By this time the habits of sailors were probably firmly fixed. Some Confederate Navy surgeons wanted to have the daily ration of spirits served with breakfast, apparently on the grounds that the stimulating effects would help to get the work day off to a good start, much like latter-day sailors and city dwellers depend on a cup of hot coffee for a similar boost. They may also have reasoned that the hard work would help to wear off the effects of alcohol sooner than a period of rest. But whatever their suppositions might have been, Confederate line officers were opposed to grog at breakfast for fear that it would lead to a deterioration of discipline. At least one Confederate official, John De Bree, the Chief of the Bureau of Provisions and Clothing, opposed the grog ration on the grounds of its cost. In a effort to deal with this problem the Confederate Navy established a distillery in Augusta, Georgia, to process the grain and corn.[15]

Regulations also prescribed that the men should have a daily allowance of one gallon of water unless the commander of the ship concluded that the needs of the service required an exception to this rule. One of the duties of the commander of a ship was to inspect the water and not allow the men to drink it 'until the mud and other impurities it my contain shall have time to settle.' In the *Alabama* a daily supply of fresh water was available through the ship's condensing apparatus. When the portion needed for the cook's use was deducted from the daily gallon, there was little left for drinking and washing. The condenser broke down while the ship was off the coast of Africa, and until the apparatus could be repaired the *Alabama* had to depend on three vessels sailing with it for fresh water. Fortunately the condenser was repaired in a short time. If it had not been, the ship would have had to make for the nearest port to ensure a continuous supply of water.[16]

The *Shenandoah* replenished its fresh water and saved the coal that powered the condenser by collecting the ice that had formed on the running rigging as it sailed in the Okhotsk Sea off Siberia. Using wooden billets, crewmen knocked off the ice on to the deck. It was then collected in tanks, casks and any other vessels that could hold the ice. In this way the ship acquired several thousand gallons of drinking water.[17]

In the Savannah squadron the main staples of the sailors diet were fresh beef, rice and bread. Generally salted beef, pork or bacon were issued at least four days a week and fresh meat and vegetables at least three days a week. Fresh bread was delivered to the squadron weekly. Later in the war the deliveries of food became less reliable. Two months after reporting on board the ironclad *Savannah*, Thomas Watson got his first fresh food on May 10, 1864. At that time corn meal and flour were so scarce that rice was substituted. Yet in October 1864 the squadron had an eight-weeks' supply of bread on hand and as a result it was able to lend 620 barrels of flour to the Army. In February 1865 at least one member of the Savannah squadron was reduced to selling some of his clothes to buy additional food.[18]

Rewards and pleasures

Navy regulations stated that commanders were to encourage men who distinguished themselves by 'meritorious behavior'. In the case of Raphael Semmes of the *Alabama*, he hoped to win the loyalty and dedication to duty of his largely British crew by promising them double the wages normally paid by their own government and in gold, designated shares in the prize money from ships captured or bonded, the grog ration twice a day, a daily ration of food of a higher quality and a more generous amount

Civilians being entertained aboard the *Shenandoah* at Melbourne, Australia. (*Illustrated Australian News*)

than in any other navy, plenty of tobacco and generally good treatment. Semmes was as good as his word, and he seems to have been respected and in at least some cases, admired by the men who served under him. The regard in which his men held Semmes no doubt increased in November 1862 when he gave his men a pay rise.[19]

The common pursuits of the men in their off-duty hours have been briefly noted earlier. Music, dancing, theatricals, spinning yarns and smoking filled many a free hour. Semmes supplied the men of the *Alabama* with musical instruments such as the violin and tambourine. With music available, there was an inducement to dance. Shot racks, coils of rope and other impediments were moved to create a dance floor. Some of the men would tie handkerchiefs or aprons around their waists to indicate that they were the 'ladies' for the occasion. With couples in place, the dance proceeded with all the formality and ceremony associated with a

similar event on shore. The 'ladies' tried to move with grace and dignity, and to speak in high voices. Those on the sidelines who watched the performances of the dancers and the efforts of their shipmates to assume a new identity enjoyed many a hearty laugh at the spectacle. During the visits of the *Alabama* to Cape Town and Singapore, some members of the crew learned new dance steps from the local women and introduced them to others during the shipboard dances.[20]

Minstrel shows and theatrical performances were staged in some ships. The plays were written or adapted by the men and probably involved some type of costuming when men played women's roles.[21]

In the *Alabama*, some of the officers formed a glee club that performed for both officer and enlisted audiences. Its repertoire included nautical and sentimental songs as well as a few Confederate tunes such as 'Dixie' and 'The Bonny Blue Flag'. The theatre arrangements for the concerts consisted of camp stools, which were designated as 'private boxes' for the officers, and the forecastle and higher parts of the deck which were called the 'gallery'. This was also the portion of the ship where pipes and

A diorama showing ironclads *Charleston* and *Chicora*, Charleston Harbor, rigged for summer comfort with sun awnings and ventilators. The small rectangular structures on the flush decks are water closets. (WMCWNH)

cigars could be enjoyed during the performance. Everything had to end when the starboard watch was piped at eight bells or 8pm.[22]

Another source of pleasure that was enjoyed by both the officers and men in the *Alabama* was the ship's library. The captain's secretary was in charge of it, and he was a popular man with his shipmates. When the *Tuscaloosa* and the *Alabama* met in the harbor of Cape Town, there was visiting between the crews of the two ships, and the *Tuscaloosa* received a small collection of books from the *Alabama*'s library.[23]

Pets have always been popular with sailors, and Semmes allowed his men to purchase parrots and monkeys. One of the crew brought a cat with him when he enlisted. Once a black bird about the size of a field lark was rescued from the sea and became a favourite of all in the *Alabama*. Named 'Johnny Raw', the bird hopped around the deck, snapped up choice morsels of food and adjusted to shipboard routines until it was washed overboard one rough day.[24]

Sometimes boxing matches were held as a means of settling disputes between enlisted men, as well as relieving tensions. On one occasion, two of the powder monkeys, or young boys who carried gunpowder to the guns, in the *Alabama* had a sparring match to work off an old grudge. First Lieutenant John McIntosh Kell, the Executive Officer of the ship, acted as a referee, called the time, and after a little blood had been shed, brought an end to the match.[25]

The seizure and destruction of prizes sometimes resulted in the arrival of women on the commerce raiders. They were not considered as prisoners, but were given accommodation in spaces normally reserved for sea officers. The displaced officers found temporary quarters in other parts of the ship. While they were

aboard, the women were treated with dignity and respect by all. Normally only the officers had any extended conversation with them but their presence on board for several days, until they could be transferred to another ship or landed at a port, was a source of interest despite the temporary disruption they caused.[26]

When the *Alabama* was approaching the equator, the boatswain improvised a bathhouse for the officers and men. This consisted of a large square sail that was spread a few feet under the surface of the ocean and held there by a solid shot in the center of the canvas. The top, bottom and sides of the sail were tied up to form a huge bag. By sitting in this contrivance in comfort and safety, a man could get a little relief from the scorching sun.[27]

Of all the pleasures of naval life, none surpassed shore leave. The place, time and duration of the leave were usually known to the crew only at the last minute. Anticipation built up expectations, and the understanding that this time away from the ship could not last for long made this time of freedom an intense and carefree one. Sailors headed for the bars, the brothels and the available women. Usually leave was granted to one watch at a time, So, when the starboard watch returned from leave, somewhat the worse for the experience, its members were able to advise their shipmates in the port watch what to look for and what to watch out for.[28]

Lieutenant Arthur Sinclair remembered the way the jack tars of the *Alabama* spent their shore leave in Cape Town:

> Jack and his chum from the English fleet are to be seen arm-in-arm standing before the wind with light kites out alow and aloft, bound to sailor-town, the new-found mate from the Narcissus being the pilot. All Cape Town is agog; and the sailor boarding-house keeper, and the

ladies of the 'east end', are on the tip-toe of expectation, the latter drawing heavily on their stock of ribbons and furbelows for the evening ball.[29]

A more serious situation developed when the men of the *Alabama* were exposed to 'samshee', a Chinese liquor made from rice, which was very potent and which they first tasted in Singapore. Lieutenant Sinclair said that its rapid and effectual work 'would cause "Jersey lightning" to blush. The number of "snakes" in it would make a head of hair for Medusa.'

Its effect on the men of the *Alabama* was very noticeable:

> Our vagabonds are in every stage of drunk, from kitten playfulness to fighting trim, and are to be found scattered from the dock along the broadway into the city. No occasion for money to keep up the sport (so-called); for our Jacks are the pets of the people, and money don't count in it. Here you will see an old sea-dog, making 'half boards' to windward, coming up to the wind, and shivering his canvas, then steadying and filling away again. Another making better weather and standing before it. Our friends the cabmen are busy, too, with the blackguards, voyaging them from point to point. Our officers are hard at it, boarding and capturing the runaways; the principal difficulty in the way being the so-called attentions and hospitality of the towns-people , who are making heroes of our worthies, hiding them away without thought of the seriousness of the fun to us, and supplying the liquid refreshments *ad libitum*. Our worst fears as to the loss of our crew here are not realized. We finally secure most of them, and alto-gether through the efforts of our own young officers, without the assistance of the police-force.[30]

On the other hand, not every port appealed to the sailor. The French island of Condore in the South China Sea, south of the Mekong River, was a tropical paradise, but it had no rum and no dancehall. Coconut milk could be had in abundance, but this had no appeal for the sailors. There was no need to worry about deser-tion here. A similar experience took place when the ship visited the Comoro Islands, off the eastern coast of Africa.[31]

Contacts with the shore usually involved attempts by members of the crew to smuggle liquor on board. Officers of the deck had to be very wary of contacts between members of the crew and the bumboat men, or merchants who brought items of food to the ship to sell to the sailors. Men returning from a frolic ashore often tried to smuggle liquor on board. The *Alabama* had a marine officer but no marines, so the duty of guarding against smuggling was up to the duty officer and the master-at-arms. If a sailor was success-ful in getting liquor into the ship, it led to drunkenness and to breaches of discipline. One of the objections to serving grog in the US Navy, and which led to the abolition of the practice in 1862, was that the daily ration of liquor created a craving which the men would go to almost any length to satisfy.[32]

In view of this state of affairs, the officers of the *Alabama* faced a problem of how to deal with a prize whose cargo consisted of wines and brandies as well as sardines, olives and other foods. Lieutenant Sinclair decided to take the captain's cockswain into his confidence and told him the nature of the cargo and the need to keep the men from looting the liquor. He then explained his plan. Drawing on the ship's stores and the cargo of the captured ship, a lunch would be spread on the cabin table consisting of sardines, cheese, olives and other food as well as bottles of brandy, claret and burgundy. Men working in the hold were told that they could eat and quench their thirst with the items in the cabin. They did so in an orderly manner and without any breaches of discipline.[33]

In the ironclad *Atlanta* at Savannah, members of the crew were given liberty whenever possible, though in some cases it was only liberty to visit another ship. Here the assumption seems to have been that any change of scene was better than no change.[34]

Medicine and health

Under Confederate Navy regulations the commanding officer was to make a personal inspection of the ship every day, accompanied by his executive officer, and he was obliged to satisfy himself that everything that contributed to the health of the crew and the effi-ciency of the ship was being done. The commanding officer was not to allow his men to sleep in wet clothes or bedding. The decks where the men slept were to be as thoroughly dried as possible before the men took their meals there or carried their bedding below. At least once every two weeks the commander was to see that the crew's bedding and clothes were opened, cleaned and dried. In warm climates or good weather the procedure was to be followed more frequently. Men were not allowed to sleep on the deck where they might be exposed to rain or morning dews. The commander was to see to it that the men washed themselves and bathed frequently, especially when the weather was warm. He was to see to it that they had clothing that was appropriate to the cli-mate in which they were serving and which was conducive to good health. It was also his responsibility to see that members of the crew did not eat too much fruit or other items that might endanger their health.[35]

According to the regulations, the surgeon was to report daily to the captain of the ship on a prescribed form the names and condition of the sick, and to suggest any measures that he regarded as important for the health of the crew. A list of the men whose physical condition required them to be excused from duty was to be posted on the binnacle. This list became the basis for determining which men would have their daily allowance of grog stopped until they were fit for duty. For assistance in preparing various kinds of nourishment for the sick, the surgeon was to apply to the commanding officer. A person or persons might be assigned to the surgeon to assist him in various tasks and to provide comfort to the sick. When a battle was in the offing, the surgeon was expected to have everything ready to treat the wounded.[36]

During most of their two years of active service, the crew in the *Alabama* suffered only minor injuries and ailments. Six men were invalided and sent back to England. On one occasion a member of the crew who had been ill for some time and who was then convalescing was carried out to the deck to enjoy some sun and air. Through some mishap, he fell overboard. the cry of 'man overboard!' was sounded. Orders were given to slow down the ship, to throw a life-buoy to the man, and to lower a boat to rescue him. While all this was going on, the cockswain sized up the situation instantly, realized that there was no time to be lost, threw a wooden hull grating over the side and jumped in after it. Pushing the grating in front of him, he swam to the invalid sailor and placed the grating under him. The two then waited for the lifeboat to bring them back to the ship. When all were back on board, and the ship was moving again, Captain Semmes mustered the officers and crew on the quarterdeck and praised the gallantry of the rescuer, an Irishman named Michael Mars.[37]

A different kind of luck prevailed while the *Alabama* was being repaired at Saldanha Bay, a harbor on the west coast of Africa sixty miles from Cape Town. Three officers from the ship went duck hunting on shore and as they were returning to the ship, Engineer Simeon W Cummings accidentally shot himself and died instantly. The body was carried below where it was examined by Acting Surgeon D Herbert Llewellyn. The next day the unfortunate officer was buried on shore.[38]

When the *Alabama* stopped at the Comoro Islands north of Madagascar, the Acting Surgeon was in great demand by all classes of the people who sought advice and medicines for their physical problems. Llewellyn was informed that most of the ailments

affecting the populace were the results of visits by American whalemen. The doctor did what he could to help these people.[39]

A sense of duty kept Surgeon Llewellyn in the cockpit of the *Alabama* during the fight with the USS *Kearsarge*, even when he was standing in water. Advised by Lieutenant Sinclair that he must soon get the wounded and himself off the ship, Llewellyn replied that he must wait for orders. These came soon after this and the wounded were placed in a boat. The surgeon did not go with them but stayed behind. Unable to swim, his shipmates tried to save the surgeon by affixing a wooden ammunition box on each arm before he entered the water. While a ship's boat was moving to rescue him, the ammunition boxes shifted and the surgeon drowned. During the battle nine men were killed and twenty were wounded, including Semmes and two other officers. Twelve were drowned.[40]

The general good health that prevailed in the *Alabama* for most of its cruise was not shared by the CSS *Florida*. While Lieutenant John L Maffitt was preparing his ship for sea in the Bahamas in August 1862, it was necessary for both officers and men to engage in the hard work of transferring arms and stores. During this process one man died and was buried ashore. Later that month, when the *Florida* had begun its cruise, several cases of yellow fever appeared in the ship. There was no surgeon on board so Maffitt personally attended to the sick. As the sick list grew, the quarterdeck became a hospital. Maffitt worked night and day to attend the crew. The working force of the ship was down to one fireman and four deck hands when it entered the harbor of Cardenas, Cuba, and Maffitt requested and received permission to remain in port. The next day he sent an officer to Havana to find the local Confederate agent, and through him to get a doctor and some men for the ship. By the time a Cuban physician reached the ship, Maffitt was also sick with the fever. While in this state he did what he could for himself and wrote out minute directions for those around him including what to do in the event of his death. The Cuban physician told Maffitt that he would die. Maffitt replied that he would survive, and he did. With a dozen men acquired in Havana to replace those who were sick, Maffitt took the *Florida* to Havana and then to Mobile.[41]

En route to Mobile the ship was fired on by the Union blockading force. An 11-inch shell passed through the coal bunkers, bounced off a forward boiler and decapitated a seaman. Several men were wounded by gunfire. When Maffitt arrived at Mobile the next day many of the officers and crew were prostrated by yellow fever and a lieutenant died of the disease. Officers and men were quarantined for a time.

Later, when the *Florida* was at Rocas Island off the coast of Brazil awaiting the arrival of tender with coal, three men were lost, one by illness and two by drowning. One of those drowned was Joseph D Grafton, the ship's surgeon, whose body was not recovered. Less than two months later, the Assistant Paymaster died of consumption. He was buried in Bermuda.[42]

When the *Shenandoah* was cruising in the Okhotsk Sea, the medical officers were concerned that the cold weather would lead to the sickness of many on board. A stove therefore was taken from a captured whaler and placed in the cabin. The ship was kept under easy sail to limit any unnecessary exposure of the crew to the weather. In addition:

The men were required by our very excellent Surgeon [Charles E] Lining to clothe themselves warmly and keep themselves dry. Extra rations of hot coffee and grog were served at regular hours, and the surgeon, with his efficient assistant, Dr McNulty, inspected the food for the crew before and after it was prepared. Indeed the surgeon cannot be recommended too highly for his discretion in preserving the sanitary condition of the Shenendowah. [*sic*][43]

Discipline and desertion

The police duties in a warship were performed by a chief petty officer known as the master-at-arms, who was assisted by a petty officer whose rank was the ship's corporal. It was their responsibility to see that the galley fire and all unauthorized lights were put out. Where lamps were authorized they were to see that they were in place, lighted and properly trimmed. At the appropriate time, they extinguished all lights. When it was necessary to renew the lights and fires, the master-at-arms had to get the permission of the commanding or the executive officer to do so.

The master-at-arms and the ship's corporal took the names of any members of the crew who violated any of the ship's or the Navy's rules and regulations. The man was reported to the commanding officer who decided on the appropriate punishment.

On the whole, discipline in the Confederate Navy was mild. Some of this was no doubt due to the fact that in 1850 the US Navy abolished flogging as a punishment and at the time of the Civil War there had been ten years experience with substitutes. One example of a substitute punishment took place in the CSS *Chattahoochee* off Saffold, Georgia in January 1863. Lieutenant George W Gift was disturbed to find that the non-commissioned

officers in the steerage had fallen 'into the disagreeable and disreputable practice of loud swearing, coupled with many bad expressions.' He therefore punished one of the offenders, who was also one of the best men in the ship, by tying him by the wrists to a hammock hook for four hours.[44] Presumably this example made the others more careful about when and where they used profanity.

The British subjects who made up the crews of Confederate commerce raiders, such as the *Alabama*, were generally accustomed to harsh discipline, including flogging. The change of approach in the Confederate service must have been most welcome. Of the crew of the *Alabama*, Semmes wrote in December 1862 that:

Many of my fellows no doubt thought they were shipping in a sort of privateer, where they would have a joy good time and plenty of license. They have been woefully disappointed, for I have jerked them down with a strong hand, and now have a well disciplined ship of war. Punishment *invariably* follows immediately on the heels of the offence. It has taken me three or four months to accomplish this; but when it is considered that my little kingdom consisted of one hundred and ten of the most reckless sailors from the groggeries of Liverpool, this is not much.[45]

Semmes expressed his philosophy of discipline with the words 'a tight rein and plenty of work'. In January 1863 he noted that: 'My men will rebel a little yet. I was obliged to-day to trice one of them up for a little insolent behaviour'.[46] But his usual pattern was to punish a man by placing him in irons for a day or two.

Semmes understood that a sailor was a creature of habit and one conditioned to familiar routines. He used this knowledge when early in the career of the *Alabama* he was faced with what looked like the makings of a mutiny, or at least gross insubordination. It seems that when the ship was off Fort de France, on the island of Martinique, in November 1862, liquor was successfully smuggled on board and several of the men became drunk. In this condition they became insubordinate, or as Lieutenant Arthur Sinclair expressed it, they forgot who commanded the ship. An officer who attempted to quell a disturbance was abused, threatened and had a belaying pin thrown at him. Semmes dealt with the problem by having beat to quarters sounded by the ship's bell. The men went to their duty stations where they answered to a roll call. Whenever Semmes saw a drunken man he had his shipmates arrest him and the man was then put in irons. About twenty men were apprehended in this fashion. The culprits were then taken to the gangway where two or three of the quartermasters were ordered to empty buckets of water on them in rapid succession. This treatment soon put a stop to the insolent language and sobered the men. The men under arrest began to beg for mercy and promised to behave in the future. When Semmes was convinced that they had learned their lesson, he had the irons removed and sent the men to their hammocks to sleep. Meanwhile the rest of the officers and men stood at their guns and stations until the punishments were completed, which lasted about two hours.[47]

Later one of the men, Seaman George Forrest, was tried by court martial. Forrest had earlier served in the *Sumter* and had deserted. He was subsequently apprehended, tried and found guilty. His sentence was to forfeit all his pay and prize money earned up to that time and to serve out his time. In the second trial he was found guilty of procuring liquor, giving it to crew members and inciting them to mutiny. His sentence was to forfeit his prize money and be dismissed from the Confederate service in disgrace. All hands were mustered aft at 7:15pm to hear the sentence read and after a short speech by Semmes, Forrest was placed in a boat and rowed to shore where he was left.[48]

Men who overstayed their shore leave were rounded up by the officers and were briefly confined to the brig for their infractions of the rules. While the *Alabama* was at Jamaica, Semmes was confronted with the disturbing news that one of his officers had gone over to the enemy. Paymaster Clarence R Younge was in communication with the US consul at the port and had meetings with paroled Union seamen. Through the paymaster's influence with the crew and the assistance of the consul, several valuable men were induced to desert the Confederate service. When word of this reached Semmes, he sent an armed party ashore and arrested the paymaster. He was then dismissed from the service and drummed out of the ship. On the whole it was a rather humane approach to a serious breach of trust, if not a case of treason.[49]

A similar situation arose in the *Sumter*. The ship had a good crew, but while it was at Gibraltar there were some problems with the men, and one seaman, George A Whipple, deserted. He was arrested and punished, but later enlisted in the Union Navy and was in the *Kearsarge* at the time of the battle with the *Alabama*.

Earlier in the war, when Semmes commanded the CSS *Sumter*, a marine was tried by court martial for sleeping on duty. When he was found guilty of this crime, he was discharged and put ashore in Cadiz, Spain.[50]

In the *Tuscaloosa* the lack of activity led to boredom and irritation among members of the crew. When a lieutenant ordered a mate to take in and close reef some sails, the mate refused and cursed the officer. The mate was punished by being confined in double irons for two days and reduced in rank to a seaman. A week later the man had his old rate back, and when a seaman refused to obey his order, the mate struck him with his fist and knocked him down. The seaman was put in the brig and the mate was suspended from duty. The next morning both were back on duty.[51]

These examples of discipline may be compared to that dispensed in the CSS *Chattahoochee* off Saffold, Georgia in 1863. The captain's steward was found guilty of noisy and boisterous conduct on the berth deck and sentenced to carry a 32lb shot while he paced the deck for three hours a night for four nights. In another case, two galley cooks fought each other on the berth deck and created a mess. They were condemned to wear double irons and to be 'triced up' (probably to a hammock hook) for every other four-hour period. Presumably this lasted only a day or for a couple of watches. Things reached a more serious level when a conscript C V McKenny was found guilty of 'maliciously and slanderously' defaming the good character and reputation of the boatswain's mate and the master-at-arms. Because the defendant had said that the boatswain should have his hide scrubbed with a hickory broom, it seemed appropriate that that item should be a part of the punishment. Six men were to administer the punishment, two had hickory brooms, two had pieces of canvas, and two had sand. They were ordered to scrub the conscript 'until they were thoroughly satisfied' (presumably until he was clean). He was then to be taken half way up the main rigging of the ship, spread-eagled and left to dry.[52]

When it came to desertion, the Confederate commerce raiders *Sumter*, *Alabama* and *Shenandoah* all had to deal with the fact that US consuls and their agents at several ports made serious efforts to get seamen to desert. Sometimes only a few would be convinced to do this, but almost every success meant that the Confederate ship lost a trained and valuable man. But not all desertions were the result of the actions of Union men; sometimes sailors were overworked. As early as December 1862, Semmes wrote of the men of the *Alabama* that: 'Constant cruising, vigilance against being surprised by the enemy, salt provisions, and a deprivation of the pleasures of port, so dear to the heart of the seaman, are probably what most of them did not expect'.[53]

In August 1864 Seaman Robert Watson of the ram *Savannah* at Charleston was talking to a sailor named John Lowe, who had

Sailor on the Confederate monument at Montgomery, Alabama. (Robert Holcombe)

recently served in the CSS *Tallahassee*. Lowe told him that since there were only three experienced seamen on board, they all had to work very hard both day and night. When the ship reached Halifax, Nova Scotia, twenty-seven of the men deserted.[54]

Hard work in a tropical climate was also necessary when the *Florida* coaled in the Bahamas in January 1863. Twenty-six men deserted. Lieutenant John Newland Maffitt, the captain of the ship, replaced them with new men who were received outside the three-mile limit of the island. A short time later, when the ship was at Bridgetown, Barbados, some observers considered it a well-disciplined ship. The officers were young, polite and attentive, and the men were well-behaved and orderly. Members of the crew seemed to have a high regard for their captain.

No one understood better than Maffitt how a break in routine could cause problems. In May 1863 he was forced to coal his ship at sea by means of small boats, a procedure he disliked because the lack of formality in the process produced a 'general laxity.' A few weeks later the *Florida* spent two weeks awaiting the arrival of a tender with a fresh supply of coal. While waiting Maffitt kept the crew as busy as he could by cleaning and painting the ship, but the prolonged period of inactivity undermined morale. Maffitt finally concluded that the tender had been captured or lost and he sailed without his coal.[55]

At Savannah in January 1863, Midshipman Dabney Scales of the ironclad CSS *Atlanta* found five cases where a man who was carried on the rolls as a marine was actually a deserter from the Army. Such men were turned over to the Army.[56]

In March 1863 a guard boat under the command of a master's mate was sent to guard the North Channel approach to Savannah. A report was later received that the boat and its crew had been captured. In the *Atlanta* there was a general supposition that the crew had mutinied and took the boat and its officer over to the Union forces.[57]

Generally speaking, the quality of the conscripts that were assigned to the ironclads, rams and other river craft was such that a great deal of patience and tolerance was necessary on the part of the officers. With sufficient drill and supervision they could be moulded into an effective force. But no matter how effective they were, they could not be kept in ignorance about the ever-increasing signs of Union might and of the growing plight of the Confederacy. News of Federal successes gradually became known to seafaring men in Great Britain as well. Late in the war the steamer *Ajax* was purchased in England with a view to converting it into a gunboat for service in the Cape Fear River in North Carolina. *En route* to that destination the ship stopped at the Irish port of Kingston where fifteen of the twenty-one crew members refused to do their duty on the grounds that the ship was unseaworthy. The captain accused the men of mutiny and appealed to the local police for help. The police arrested one member of the crew who said that the real reason for the disobedience was that the men had learned that the ship was to become a Confederate gunboat. A judge sentenced the crew member to thirty days in jail. On the same day two other deserters were arrested and given sentences of six weeks. The captain signed on fifteen new members of the crew and sailed for Nassau in the Bahamas. After reaching there on March 11, 1865, arrangements were made to discharge the captain and the crew and to sell and re-register the ship.[58]

Confederate naval regulations required commanders to report monthly all persons who died, deserted or were discharged during the reporting period. Such information was vital for determining pay and keeping track of men in the service. The regulations also required quarterly reports of all punishments inflicted on board as well as the nature of the offence, the extent of the punishments and any other explanatory information that might be needed. Just how much attention was paid to these reports in the Navy Department cannot be ascertained. There seems to be few indications that the authority to punish was abused in the Confederate Navy.[59]

Dr Harold D Langley

Chapter Ten
STRATEGY AND TACTICS

While Navy Secretary Stephen R Mallory was creating a navy for the South, he was also devising a strategy for its use. Despite his previous experience as a member of the United States Committee on Naval Affairs, Mallory had no background in either strategy or tactics. This is hardly surprising. Admiral Bern Anderson observes that before the Civil War, 'no study of naval strategy existed, and the works on naval tactics were largely obsolete, as they dealt with the disposition and fighting of sailing ships'.[1] Mallory's biographer notes that at the time he took office, he 'had acquired no more knowledge and skill in naval matters than were sufficient to place him in the class of a clever amateur in the field'.[2] Mallory had no Alfred Thayer Mahan to advise him on strategic and tactical matters. In 1861 Mahan was only a junior officer in the United States Navy and his important works (based in large part on his personal observations during the Civil War) were still years in the future. But, in any case, Mallory would have disagreed with many of Mahan's theories even had he known of them. Or, more likely, he would have redefined them to suit his own purpose. One Mahan maxim would have especially amused Mallory: 'The proper main objective of the Navy is the enemy's Navy.'[3] In Mallory's redefinition, it would not be 'the enemy's Navy', but instead their merchant fleet that would be his objective. Gideon Welles, the United States Navy Secretary, would have found Mahan's theories more to his liking. He could well afford to do so.

Mallory had no choice but to develop a strategy based on the pressing needs of the South. Although in the end this strategy failed, it is doubtful whether any alternative strategy could have done much better. Diplomatic historian Frank Merli is among those who credit the Navy Secretary with achieving impressive results because of his 'demonstrated intellectual flexibility' and 'a capacity for growing with the job'.[4] It should be noted, however, that there was another side to Mallory, and he has been strongly criticized for failure to articulate his ideas, leaving subordinates perplexed and bewildered 'as to the desires of a noncommittal senior pursuing an unknown plan'.[5] In the final analysis, Mallory

Stephen R Mallory. (Scharf, *Confederate States Navy*)

Admiral Raphael Semmes, commander of the *Alabama* and most proficient of the commerce raider captains. (Scharf, *Confederate States Navy*)

must be judged by his accomplishments as well as his failures. The fact remains that the obstacles that confronted the Navy Secretary would have sorely tried any man.

Confederate overall naval strategy

Since President Davis's overall military strategy was one of defense, so too was the Navy's. However, Mallory would also use the offensive while pursuing this defensive strategy. An underdog Confederate Navy would use both traditional (eighteenth-century) and 'modern' (mid-nineteenth-century) methods of strategy. Mallory was not troubled that the major maritime nations (although not the United States) had condemned both privateer-

ing and commerce raiding in the 1856 Declaration of Paris. Without hesitation, he would eagerly use both of these. In addition, Mallory would utilize the latest shipbuilding technology and produce ironclad warships for his Navy, as both England and France were already doing. Ironclads could be used to defend the South's rivers, harbors and ports, and of course the Confederate capital itself, which was vulnerable to attack by water. Mallory believed that ironclads, together with the privateers and commerce raiders, could keep open the Confederacy's vital coastal and transatlantic trade.

In short, the Navy Secretary was willing to try whatever would work. It would be a 'David versus Goliath' situation in which the South's objective was not to slay the giant, but rather to hold it at bay until Southern independence could be guaranteed. Although Mallory was treated with 'massive indifference'[6] by the Richmond government, at least this allowed him to conduct his office with virtually a free hand. And, Mallory could usually count on President Davis to support him on major issues. But Davis's 'land-mindedness' meant that the interests of the Navy would often be short-changed.

On tactical matters Mallory would defer to his experienced captains, men such as French Forrest, Josiah Tattnall, Catesby ap Roger Jones, Matthew F Maury, Franklin Buchanan, Raphael Semmes and James D Bulloch.

Privateering

The quickest and cheapest way for the South to produce a navy was by privateering – relying upon civilians motivated by Southern patriotism, but chiefly at the prospect of getting rich. The fact that the United States had not signed the 1856 Declaration of Paris condemning privateering served only to reinforce Davis's and Mallory's belief that it was a good idea. Among the South's earliest supporters of the use of privateers was Raphael Semmes, who soon gained a reputation of his own as a destroyer of Northern commerce. Writing to a Southern congressman, Semmes advised that 'it is at ships and shipping that you must strike; and the most effectual way to do this is by means of an irregular force'.[7] But, Semmes warned, because of 'private cupidity', legal restraints would be necessary to prevent privateering from 'degenerating into piracy'.[8]

On April 17, 1861, only days after the firing on Fort Sumter, President Davis issued an official proclamation inviting private

JEFFERSON DAVIS,
President of the Confederate States of America.

To all Who shall see these Presents---Greeting:

Know Ye, That by virtue of the power vested in me by law, I have commissioned, and do hereby commission, have authorized, and do hereby authorize the _____ or vessel called the _____ (more particularly described in the schedule hereunto annexed,) whereof _____ is Commander, to act as a private armed vessel in the service of the CONFEDERATE STATES, on the high seas, against the United States of America, their Ships, Vessels, Goods and Effects, and those of their citizens, during the pendency of the War now existing between the said CONFEDERATE STATES and the said United States.

This Commission to continue in force until revoked by the President of the CONFEDERATE STATES for the time being.

Schedule of Description of the Vessel.

Name, _____

Tonnage, _____

Armament, _____

No. of Crew, _____

BY THE PRESIDENT:

Given under my hand and the Seal of the CONFEDERATE STATES at Montgomery, this _____ day of _____ A. D. 1861.

_____

Secretary of State.

Privateer Letter of Marque. (WMCWNH)

parties to apply for letters of marque and reprisal. Those who qualified for these letters would be authorized to capture Northern naval and merchant vessels. Owners, captains, and crews of these privateers would share lucrative profits from the sale of prizes and their cargoes. The government agreed to pay 20 per cent of the value of any Federal warships destroyed by privateers. The captains of privateers were required to keep detailed journals of their actions at sea; these, along with their commissions, were to be presented to the collectors of customs at every Confederate port they entered. In addition, all applicants approved were required to post bonds of from $5,000 to $10,000 to ensure that they would follow only 'legitimate' privateering practices. By these means Confederate authorities believed they could prevent privateering from degenerating into piracy.

On May 6, 1861 the Confederate Congress approved the use of privateers. Even before the policy had become official, more than 3,000 applications had been submitted to state and Confederate authorities, including some from New England! Companies were formed to finance the purchase, arming, and manning of private vessels, and all manner of craft were converted into 'warships'.

The success of the first of these privateers operating out of New Orleans – a converted tugboat, *Calhoun* – was encouraging. In just one month, May 1861, she took six prizes. The enthusiasm for privateering led to the boast of one leading New Orleans journal that with some 750 such vessels, armed with four guns apiece, the South would 'wage war upon the Northern commerce, blockade Northern ports, cripple Northern strength and destroy Northern property'.[9] Secretary Mallory, however, had something else in mind; he believed that the panic created among Northern merchants and coastal residents would force his adversary to divert warships from the blockade. Mallory was correct about the panic but misjudged Secretary Welles's determination to maintain and strengthen his own blockade strategy despite mounting alarm in the North. The turning point for New Orleans privateering came in July 1861, when the steam sloop USS *Brooklyn* took her station at the mouth of the Mississippi.

Enthusiasm for privateering waned as the Federal blockade became more effective and Southern ports were no longer safe havens. Nor were neutral ports an alternative for the privateers to bring their prizes. Privateering became even riskier after President Lincoln decreed that individuals captured in the act would be considered 'pirates' and treated accordingly. As a result, blockade running, for all its hazards, seemed to many to be a safer and more lucrative enterprise. By early 1862 all but the most intrepid mariners had given up privateering, and their vessels were either converted to blockade runners or used by naval authorities for coast defense.

In his classic study of the Confederate privateers, William Robinson observes that by the coming of the Civil War 'the day of privateers had passed', although this was not generally realized at the time.

> They achieved individual successes, but the institution of privateering was obsolete, and no amount of industry and valor could save it. It belonged to a vanished order of things, like the very political and social structure which the Confederate states themselves typified.[10]

Commerce raiding

Privateering was, of course, one form of commerce raiding. Mallory had something far grander in mind for his strategy of defense – offense. He wanted commissioned Confederate warships to wage war, not on enemy warships, but on Northern commerce. These vessels would take commerce raiding to all the oceans of the globe. They would be better suited than the privateers to inflict crippling damage on the North's economy, and so alarm Northern merchants and the northeast coastal population that

Ransom bond of the Union merchantman *Washington*, captured by the CSS *Alabama*, February 27, 1863. (W S Hoole Special Collection Library, The University of Alabama).

Welles would have no choice but to divert warships from the blockade in pursuit of them.

For the purpose he had in mind, Mallory needed the kind of ship that could not be built in the South. They would be fast vessels that could spend long periods at sea. With no ports to which

Know all men by these presents, that whereas the ship *Washington*, of New York, under my command, was this day captured on the high seas as prize of war by the C.S. steamer of war *Alabama*, R. Semmes, commander; and whereas I, Joseph G. White, master of said ship as aforesaid, am desirous of ransoming said ship for the benefit of myself and of the owners thereof, to wit, William T. Frost, James M. Hicks, George Bell, Thomas Eggleston, Joshua Battel, Horace Wright, David L. Young, Robert L. Taylor, Pitkin Page: Now, therefore, I, Joseph G. White, master of the said ship as aforesaid, acting for myself and the above-named owners, as I am empowered to do by the laws of nations, for and in consideration of the release of said ship by the captor, the release whereof is hereby acknowledged, do acknowledge myself and the aforesaid owners, to wit, William T. Frost, James M. Hicks, George Bell, Thomas Eggleston, Joshua Battell, Horace Wright, David L. Young, Robert L. Taylor, Pitkin Page, jointly and severally indebted to the President of the Confederate States of America, and his successor and successors in office, in the sum of $50,000, which said sum of $50,000 well and truly to pay unto the President of the Confederate States of America, his successor and successors in office, within thirty days after the conclusion of the present war between the said Confederate States and the United States, I hereby bind myself and the above-named owners, jointly and severally, and my and their heirs, executors, administrators, and assigns. And I do hereby hypothecate the said ship, her tackle and apparel for the payment of this bond.

Done this the 27th day of February, in the year of our Lord 1863, at sea, on board the C.S.S. *Alabama*.

JOSEPH G. WHITE [SEAL.]
Witness: W.B. SMITH, Commander's Clerk.

they could bring their prizes, they would have to dispose of them at sea. American-owned vessels and American-registered cargoes would be burned or scuttled after the removal of crew and any passengers and the transfer of supplies that could be used aboard the cruiser. When the cargoes of American merchant ships were determined to belong to foreign nationals, the vessels would then be released on ransom bond, a document which stated that the value of the vessel would be paid to the Confederacy at the end of the war. Unlike commerce raiding in previous wars, cruiser captains were instructed to avoid contact with enemy warships, unless impossible to avoid. 'Commerce destruction, not victorious naval duels, was the paramount object of cruiser warfare.'[11] Cruisers were too valuable to risk losing by the rash action of a daredevil commander.

Another difference between privateering and government-run commerce raiding was motivation. Whereas the privateers were driven to action by the prospect of easy riches, naval personnel aboard the cruisers — certainly the officers — were, above all, Southern patriots motivated by love of country.

The first of the Confederate commerce raiders, the *Sumter*, was a former passenger — cargo steamer converted for use as a cruiser at New Orleans. Ironically, Raphael Semmes, who eagerly requested command of the *Sumter*, had once denounced privateering and commerce raiding in the strongest terms: 'The crews of these vessels are little better than licensed pirates; and it behoves all civilized nations… to suppress the practice altogether.'[12] The 'civilized nations' (although not the United States and Spain) *had* made an effort to 'suppress the practice' by the 1856 Declaration of Paris. But circumstances had changed by 1861, and Semmes was now a leading advocate for their use. A letter to that effect from Semmes to Mallory written in April 1861 helped to get things moving.

Although the *Sumter* proved inadequate for continued use as a commerce cruiser, the eighteen captures she made during only six months at sea convinced both Semmes and Mallory of the value of the commerce-raiding strategy. A former passenger liner became the *Nashville*, but she too proved unsuitable for use as a commerce cruiser. The limitations of the *Sumter* and *Nashville* only served to reinforce Mallory's conviction that the type of ship he needed could not be obtained in the South. In May 1861 he sent James Dunwoody Bulloch abroad as special naval agent to secure cruisers in England and France. Three other naval officers — James H North, George T Sinclair and Matthew F Maury — were also sent to England for the same purpose. But it was Bulloch who impressed Mallory as the best man to get the job done. Weighing

Bulloch's considerable accomplishments, it is not surprising that he has been characterized as a man of 'competence and courage, ingenuity and integrity, discretion and determination'.[13] Only a skilled negotiator — and Bulloch proved to be one — could 'find and exploit loopholes in British neutrality laws and capitalize on sympathy for the South'.[14] Bulloch soon became the Navy Department's indispensable man abroad. Although Bulloch yearned for active command, Mallory could not afford to lose his enterprising agent. He had a surplus of officers available to command cruisers.

At Birkenhead Bulloch contracted for the building of two cruisers, after being unable to find any suitable ships for sale. All the while, he was kept under surveillance by spies employed by Thomas Dudley, the United States Consul at Liverpool. Bulloch's first cruiser was the *Oreto*. After departure from England on March 22, 1862, the *Oreto* made a prearranged rendezvous with the steamer *Bahama* (chartered by Bulloch) in the Bahama Islands. There she received her guns, enlisted a crew, and was formally commissioned CSS *Florida*. Bulloch had been careful to avoid violating England's Foreign Enlistment Act, which prevented him from enlisting a crew in England. His second cruiser, the *Enrica*, made her escape from Birkenhead only hours before she was to be seized for violation of English neutrality. Dudley had secured the evidence that the vessel was intended as a Confederate cruiser. At Terceira, in the Azores, guns were transferred from the *Bahama* to the *Enrica*, and sailors brought from England aboard both ships were enlisted as crew of the commissioned Confederate warship CSS *Alabama*, the former *Enrica*. Bulloch had a major asset in having ships built and enlisting crews with the promise of gold. In order to obtain a crew of Englishmen, the only men available, Semmes agreed to pay them wages twice what the men would receive in the Royal Navy, along with grog served twice a day, and prize money to be distributed at the end of the cruise. Semmes told them he wanted men who were not afraid to fight, as they might encounter a United States warship. As seen by many of the sailors who signed to serve aboard the *Alabama*, the experience would be similar to privateering (or even piracy), offering them an opportunity to get rich.

Once operating at sea, both the *Florida* and the *Alabama* appeared to offer clear evidence of the successful cruiser strategy. The *Florida*, initially under the command of daredevil John N Maffitt, captured thirty-seven merchant ships, and the *Alabama* an even more impressive record — sixty-five prizes captured. Semmes, Maffitt, and other cruiser captains used a 'hit-and-run' strategy,

CSS *Alabama*, the most successful of the Confederate cruisers. (*Harper's Weekly*)

appearing in one ocean, disappearing, then reappearing in another, confusing their pursuers and prey alike.

Both Semmes and Maffitt converted one of their prizes into a 'satellite cruiser' at sea. Semmes had the *Conrad* armed, then, manned by fifteen of his sailors and a lieutenant; she became the *Tuscaloosa*. In this case, the effort was hardly worth it. Arriving at Simon's Bay after a disappointing six months at sea, the *Tuscaloosa* was seized for alleged violation of British neutrality. Although she was eventually released by court order, by that time there were no Confederates around to claim her.

The satellite cruiser created by Maffitt aboard the *Florida* had a far different experience. The *Clarence*, commanded by Lieutenant Charles W Read, was sent to the New England coast. In only weeks, Read had captured fifteen vessels, including Gloucester fishing boats. After transferring his crew and howitzer to the captured schooner *Archer*, Read conducted a daring night raid into

Portland harbor. Finding the revenue cutter *Caleb Cushing* at anchor, Read and his men boarded and captured her. While attempting to escape with their valuable prize, they were captured but not before they had set her afire.

Only three of the eight Confederate cruisers – Bulloch's *Florida*, *Alabama*, and the *Shenandoah* – were of the caliber that Mallory had envisioned. But then, not all of the others got to sea. Matthew Maury succeeded in purchasing and getting to sea two cruisers – the *Georgia* and the *Rappahannock* – but neither was suited for commerce raiding. The *Georgia* had an iron hull that required frequent repair, and the *Rappahannock* was so handicapped by engine breakdowns that she was useless at sea. Brought to Calais for repairs, the *Rappahannock* remained in dry-dock for the remainder of the war. Sinclair's cruiser, the *Canton*, was potentially another *Alabama*, but she never made it to sea as a raider. Once they were convinced as to her identity, British authorities had her seized for

CSS *Alabama* burning the American bark *Virginia*, September 17, 1862. (*Pictorial War Record*)

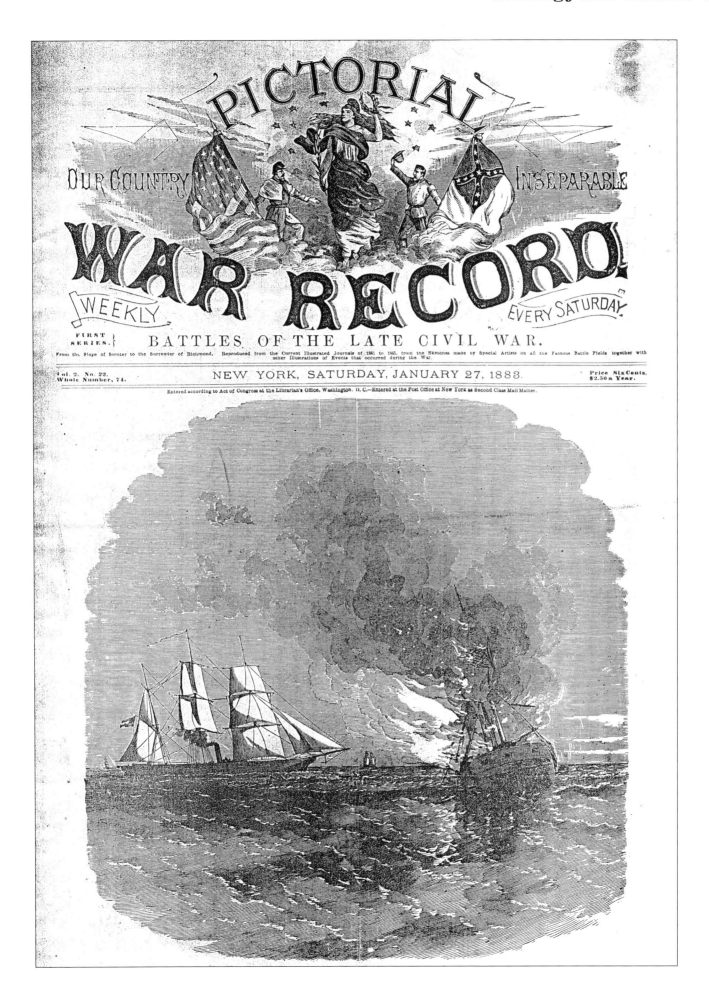

PICTORIAL

OUR COUNTRY — INSEPARABLE

WAR RECORD
WEEKLY — EVERY SATURDAY

FIRST SERIES.} BATTLES OF THE LATE CIVIL WAR.

From the Siege of Sumter to the Surrender of Richmond. Reproduced from the Current Illustrated Journals of 1861 to 1865, from the Sketches made by Special Artists on all the Famous Battle Fields together with other Illustrations of Events that occurred during the War.

Vol. 2. No. 22. Whole Number, 74.   NEW YORK, SATURDAY, JANUARY 27, 1883.   Price Six Cents. $2.50 a Year.

Entered according to Act of Congress at the Librarian's Office, Washington. D. C.—Entered at the Post Office at New York as Second Class Mail Matter.

violation of the Foreign Enlistment Act. Still another potential cruiser, the *Alexandra*, built in England as a gift for the Confederacy, was also seized by British authorities. North, too, was unsuccessful in getting his ship, an ironclad built at a Glasgow shipyard, to sea as a cruiser.

After the *Alabama* and the *Florida* were lost to the Confederacy in 1864, Bullock was hard-pressed to find a replacement for them. He eventually succeeded in purchasing the *Sea King*, which met the standards he felt were necessary in a cruiser. The CSS *Shenandoah*, last of the Confederate cruisers, brought commerce raiding into the Pacific and to the Arctic Ocean where, even though the war had ended, she destroyed thirty-two vessels of the whaling fleet. It was a catastrophe from which the American whaling fleet never recovered. After finding out that the war had ended, the *Shenandoah*'s captain, James I Waddell, succeeded in bringing his ship to England, where he surrendered her.

Two other Confederate commerce raiders were the *Tallahassee* and the *Chickamauga*, both former blockade-runners operating out of Wilmington, North Carolina. The *Tallahassee*, under John Taylor Wood, made two successful cruises along the northeast coast but the problem of coaling and the coolness of Canadian officials toward the Confederacy late in the war brought an end to her activities. The *Chickamauga*, which completed only one cruise, was

faced with the same obstacles. Both vessels were returned to their former function as blockade runners.

The Confederate commerce raiders inflicted considerable damage on Union shipping, especially the New England whaling industry, with more than two hundred vessels destroyed. The direct losses in ships and cargoes were as high as $25,000,000. The raiders were responsible, directly and indirectly, for the capture, destruction, or sale to foreign owners of nearly a million tons of American merchant shipping. Exorbitant insurance rates resulted in hundreds of vessels remaining in port. Those aboard the cruisers felt optimistic even after it became increasingly difficult to find Union merchant ships at sea. In December 1863, an *Alabama* officer explained to an English sympathizer at New Harbour, Singapore: 'We don't care much whether or not we succeed in destroying any more of the enemy's merchant-men; we have done enough already; our presence alone in these waters will now suffice to ruin the eastern commerce of the Federal states.'[15] The officer's optimism was understandable but short-sighted. Although the damage inflicted by the cruisers was indeed serious, the American

Confederate cruiser *Tallahassee*, altered from the blockade-runner *Atalanta*. (*Illustrated London News*)

merchant marine merely 'diverted the ocean carrying trade to British and other neutral shipping, without diminishing in the slightest the flow of munitions and other goods into the United States.'[16] The economy of the United States was strong enough to withstand the losses inflicted by the cruisers. And, despite 'cruiser fever' along the northeastern seaboard, Welles refused to weaken the blockade, as Mallory had counted on.

Although Southerners could feel pride in the achievements of the commerce raiders, and satisfaction in knowing that they were helping to settle scores for the destruction of Southern property by invading Northern armies, this was of little consequence to the end result. In analyzing Confederate naval strategy, Harold and Margaret Sprout support the thesis of Alfred Thayer Mahan when they conclude: 'In the realm of strategy, the war had but repeated the lessons of earlier conflicts. Confederate commerce-raiding, although well planned and skilfully executed, had not affected the outcome in the slightest.'[17]

Coastal defense

Even while Mallory waited for positive results from his commerce raiding policy, 'homewater defense' remained the principle focus of his strategy. Archer Jones explains:

> Protecting the coast from the demonstrated menace of landings became a major element in Confederate strategy as the War Department concentrated many of its newly raised troops along the eastern seaboard and Gulf coast to meet this expected Union threat. Protecting Southern ports became a major mission for the newly organized Confederate Navy. [18]

The Confederate capital, Richmond, on the James River, was among those Southern cities vulnerable from both land and sea. But, on the other hand, so were the North's coastal cities, if the Confederate Navy had the opportunity to act offensively.

In February 1861, the Confederate Congress passed several bills authorizing the construction of gunboats for coast defense. Matthew Maury was a strong proponent of their use. Not long afterwards, Mallory sent Raphael Semmes to New York to locate and purchase suitable vessels for coast defense. When Semmes returned unsuccessful, the Navy Department launched a top-priority building programme in the South. Former river steamers, armed and reinforced with bales of hay and cotton, became improvised gunboats while the building went on. Coastal fortifica-

tions were often manned by both Army and Navy personnel. The Confederacy would also use new technology – ironclads, submarines, torpedoes (mines), and torpedo boats – in coastal defense.

Ironclads were very much on Mallory's mind when he made an urgent appeal to the Confederate Congress on May 9, 1861:

> I regard the possession of an iron-armed ship as a matter of the first necessity … If we build wooden ships, we shall have to construct several at one time; for one or two ships would fall an easy prey to her comparatively numerous steam frigates. But inequality of numbers may be compensated by invulnerability; and thus not only does economy but naval success dictate the wisdom and expediency of fighting with iron against wood, without regard to first cost.[19]

Impressed by Mallory's argument, Congress immediately appropriated $2,000,000 to purchase ironclads in England and France. While waiting for his reliable agent Bulloch to secure them, Mallory decided to have other ironclads built in the South. It soon became evident that ironclads could not be purchased abroad and would have to be built there too.

When Federal forces hastily abandoned the Gosport Navy Yard at Norfolk, Virginia on April 20, 1861, they left behind the charred hull of the steam frigate *Merrimack*. On learning that the hull was salvageable, Mallory seized the opportunity and had her converted to the ironclad *Virginia*. In his history of the famous ironclad, R W Daly contends that the *Virginia* was not built to break the blockade, but instead was '*a harbor defense vessel*, more elaborate in construction but little different in principle from the floating iron battery employed by the South Carolinians in the attack on Fort Sumter'.[20] It was indeed the purpose of the *Virginia*'s attack on the Union fleet, on March 8, 1862, 'to gain undisputed control of Hampton Roads and the James River in order to protect Norfolk and the river approaches to Richmond'.[21] But the initial success of the *Virginia* against her wooden opponents led Mallory to believe that she was capable of attacking Washington, New York, and other Northern coastal cities. If it could be done, it would add a whole new dimension to his strategy. Captain Franklin Buchanan, CSN, the *Virginia*'s first commander, knew better. He was well aware of the ironclad's unseaworthiness and advised the Secretary accordingly.

Four other ironclads built early in the war were intended for offensive use: the *Arkansas* and the *Tennessee*, built at Memphis, and the *Mississippi* and the *Louisiana*, built at New Orleans. Only the *Arkansas* and *Louisiana* were used, as the *Tennessee* and *Mississippi* were destroyed by the Confederates before their completion.

CSS *Tennessee*, one of the most powerful ironclads built in the South and Admiral Buchanan's flagship at Mobile Bay. (National Archives)

During her brief but eventful career the *Arkansas* was used offensively on July 15, 1862 when she passed through a Federal fleet anchored above Vicksburg with her guns blazing. The Confederates next planned to use her in an attempt to recapture Baton Rouge, but when her engines failed, she was set afire by her crew to prevent capture. By this time – the summer of 1862 – Mallory had given up his idea of using the Southern-built ironclads for offensive action. Until the end of the war, they would be used only for river, harbor and coast defense. However, since people in the South continued to believe that the ironclads were intended to break the blockade, they were sorely disappointed when their expectations were never realized.

John Porter, naval constructor of the Confederacy, developed a design for small, shallow-draft vessels better suited for harbor defense. Of the approximately forty Porter-designed hulls that were laid down, half were completed. The 150ft *Richmond*, the first of these, was a model for several others, including the 310ft *Nashville*. Porter also designed a smaller 139ft ironclad specially for use in the North Carolina sounds. The only two of these actually completed were the *Albemarle* and the *Neuse*. (The *Albemarle* was destroyed, not by the Confederates, as was usual, but as a result of a daring night raid planned and executed by Lieutenant William B Cushing, USN.) Of the twenty-two Confederate ironclads completed and more than thirty others laid down but never finished, four were captured, the *Albemarle* destroyed by the enemy, and all the others destroyed by the Confederates to prevent their capture. William Still notes the consequence: 'This, more than anything else, explains the unpopularity of the Navy throughout the war.'[22]

A model of CSS *Missouri*, a centerwheel ironclad built at Shreveport, Louisiana., 1862-4. (WMCWNH)

(This negative image, however, did not extend to the Confederate cruisers operating on the high seas. They, at least, provided Southerners with better evidence of success.) Since Mallory never doubted the wisdom of his ironclad strategy, he continued to have them built even during the fall of 1864 and winter 1865.

Overseas, in Liverpool, the ever-resourceful James Bulloch was determined to produce powerful ironclads capable of breaking through the blockade and opening up Southern ports. Unable to purchase them, he contracted with John Laird & Son, shipbuilders, for two ironclads. Mallory was so optimistic that these 'rams' would be a turning point in the war that he sent Flag Officer Samuel Barron to England to assume command even as they were still under construction. The two twin-turreted ironclads, with strengthened iron rams protruding seven feet beyond their prows, and capable of speeds up to 10 knots from their 350-horsepower engines, would surely have proved formidable had they ever

reached the Confederacy. But Bulloch, for all his success in getting the *Florida* and *Alabama* to sea, was unable to prevent the seizure of the ironclads by British authorities. Instead of becoming Confederate warships, they became HMS *Scorpion* and HMS *Wivern* in the Royal Navy. Bulloch had better luck in securing one of the two ironclads he had built in France. After first selling the ironclad to Denmark to avoid having her seized by the French, Bulloch managed to have her returned to him. The 172ft long *Stonewall*, covered by 3.5 inches of iron, was intended to raise the blockade of Wilmington, intercept California gold steamers, attack Northern ports, and destroy the North's fishing fleet. She was the Confederacy's last hope. The *Stonewall*, commanded by Thomas J Page, CSN, eventually reached Havana, Cuba after the war had ended; she was surrendered to Spanish authorities there. Despite the invincible 'monster' the *Stonewall* appeared to be, her ocean crossing had shown her to be unseaworthy. She leaked badly and was extremely difficult to manoeuvre.

It is difficult to judge the effectiveness of Mallory's 'home water defense' strategy. Archer Jones points out that 'the Federal Navy could concentrate against a port and, though the Confederate Army could move men to counter this, the port defense ships could not make sea voyages to carry out a corresponding concentration.'[23] Paul Lockhart criticizes Mallory's 'home-defense' strategy as 'irrational', a 'non-strategy' that lacked clearly defined goals other than the defense of the coastline and rivers. Lockhart also criticizes Mallory for not realizing that 'since Confederate naval vessels were incapable of defending themselves against Federal ironclads, they could hardly defend major harbors against entire fleets of ironclads'.[24] But, despite the weaknesses in the Confederate ironclads, Federal naval commanders took them seriously. Their respect for the ironclads resulted in 'ram fever', which influenced their own actions. The actual power of the ironclads tended to be magnified in most people's minds, both civilians and military alike, although General Beauregard had a poor opinion of them. Those who actually served aboard the ironclads were well aware of their deficiencies.

Despite their technical flaws, the Confederate ironclads definitely made a contribution to the war effort, but it is uncertain to what extent. Paul Lockhart dismisses them as ineffectual. 'Not once during the war was a Union naval assault defeated or deterred by the presence of Confederate naval forces.'[25] William Still, on the other hand, makes a strong case that the ironclads *did* serve as a deterrent. In his *Iron Afloat*, the foremost authority on the Confederate ironclads explains:

> As 'fleets in being', Confederate ironclads also tied down Union vessels as well as large numbers of troops that could have been used elsewhere. Farragut's attack on Mobile was delayed more than a year because the monitors ordered to reinforce his squadron for the operation were held at Charleston; they were supposed to proceed to join him after the attack on the city in April 1863 but did not, primarily because of the presence of Confederate armored vessels there and at Savannah. In fact, he never did receive the monitors originally ordered to him.
>
> Of the five seaports – Savannah, Charleston, Wilmington, Mobile, and Galveston – taken in the last six months of the war, two were taken by land forces from the rear, and two indirectly as a result of pressure from the rear. In all the cities but one, Galveston, the Confederate Navy had ironclads as part of the harbor defense. If time had allowed, the Confederate ironclads might have made a more significant contribution to the Southern war effort. As it was, they certainly achieved some success in the overall strategy of defense.[26]

Unconventional warfare — mines, torpedoes and submersibles

In addition to ironclads, the Navy eventually realized the value of torpedoes (mines) in both defense and offense. The 'Father of Mine Warfare' was also 'The Pathfinder of the Seas', the distinguished scientist–sailor–oceanographer Matthew Fontaine Maury of Virginia. After demonstrating to Mallory that using torpedoes was feasible, Maury became the head of the newly created

Torpedo Bureau in Richmond. There he concentrated on developing electrical torpedoes, which, when fitted with electrical detonators, were connected to shore stations from where they could be fired. In June 1862 Maury was sent to England to obtain cruisers for the Confederacy, and there he continued his experiments with torpedoes. His able successor, Lieutenant Hunter Davidson, continued Maury's work at a time when there was a desperate need to protect Richmond by mining the James River approaches.

Of several types of torpedo devised, the 'keg' and 'frame'

weapons were the ones most commonly used. They played a sig- nificant role in the defense of Charleston, Mobile and Richmond, and were actually more effective than the Confederate ironclads and gunboats. Mallory has been criticized for not realizing their potential sooner than he did. He has also been criticized for send- ing Matthew Maury to England where his great talent was largely wasted. Neither of the two ships that Maury purchased was suit- able as a commerce raider. But not everyone favoured the use of torpedoes. Some Southern military leaders 'did not regard torpedo

warfare as worthy of consideration',[27] believing them to be too 'barbaric' to be used by a civilized people.

The destruction inflicted by Confederate torpedoes on the Union Navy is impressive: seven ironclads and twenty-two wooden gunboats sunk, and fourteen others damaged. The Union ironclad

CSS *Stonewall,* **from a photograph taken after the war, probably in Washington, DC. (WMCWNH)**

HMS *Wivern*, one of the Laird Rams. (CPL)

Cairo of the Western Gunboat Fleet struck two torpedoes while participating in a naval operation up the Yazoo River and sank within minutes. In addition to destroying enemy ships, torpedoes diverted 'large forces of men and material from other important duties in order to neutralize the devastating effect of the new weapon'.[28] Also important was their psychological effect – 'torpedo fever' – on Union forces. According to Milton Perry, the Confederate torpedoes had a significant effect on the war:

> Nowhere did Confederate mines and torpedoes actually change the outcome of a major battle; but at various places they permitted the Confederates to achieve offensive capabilities in essentially defensive operations, and in some actual encounters of major importance, mines delayed the decision sufficiently to give the Confederates time to regroup or escape. For example, off Charleston and Hampton Roads, the Federals cruised at will during daylight, but after nightfall, they gathered their capital ships behind circling boats, log and rope obstructions, and calcium lights. At Williamsburg and Fort Wagner, land mines assisted in slowing Federal advances so that the Southerners escaped completely.[29]

Both Navies experimented with submersibles, but these were unreliable and dangerous to their crews. The Southern Navy took a greater interest in 'submarines', as they could also be used as gunboats. The CSS *Pioneer*, built at New Orleans, was originally intended to be a privateer, but became a two-man submarine. After being commissioned in March 1862, she was put to the test in Lake Pontchartrain. The *Pioneer* never had the opportunity to be battle-tested, as she was sunk by the Confederates when the Federals captured New Orleans. A second submarine – *Pioneer II* – was built at Mobile and, when ready, was brought to Fort Morgan for a planned attack on the Federal fleet. Unmanageable in rough seas, the *Pioneer II* sank, although all hands aboard were saved.

The best known of the Confederate submarines is the *H. L. Hunley*, the creation of Horace L Hunley and other engineers and entrepreneurs. Built from a 25ft long boiler cylinder, the *Hunley* was equipped with a bared spike for ramming and armed with a torpedo that contained 90lb of gunpowder. Hunley's submarine was brought overland from Mobile, where she was built, to

Commander Matthew F Maury, early proponent of submarine torpedo warfare in the South. (Naval Historical Center)

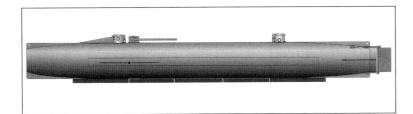

CSS *H.L. Hunley* (see illustration on p63)

Charleston to be used against the blockaders there. The *Hunley* soon earned her nickname – 'peripatetic coffin' – after trial runs in which she was unable to surface. Hunley himself became a fatality, along with three volunteer crews. Finally, General Beauregard forbade further diving, and the *Hunley* was used as a surface gunboat. On the night of February 17, 1864, the *Hunley* stealthily moved outside the harbour, where her torpedo was exploded against the wooden hull of the Union frigate *Housatonic*. Historically, this encounter is recorded as the first time that a ship was sunk by a 'submarine'. Strictly speaking, however, the *Hunley* was not a 'submarine' at the time of the encounter, but rather a submarine being used as a surface gunboat. The *Hunley* apparently survived the explosion, but sank for unknown reasons during her return to Sullivan's Island.[30]

Despite the fate of the *Hunley* and her unfortunate crews, a five-man submarine – *St Patrick* – was built at Selma, Alabama during late 1864. Brought from Selma to Mobile, she was used as a surface gunboat in an attack on the *Octarara* of the blockade squadron. The *St Patrick's* spar torpedo failed to explode, and she returned to Mobile.

The Confederate Navy built other iron surface torpedo boats equipped with spar torpedoes. In 1863, the 50ft long *David*, armed with a torpedo attached to her 10ft spar, was built in Charleston. On the evening of October 5, 1863, *David's* four-man crew targeted the Federal blockader *New Ironside*, but she was able to remain afloat. Five months later *David* was used in an attack on the *Memphis*, but this time her torpedo failed to detonate. The torpedo boat and her crew were able to return to port safely.

Other 'David'-design torpedo boats were built but apparently never used. Several of these were seized by the Federal forces that captured Charleston close to the end of the war.

Commander Hunter Davidson. Commanded the Naval Submarine Torpedo Battery Service after Matthew Maury was sent abroad in 1862. (Naval Historical Center)

Replica keg (left) and demi-john torpedoes; two crude but successful underwater explosive devices employed by the Confederates. (WMCWNH)

A stake torpedo from the Mobile area. (WMCWNH)

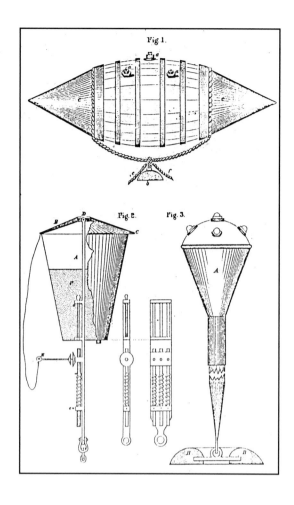

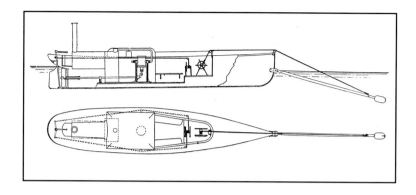

Torpedo boat *Squib*. Under the command of Lt Hunter Davidson, *Squib* torpedoed the USS *Minnesota* April 9, 1864. (*Official Records, Naval*)

Types of Confederate torpedoes. (Barnes, *Submarine Warfare, 1869*)

Warship tactics

Although overall strategy for the Navy was Secretary Mallory's responsibility, battle tactics were left to individual commanders. Only a few of the Confederate ironclads and only one of the commerce cruisers – the *Alabama* – engaged in combat. And then, only rarely did the Confederates have the advantage, as with the *Virginia* in her initial encounter with the wooden blockade fleet at Hampton Roads and the *Alabama* winning her one victory against a Federal warship. The *Virginia* was the first Confederate ironclad to be battle-tested at a time when nobody quite knew how to handle her. It was not until 1865 that British naval Commander Philip H Colomb outlined the tactical use of ironclads in his essay on 'Modern Naval Tactics'. Before the *Virginia*'s engagement with the Union fleet, Mallory was purposely vague in his instructions to her captain:

> The *Virginia* is a novelty in naval construction, is untried, and her powers unknown, and the Department will not give specific orders as to her attack upon the enemy. Her powers as a ram are regarded as very formidable, and it is hoped that you may be able to test them. [31]

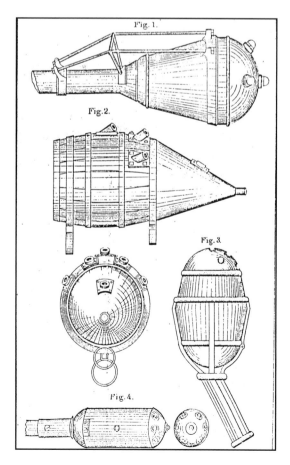

Types of Spar torpedoes. (Barnes, *Submarine Warfare, 1869*)

It was the *Virginia*'s captain, Franklin Buchanan, and her other officers who had to improvise the tactics that proved so successful against the blockaders. Her next commander, Josiah Tattnall, did likewise in his engagement with the *Monitor*. These officers soon realized serious deficiencies in the ironclad that severely limited her capabilities. R W Daly has described the *Virginia* as strictly a defensive weapon similar to the type of floating battery that the Confederates had earlier used at Charleston against Fort Sumter.[32] These so-called 'floating batteries' had been used by navies since the eighteenth century. Guns were mounted on floats which were towed into position for action. Since these floating batteries were unable to manoeuvre, they had to be protected, usually with iron plate. The 100ft-long floating battery used by Confederate forces at Charleston was protected by two layers of railroad iron. Two of the Confederate ironclads – the *Georgia* and the *Louisiana* – were so unmanageable that they had to be towed into position, thereby serving as floating batteries. The *New Orleans* briefly served as a Confederate floating battery on the Mississippi before being scuttled to prevent her capture. According to Robert Suhr, the floating batteries were not very effective: 'A stationary target covered with iron plate was no match for the Union Navy'.[33]

A large number of the Confederate ironclads, however, had one offensive weapon, the ram. In fact, many of them were called 'rams'. The *Virginia* was the first Confederate vessel to incorporate an armoured prow, and her success in the Battle of Hampton Roads persuaded the Navy Department to include rams as part of the armament for more than half the armourclads laid down. As a result, ramming an enemy vessel became a standard tactic employed by Confederate ship commanders whenever possible.

In addition to ramming, Confederate naval officers gave some thought to other tactics against monitor-type vessels. Commander Catesby ap R Jones, who fought the *Virginia* against the *Monitor*, advocated firing rifled bolts at a turret's base, hoping to damage it so that it could not rotate. There is no evdience that this tactic was successfully carried out by a Confederate warship.

Confederate cruisers, especially the *Florida* and the *Alabama*, were virtually irreplaceable, far too valuable to the South to risk losing in battle, and their captains were under strict orders to avoid engaging Federal warships. Orders were clear: destroy Union commerce on the seas. The cruisers would fly the flags of either the United States or Great Britain or alternate between them, while hunting for their prey. Only when an unarmed Union merchant vessel or whaling ship was overtaken would the Confederate colours be raised and her identity revealed. First, a blank shot was

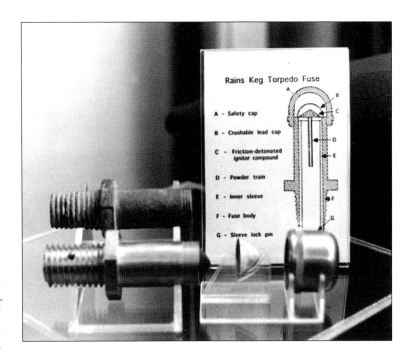

Torpedo fuze-type developed by General Gabriel J Rains, CSA. (WMCWNH)

fired as a signal to surrender, and, if there was no response, a live shell was then fired over the victim's bow. Raphael Semmes may have been the only cruiser captain to deliberately burn prizes at night, knowing that the law of the seas dictated that other captains would respond to a vessel in distress. By the use of such 'bait', Semmes would set his trap. However, not all cruiser captains

Sinking of the US tinclad *Rodolph* by a torpedo near Mobile, April 1, 1865. (Naval Historical Center)

operated in the same manner as Semmes. Lieutenant William Maury, while commanding the *Georgia*, swore that he would rather be court-martialed than 'burn the ship of a man who had come on an errand of mercy'.[34]

Semmes was the only cruiser captain to fight enemy warships, winning one engagement and losing the other. Infuriated by continual barbs in the Northern press denouncing him as 'coward' and 'pirate', Semmes desperately wanted to perform a heroic deed in the manner of a Francis Drake or John Paul Jones. While cruising the north Atlantic, he drafted a plan to brazenly bring the *Alabama* into New York City's outer harbor at night and either set fire to the Union merchant fleet there or hold it for ransom. He was convinced that such a daring deed would prove to be a turning point in the war.[35] (John Taylor Wood, while commanding the commerce raider *Tallahassee* off the northeast coast, devised a similar plan, a surprise night raid into New York harbor to attack shipping and the Brooklyn Navy Yard. Lacking a pilot, however, Wood gave up the idea.) The *Alabama* encountered a cyclone which caused sufficient damage to make Semmes abandon his plan. But not completely. Later, entering the Gulf of Mexico, he decided to modify the plan and attack the Union force at Galveston. He had learned from captured newspapers that the Federals had taken the city. On January 11, 1863, approaching Galveston, Semmes was surprised to find a Federal naval squadron blockading the city. Only then did he realize that the Confederates had recaptured Galveston. It was too late for him to escape, so he decided to bluff. One of the ships of the squadron – the *Hatteras* – left her position to investigate the unidentified vessel flying the British flag. Semmes gradually distanced himself from the squadron, finally

Spar torpedo arrangement on the bow of a model of the CSS *Atlanta*. (WMCWNH)

A model of the CSS *David*, the first operational steam torpedo boat. (WMCWNH)

allowing his pursuer to close the distance between them. Although darkness made visibility more difficult, it favoured the Confederates. While a boarding party was being launched from the *Hatteras*, Semmes finally identified himself as the British ship *Petrel*, followed immediately by the order to his sailors: 'Fire!' It took only thirteen minutes for the *Alabama* to defeat the *Hatteras*, then rescue all her survivors. Not surprisingly, Semmes relished this opportunity to do battle on his terms with a decidedly inferior opponent. The *Hatteras*, a side-wheel steamer, was a former passenger ship converted into a warship.

Seventeen months following the sinking of the *Hatteras*, Semmes was prepared to relinquish command of the *Alabama*. Worn out from the stress of months at sea, he arrived at Cherbourg, France on June 13, 1864. He planned to have the *Alabama* dry-docked and his men allowed leave until she was ready for sea under a new commander. But, when the USS *Kearsarge* arrived, Semmes welcomed the opportunity for a fight. Having observed the *Kearsarge* closely two years earlier when he was aboard the *Sumter* at Gibraltar, he felt confident that the two ships were evenly matched. When Commodore George T Sinclair arrived from Paris, both he and Semmes conferred on tactics for the pending engagement. Disappointed that the French authorities would not let him join Semmes for the fight, Sinclair cautioned his fellow officer to keep at a distance from the *Kearsarge*, well out of range of her powerful 11in guns. Semmes replied, 'I shall feel him first and it will all depend on that.'[36]

Seven miles out to sea from Cherbourg, Semmes had his gunners commence firing at 2,000 yards. Most of her shot and shell were fired wildly and missed their mark, while the *Kearsarge* waited to shorten the distance before firing. Semmes was hoping for a well-placed shell to cripple his opponent. (He was also prepared to have his men board the *Kearsarge* if all else failed.) Semmes's 'lucky shot' finally struck, lodging in the *Kearsarge*'s sternpost, but

through the winter of 1865. Mallory continued to believe that his cruiser – ironclad strategy would succeed. But, it was too late to make any difference in the war's outcome. The Confederate Navy by itself could not have won Southern independence, although its achievements were remarkable. Frank Merli reveals the fatal flaw in Confederate naval strategy:

> The leaders of the South were narrowly self-centered in their approach to international affairs; and they were 'landminded'. As David M Potter once pointed out, President Davis made many mistakes during the war, but none was more fraught with danger than his failure to support his naval assistants. He apparently did not understand – and made little effort to understand – the significance of seapower in the South. The long, fatal delay in implementing the Navy's plan for government-sponsored blockade runners is a case in point. Suggested in 1862, it did not go into operation for another two years, by which time 'one of the most intelligent bits of strategy ever formulated by the Confederacy' faced too many formidable obstacles. 'The whole that could be accomplished', Bulloch sadly concluded, 'was not sufficient to turn the scale or to greatly delay the final result of the war.' The fatal mistake of the Confederacy, according to one post-war account, was neglect of the Navy.[38]

Dr Norman C Delaney

Admiral Franklin Buchanan, first of only two admirals in the Confederate Navy, was severely wounded at Hampton Roads and Mobile Bay. (Scharf, *Confederate States Navy*)

failed to explode. Semmes and his officers remained convinced that, had the shell exploded, it would have put the *Kearsarge* out of action and won the day for the Confederates. It had failed to explode, they believed, because much of the *Alabama*'s powder had deteriorated from dampness during the long cruise. Also, following his defeat, Semmes accused his opponent – *Kearsarge*'s captain John Winslow – of having 'cheated', by having (unknown to Semmes, or so he claimed) had chains slung over the sides of his ship, covering them over with boards, and thus engaging the *Alabama* as an 'ironclad'.[37]

Conclusion

The loss of the *Alabama* did not bring an immediate end to Confederate commerce raiding, which continued for another year. And, within the Confederacy, ironclad construction continued

Alabama fighting the USS *Hatteras* off Galveston, January 11, 1863. (Semmes, *Memoirs of Service Afloat*)

Chapter Eleven
OPERATIONS

The Atlantic

Confederate naval operations generally followed strategic priorities that to a great degree were determined by Union military operations. Defending the area that comprised the newly proclaimed nation was the Navy's major responsibility in co-operation with Southern land forces. Challenging the Union blockade was secondary, but as the number of blockaders on station increased and ships with badly needed supplies were captured or destroyed, it increased in importance. Nonetheless, the blockade was rarely attacked by Confederate warships operating in home waters; they were far more involved in defending these waters from Union combined/amphibious operations.[1]

Ten vessels, carrying a total of fifteen guns, formed the nucleus of the Confederate States Navy when it was organized in February 1861. The Confederacy acquired by purchase or capture four revenue cutters, three slavers, two small privately-owned coastal steamers, and the *Fulton*, an old sidewheel warship seized at the Pensacola (Florida) Navy Yard. The incorporation of several state navies added additional vessels. Georgia and South Carolina each supplied two small gunboats, and after secession both Virginia and North Carolina transferred five ships to Confederate service.[2] It was with these vessels that the Confederate Navy had to fight off any Union naval challenge until additional warships could be converted or built. The first test came in the fall of 1861.

In early November 1861 a large army and navy expedition under the joint command of Flag Officer Samuel F Du Pont and

Brigadier General Thomas W Sherman assaulted Port Royal, South Carolina. Union Secretary of the Navy Gideon Welles selected the target because of its deep water and geographical proximity to Charleston and Savannah, major objectives of the blockade. A Confederate flotilla of four small converted steamers under the command of Commodore Josiah Tattnall attempted to co-operate with the land defenses. Facing a much too powerful force of Union warships, Tattnall's 'mosquito fleet' simply fired a few random shots and retired to safety. A somewhat larger Confederate naval force did little better in North Carolina waters.

In the summer of 1861 North Carolina created another 'mosquito fleet' to guard the vital sounds, the large bodies of water that

B̲ombardment of Fort Walker, Hilton Head (*Harper's Weekly*)

separated the Outer Banks from the rest of the state. Control of the sounds was essential to the defense of North Carolina and also southeastern Virginia, including the important port of Norfolk. The North Carolina 'navy', consisting of four converted steamers carrying a total of five guns, was turned over to the Confederate Government. They were placed under the command of Captain Samuel Barron and later Commodore William F Lynch. On July 21, the CSS *Beaufort* with her single gun exchanged fire with the blockader USS *Albatross* across a spit of land at Oregon Inlet. Outgunned, the Confederate vessel withdrew after an hour of firing. No hits were made by either ship. In August the sounds were opened to Union invasion with the capture of Hatteras Inlet and the forts guarding it. Although Lynch's flotilla made no attempt to challenge the invasion, it later achieved some success when the steamer *Fanny* was captured in Pamlico Sound with Union troops on board.[3] This would be the 'squadron's' only 'victory' during the few remaining months of its existence.

Battle of Roanoke Island, February 7-8, 1862. (*Official Records, Naval*)

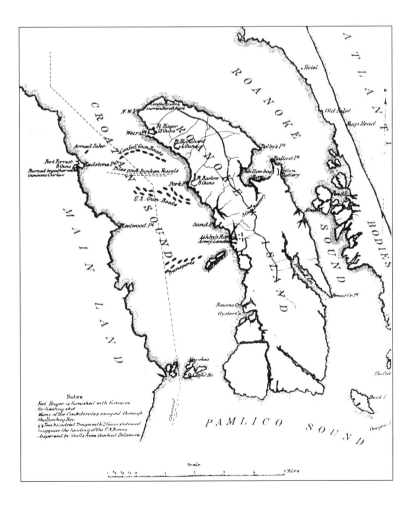

The flotilla's demise came as a result of the 'Burnside Expedition', an operation designed to capture Roanoke Island and use it as a base to control coastal North Carolina and threaten Norfolk. Led by Major General Ambrose E Burnside and convoyed by units of the North Atlantic Blockading Squadron, the island was secured early in February 1862. Lynch's small gunboats joined in the island's defense, but were ineffective. The Confederate force made no attempt to close with the far more powerful Union warships and fired at long range until its ammunition was exhausted. The flotilla then retired up the Pasquotank River to Elizabeth City. For their efforts no Union ship was hurt by the Confederate naval fire, and one of Lynch's ships, the *Curlew* was hit at the waterline and abandoned.[4]

On February 10 the day after the fall of Roanoke Island, fourteen Union warships steamed up the Pasquotank in pursuit of the Confederate vessels. At Elizabeth City, some twelve miles from the river's mouth, they found Lynch's flotilla lined across the river. The Union attack was swift and decisive; with negligible damage to the Federal vessels, the CSS *Ellis* was captured, the CSS *Seabird* was sunk, and the CSS *Black Warrior, Fanny* and *Forrest* (on the stocks) burned to prevent capture. Only the *Beaufort* escaped, fleeing through the Dismal Canal to Norfolk.

The destruction of Lynch's command left the government without any naval vessels to defend eastern North Carolina. The exception to this was in the Cape Fear River which flowed direct into the ocean at the southern end of the state. There a naval force was being created to defend Wilmington, the state's most important port.

The Federal Navy also gained control of two canals, the Dismal Swamp and the Albemarle & Chesapeake that provided a vital link with the Chesapeake Bay area. The Bay was also closely blockaded by units of the North Atlantic Blockading Squadron. The secession of Virginia in the spring of 1861 had led to the immediate blockade of the Bay, followed by the Union Navy's gaining control of Hampton Roads, the strategically important body of water at the Bay's entrance. For nearly a year the Confederacy could do little to challenge Federal ascendancy in the Roads. Despite the capture of the Gosport Navy Shipyard at Norfolk, Confederate naval forces in the area were extremely weak, consisting of a few converted steamers.[5] This changed in early March 1862 when the Confederate armourclad *Virginia* appeared in Hampton Roads.

Hampton Roads is the body of water where the James, Elizabeth, and Nansemond Rivers converge and flow into

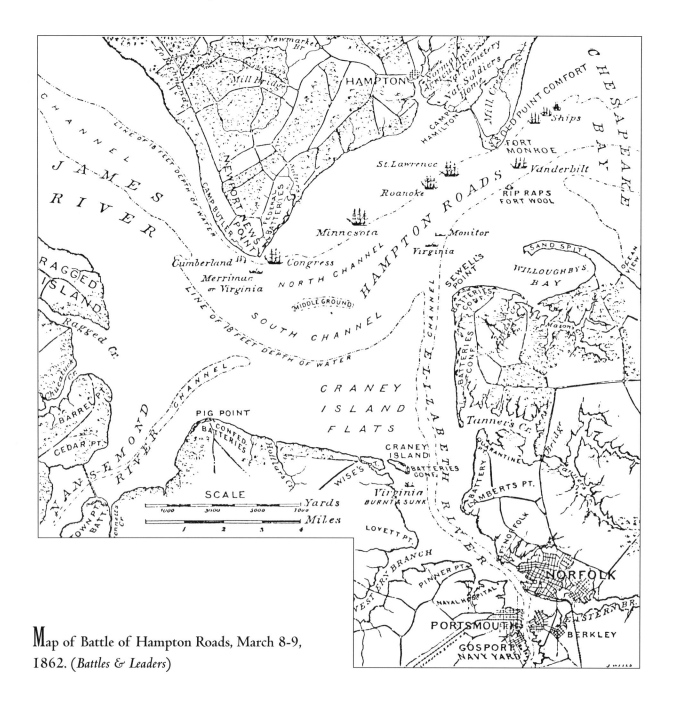

Map of Battle of Hampton Roads, March 8-9, 1862. (*Battles & Leaders*)

Chesapeake Bay, and from there into the Atlantic Ocean. It is approximately six miles at its widest point and has been described as a 'natural naval amphitheatre'. Thousands of Union and Confederate soldiers as well as civilians therefore had the unique opportunity on March 8–9 to witness a naval engagement. The north shore was held by Federal forces and Confederate troops were in control of the south bank.

Union naval officials had long known that the Confederates were converting the *Merrimack* into an armourclad. Nevertheless, Buchanan achieved tactical surprise. Only a few of the fifty-odd vessels that comprised the North Atlantic Blockading Squadron were in Hampton Roads on March 8. Nonetheless, the Union

naval force present in the Roads was still impressive, consisting of the 50-gun screw frigates *Minnesota* and *Roanoke*, the 44-gun sailing frigates *St Lawrence* and *Congress*, and the 24-gun sailing sloop *Cumberland*. The *Congress* and the *Cumberland* were the closest to the Confederate naval force; the others were at some distance and, in fact, because of shallow water were unable to join in the action. The *Minnesota* and *Roanoke* grounded in trying to get under way and the *St Lawrence* was helpless because of the light wind.

Buchanan intended to ram the *Cumberland* first — she had a much heavier battery — then turn on the *Congress*. When the *Virginia* turned towards the *Cumberland* the *Beaufort* and *Raleigh* engaged the *Congress*. The remainder of the Confederate squadron steamed across the Roads and opened fire on Union shore batteries near Newport News.

The *Cumberland* opened fire on the approaching warship, but the shot and shell bounced off the *Virginia*'s armour. The ironclad's fire was far more effective, penetrating the sloop-of-war's wooden side and exploding among her crew. The *Virginia* then rammed the Union vessel, crushing her hull. The *Cumberland* sank carrying the ironclad's ram with her. After destroying the *Cumberland* the Confederate ironclad turned her attention to the *Congress*.

While the *Virginia* engaged the *Cumberland* the Confederate gunboats continued to fire on the Union frigate, but did no appreciable damage. The *Congress* was grounded with her bow towards the north shore. She could bring only two guns to bear on the approaching ironclad. The *Virginia*, without a ram, had to destroy the frigate by gunfire. She steamed to within two hundred yards of the helpless Union warship and opened a devastating fire with hot shot and incendiary shell. The *Beaufort, Raleigh*, and *Patrick Henry* moved in closer to add their fire to that of the ironclad. The battle lasted for nearly an hour before the *Congress* struck. When Union shore batteries opened fire on Confederate gunboats moving alongside the surrendered frigate, Buchanan ordered them to resume firing. The burning warship was then destroyed. Buchanan was wounded in the action and command passed to Lieutenant Catesby Jones, the *Virginia*'s executive officer.[7]

Jones attempted to engage the stranded *Minnesota* but shoal waters prevented the ironclad getting into effective range and, with twilight approaching and a falling tide, he decided to retire until the following day. The Confederate force withdrew in relatively good shape, only the *Virginia* suffering any damage. With the exception of the lost ram and two disabled guns, damage was negligible. Casualties for the entire squadron were fewer than sixty killed and wounded.

At 6am on March 9 the *Virginia* followed by the *Patrick Henry, Jamestown*, and *Teaser*, got under way from the Elizabeth River and stood for the still grounded *Minnesota*. As they steamed into the Roads the Confederates observed a strange looking craft alongside the *Minnesota*. This was the USS *Monitor* which had fortuitously arrived the night before. As the ironclad drew within range, she fired a shot through the rigging of the *Minnesota*. The *Monitor* immediately headed for the armourclad, determined to keep her away from the helpless frigate. The three Confederate wooden gunboats stayed clear of the action. They were no match for the *Minnesota*. Nor did they attempt to engage the *Monitor*.

For the next four hours the two armoured ships pounded each other mercilessly. Throughout most of the encounter the range was brutally short – less than a hundred yards. Neither could damage the other, partly because of weak powder charges and partly because of gun problems. The *Monitor* could fire only one gun at a time, with a lapse of seven to eight minutes per gun as the gun crews had to raise and lower heavy iron shutters each time the gun fired and recoiled into the turret. The turret was also a problem, rotating slowly with much difficulty. The *Virginia* fired only shells that day, having anticipated engaging wooden vessels only. The Confederate ironclad used her prow to ram once, but the *Monitor* turned in time and received only a glancing blow. The *Virginia* ran aground but the lighter Union armourclad, despite her manoeuvrability, was unable to seriously hurt her opponent. Shortly before the Confederate ship worked her way free, a shell exploded against the *Monitor*'s pilothouse and severely wounded the commanding officer. This ended the action. The Union vessel withdrew while her captain was attended to. Jones, after deciding against renewing the attack on the *Minnesota* because of the falling tide, steamed back into the Elizabeth River, followed by the wooden gunboats.

The two-day battle of Hampton Roads was over. The first day was clearly a Confederate victory; the second a Union victory since the *Minnesota*, the Confederate's objective, was not destroyed. Strategically both sides benefited. After the engagement the Confederates made no serious effort to challenge Union control of Hampton Roads for the remainder of the war. At the same time the *Virginia* and her wooden consorts were able to block the mouth of the James River and were a factor in persuading Major

Battle between *Virginia* and *Monitor* at Hampton Roads, March 9, 1862. (WMCWNH)

General George B McClellan to delay his Peninsula Campaign. In May Norfolk was captured by Union forces. Confederate naval forces, including the unfinished ironclad *Richmond* under tow, ascended the James to the Confederate capital. The *Virginia*'s draft, however, was too deep and she had to be destroyed by her own crew. Until the spring of 1864 the Confederate naval squadron in the James River stayed inactive, remaining above obstructions in the river a few miles below Richmond.

By then the James River Squadron had become one of the most powerful naval forces in the Confederacy, consisting of the wooden gunboats *Nansemond*, *Hampton*, and *Drewry*, and the small steam launches *Torpedo*, *Scorpion*, *Wasp*, and *Hornet*.[8] In 1863 the gunboat *Patrick Henry* was converted into the home of the Confederate Naval Academy, and the gunboat *Teaser*, also a participant in the Battle of Hampton Roads, had been captured by Federal forces in 1862. The nucleus of the squadron, however, was three armour-clads: the *Richmond*, completed in 1863 and the *Fredericksburg* and *Virginia II* in 1864. The squadron's long period of inactivity ended with the initiation of the Union's grand strategy in May 1864.

This plan included a campaign for the destruction of the Army of General Robert E Lee in Virginia. A Federal Army operating under the command of General Ulysses S Grant would attack Lee's forces concentrated in northern Virginia. Another Union force would move up the James River from its base on the Chesapeake Bay and attempt to capture Richmond. This force would be supported by units of the North Atlantic Blockading Squadron.

The Federal Army advancing up the James was stopped short of Richmond, but Grant's troops protected by Union warships passed safely across the river to attack Petersburg. Although early in May a passage through the obstructions in the river a few miles below Richmond was cut, allowing the Confederate squadron access to the lower James, no attempt was made to challenge the Union naval force guarding the crossing. Units of the squadron, including the three ironclads, did pass through the obstructions but did not move downstream for nearly a month. Throughout the remainder of 1864 the Confederate vessels occasionally exchanged fire with the Federal gunboats and shore batteries with negligible results. In late January 1865 the Confederate squadron, attempted to pass Union obstructions in the river and attack the large supply

Virginia sinks the USS *Cumberland* at Hampton Roads, March 8, 1862. (WMCWNH)

depot at City Point. The attempt failed. Only the *Fredericksburg* got through the obstructions safely; the others grounded and the wooden gunboat *Drewry* was destroyed before she could break free. Under attack from Union shore batteries and the monitor *Onondaga*, the squadron retired back up the river. This was the last action by the squadron. When Richmond was abandoned early in April, the vessels of the squadron were destroyed. Self-destruction was also the fate of the Confederate squadron at Savannah, Georgia.

The Georgia Government had created a small naval force shortly after the state seceded. It consisted of three small convert-ed tugboats, the *Savannah, Sampson* and *Resolute*, armed with one 32-pdr smoothbore each. Under the command of Commodore Josiah Tattnall, they were placed under Confederate command. In November 1861 they participated in the futile attempt to prevent Federal occupation of Port Royal, South Carolina. Afterwards they returned to the Savannah River to co-operate in the defense of the port of Savannah. For more than a year these vessels along with two additional converted steamers harassed the Union

B*attle of Port Royal, November 7, 1861. (WMCWNH)*

blockading force off Savannah, allowing an occasional blockade runner to slip in or out of the port.[9] Later another small wooden gunboat, the *Firefly*, reinforced the squadron from Charleston. In the meantime the Confederate Navy was building new warships, both wooden and ironclad, in Savannah.

Five wooden gunboats were laid down in the Savannah ship-yards, but only two, the *Macon* and *Isondiga*, were commissioned and placed in operation. *The Virginia – Monitor* battle was a major factor in the Confederate Navy's decision to cancel the construction of wooden gunboats and concentrate on building armoured vessels. Within two months of the battle twelve new ironclads had been contracted for, including four in Savannah. Three would be new construction and the fourth would be converted from a merchant steamer. Two were commissioned in the fall of 1862: the floating battery *Georgia* and the *Atlanta*, formerly the English merchant steamer *Fingal*. The *Savannah* joined the fleet the following year.

The *Georgia* was completed first but her machinery was so inadequate that she could not move under her own power. For most of the war the ironclad was moored in a log 'crib' near an island where she could, by warping, bring a broadside to bear on either channel of the Savannah River. The *Atlanta* was the first of the ironclads in the Savannah Squadron to go into action. Tattnall

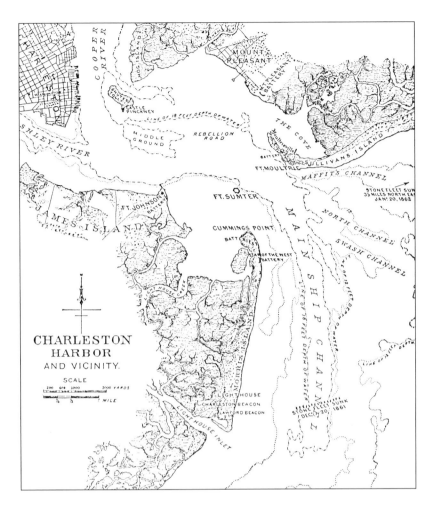

Charleston Harbor, South Carolina. (*Battles & Leaders*)

determined to use the powerful warship to clear the sounds south of the Savannah River of Federal warships. In mid June 1863 the *Atlanta*, while attempting to enter the sounds, ran aground and was forced to surrender. While stranded the Union monitor *Weehawken* closed to within 300 yards before opening fire with her 15in guns. Four hits were made on the Confederate ironclad. Listing to port, the *Atlanta* fired seven shots. None was effective. After fifteen minutes of the unequal contest, the *Atlanta* struck.

The *Atlanta*'s capture ended the squadron's offensive operations. After that the Confederate Navy concentrated on co-operating with the Army in defending the port. The *Georgia* remained stationary in her 'crib' near obstructions across the river. The *Savannah*'s duty station was several miles below the port where she was in position to reinforce the defenses guarding the river obstructions. The wooden vessels rotated on picket duty above the obstructions.

Confederate defenses for Savannah were planned with the con-

viction that Union efforts to take the port would come from the sea. Until the fall of 1864 this proved to be correct. Other than the occupation of the land and waters directly adjacent to the ocean, Federal forces did not seriously threaten the city from that direction. The major threat, however, came from the west. By December 1864 Major General William T Sherman's powerful Army was approaching Savannah. Two of the Confederate's wooden gunboats, the *Macon* and *Isondiga*, were sent to guard bridges above the city. The *Macon*, joined by two other wooden gunboats (the ironclads drew too much water), steamed further up river to reconnoitre. While steaming back downstream they were ambushed. The *Resolute* was captured and the others cut off from the rest of the squadron. Shortly before Christmas, as Sherman's soldiers neared the port, the Confederate warships were destroyed by their crews. Only the *Sampson* and *Macon*, isolated above the city, escaped to Augusta where they remained until the end of the war.

After taking Savannah, Sherman's Army crossed the Savannah River into South Carolina. As at Savannah, the port of Charleston was threatened from the rear, and as at Savannah, Charleston's defenses primarily faced seaward. These included a naval squadron of several wooden vessels and four ironclads.

South Carolina was the first state to secede from the Union and the first state to organize a naval force. In December 1860 four Federal vessels, all sailers, were seized by state officials. In January a steamer, the *General Clinch*, was purchased and armed with two small guns. Later two additional steam vessels were taken over by the state. All of them were turned over to the Confederate Navy in April.[10] These vessels were too weak to engage the Federal blockaders off the harbor. However, the addition of two ironclads led to the first offensive action off Charleston.

In the fall of 1862 the armoured vessels *Chicora* and *Palmetto State* were commissioned. During the night on the last day of January 1863, at the urging of Major General P G T Beauregard, in command of the Charleston defences, the two armoured vessels crossed the bar at the harbor's entrance and attacked the Union blockading force off the port. The *Palmetto State* rammed the USS *Mercedita* forcing the sinking gunboat to surrender. The *Chicora* engaged the USS *Keystone State*, badly damaging her and forcing another blockader to take the wooden gunboat under tow 'in a sinking condition'.[11] After exchanging shots with several other Union warships, the two Confederate ironclads retired into the harbor. The blockade, however, remained intact and in fact was strengthened by the addition of monitors and the armoured ship *New Ironsides*. After this attack the surface units in the Confederate

Ironclads *Chicora* and *Palmetto State* sortie from Charleston Harbor, January 31, 1863. (*Illustrated London News*)

Charleston Squadron reverted to their more realistic role of harbor defense for the rest of the war. The *Chicora* and *Palmetto State*, reinforced by two additional ironclads the *Charleston* and *Columbia*, alternated in guarding the channels between the forts guarding the harbour.

Nevertheless, using underseas warfare the Confederate Navy did continue challenging the Union blockade off Charleston. In October 1863 the *David*, a small, semi-submergible torpedo boat, attacked and badly crippled the powerful ironclad *New Ironsides*. The *David*'s success led the Confederate Navy to construct similar craft at Charleston and elsewhere in the South, but none matched the original *David*'s accomplishment.[12] The Confederacy had even more success with its submarine, *H. L. Hunley*. Built in Mobile, Alabama and transported by rail to Charleston, it underwent a series of tests, fatal for most of the crews, before torpedoing and

sinking the USS *Housatonic* in February 1864. The submarine was apparently damaged in the attack and also sank with the loss of her crew.[13] The two underwater attacks, while spectacular, did not effectively weaken the blockade off Charleston.

As with Savannah, Union efforts to take Charleston from the sea failed. Once again it was Sherman's troops marching up the coast that captured the city. Confederate naval forces were destroyed shortly before Union forces reached the port.

After seizing Charleston and the state capital at Columbia, Sherman's Army continued up the coast, entering North Carolina early in March 1865. By that date Wilmington had fallen as the result of an amphibious assault on the forts guarding the river entrance to the port. The remaining Confederate naval forces in the state had also been destroyed.

The Federal occupation of coastal North Carolina in the spring of 1862 left Wilmington as the state's only remaining major outlet to the sea. Wilmington also became a key blockade-running port in the Confederacy. The fall of New Orleans and the strengthening of the blockade off the other key southern

ports, the difficulties of blockading Wilmington, the close proximity of the North Carolina port to the front in northern
Virginia, as well as the British shipping centre in Bermuda, all were
factors in Wilmington's importance. The port was guarded by two
pre-war forts and Fort Fisher, a powerful log and earthwork forti-
fication constructed on the north bank of the Cape Fear River,
the water entrance to Wilmington. A naval force was also established to aid in the port's defense.

Two small wooden vessels, *Casewell* and *Uncle Ben*, were the only
units of the Confederate Navy in the Cape Fear River until two
ironclads were completed. The *North Carolina* and *Raleigh* were commissioned in the spring of 1864. They were probably the most
defective of all the armoured vessels built within the Confederacy.
Because of serious imperfections with her machinery, the *North
Carolina* was used mainly as a floating battery. She was anchored
near one of the inlets to the Cape Fear and there sunk at her
moorings as a result of a worm-eaten bottom. The *Raleigh*, however, did attempt to challenge the blockading squadron off the
river's inlets. During the night of May 7, 1864 the ironclad with
two wooden consorts crossed the bar at the river's mouth.
Throughout the night the Confederate vessels exchanged fire with
several blockaders; no ship on either side was hit. The following
morning the ironclad and the wooden gunboats recrossed the bar.
While steaming up river, the *Raleigh* grounded and was lost. There
were no further engagements between Union and Confederate
naval forces in the area.[14]

On the day the *Raleigh* stranded fatally, the CSS *Albemarle*
clashed with a Union naval force in Albemarle Sound. The
Albemarle and a sister ironclad, the *Neuse*, were built to co-operate in
regaining control of North Carolina's coastal area. The *Albemarle*
was constructed on the Roanoke River and the *Neuse* on the Neuse
River. The *Neuse* accomplished nothing; her draft was too deep to
move down the shallow stream. She was scuttled to keep her from
falling to Union forces. The *Albemarle* had a more spectacular
career and was one of the more successful Confederate armoured
vessels in combat with Union naval forces. In April 1864 the
Albemarle, co-operating with Confederate troops, attacked and
retook Plymouth, North Carolina. During the attack, the
Confederate ironclad sank one Union gunboat and drove the
remainder out of the river. On May 5 the *Albemarle* steamed down
the river. Her objective was to clear the sounds of Union vessels
and then co-operate with Confederate troops in retaking the port
of New Bern. The ironclad accompanied by two wooden vessels
entered Albemarle Sound where they were attacked by a Union
flotilla of seven vessels. In the battle that followed one of the
Confederate wooden vessels, the *Bombshell*, surrendered; the second
fled back into the river. The Union gunboats then concentrated on
the *Albemarle*, surrounding her and at close range pouring broadside
after broadside at her iron casemate. The *Sassacus* rammed the
Confederate ship, but damaged herself more than the ironclad.
Nevertheless, the *Albemarle* was damaged and limped back to
Plymouth. The Confederate Navy never threatened Union control
of the North Carolina sounds after the May 5 battle. The
Albemarle remained in the river and a threat until torpedoed and
sunk by a volunteer crew in a small open launch.[15]

Bombardment of Fort Fisher. (*Harper's Weekly*)

The western rivers

In the months after the fall of Fort Sumter the United States formulated its strategy to recover the South. Naval responsibilities
included the blockade along the Southern coast and the capture of
the main transportation arteries from Ohio to the Gulf. Control
of the Mississippi River and its tributaries was, as Abraham
Lincoln said, 'the key to the whole situation'. Since the rivers were
at once natural highways for invasion and barriers against it, they
should have been defended jointly by Confederate Army and naval
forces. For its part, the Army did attempt to block the arteries at
several points, but naval power was noticeably absent. The Navy
was far more concerned about the blockade and defending the
lower Mississippi and the important port of New Orleans.[16]

Naval battle below New Orleans, April 1862. (WMCWNH)

In 1861 New Orleans shipyards converted or laid down an impressive number of wooden vessels-of-war including the floating batteries *New Orleans* (20 guns), *Memphis* (18 guns); and the gunboats *General Polk* (3 to 7 guns), *McRae* (7 guns), *Maurepas* (5

Passing of the forts below New Orleans, April 24, 1862. (WMCWNH)

guns), *Livingston* (6 guns), *Ponchartrain* (6 guns), *Carondelet* (6 guns), *Morgan* (3 guns), *Pickens* (3 guns), *Pamlico* (1 gun), *Oregon* (1 gun, 2 howitzers), *James L. Day* (1 gun), and the *Ivy* (2 guns) along with several operated by the Army and the state of Louisiana. Two ironclads were laid down and a third, the privateer *Manassas,* was commandeered by the Navy.

The *Ivy* was the first to see action. On October 9, 1861 she opened fire on Union blockaders at the Head of Passes, the entrance from the Gulf of Mexico to the Mississippi River. No damage occurred in the long-range bombardment. Two days later the ironclad ram *Manassas* led a small force of four wooden gunboats, and two tugs pulling fire rafts to the Head of Passes. The four wooden vessels did not enter the Head of Passes; the fire rafts were ignited and set free to float with the current but reached no target. Only the *Manassas* was successful; she rammed one Union warship, damaging her, and caused the entire Federal force to cross the bar back into the Gulf. At daybreak the Confederate wooden vessels opened fire on the retiring ships but none were hit. These were the only attacks against the Union force concentrated at the Mississippi's mouth until the following April when a much more powerful Union fleet crossed the bar and steamed up the river.

During the night of April 24 Flag Officer David G Farragut led a force of eighteen warships through the obstructions and past

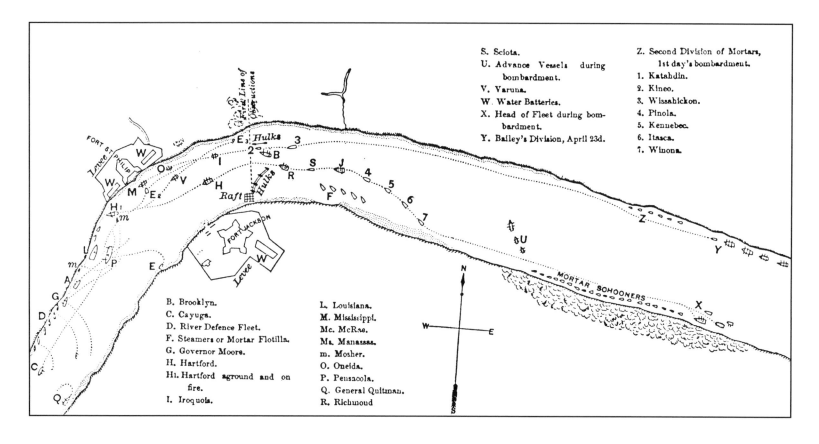

the forts that guarded the river approach to New Orleans. A Confederate naval force of thirteen vessels was assembled above the obstructions. Only three of them, the *McRae, Manassas* and the uncompleted armourclad *Louisiana*, were units of the Confederate Navy; the remainder were state vessels or belonged to the Army's 'River Defense Fleet'.[17] The *Louisiana*, without adequate power to move but armed with a heavy battery of 16 guns, had been towed down the river and moored alongside one of the forts. As

Map of Head of Passes, Mississippi River, where the *Manassas* attacked the Union fleet on October 12, 1861. (Mahan, *Gulf and Inland Waters*, 1883)

Admiral Farragut's Federal fleet fights past the forts below New Orleans, April 1862. (WMCWNH)

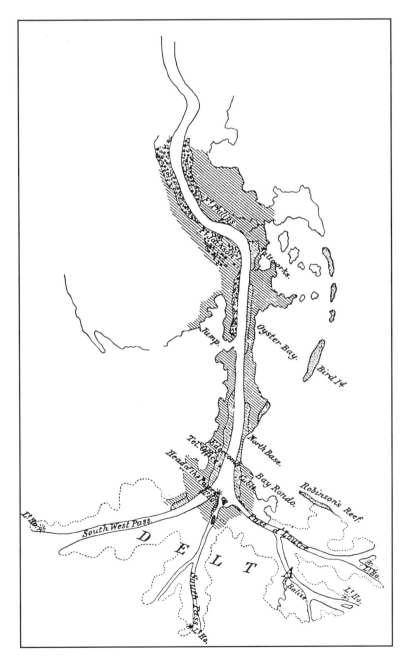

Farragut's fleet steamed by the forts the stationary ironclad fired through the darkness and smoke at the Union vessels. The *Manassas* moored to the bank above the forts headed for the gun flashes. In the darkness she grazed one of the Federal warships churning up the river, then struck the USS *Mississippi* a glancing blow. The slightly damaged Union vessel continued up the river. The *Manassas* then rammed the *Brooklyn*, but again damage was minimal. By this time the Union fleet was above the ram. Unable to make sufficient headway against the current to mount a serious attack (having only one small gun she had to depend upon the ram), and with two Union warships approaching, the ironclad was run ashore and abandoned by her crew. On the opposite side of the river the *McRae* became heavily engaged with several Union vessels. She exchanged broadsides with the *Iroquois* in the van of one of the Federal columns. Within a brief period the Confederate ship was under fire from several of the Union vessels; a shell from one of them started a large fire in the sail locker. As she steamed towards the other bank, she was hulled several times and her smoke stack nearly carried away, she was then beached and abandoned by her crew. On the 28th, the day the river forts surrendered to Federal forces, the *McRae* and *Louisiana* were destroyed to prevent their capture. The bitterest fight was carried on not by a Confederate naval or military gunboat, but by the *Governor Moore*, commanded by a naval officer but owned by the state of Louisiana. During the battle the state gunboat twice rammed the *Varuna* while raking her deck. She then attacked the *Cayuga* while coming under intense fire from several Union vessels. With

The naval battle below New Orleans, April 24, 1862. (WMCWNH)

One ironclad, the CSS *Arkansas*, under construction on the Yazoo River, was nearly operational.

The *Arkansas* was one of two large armoured vessels laid down at Memphis. When Union forces approached the city, one still on the stocks was destroyed, and the other, the *Arkansas*, was towed down the Mississippi and up the Yazoo River. There she was completed and placed in operation early in July 1862. On July 15 the ironclad was involved in one of the Confederate Navy's most dramatic successes. Steaming down the narrow Yazoo she encountered three Union gunboats, including one ironclad coming upstream. Under fire from the Confederate vessel's bow guns, the Union warships reversed course and headed for the river's mouth. The Union ironclad's steering cables were damaged and she ran ashore, exchanging fire with the *Arkansas* as she passed. The two wooden gunboats were able to outdistance the Confederate ship and enter the Mississippi. The *Arkansas* followed and within minutes upon rounding a bend a large concentration of ships was observed.

The Yazoo flows into the Mississippi some twelve miles above Vicksburg. Approximately half way between the river's mouth and the port lay a powerful Union naval force of more than thirty warships, the combined squadrons of flag officers Farragut and Charles H Davis. After seizing New Orleans and the lower Mississippi, Farragut's vessels had ascended the river, finally arriving below Vicksburg in late May. On June 28 his squadron

sixty-four of her crew dead or dying, she drifted ashore where she was set afire by her surviving crew. With the Confederate warships destroyed or cut off, New Orleans surrendered to Farragut.

While Admiral Farragut's fleet was gaining control of the lower Mississippi, a naval force of wooden gunboats and ironclads was created on the upper Mississippi and its tributaries. In the fall of 1861 units of the Confederate Navy in New Orleans under Commander George N Hollins were sent to co-operate with Confederate defenses established near the Kentucky – Tennessee border. In early 1862 joint Union Army and Navy operations began on the Mississippi, capturing Confederate strongholds as the force descended the river. Hollins's weak flotilla made no attempt to challenge the Federal onslaught, but retired downstream. Confederate Army gunboats, however, did engage the Union vessels but with little success.[18] By the middle of June 1862 Federal forces held most of the Mississippi. Only the bastion of Vicksburg was left to deny Union domination of the entire Mississippi River area. After the loss of New Orleans and Memphis (June 6), the Confederate Navy in the west consisted of a few wooden gunboats scattered up the Mississippi's tributaries.

successfully ran the Confederate batteries massed on the bluffs at Vicksburg. Two days later the wooden gunboats and ironclads of Davis's squadron arrived from Memphis. The ships were anchored generally in two lines, one on each side of the river.

The *Arkansas*, damaged from the previous encounter on the Yazoo, fired broadsides at the anchored vessels as she steamed sluggishly between the lines. Some of the surprised Union warships were able to unmask their batteries and open fire at the slowly moving ironclad, others did not. The *Arkansas* was hit repeatedly, but most of the shot and shell bounced off her armoured sides. One shell, however, penetrated and exploded on the gundeck, killing and wounding a number of men. The Union vessels also suffered damage, but only the wooden ram *Lancaster* was seriously hurt. No ships were sunk. Although it took the *Arkansas* thirty minutes to reach the end of the lines, only two of the Federal warships were able to get up steam and pursue the Confederate armourclad. However, she was able to get under cover of

A model of the CSS *Arkansas*. (WMCWNH)

Confederate land batteries at Vicksburg before they could close within range.

Farragut, concerned over the Confederate warship's presence between his squadron and the lower Mississippi, decided to attack the *Arkansas* that night. Under the cover of darkness his vessels steamed in column as close to the Vicksburg side as possible and fired at the *Arkansas*'s estimated position. Only one shell hit the

CSS *Manassas* at the naval battle below New Orleans, April 1862. (*Battles & Leaders*)

moored ironclad, piercing the port side a few inches below the waterline. Although the Confederate gunboat was no longer between Farragut's ocean-going vessels and New Orleans, she was intact and apparently operational. The Union naval commanders were still determined to destroy her. On July 22 two warships of the upper fleet, the Army ram *Queen of the West* and armourclad *Essex* attacked the *Arkansas* while the two squadrons engaged the land batteries. The *Essex* was able only to graze the ironclad's side as the Confederate crew threw off lines allowing her bow to swing out towards the approaching Union vessel. The Union vessel grounded alongside the *Arkansas* and for ten minutes the ships exchanged fire at point-blank range. Neither was seriously damaged, although one shot penetrated the Confederate gunboat killing and wounding several men. The Union ironclad was hit forty-two times by the *Arkansas*'s guns and land batteries, before she was able to pull free and steam downstream. The *Queen of the West* also attempted to ram, but with little more success. Ramming the Confederate ship from downstream and against the current,

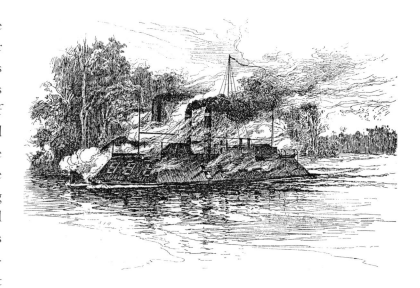

Arkansas and *Carondelet* engaged in battle on the Yazoo River, July 15, 1862. (*Battles & Leaders*)

Commander Isaac N Brown, commander of the *Arkansas*. (*Battles & Leaders*)

the *Arkansas* rolled heavily but her hull was not penetrated. The 'ram' in return was raked from stem to stern, although she was able to back clear and return upstream.

Two days later Farragut's squadron stood down the river. Four ships, including the ironclad *Essex*, were left at Baton Rouge in case the *Arkansas* came down. Less than two weeks later she did. The Confederate ironclad was to participate in an attack on Louisiana's capital. The *Arkansas*, however, never joined in the assault. Her machinery broke down as she approached the town. Under fire from the *Essex* the helpless ironclad was set afire and abandoned by her crew. She blew up after drifting downstream for more than an hour.

The *Arkansas*'s destruction left the Confederacy with no operational naval force of any consequence on the Mississippi and its tributaries. The remnants of Hollins's former fleet, two on the Yazoo and one on the White River were destroyed in June – July 1862. A fourth wooden gunboat, the *Ponchartrain*, was destroyed in 1863, blockaded far up the White River. Ironclads under construction on the Yazoo River were also destroyed to prevent their capture. In 1865 the Confederate Navy in the west consisted of two warships, the former Army ram, *Webb*, and the ironclad *Missouri*, both on the Red River.[19] In April 1864 a combined Union force ascended the Red River. The two Confederate ships were supposed to co-operate in the defense of the river port of Alexandria, but low water held them incapacitated at Shreveport. They were not needed, however, as the Confederate Army defeated

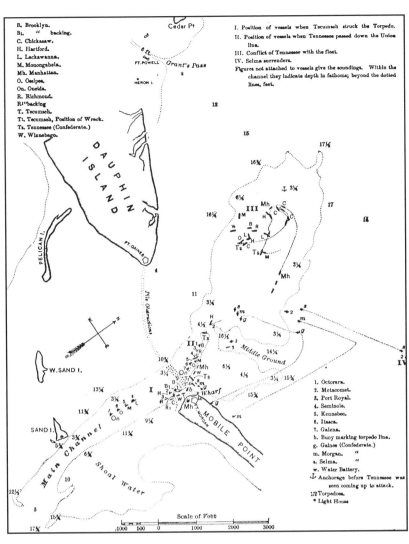

B. Brooklyn.
Bᴸ. " backing.
C. Chickasaw.
H. Hartford.
L. Lackawanna.
M. Monongahela.
Mh. Manhattan.
O. Ossipee.
On. Oneida.
R. Richmond.
Rᴸ backing.
T. Tecumseh.
Tᴸ. Tecumseh, Position of Wreck.
Ts. Tennessee (Confederate.)
W. Winnebago.

I. Position of vessels when Tecumseh struck the Torpedo.
II. Position of vessels when Tennessee passed down the Union line.
III. Conflict of Tennessee with the fleet.
IV. Selma surrenders.
Figures not attached to vessels give the soundings. Within the channel they indicate depth in fathoms; beyond the dotted lines, feet.

1. Octorara.
2. Metacomet.
3. Port Royal.
4. Seminole.
5. Kennebec.
6. Itasca.
7. Galena.
b. Buoy marking torpedo line.
g. Gaines (Confederate.)
m. Morgan. "
s. Selma. "
w. Water Battery.
⚓ Anchorage before Tennessee was seen coming up to attack.
⚓ Torpedoes.
* Light House

Map of the Battle of Mobile Bay, August 5, 1864 showing positions of ships. (Mahan, *Gulf & Inland Waters*)

the Federal force. It was nearly a year before the water in the river rose to where the ironclad could descend the river to Alexandria. There she surrendered in June, never having fired a shot in anger. The *Webb* did evade the Union blockade at the Red River's mouth, but failed in a desperate attempt to descend the Mississippi into the Gulf of Mexico. She was hotly pursued by Union naval vessels and forced ashore where she was fired by her crew and abandoned.

The Gulf of Mexico

The Union blockade of the rebellious Southern states, more than 3,400 miles in length, included the shores of the Gulf of Mexico from the Florida Keys to the Rio Grande River. Initially one squadron had the responsibility for the entire area, but in the fall of 1861 it was divided, with the East Gulf Blockading Squadron patrolling the waters from the Keys to Pensacola, Florida, while

Battle of Mobile Bay, August 5, 1864. (Porter, *Naval History of the Civil War*)

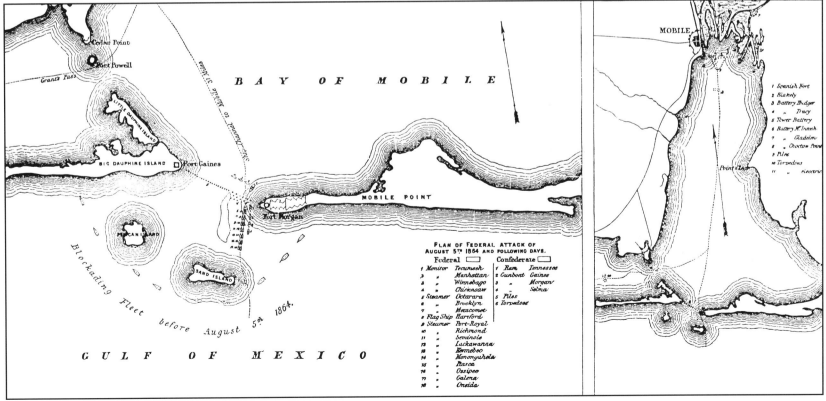

USS *Metacomet* captures CSS *Selma* at Mobile Bay, a painting by Xanthus Smith. (WMCWNH)

Pensacola and the waters west were to be watched by the West Gulf Blockading Squadron.

With the exception of Pensacola, site of a pre-war naval yard, Florida's west or Gulf coast was empty of commercial shipping. The waters were notoriously shallow, and only a few fishing and lumber shipping ports dotted the long coast. For that reason throughout the war the Union squadron operating in those waters included very few vessels.[20] It had a low priority with the Confederate Navy as well. When Pensacola was retaken by Federal forces in May 1862, the only Confederate naval facilities remaining in the area were on the Chattahoochee River, which flowed into Apalachicola Bay and the Gulf. Two vessels, the wooden gunboat *Chattahoochee* and the ironclad *Jackson*, were laid down at yards on the river. The wooden gunboat was completed

first and had the onerous responsibility of defending the Apalachicola–Chattahoochee–Flint river system against expected Federal military operations.[21] Although inoperable for an extended period because of a boiler explosion and subsequent sinking, she nevertheless was the only Confederate naval vessel completed and commissioned on the Chattahoochee River. The *Jackson* never became operational.

The West Gulf Blockading Squadron, in contrast to the Union force in Florida waters, was faced with blockading a large geographical area which included some of the most important ports in the Confederacy. These included New Orleans, Mobile and Galveston, Texas. New Orleans was captured in April 1862, but Mobile and Galveston (except for three months in the fall–winter 1862) remained in Confederate hands throughout the war. The Confederate Navy was not involved in the defense of Galveston, but played a major role in Mobile Bay.[22]

The port city of Mobile was on the northern shore of Mobile Bay about thirty miles from the Gulf itself. The entrance to the

The USS *Lackawanna* rams the ironclad *Tennessee* at Mobile Bay, August 1864, a painting by Zanthus Smith. (WMCWNH)

Bay was guarded by two forts and a naval squadron. In 1861 the Mobile Squadron consisted of two converted gunboats, the *Alert* (1 gun) and the *Florida* (4 guns), later named the *Selma*. In 1862 three additional warships joined the squadron, the ironclad *Baltic*, financed by the state of Alabama, and the wooden gunboats *Morgan* and *Gaines*. Early in April the four wooden gunboats made a half-hearted attack on Union blockaders off the Bay. After firing a few shots in the general direction of the Union vessels, the Confederate squadron withdrew.[23] Confederate officials considered the squadron too weak to seriously challenge the Union force off the Bay until it had been reinforced by new vessels including ironclads. By the fall of 1862 seven armoured vessels were under construction on the rivers flowing into Mobile Bay. Four of them, the floating batteries *Huntsville* and *Tuscaloosa*, and the large rams

Nashville and *Tennessee*, were commissioned and became operational in 1863 – 64. The other three were never completed. Only the *Tennessee* actually entered the Bay; the others were considered too weak. The Confederate Navy was forced to face a powerful Union force being assembled off the Bay with one ironclad and three small wooden gunboats.

Admiral Farragut had wanted to attack Mobile immediately after the fall of New Orleans, but operations on the Mississippi delayed him until the summer of 1863. By then, however, he had become convinced that ironclads were needed as well as troops, and none were available at that time. It was early August 1864 before all was ready to attack. On August 5 the Union fleet in two columns entered the Bay. One column consisted of fourteen wooden warships lashed together; the second of four monitor-type vessels. The channel was on the east side of the Bay where it passed close to Fort Morgan, one of the two bastions guarding the entrance. The monitors led by the *Tecumseh* were in the column nearer the fort and were the first to open fire. After firing only two shots the Confederate squadron was observed steaming to intercept the Union columns. The *Tecumseh* immediately broke off engaging the fort and headed for the Confederate squadron. The monitor crossed in front of the second column and steamed directly for the ironclad *Tennessee*. Before coming in range of the Confederate ironclad, she struck a mine and went down.

Rear Admiral Franklin Buchanan, who had commanded the ironclad *Virginia* on the first day of the battle of Hampton Roads, was in the *Tennessee*, flagship of his small squadron. Because the attack had been expected for some time, the *Tennessee, Gaines, Selma*

USS *Montauk* destroys the Confederate privateer *Rattlesnake* (ex-CSS *Nashville*) in the Ogeechee River, Georgia, February 1863. (*Harper's Weekly*)

and *Morgan* had been on station just north of Fort Morgan for over two months. When Farragut's fleet was observed entering the channel, Buchanan ordered his ships to steam abreast towards the approaching enemy. Buchanan at first ignored the monitors intent upon ramming the leading wooden warship. The flagship *Hartford* was in the van, having assumed this position when the leading vessels were thrown into confusion by the *Tecumseh*'s disaster. The lumbering Confederate ironclad was no match for the much faster *Hartford* which easily manoeuvred around her. The *Tennessee* also tried unsuccessfully to strike the *Brooklyn*, the next in line and then engaged each of the large ships as they passed. The *Monongehela*, fourth in the column, attempted to ram the Confederate ironclad amidships, but the *Tennessee*'s helmsman swung her hard a-starboard and the collision occurred at an angle. The two vessels momentarily hung side by side with the gunboat *Kennebec* sandwiched between

them. The *Tennessee's* small boat was torn from its davits, while the ironclad fired a broadside into the wooden gunboat. A few men were killed and wounded but damage was negligible. The *Tennessee* then continued down the column firing into the Union vessels as her guns came to bear. The *Oneida* – last in the line – was seriously damaged – a broadside from the ironclad carried away much of her lower rigging and severely wounded her captain and a shot from the *Morgan* exploded one of her boilers.

Buchanan's three wooden gunboats had followed the flagship into the fray. The *Hartford* was hard hit, particularly by the *Selma*, which poured a raking fire into her. Farragut's flagship had more than twenty killed and many wounded. The *Morgan* and *Gaines* exchanged shots with the Federal ships as they came within range. The accurate Union fire seriously damaged the *Gaines*. Her steering wheel was destroyed and she was hulled several times. Sinking, she was run ashore near Fort Morgan. Badly outgunned, the *Selma* and *Morgan* broke off the engagement and retired up the Bay. The smaller Union gunboats immediately gave chase. The *Selma* was forced to surrender, but the *Morgan* eluded capture and eventually reached the safety of Mobile.

Only the *Tennessee* continued the fight. After running through the gauntlet of the fort's batteries, the minefields, and Buchanan's squadron, the Union fleet assembled about four miles up the Bay. The Confederate ironclad followed as quickly as she could. As the ram approached, signals flew from the flagship, ordering the monitors and larger vessels to attack. The *Monongehela* and *Lackawanna* both rammed the ironclad but received far greater damage than they inflicted. The *Hartford* was the third ship to crash into the *Tennessee*, but while circling for another try, she in turn was rammed by the *Lackawanna*. Meanwhile the monitors had finally entered the mêlée. The *Manhattan* crept up to less than a hundred yards before firing its 15in gun at the ironclad's casemate. The shot penetrated the armour plate and wood backing. The river monitor *Chickasaw* manoeuvred into position astern of the ram and pounded her mercilessly. Shots from the monitor's two 11in guns jammed port shutters, cut the exposed wheel chains and relieving tackle, and wounded and killed several men, including Buchanan. The *Tennessee* rapidly became helpless, almost dead in the water. At 10am after nearly three hours of fighting, the Confederate ship surrendered. The Confederates had lost four of their five ships, twelve killed, twenty wounded, and the crews of the *Tennessee* and *Selma* captured. Farragut lost no ships, but all of the wooden ships were damaged to some extent. He also lost 145 killed and 170 wounded. Federal forces were in control of the Bay, the gateway to Mobile. The city,

however, would not surrender until April 1865, nearly nine months later. During that nine months the Confederate Navy continued to play a major role in Mobile's defense.

In March 1865 a large Union force of over 45,000 men attacked the fortifications guarding the city on the upper bay and rivers flowing into it. Two Confederate ironclads, the *Huntsville* and *Nashville*, and the wooden gunboat *Morgan* operating in the rivers supported the Confederate defense positions by shelling Union troops. This bombardment continued for over two weeks, until the vessels were out of ammunition. The Confederate fortifications were breached and on April 12 the city surrendered. The surviving vessels of the Mobile squadron were then scuttled.

Distant waters

Quite early in the war the Confederate Government attempted to obtain warships, both wooden and armoured vessels, in Europe, either by the purchase and conversion of existing vessels or new construction. Only one ironclad, the CSS *Stonewall*, reached Confederate hands. She arrived at Cuba in 1865 only to discover that the American Civil War was over. The Confederates were more successful with their wooden vessels, nearly all of which became commerce cruisers. During the war agents of the Southern Government in Europe purchased or contracted for eighteen vessels that were designated or intended to be cruisers. Six became operational as raiders, the *Alabama, Georgia, Florida, Rappahannock, Shenandoah* and *Tallahassee*. The remainder became blockade runners, were seized by the British and French Governments, or were not completed during the war.[24] Commerce raiders were also converted from merchant ships, blockade runners or built within the Confederate states. Seven became operational: the *Archer* and *Clarence* captured by the *Florida*, and in turn the *Tacony* seized by the *Clarence*, the *Tuscaloosa* fitted out by the *Alabama*, the *Chickamauga, Nashville* and the *Sumter*.[25]

The *Sumter* was actually the first Confederate commerce cruiser. Originally the barque-rigged steamer *Habana*, she was converted into a raider and under the command of Raphael Semmes sailed from New Orleans, Louisiana in June 1861. Successfully eluding the Federal blockade, she made her first capture on July 2. Cruising in the Gulf of Mexico, Caribbean and down the coast of South America to Brazil, she seized more than a dozen more ships. Continuing to evade Union warships, she crossed the Atlantic and

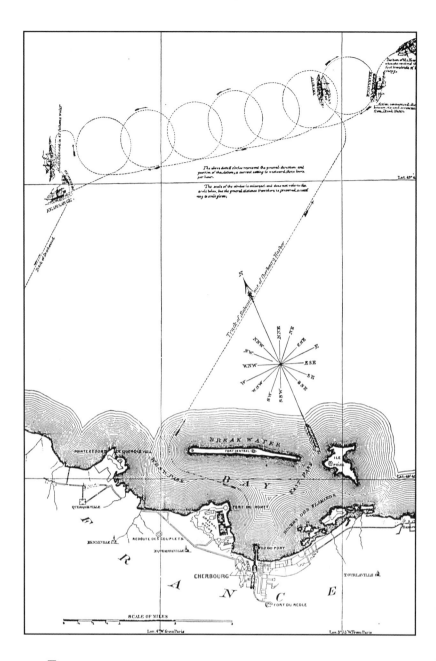

Track of the battle between *Alabama* and *Kearsarge*, June 19, 1864. (Porter, *Naval History of the Civil War*)

entered Cadiz, Spain for repairs. Unable to repair his ship there, Semmes sailed for Gibraltar. There she was finally cornered and blockaded. Unable to escape Semmes abandoned the *Sumter*. During her approximately six-months career as a commerce cruiser, she captured altogether eighteen ships.[26]

The *Archer, Nashville* and *Tuscaloosa* were not particularly successful; only five captures were made by them. The *Clarence* and her

Alabama sinks after a fight with the USS *Kearsarge* off Cherbourg, France, June 19, 1864. (*Harper's Weekly*)

A model of the CSS *Shenandoah*. (WMCWNH)

prize, the *Tacony*, were more successful. Ranging up and down the east coast of the United States, the *Clarence* took seven and the *Tacony* fourteen merchant ships.[27]

Two were converted from blockade runners in Wilmington, North Carolina. In October 1864 the *Chickamauga* put to sea, cruised as far north as Long Island Sound, then to St Georges, Bermuda before returning to Wilmington. She captured and sank four prizes. She never put to sea again but rendered support to Fort Fisher when it was attacked early in 1865. The *Tallahassee* was the most accomplished of all the 'home water' commerce raiders. Converted from the blockade runner *Atlanta*, noted for her speed, the *Tallahassee* was commissioned in the Confederate Navy in 1864. The cruiser, under the command of Commander John Taylor Wood, slipped out of Wilmington and turned north. In a brief but brilliant nineteen-day cruise up the coast as far as Halifax, Nova Scotia, she seized thirty-five vessels, nearly all of which were destroyed. After returning to Wilmington her name was changed

to the CSS *Olustee*, and under a new commanding officer she once again headed into the Atlantic. This time she took six vessels before being chased by blockaders back into Wilmington. Her name was changed for a fourth time and as the blockade runner *Chameleon* she tried unsuccessfully to bring military supplies into the port. The *Chameleon* eventually returned to Great Britain where she had been built and was seized by the British Government.[28]

Five of the cruisers purchased in Great Britain became operational. The *Rappahannock*, however, was disabled shortly after leaving Sheerness on her maiden voyage as a cruiser and spent the remainder of the war in Calais.

The *Georgia* was another disappointment to the Confederate authorities. Constructed in 1862 as the merchantman *Japan*, she was purchased by the Confederates at Dumbarton in Scotland in March 1863. On April 1 the ship left Scotland reputedly bound for the East Indies, but off Ushant, France, she rendezvoused with a steamer carrying arms and supplies. She was then placed in commission as the CSS *Georgia*. The raider made one long cruise, sailing across the Atlantic to Brazil and Trinidad, and from there back across the ocean to Simon's Bay, Cape Colony in South Africa.

The cruise ended at Cherbourg, France, which port she entered in October for repairs. For various reasons, principally concerning her iron hull, it was decided that she was unsuitable as a cruiser. The ship was taken to Liverpool and sold.

The *Florida*, *Alabama* and *Shenandoah* were the most successful and best known of all the Confederate commerce raiders. All three were British-built, the first two from the keel up as Confederate ships and the third, the *Shenandoah*, was formerly a merchant vessel designed as a troop transport.

The *Florida*, often referred to as the *Oreto*, sailed from Birkenhead in England on March 22, 1862.[29] In the Bahama Islands the cruiser took on coal and some arms and ammunition. However, with crucial parts of the guns missing and with many of the crew, including the commanding officer John Newland Maffitt, incapacitated because of yellow fever the *Florida* was forced to run the blockade into Mobile. In January 1863, once more ready for sea, she again ran the blockade and for more than six months cruised off North and South America and in the West Indies, eluding Federal warships while capturing merchant vessels. In July 1863 the raider stopped off in the Bermudas for fuel and repairs and after another brief cruise in the North Atlantic entered Brest, France, for an extensive refit. In February 1864, with a new captain on board, the *Florida* sailed for the West Indies. Searching for prizes she sailed east to the Canaries and from there to Bahia, Brazil. While anchored in Brazilian waters she was taken in a night attack by the USS *Wachusetts*, and sent to the United States as a prize, despite Brazil's protest at this violation of neutral rights. In November 1864 she was sunk in Hampton Roads, Virginia, as a result of a collision.

The CSS *Alabama* is perhaps the most famous commerce cruiser in history and possibly the most successful. Under the command of Raphael Semmes she would make a two-year odyssey encompassing a large part of the world. Leaving Liverpool late in July 1862 for what was supposed to be a trial run, the ship, under the name *Enrica*, slipped away and rendezvoused in the Azores with steamers carrying officers and arms. There she was fitted out as a cruiser and commissioned the *Alabama*. For the next two months the Confederate ship ranged the North Atlantic, burning whalers and grain ships bound for Britain. Having destroyed twenty ships she then made her way to the West Indies to replenish coal. In January 1863 the cruiser headed for the coast of Texas where Semmes hoped to intercept a fleet of Union transports. Off Galveston he was challenged by the USS *Hatteras*. In an engagement lasting only a few minutes the blockader was sunk. Semmes

returned to the West Indies and gradually moved south to the Brazilian coast. The *Alabama*'s captain decided to shift his hunting grounds to the shipping lanes around the Cape of Good Hope. In July 1863 the ship arrived in Cape Town. Few prizes were taken so the cruiser continued into the Indian Ocean and Far Eastern waters. The *Alabama* would spend six months in a cruise to the South China Sea and back to Cape Town; few ships were sighted and only seven prizes taken. In March 1864 the cruiser, in bad need of an overhaul, set sail for France. On June 11 she arrived in Cherbourg. Shortly afterwards the USS *Kearsarge* arrived off the port. On June 19 the *Alabama* stood out of Cherbourg. Outside French waters the Union warship waited and opened fire as the range closed to within a thousand yards. The range continued to close as the two ships circled and fired their guns as rapidly as possible. The *Kearsarge*'s fire was far more effective, seriously damaging the Confederate vessel. After nearly an hour of fighting the *Alabama*, in a sinking condition, struck. The Confederates lost nine killed, several drowned, and twenty-two wounded; the *Kearsarge* lost only three wounded, one of whom later died. During her career the *Alabama* captured sixty-nine vessels, the overwhelming majority of which were destroyed.

The *Shenandoah* was the last Confederate raider and probably the last ship to fly the Southern flag. In October 1864 she departed from London and, as with the *Florida* and *Alabama*, received her guns along with officers at a rendezvous with a chartered vessel. Legitimate targets were scarce by the fall of 1864, particularly in the usual shipping lanes, so the Confederate Secretary of the Navy ordered the cruiser's commanding officer, James I Waddell, to concentrate on the Cape of Good Hope – Australia route and the Pacific grounds of the whaling fleet. She sailed around the Cape of Good Hope and arrived in Melbourne, Australia, in January 1865, having taken a number of prizes *en route*. The *Shenandoah*, enthusiastically received 'down under', was able to fill her bunkers and storerooms and refresh her crew before departing for the Pacific whaling grounds. In the spring the ship entered the Bering Sea and destroyed a large number of whalers. In June Waddell was informed by the master of a captured vessel that General Robert E Lee had surrendered, the capital at Richmond was taken, and the war was probably over. The cruiser's captain refused to give up. The raider moved south to intercept traffic from the West Coast of the United States to Latin America and the Far East. In August a British ship confirmed that the war had ended. Waddell decided to surrender in England. Disguised as a merchant ship, the *Shenandoah* skirted the Cape of Good Hope and arrived in

Liverpool on November 6, 1865. There she was surrendered to British authorities. The *Shenandoah* had remained at sea for twelve months and seventeen days, had travelled 58,000 miles, and had captured thirty-eight prizes, mostly whalers, two-thirds of them after hostilities ended.[30]

Conclusion

How successful was the Confederate States Navy? It certainly failed in its mission to preserve the Southern states' efforts to achieve independence. It never had the resources to seriously challenge Union sea power. Only a half dozen Federal warships were actually sunk in action by Confederate naval vessels. The Union blockade was far from being a major factor in the Confederacy's collapse, but this was not due to the Confederate Navy, but rather to the enormous difficulties in blockading the lengthy shoreline of the Southern states and to the logistical and technological problems in maintaining warships on this coastline for extended periods.[31] Nevertheless, the Confederate Navy did contribute significantly to the Southern war effort. Torpedoes (mines) proved to be the most successful weapon used against Union ships. Mor than sixty ships, including armoured vessels, were sunk by Confederate torpedoes during the war. Of the five seaports – Savannah, Charleston, Wilmington, Mobile and Galveston – taken in the last six months of the war, two were taken by land forces from the rear and two indirectly as a result of pressure from the rear. In all of the cities but one, Galveston, the Confederate Navy was intimately involved in their defense. The commerce cruisers destroyed some 5 per cent of the Union merchant fleet and seized or destroyed millions of dollars in cargo. For every vessel the Confederate raiders destroyed or seized, the Union merchant fleet lost eight others as an indirect result. Exorbitant insurance rates caused by war risks resulted in hundred of vessels remaining in port. In addition, nearly a thousand were transferred to other flags, principally British. Nevertheless, the Confederate raiders had little of the hoped-for-influence on Union policy; the blockade was not weakened and President Lincoln and his advisers gave no thought to a negotiated peace. In the final analysis the Confederate Navy was too weak and too ineffective to influence the war's outcome.

Dr William N Still, Jr

APPENDICES

Appendix to Chapter 6

RESIGNATION OF NAVAL OFFICERS*
(1860-61)

[Each rank is followed by the total number of resignations tendered by officers of that rank]

CAPTAINS (93)

Resigned-Accepted (9)

Randolph, Victor M
Ingraham, Duncan N
Rousseau, Lawrence
Tattnall, Josiah
Newell, Thomas M (Inactive)
Lynch, William F
Cooke, Harrison H
Page, Hugh N (Inactive)

Resigned-Dismissed (6)

Forrest, French
Buchanan, Franklin
Barron, Samuel
Magruder, George A
Mayo, Isaac
Hollins, George N
Sterrett, Isaac S

COMMANDERS (127)

Resigned-Accepted (16)

Harstene, Henry J
Brent, Thomas W
Farrand, Ebenezer
Semmes, Raphael
Henderson, James L
McBlair, Charles H
Thorburn, Robert D
Minor, George
Myers, Joseph
Pinkney, Robert F
Chatard, Frederick
Hunter, William W
Green, William
Mason, Murray
Whittle, Willliam C
Manning, John

Resigned-Dismissed (18)

Robb, Robert G.
Fairfax, Archibald
Page, Richard L
Sinclair, Arthur
Tucker, John R
Rootes, Thomas R
McBlair, William
McIntosh, Charles F
Lee, Sidney Smith
Page, Thomas J
Hunter, Thomas T
Maury, Matthew, F
Muse, William T.
Mitchell, John K
Kennedy, Charles H A H
Handy, Edward L
Boutwell, Edward B
Chandler, William

LIEUTENANTS (351)

Resigned-Accepted (51)

Hamilton, John R
Law, George E
Dozier, William G
Warley, Alexander F
Selden, Robert
Stribling, John
Pelot, Thomas P
North, James H
Chapman, Robert T
Renshaw, Francis B
Eggleston, John R
Kell, John
Fry, Joseph
Porcher, Philip
Walbach, J J B
Rutledge, John
Morris, C Manigault
Simons, Maurice
Bradford, William L
Fitzgerald, William B
Kennard, Joel S
Tilghman, Richard L
McLaughlin, Augustus M
Hunter, Bushrod W
McGary, Charles P M
Carter, Jonathan
Dunnington, John W
Wayne, William A
Maffitt, John N
Cooke, James W
Jones, Catesby ap R
Maury, William L
Kennon, Beverly
Johnston, James D
Harrison, George W
Taylor, John S
Bier, George H
Daniels, Joseph D
Webb, William A
Porter, Thomas K
Campbell, William P A
Stevens, Henry K
Loyall, Benjamin P
Butt, Walter R
Myers, Julian
DeBree, Alexander M
Forrest, Dulaney A
Glassell, William T
Van Zandt, Nicholas
Waddell, James I
McArann, Robert M

Resigned-Dismissed (38)

Wood, John Taylor
Fauntleroy, Charles M
Sinclair, George T
Gwathmey, Washington
Peagram, Robert B
Sharp, William
Spottswood, Charles F
Poindexter, Carter B
Maury, John S
Rochelle, James H
Bennett, John W
Wilkinson, John
Lewis, Henry H
Parker, William H*
Powell, William L
Brooke, John M
Murphy, Peter U
Murdough, William H
Winder, Edward L
Simms, Charles C
Minor, Robert D
Johnston, Oscar D
Davidson, Hunter
Brown, Isaac N
Bent, Silas
Jones, J Pembroke
McCorkle, David P
Lewis, James B
Barney, Joseph N
Barbot, Alphonse
Shyrock, George S
Hays, Charles W
Morgan, Van Rensellaer
Dalton, Hamilton H
Alexander, Joseph W
Shepperd, Francis E
Guthrie, John J
Ward, William H

SURGEONS (69)

Resigned-Accepted (6)
Spottswood, W A W
Steele, Thomas B
Patton, William F
Mason, John T
Blacknall, George
Cornick, James

Resigned-Dismissed (9)
Minor, Lewis W
McClenahan, Wm F
Sinclair, W B
Mason, Randolph
Green, Daniel S
Harrison, James F
Jeffery, Richard W
Page, Wm M
Fahs, Charles F

PASSED ASSISTANT SURGEONS (43)

Resigned-Accepted (6)
Lynah, Arthur M
Carrington, Wm F
Galt, Francis L
Ward, John
Phillips, Dinwiddie
Beck, Morris B

Resigned-Dismissed (4)
Williamson, Charles W
Wysham, William E
Washington, H W M
Greenhow, J W B

ASSISTANT SURGEONS (36)

Resigned-Accepted (3)
Charlton, Thomas J
Lining, Charles E
Sheldon, H Lawrence

Resigned-Dismissed (10)
Grafton, Joseph D
Van Bibber, Frederick
Lowndes, Charles Jr
Garnett, Algernon S
Green, Bennett W
Sanford, John W Jr
Freeman, Robert J
Christian, Marcellus J
Lindsay, James E
Herty, James W

PAYMASTERS (64)

Resigned-Accepted (4)
Kelly, W W J
Myers, Henry
Nixon, John W
Ritchie, George

Resigned-Dismissed (9)
Clark, George W
Johnston, John C
Allison, Richard T
DeBree, John
Harwood, James K
Morris, Miles H
Senac, Felix
Ware, Thomas R
Semple, James A

MASTERS IN LINE OF PROMOTION (37)

Resigned-Accepted (4)
Mills, Thomas B
Evans, William E
Kerr, William A
Whittle, William C

Resigned-Dismissed
None

MASTERS NOT IN LINE OF PROMOTION (9)

Resigned-Accepted (2)
Pearson, John
Young, H A F

Resigned-Dismissed
None

CHAPLAINS (24)

Resigned-Accepted (1)
Thomas, Charles W

Resigned-Dismissed
None

BOATSWAINS (43)

Resigned-Accepted (9)
None

Resigned-Dismissed (2)
Hasker, Charles H
Miller, James M

GUNNERS (47)

Resigned-Accepted
None

Resigned-Dismissed (4)
Oliver, Charles B
Moran, Charles
Owens, John
Lovatt, John A

CARPENTERS (45)

Resigned-Accepted (2)
Knight, William
Kinnear, James

Resigned-Dismissed (5)
Holmes, Lewis
Bain, Robert M
Williams, Edward
Thomas, Henry G.
Hoover, John B

SAILMAKERS (40)

Resigned-Accepted (3)
Turner, Samuel V
Bennett, William
Wightman, George A

Resigned-Dismissed (3)
Mahmey, William M
Boutwell, Samuel H
Blackford, George D

CHIEF ENGINEERS (28)

Resigned-Accepted (1)
Archibold, Samuel

Resigned-Dismissed (4)
Williamson, Wm P
Jackson, Thomas A
Patterson, Nathaniel P
Warner, James H

1st ASSISTANT ENGINEERS (43)

Resigned-Accepted (1)
Alexander, George W

Resigned-Dismissed (7)
Stump, T B C
Manning, Edward W
Ramsay, Henry A
Schraeder, Charles
Potts, Richard C
Freeman, Virginius
City, George W

2nd ASSISTANT ENGINEERS (29)

Resigned-Accepted (3)
Lining, George D
Campbell, Loudon
Wright, James D

Resigned-Dismissed (4)
Tynan, John W
Jordan, Marshal P
Levy, Charles H
Copeland, Robert W

3rd ASSISTANT ENGINEERS (92)

Resigned-Accepted (5)
Plunkett, James
Tennent, George W
Miller, William
Lawrence, Henry W
Fuller, William H

Resigned-Dismissed (7)
Patten, Edwin C
Jordon, Charles
Tucker, John T
Wright, Henry X
Dick, Edward L
Herring, Benjamin
Fagan, Henry

PASSED MIDSHIPMEN (55)

Resigned-Accepted (3)
Grimball, John
Read, Charles W
Hall, Wilburn B

Resigned-Dismissed (12)
Read, Edmund G
Dornin, Thomas L
Hoole, James L
Hoge, Francis L
Averett, Samuel W
Tayloe, James L
Hackett, Samuel H
Borchert, George A
Harrison, Thomas L
Claiborne, Henry B
Cenas, Hilary
Wharton, Arthur D

ACTING MIDSHIPMEN (267)

[Note: all resignations in this category were accepted.]

Resigned-Accepted (111)

Foute, Robert C
Bacot, Richard H
Walker, John T
Wilkinson, William W
Haward, Ochran H
Flournoy, Robert
Smith, Napoleon
Stone, Sardine G Jr
Roby, Francis M
Price, John R
Robinson, Wm F
Baldwin James G
lcombe, Isaac C
Hill, Hugh L
Payne, RobertM
Merriwether, James A
Moses, Raphael J Jr
McClintoc, Horatio G
Pinckney, William E
Carter, Barron

Berrien, Thomas M
Moody, David
Armstrong, Richard F
Comstock, Wm Van
Comstock, John H
Carnes, William W
Goodwyn Matthew, P
Ingraham, John H
Scales, Dabney M
Garrett, Thomas G
Reber, John M
Wilson, Joseph D
Holden, John F
Hicks, William A
Lee, William Piercy
Hudgins, Albert G
Dougherty, Harvey H
Dalton, William R
Bryan, George D
Appleton, Giles F
Daniels, Charles H
Ahl, James W
Fortune, John C
Willet, Silas S

Young, William W
Hopkins, John A
Heath, Benjamin
Fagan, Louis
Guthrie, Edward P
Dick, James A
Carmody, Robert E
Hivling, Wm H
Marmaduke, Henry
Ruggles, Edward S
Telfair, David A
Osterloh, William C
Ames, William L
Livingston, John S
Washington, Leroy H
Williams, Henri S H
Heath, Lucius E
Cushing, William B
Meyer, Cassius
Blake, H J
Fisk, James E
Morgan, James M
McDermott, Edward J
Moore, Thomas L
Howard, George A
Mason, William
Holt, Henry C
Benton, Mortimer M
Trigg, Daniel
Chew, Francis T
Claybrook, Joseph P
Beirne, Andrew P
Hutter, William C
Camm, Robert A
Floyd, Richard S
Carroll, Daniel

Peters, JA
Long, James C
Peyton, Joseph B
Spencer, Julian M
King, Charles K
Jackson, William C
Read, William W
Gardner, Joseph M
Sevier, Charles F
Wright, Augustus O
Sturdivant, Theodore
Foreman, Ivey
Mason, Alexander M
Worth, Algernon S
Littlepage, H Beverly
Stafford, James M
Cook, Henry S
McDaniel, Henry C
Pearson, James M
Carroll, William J
Mayo, Wyndam R
Browne, Orris A
Vaughan, Henry L
Sparks, Gale W
Mayo, Wyndam R
Browne, Orris A
Vaughan, Henry L
Sparks, Gale W
Good, William D
Phelps, Jefferson
Pipkin, William M
Evans, R
English, Gustavus
Craig, William J
Schulz, Charles L

Resigned-Dismissed: None
* From a list in Dudley, *Going South*, pp34-53

EXCERPT FROM
Adjutant and Inspector General's Office,
UNIFORM AND DRESS OF THE ARMY [AND NAVY]
OF THE CONFEDERATE STATES,
Richmond, Virginia, 1861

[Note: Regulations for civil officers are not included]

Undress [Sea Officers] Coats

For a Flag Officer, shall be a frock coat of steel gray cloth, faced with the same and lined with black silk serge, double breasted, with two rows of large navy buttons on the breast, nine in each row, placed four inches and a half apart from eye to eye at top, and two inches and a half at bottom. Rolling collar, skirts to be full, commencing at the top of the hip bone and descending four-fifths thence towards the knee, with one button behind on each hip and one near the bottom of each fold. The cuffs to be two inches and a half deep, with one strip of gold lace one-half an inch wide below the seam, but joining it; three strips of lace of the same width on the sleeves above the cuffs, separated by a space of three-eights of an inch from each other, the upper one with a loop three inches long, and a strip of lace half an inch wide, from the lower button to the end of the cuffs on the upper side of the opening, and four small sized buttons (navy buttons) in the opening.

For a Captain, the same as for a Flag Officer, except that there shall be but three strips of lace around the sleeve and cuff, including the looped strip.

For a Commander, the same in all respects as for a Captain, except that there shall be but two strips of lace around the sleeve and cuff, including the looped strip, and three small buttons in the opening.

For a Lieutenant, the same in all respects as for a Commander, except that the cuffs shall have but one strip of gold lace, looped, around the upper edge.

For a Master, the same as for a Lieutenant, except that the cuffs shall have but one strip of lace one-fourth of an inch wide, without a loop, around the upper edge.

For a Passed Midshipman, the same as for a Master, except that the cuffs shall have, instead of lace, three medium sized navy buttons around the upper edge.

For a Midshipman, the same as for a Passed Midshipman, except that medium sized buttons shall be substituted for the large buttons (*sic*).

Vests

For all officers, steel gray or white, single breasted, standing collar, with nine small buttons in front, and not to show below the coat.

Pantaloons

For all officers, shall be of steel gray cloth or white drill, made loose to spread well over the foot and to be worn over boots or shoes.

Shoulder Straps

For a Flag Officer, of sky-blue cloth, edged with black, four inches long and one inch and three-eighths wide, bordered with an embroidery of gold one-quarter of an inch in width, with four stars in line at equal distances, the two on the ends six-tenths of an inch in diameter, and the two intermediate six-eighths of an inch in diameter.

For a Captain, the same as for a Flag Officer, except that there shall be three stars at equal distances, each six-tenths of an inch in diameter.

For a Commander, the same as for a Captain, except that there shall be but two stars.

For a Lieutenant, the same as for a Commander, except that there shall be but one star, in the centre.

For a Master, the same as for a Lieutenant, except that there shall be no star.

Caps

Cap of steel gray cloth, to be not less than three inches and a half, nor more than four inches in height, and not more than ten nor less than nine inches and a half at top, with patent leather visor, to be worn by all officers in service dress. *For a Flag Officer*, the device shall be a foul anchor in an open wreath of live oak leaves, with four stars above the anchor, embroidered in gold as per pattern, on the front of the cap above a band of gold lace one inch and three quarters wide. *For a Captain*, the same as for a Flag Officer, except that there shall be but three stars above the anchor, and the gold band shall be one and one half inches wide. *For a Commander*, the same as for Captain, except that there shall be but two stars. *For a Lieutenant*, the same as for a Commander, except that there shall be but one star. *For a Master*, the same as for a Lieutenant, except that there shall be no star. *For a Passed Midshipman*, a foul anchor without the wreath.

Buttons

Buttons shall be of three sizes: large, medium, and small and all of the same device, as per pattern.

Summer Frock Coats

In summer or in tropical climates, officers may wear frock coats and pantaloons of steel gray summer cloth of the style and pattern herein prescribed, with medium size navy buttons.

Jackets

Jackets may be worn as service dress by all officers when at sea, except when at general muster, to be of steel gray cloth or white drill linen with the same, double breasted, rolling collar, same number of small sized buttons on breast as for undress coat, open fly sleeve with four small buttons in the opening, with shoulder straps for appropriate grades.

Straw Hats

In summer or in tropical climates, officers may also wear, except at general muster, white straw hats. The body of the hat to be six inches in height, and the rim three and a half inches in width.

Over Coats

For all officers, shall be of steel gray cloth, double breasted, rolling collar, skirts to descend three inches below the knee, the same number of navy buttons, and similarly arranged as for undress coat. No buttons to be worn on the cuffs or pocket flaps. Officers entitled to shoulder straps will wear the same on their overcoats as directed for undress coats. Gray cloth cloaks may be worn in boats.

SOURCES

Selected Bibliography

Adjutant and Inspector General's Office, *Uniform and Dress of the Army and Navy of the Confederate States of America*, Richmond, VA, 1861

Anderson, Bern, *By Sea and by River: The Naval History of the Civil War*, New York: Knopf, 1962

Barnes, John S, *Submarine Warfare*, New York: Van Nostrand, 1869

Baxter, James P, *The Introduction of the Ironclad Warship*, Hamden, CT: Archon Books, 1968 [originally published: Cambridge, MA: Harvard University Press, 1933]

Bergeron, Arhur Jr., *Confederate Mobile*, Jackson, MS, University of Mississippi Press, 1991

Beringer, Richard E, Herman Hattaway, Archer Jones and William N Still, *Why the South Lost the Civil War*, Athens, GA: University of Georgia Press, 1986

Bradlee, Francis B C, *A Forgotten Chapter in our Naval History: A Sketch of Duncan Nathaniel Ingraham*, Mass: Essex Institute, Salem, 1923

Bright, Leslie, S, et al., *CSS Neuse: A Question of Iron and Time*, Raleigh, NC: North Carolina Division of Archives and History, 1982

Brooke, George M, *John M. Brooke: Naval Scientist and Educator*, Charlottesville, VA: University Press of Virginia, 1980

Browning, Robert M Jr, *From Cape Charles to Cape Fear: The North Atlantic Blockading Squadron During the Civil War*, Tuscaloosa: University of Alabama Press, 1993

Bullard, Thomas R, *Arman's Confederate Rams*, Oak Park, IL: the author, 1989

Bulloch, James Dunwoody, *The Secret Service of the Confederate States in Europe, or How the Confederate Cruisers Were Equipped*, New York: Putnam, 2 vols, 1884 [reprinted New York: Burt Franklin, 1972]

Bulloch, James D, *The Secret Service of the Confederate States in Europe*, 2 vols. New York, G. P. Putman's Sons, 1884

Buker, George E, *Blockaders, Refugees, & Contrabands: Civil War on Florida's Gulf Coast, 1861–1865*. Tuscaloosa: University of Alabama Press, 1993

Burton, E Milby, *Siege of Charleston, 1861–1865*, Columbia, SC: University of South Carolina Press, 1970

Combs, Edwin L, 'On Duty at Wilmington: The Confederate Navy on the Cape Fear River', MA thesis, East Carolina University, Greenville, NC, 1996

Confederate States Navy Department, *Ordnance Instructions for the Confederate States Navy*, 3rd edn, 1864

Confederate States Navy Department, *Register of the Commissioned and Warranted Officers of the Navy of the Confederate States to January l, [1862]*, 1862

Confederate States Navy Department, *Regulations for the Navy of the Confederate States*, 1862

Confederate States of America, *Report of Evidence Taken before a Joint Special Committee of Both Houses of the Confederate Congress to Investigate the Affairs of the Navy Department*, Richmond, VA: GP Evans, 1863

Coski, John M, *Capital Navy: The Men, Ships, and Operations of the James River Squadron*, Campbell, CA: Savas Woodbury, 1996

Current, Richard N, & et al. *Encyclopedia of the Confederacy*, 4 vols. New York: Simon & Schuster. 1993

Daly, Robert W, *How the Merrimac Won: The Strategic Story of the CSS Virginia*, New York: Crowell, 1957

Dalzell, George W. *The Flight from the Flag: The Continuing Effect of the Civil War upon the American Carrying Trade*, Chapel Hill: University of North Carolina Press, 1940

Daniel, Larry J and Riley W Gunter, *Confederate Cannon Foundries*, Union City, TN: Pioneer Press, 1977

Davis, William C, *Duel between the First Ironclads*, Garden City, NY: Doubleday, 1975

Davis, William C, *Rebels and Yankees: the commanders of the Civil War*.

Delaney, Norman C, *John McIntosh Kell of the Raider Alabama*, University, AL: University of Alabama Press, 1973

Dew, Charles B, *Ironmaker to the Confederacy: Joseph R. Anderson and the Tredegar Iron Works*, Wilmington, NC: Broadfoot, 1987 [originally published 1966]

Donnelly, Ralph W, *Biographical Sketches of the Commissioned Officers of the Confederate States Marine Corps*, Alexandria, VA: the author, 1973

Donnelly, Ralph W, *Service Records of Confederate Enlisted Marines*, Washington, NC: the author, 1979

Donnelly, Ralph W, *The History of the Confederate Marine Corps*, Washington, NC: the author, 1976

Dudley, William S, *Going South: US Navy Officer Resignations and Dismissals on the eve of the Civil War*, Washington DC, Naval Historical Foundation, 1981.

Dufour, Charles L. *The Night the War was Lost*, Garden City: Doubleday, 1960

Durkin, Joseph T, *Stephen R. Mallory: Confederate Navy Chief*, Chapel Hill, NC: University of North Carolina Press, 1954; reprinted Columbia, SC: University of South Carolina Press, 1987

Elliott, Robert G, *Ironclad of the Roanoke, Gilbeert Elliott's Albemarle* Shippensburrg, PA: White Mane Publishing Co, 1994

Flanders , Alan B. *The Merrimac: The Story of the Conversion of the USS Merrimac into the Confederate Ironclad Warship CSS Virginia*, Portsmouth, VA: Navy Yard Museum, 1982

Gardiner, Robert (ed), *Steam, Steel and Shellfire: The Steam Warship 1815–1905*, London: Conway Maritime Press, 1992

Harwell, Richard (ed.), *A Confederate Marine*, Tuscaloosas: Confederate Publishing Co, 1963

Hearn, Chester G, *Gray Raiders of the Sea: How Eight Confederate Warships Destroyed the Unions High Seas Commerce*, Camden, ME: International Marine Publishing, 1992

Holcombe, Robert, 'Evolution of Confederate Ironclad Design', MA thesis, East Carolina University, Greenville, NC, 1993

Holcombe, Robert, *Notes on the Classification of Confederate Ironclads*, Savannah, GA: US Army Corps of Engineers, 1980

Hoole, William S, *Four Years in the Confederate Navy: The Career of Captain John Low on the CSS Fingal, Florida, Alabama, Tuscaloosa, and Ajax*, Athens, GA: University of Georgia Press, 1964

Horan, James D (ed), *CSS Shenandoah: The Memoirs of Lieutenant Commanding James I. Waddell*, Crown Publishers, 1960

Horn, Stanly F, *Gallant Rebel: The Famous Cruise of the CSS Shenandoah*, New Brunswick, NJ: 1947

Hunter, Lewis C, *Steamboats on Western Rivers*, Cambridge, MA: Harvard University Press, 1949

Jeter, Katherine B, *A Man and his Boat: The Civil War Career and Correspondence of Lieutenant Jonathon H. Carter*, CSN. Lafayette, La: Center for Louisiana Studies, 1996

Johnson, Robert U and Clarence C Buel (eds), *Battles and Leaders of the Civil War*, New York: Century, 1887–88, 4 vols [subsequent reprints]

Jones, Wilbur D, *The Confederate Rams at Birkenhead: A Chapter in Anglo-American Relations*, Tuscaloosa, AL: Confederate Publishing Co, 1961

Kell, John McIntosh, *Recollections of a Naval Life*, Washington, DC: Neale Publishing Co, 1900

Kennington, John W, 'Gray Jackets in Savannah: The Enlisted Sailor in the Confederate States Navy on the Savannah River, 1861–1864', MA thesis, East Carolina University, Greenville, NC, 1994

Kerkis, Sidney C and Thomas S Dickey, *Heavy Artillery Projectiles of the Civil War, 1861–1865*, Kennesaw, GA: Phoenix Press, 1972

Kloeppel, James E, *Danger beneath the Waves: A History of the Confederate Submarine H.L. Hunley*, Orangeburg, SC: Sandlapper, 1992

Benjamin LaBree, *The Confederate Soldier in the Civil War*, Louisville, KY, 1895

Langley, H D, *Social Reform in the US Navy, 1798-1862*, Urban, ILL: University of Illinois Press, 1967

Lewis, Charles L, *Admiral Franklin Buchanan*, Baltimore, MD: The Norman Remington Co, 1929

Luraghi, Raimondo, *A History of the Confederate Navy* (trans Paolo E Coletta), Annapolis, MD: Naval Institute Press, 1996

Mahan, Alfred T, *Gulf and Inland Waters*, New York: Schribners, 1883.

Marvel, W, *The Alabama and the Kearsarge: The Sailor's Civil War*, Chapel Hill, The University of North Carolina Press, 1996

Melton, Maurice, *The Confederate Ironclads*, New York: Yoseloff, 1968

Melton, Maurice, 'Major Military Manufacturing by the Confederate Government.' PhD dissertation, Emory University, 1978

Merli, Frank J, *Great Britain and the Confederate Navy, 1861–1865*, Bloomington, IN: Indiana University Press, 1970

Merrill, James M, *Battle Flags South: The Story of the Civil War Navies on the Western Waters*, Rutherford, NJ: Fairleigh Dickinson University Press, 1970

Milligan, John D, *Gunboats down the Mississippi*, Annapolis, MD: Naval Institute Press, 1965

Morgan, James M, *Recollections of a Rebel Reefer*, Boston: Houghton Mifflin, 1917

Musicant, Ivan, *Divided Waters: The Naval History of the Civil War*, New York: HarperCollins, 1995

Naval History Division, *Civil War Naval Chronology, 1861–1865*, 6 vols, Washington, DC: Office of the Chief of Naval Operations, 1961–6

ORN, see US Navy Department, *Official Records of the… Navies…*

Owsley, Frank L Jr, *The CSS Florida: Her Building and Operations*, Tuscaloosa: University of Pennsylvania Press, 1987.

Parker, William H, *Recollections of a Naval Officer, 1841–1865*, New York: Scribners, 1883 [reprinted Annapolis, 1985]

Perry, Milton F, *Infernal Machines: The Story of Confederate Submarine and Mine Warfare*, Baton Rouge, LA: Louisiana State University Press, 1965

Poolman, Kenneth, *The Alabama Incident*, London: Kimber, 1958

Porter, David D, *Naval History of the Civil War*, New York: Sherman, 1886

Ragan, Mark K, *The Hunley: Submarines, Sacrifice, and Success in the Civil War*, Charleston, SC: Narwhal Press, 1995

Reed, Rowena. *Combined Operations in the Civil War*, Naval Institute Press, 1978

Robinson, William M, *The Confederate Privateers*, Columbia, SC: University of South Carolina Press, 1990 [originally published 1928]

Scharf, J Thomas, *History of the Confederate States Navy from Its Organization to the Surrender of Its Last Vessel*, New York: Rogers & Sherwood, 1887

Semmes, Raphael R, *Memoirs of Service Afloat during the War between the States*, New York: Kennedy & Sons, 1869

Semmes, Raphael R, *The Cruise of the Alabama and the Sumter*, 2 vols, London: Saunders, Otley & Co, 1864

Shingleton, Royce. G, *John Taylor Wood: Sea Ghost of the Confederacy*, Athens, GA: University of Georgia Press 1979

Shingleton, Royce, *High Seas Confederate: The Life and Times of John Newland Maffitt*, Columbia, SC: University of South Carolina Press, 1994

Sinclair, Arthur, *Two Years on the Alabama*, Boston: Lee & Shepard,1895 [reprinted 1989]

Smith, Myron J, *American Civil War Navies: A Bibliography*, Metuchen, NJ: Scarecrow Press, 1972

Spencer, Warren F, *The Confederate Navy in Europe*, University, AL: University of Alabama Press, 1983

Spencer, Warren F, *Raphael Semmes: The Philosophical Mariner*, Tuscaloosa, University of Alabama Press, 1997

Steamship Historical Society of America, *Merchant Steam Vessels of the United States, 1790–1868*, Staten Island, NY: 1975; supplements: 1978, 1982, 1984

Stern, Philip van Doren, *The Confederate Navy: A Pictorial History*, New York: Doubleday, 1962

Still, William N, Jr, *Confederate Shipbuilding*, Athens, GA: University of Georgia Press, 1969; revised edn, Columbia, SC: University of South Carolina Press, 1987

Still, William N, Jr (ed.), *Odyssey in Gray: A Diary of Confederate Service, 1863–1865*. Richmond, VA: Virginia State Library, 1979

Still, William N, Jr, *Savannah Squadron*, Savannah, 1989

Still, William N, Jr, *Iron Afloat: The Story of the Confederate Armorclad*, Columbia, SC: University of South Carolina Press, 1985 [originally published Nashville: Vanderbilt University Press, 1971]

Summersell, Charles Grayson, *The Cruise of the CSS Sumter* (Confederate Centennial Studies No 27), Tuscaloosa, AL: Confederate Publishing Co, 1965

Taylor, John M, *Confederate Raider: Raphael Semmes of the Alabama*, New York: Brassey's, 1994

Tucker, Spencer, *Arming the Fleet: US Navy Ordnance in the Muzzle-loading Era*, Annapolis, MD: Naval Institute Press, 1989

Turner, Maxine, *Navy Gray: A Story of the Confederate Navy on the Chattahoochee and Apalachicola Rivers*, Tuscaloosa, AL: University of Alabama Press, 1988

US Navy Department, *Dictionary of American Naval Fighting Ships*, Washington, DC: Government Printing Office, 8 vols, 1959–81

US Navy Department, *Official Records of the Union and Confederate Navies in the War of Rebellion*, Washington, DC: Government Printing Office, 1894–1914, 30 vol in 2 series + index vol [cited as *ORN*]

US War Department, *The War of the Rebellion: A Compilation of the Official Records of the Union and Confederate Armies*, Washington, DC: 1880–1901, 79 vols in 129 parts, 4 series + index vol and atlas

Vandiver, Frank E, *Ploughshares into Swords: Josias Gorgas and Confederate Ordnance*, Austin, TX: University of Texas Press, 1952

Wells, Tom H, *The Confederate Navy: A Study in Organization*, University, AL: University of Alabama Press, 1971

Wilkinson, John, *Narrative of a Blockade Runner*, Alexandria, VA: Time-Life, 1984 [originally published 1877]

Williams, Francis L, *Matthew Fontaine Maury, Scientist of the Sea*, New Brunswick, NJ: Rutgers University Press, 1963

Wise, Stephen R, *Lifeline of the Confederacy: Blockade Running during the Civil War*, Columbia, SC: University of South Carolina Press, 1988

Notes

Chapter One Background

This essay is almost fully based on my book: *A History of the Confederate Navy*, Annapolis: Naval Institute Press, 1996. Other sources as indicated below.

1 Even if it is quoted in the notes of my *History of the Confederate Navy*, I recall here another book of mine: *The Rise and Fall of the Plantation South*, New York, New Viewpoints, 1978.

2 Eric Foner, *Free Soil, Free Labor, Free Men: The Ideology of the Republican Party before the Civil War*, Oxford University Press, New York, 1970.

3 It seems that the Union Petty Officer in charge of firing the explosive charge did not dare to do it since the enormous stone blocks would have fallen over civilian houses in Norfolk.

4 Adolphe Lepotier, *Les Leçons de l'Histoire, 1861–1865. Mer contre Terre* (Paris, Mirambeau, 1945), quoted in my *History of the Confederate Navy*.

5 See below.

6 Lepotier, *Mer contre Terre*, p237.

7 Indeed, such interventions were not (or not only) dictated by sheer sympathy with the cause of national independence and freedom: the Napoleonic Wars had just finished; British factories, shipyards and arsenals were full of unsold weaponry and war accouterments; and the streets and taverns of discharged soldiers with no work. The insurrections of Latin American colonies offered a splendid occasion to those people and businessmen: moreover, it was in the British tradition to go fighting for 'freedom'. Spain, linked to Great Britain by a treaty, protested: hence the Foreign Enlistment Act.

8 Quoted by Jones, *Confederate Rams*, pp18–19.

9 Jones, *Confederate Rams*, pp19ff.

10 According to tradition, the name had a double meaning. The literal one, and a homage to the Governor's wife Adelaide Vance (in this instance it was spelled the *Ad-Vance*).

Chapter Two The Confederate States Navy Department

1 Scharf, *History of the Confederate States Navy*, pp27–9; Bulloch, *The Secret Service of the Confederate States in Europe*, Vol 1, p20; Durkin, *Confederate Navy Chief* (1987), p145.

2 Scharf, *History of the Confederate States Navy*, p32; US Bureau of the Census, *Historical Statistics of the United States 1789–1945*, Washington, DC, 1949, p300.

3 Durkin, *Confederate Navy Chief*, pp19, 28, 32, 133; Scharf, *History of the Confederate States Navy*, p29.

4 Entry for Mar 4, 1861, Mary Boykin Chesnut, *A Diary from Dixie*, Ben Ames Williams (ed), Cambridge, MA, 1980, pp10–11.

5 Durkin, *Confederate Navy Chief*, p180; Davis to S S Lee, Apr 2, 1862, US War Department, *The War of the Rebellion*, Ser 1, Vol 11, Pt 3, p414.

6 Entry for Aug 6, 1863, Josiah Gorgas, *The Civil War Diary of General Josiah Gorgas*, Frank E Vandiver (ed), Tuscaloosa, AL, 1947, pp58–9.

7 Entries for Nov 20, 1864, Jan 15, 1865, Gorgas, *Diary*, pp151, 165; Wilkinson, *The Narrative of a Blockade-Runner*, p109.

8 J B Jones, *A Rebel War Clerk's Diary of the Confederate States Capital*, 2 vols, Philadelphia, 1866, entry for May 31, 1861, Vol 1, p46; Mitchell to Mallory, Apr 28, 1864, *ORN*, Ser 2, Vol 2, p639; Confederate States Navy Department, *Register*, 1862, p3 (hereafter cited as CSN *Register 1862*); *Register. to January 1, 1863*, p3, (hereafter cited as CSN *Register 1863*); *Register. to January 1, 1864*, p3, (hereafter cited as CSN *Register 1864*); W W Lester and Wm J Bromsell, *A Digest of the Military and Naval Laws of the Confederate States from the Commencement of the Provisional Congress to the End of the First Congress under the Permanent Constitution*, Columbia, SC, 1864, pp199–200.

9 Wells, *The Confederate Navy*, p5; Durkin, *Confederate Navy Chief*, pp136, 180; CSN *Register 1862*, p3.

10 CSN *Regulations*, p151–*passim.*

11 Ibid, p151; Durkin, *Confederate Navy Chief*, pp136–40; Wells, *The Confederate Navy*, pp4, 13.

12 CSN *Regulations*, p152; CSN *Register 1864*, p3; Wells, *The Confederate Navy*, p14.

13 CSN *Register 1864*, pp63–71.

14 Wells, *The Confederate Navy*, pp13–14, 21; CSN *Register 1862*, p3.

15 General Order, Jul 18, 1863, CSN *Register 1864*, p87; C A Vanfelson, *The Little Red Book of Department Directory*, Richmond, 1861, p10; Mallory to Davis, Nov 30, 1863, *ORN*, Ser 1, Vol 2, p534.

16 S S Lee to Mallory, Oct 31, 1864, *ORN*, Ser 2, Vol 2, pp754–5.

17 Lester and Bromsell, *A Digest of the Military and Naval Laws*, p201; Wells, *The Confederate Navy*, pp44–5.

18 'Report of the Secretary of the Navy', Nov 30, 1863, *ORN*, Ser 2, Vol 2, p534; Mitchell to Mallory, Nov 6, 1863, *ORN*, Ser 2, Vol 2, p544.

19 CSN *Register 1862*, p3; Durkin, *Confederate Navy Chief*, pp140–1; Wells, *The Confederate Navy*, pp46, 49.

20 CSN *Register 1863* pp63–71; Parker, *Recollections of a Naval Officer*, p347.

21 Semmes, *Memoirs of Service Afloat*, pp88, 94.

22 Mallory to Wilkinson, Mar 11, 1864, *ORN*, Ser 1, Vol 8, p804; Wells, *The Confederate Navy*, p66; Wilkinson, *Narrative*, pp197–9.

23 CSN *Regulations*, pp14–15; Durkin, *Confederate Navy Chief*, pp141–2.

24 CSN *Register 1863*, p12; Wells, *The Confederate Navy*, p75.

25 CSN *Regulations*, p8; Wells, *The Confederate Navy*, p75.

26 CSN *Regulations*, pp6, 9.

27 Wells, *The Confederate Navy*, pp76–7.

28 CSN *Register 1862*, p3; Wells, *The Confederate Navy*, p74.

29 De Bree to Mallory, Nov 14, 1863, *ORN*, Ser 2, Vol 2, pp552–7.

30 Wells, *The Confederate Navy*, pp79, 81; De Bree to Mallory, Nov 14, 1863; Apr 28, 1864, *ORN*, Ser 2, Vol 2, pp552–7, 642–5.

31 CSN *Register 1863*, pp10–11; CSN *Register 1864*, pp12–13; Wells, *The Confederate Navy*, pp91–2; Durkin, *Confederate Navy Chief*, pp142–3; Spotswood to Mallory, Apr 28, 1864, *ORN*, Ser 1, Vol 2, p647.

32 Durkin, *Confederate Navy Chief*, p145; CSN *Register 1864*, p34; Wells, *The Confederate Navy*, p118; Lester and Bromsell, *A Digest of the Military and Naval Laws*, p213.

33 CSN *Register 1862*, pp1–2.

34 'Investigation of the Navy Department, Report of the Evidence Taken before a Joint Committee of Both Houses of the Confederate Congress to Investigate the Affairs of the Navy Department', *ORN*, Ser 1, Vol 1, pp431–809; Wells, *The Confederate Navy*, p7.

35 Durkin, *Confederate Navy Chief*, pp204–5; 210–11, 224, 230–*passim*; Mallory to Mitchell, Feb 24, 1862, *ORN*, Ser 2, Vol 1, p466.

36 'Report of the Secretary of the Navy', Apr 26, 1861, *ORN*, Ser 2, Vol 2, p51.

37 Mallory to C M Conrad, May 8, 1861, *ORN*, Ser 2, Vol 1, pp740–3.

38 'Investigation of the Navy Department', *ORN*, Ser 2, Vol 1, p862; Wells, *The Confederate Navy*, p97.

39 Porter to Mallory, Sep 20, 1862, *ORN*, Ser 2, Vol 2, p272; Mallory to Brown, Sep 20, 1862, *ORN*, Ser 2, Vol 2, p271; Lester and Bromsell, *A Digest of the Military and Naval Laws*, pp200, 211; CSN *Register 1864*, p32.

40 John Taylor Wood to Catesby ap R Jones, Feb 26, 1862, *ORN*, Ser 2, Vol 2, p801.

41 Durkin, *Confederate Navy Chief*, pp144–5; CSN *Register 1862*, p5; CSN *Regulations*, pp205–7.

42 Wells, *The Confederate Navy*, pp97, 107–10; CSN *Regulations*, pp208–9; CSN *Register 1864*, pp24–5.

43 Brooke to Mallory, Apr 30, 1864, *ORN*, Ser 2, Vol 2, p641–2; Mallory to Davis, Jul 1, 1864, US War Department, *The War of the Rebellion*, Ser 4, Vol 3, pp520–1; Mallory to Davis, Jul 18, 1861, *ORN*, Ser 2, Vol 2, pp76–9; Williamson to Mallory, *ORN*, Ser 2, Vol 2, pp240–1.

44 Wells, *The Confederate Navy*, pp139–41; CSN *Regulations*, pp190–1.

45 CSN *Register 1864*, pp24–5; CSN *Regulations*, pp190–1.

46 Wells, *The Confederate Navy*, pp139–41; CSN *Regulations*, pp190–1; French Forrest to J K Mitchell, Dec 4, 1863, Mar 31, 1864, French Forrest to Robert G Robb, Jan 7, 18, 1864, James River Squadron Letterbook, Virginia State Library and Archives.

47 Samual Barron to J N Barney, Nov 1, 1863, Intercepted Letters and Papers, Entry 988, Department of State Records, Record Group 59, National Archives, Washington, DC [all subsequent references to Record Groups are RG and to National Archives NA]; Mr G to F H Morse, Despatches from US Consuls in London, 1790–1906, Entry T168, RG 59, NA; Spencer, *The Confederate Navy in Europe*, p210.

48 CSN *Regulations*, pp53, 63–4.

49 Jones, *A Rebel War Clerk's Diary*, entry for May 11, 1864, Vol 2, p205.

50 'Investigation of the Navy Department', *ORN*, Ser 2, Vol 1, pp790–1; 'An Act to Authorize the Purchase or Construction of Certain Vessels of War', May 10, 1861, *ORN*, Ser 1, Vol 2, pp66–7.

51 Mallory to North, May 17, 1861, *ORN*, Ser 2, Vol 2, p70; Bulloch to Mallory, Jan 22, 1862, *ORN*, Ser 2, Vol 2, pp134–5; North to Mallory, Mar 29,1862, *ORN*, Ser 2, Vol 2, pp176–7; JM Stribling to JH North, May 29, 1862, *ORN*, Ser 2, Vol 2, p204.

52 Mallory to Bulloch, Jul 12, 1862, *ORN*, Ser 2, Vol 2, p216; Bulloch, *The Secret Service*, Vol 1, pp110–26.

53 Bulloch to Mallory, May 16, 1863, Aug 29, 1864, *ORN*, Ser 2, Vol 2, pp424, 715; *The Attorney General v Sillem and others, Claiming the vessel 'Alexandra' seized under the Foreign Enlistment Act (59) George II, Chapter 69 Report of the Trial Before the Right Honorable The Lord Chief Baron and A Special Jury* (London 1863), appendix, pIX, p133.

54 Mallory to Maffitt, Oct 25, 1862, *ORN*, Ser 1, Vol 1, pp762–3; Semmes to Mallory, Jun 16, 1862, *ORN*, Ser 1, Vol 1, pp615–16.

55 Mallory to Bulloch, Jul 12, 1862, *ORN*, Ser 2, Vol 2, p216; Durkin, *Confederate Navy Chief*, pp171–2.

56 Bulloch, *The Secret Service*, Vol 2, pp 221–2;

57 Ibid, Vol 2, pp24–5; Mallory to Bulloch, May 6, 1863, *ORN*, Ser 2, Vol 2, p416.

58 Bulloch to Mallory, May 16, 1863, *ORN*, Ser 2, Vol 2, p424; Mallory to Bulloch, Aug 8, 1862, *ORN*, Ser 2, Vol 2, p 235; Bulloch, *The Secret Service*, Vol 2, pp245, 250–3.

59 Mallory to Bulloch, Jul 30, 1864, *ORN*, Ser 2, Vol 2, p695; Freeman H Morse to William Seward, Mar 4, 5, *passim*, 1864, Entry T168, RG 59, NA.

60 Contract between Josiah Gorgas, C E Thorburn and Charles H Reid and Co, Sep 30, 1863, Entry 988, RG 59, NA.

61 Bulloch, *The Secret Service*, Vol 2, p245.

62 Stephen R Mallory, 'Last Days of the Confederate Government', *McClure's Magazine*, Vol 16, Dec 1900, p103.

Chapter Three Types of Ships

1 Baxter, *Ironclad Warship*, pp10-11; Gardiner, *Steam, Steel and Shellfire*, pp14-46.

2 Baxter, *Ironclad Warship*, pp17-32; Tucker, *Arming the Fleet*, pp170-216.

3 Baxter, *Ironclad Warship*, pp69-91; DK Brown, *Before the Ironclad: Development of Ship Design, Propulsion and Arrangement in the Royal Navy, 1815–60*, Annapolis, MD: Naval Institute Press, 1990, pp135-60.

4 Durkin, *Stephen R. Mallory*, pp61-5.

5 *ORN*, Ser 2, Vol 2, p51.

6 Robert Holcombe, 'The Confederate Navy's 1861 Gunsboat Program', paper presented to the North American Society for Oceanic History, Wilmington, NC, Mar 17, 1995.

7 Williams, *Matthew Fontaine Maury*, pp365-98.

8 David M Sullivan, 'Phantom Fleet: The Confederacy's Unclaimed European-built Warships', *Warship International*, Vol 24, No 1, 1987, pp12–32; *Civil War Naval Chronology* (*CWNC*), ppVI-191.

9 Robinson, *Confederate Privateers*.

10 Bulloch *Secret Service*; Merli, *Great Britain*; Spencer, *Confederate Navy*; Hearn, *Gray Raiders*.

11 *ORN*, Ser 2, Vol 2, pp536, 540; National Archives (NA), Entry 422.

12 Brooke, John M and John L Porter, 'The Plan and Construction of the Merrimack', in Johnson and Buel, *Battles and Leaders*, Vol 1, pp215-17; Davis, *Duel*; Catesby op R Jones, 'Services of the *Virginia*', *Southern Historical Society Papers*, Vol 11, Jan 1883, pp65–75; Still, *Iron Afloat*, pp5–40

13 Holcombe, *Notes*; Holcombe, 'Evolution of Confederate Ironclad Design'; Still, *Iron Afloat*, pp93-105; *CWNC*, ppVI-185-6.

14 Bulloch, *Secret Service*; Merli, *Great Britain*; Spencer, *Confederate Navy*; *ORN*, Ser 2, Vol 2, p518.

15 Jones, *Confederate Rams*. *El Tousson* was to be named CSS *North Carolina* and *El Monassir*, CSS *Mississippi*.

16 Bullard, *Arman's Rams*, pp32-8.

17 Spencer, *Confederate Navy*, p89; *ORN*, Ser 2, Vol 2 pp220-1, 226-7; Brooke, *Brooke*, p267.

18 Wise, *Lifeline*, pp107-11, 145; *CWNC*, ppVI-189.

19 *ORN*, 12, p840; *ibid.*, Ser II, Vol 3, pp276-8, 283; Wise, *Lifleline*, pp62, 323-4; National Archive, 'Vessel Papers,' *Theodora* File T-4.

20 Shingleton, *High Seas Confederate*, pp97-8.

21 Parker, *Recollections*, pp312-15; Perry, *Infernal Machines*, pp63-80; *CWNC*, ppVI-316.

22 Burton, *Siege of Charleston*, pp216, 219-22; 'David C. Ebaugh' pp32-36; Combs, 'On Duty at Wilmington', p85; NA, Carter Correspondence Book.

23 *ORN*, 9, p601; Ser 11, Vol ?, pp706–7; Crowley, 'Confederate Torpedo Service,' pp97-8; NA, Area 5 File; NA, Carter Correspondence Book.

24 *CWNC*, ppVI-187; Turner, *Navy Gray*, pp196, 229, 233.

25 *ORN*, Ser 2, Vol 2, pp688, 770, 790-1; Combs, 'On Duty at Wilmington,' pp129-30.

26 Dew, *Ironmaker*, p123; Perry, *Infernal Machines*, pp183-4; Sidney H Schell, 'Submersible Weapons Tested at Mobile during 'the Civil War', *Alabama Review*, Vol 44, Jul 1992, pp178-81.

27 Kloeppel, *Danger*, pp6-19, 21-3. Ragan, *The Hunley*, pp180-3. Efforts to produce an electrical propulsion system for *American Diver* failed and her builders had to revert to manpower.

28 *ORN*, Ser 2, Vol 2, p51, 53; Kerkis and Dickey, *Heavy Artillery Projectiles*, p233.

29 Still, *Iron Afloat*, pp101-4; Wells, *Confederate Navy*, pp107-17; Turner, *Navy Gray*.

248 ■ The Confederate Navy

Chapter Four Facilities

1 James D B DeBow, *The Industrial Resources, Etc., of the Southern and Western States: Embracing a View of Their Commerce, Agriculture, Manufactures, Internal Improvements, Slave and Free Labor, Slavery Institutions, Products, Etc., of the South*, New Orleans: *DeBow's Review*, 1852, Vol 2, pp27, 101, 131; Chauncey S Boucher, 'The Ante-Bellum Attitude of South Carolina Towards Manufacturing and Agriculture', *Washington University Studies*, Vol 3, Pt 2, No 2, pp247-8, 254-6; Philip G Davidson, 'Industrialism in the Ante-Bellum South', *South Atlantic Quarterly*, Vol 27, No 4, Oct, 1928, pp410-11; Greenville (S.C.) *Southern Enterprise*, Mar 1, 1860; *DeBow's Review*, Vol 21, No 1 Jan, 1852, pp42-4.

2 Melton 'Major Military Manufacturing by the Confederate Government' pp23-6; Dew, *Ironmaker to the Confederacy:* pp60, 75, 89, 90; Robert S Davis, paints an exciting picture of ante-bellum coal, copper and iron industries in Georgia, noting cities and towns all over the state boasting iron foundries, machine shops or both. Mary A DeCredico also notes the development of industry and commerce in Georgia during the ante-bellum era. But these localised studies do not address the weak and primitive nature of Southern industry; nor do they address its ability to sustain an industrial war against the United States. Davis, 'The First Golden Age of Georgia Industry, 1828–1860' in *Georgia Historical Quarterly*, Vol 72, No 4, Winter 1988, pp699-711. DeCredico, *Patriotism for Profit: Georgia's Urban Entrepreneurs and the Confederate War Effort*, Chapel Hill: University of North Carolina Press, 1988, pp1-20.

3 Of 1,412 iron foundries in the US in 1860, the South had only 96. See William N Still, 'Facilities for the Construction of War Vessels in the Confederacy', *Journal of Southern History*, Vol 31 No 3, Aug 1965, p287; Victor S Clark, *History of Manufactures in the United States*, New York: McGraw-Hill, for the Carnegie Institution of Washington, 1929, Vol I, pp498-501. Lester J Cappon, 'The Trend of the Southern Iron Industry under the Plantation System', *Journal of Economic and Business History*, Vol 2, 1930, p379. Luraghi, *History of the Confederate Navy*, pp38-9.

4 S U Ramsdell, 'The Gosport Calamity: Evacuation of the Navy Yard at Norfolk, Virginia, 21 April, 1861', MA thesis, Old Dominion University, 1986, pp1-16, 44-53; Flanders, *The Merrimac:* pp6-21; William S Dudley, *Going South: U.S. Navy Officer Resignations and Dismissals on the Eve of the Civil War*, Washington, DC: Naval Historical Foundation, 1981, pp5-6; Delaney, *John McIntosh Kell*, pp107-8.

5 John Appleyard Agency, Inc, *Pensacola's Navy Yard*, 1825-1911, privately published, nd, pp13-25. Durkin, *Stephen R. Mallory*, pp150, 186; US Navy Department, *Register of Officers of the Confederate States Navy*, Washington, DC: US Government Printing Office, 1921, 2nd edn, p160; Stephen R Mallory to President Jefferson Davis, Feb 27, 1862, *ORN*, Ser 2, Vol 2, p154.

6 Scharf, *History of the Confederate States Navy*, p133. Estimates of the guns and ordnance stores captured at Gosport vary; see William H Parker, 'Confederate States Navy' in Clement A Evans (ed), *Confederate Military History*, Atlanta: Confederate Publishing Company, 1899, Vol 12, p30; John Taylor Wood, 'First Fight of the Iron-Clads' in Johnson and Buel, *Battles and Leaders*, Vol 1, p712; Ramsdell, 'The Gosport Calamity', p2; and Scharf, *History of the Confederate States Navy*, p132; Davis, *Duel between the First Ironclads*, p6-8; Flanders, *The Merrimac*, pp22, 34-6; Mallory to Davis, Jul 18, 1861 in *ORN*, Ser 2, Vol 2, p77.

7 Gate City's proprietors, Lewis Scofield and William Markham, were natives of Connecticut. They founded the Gate City Iron Works, popularly known as the Atlanta Rolling Mill, in 1857. Mallory to Ingraham, May 20, 1861; Ingraham to Mallory, May 23, 28, 1861 in *ORN*, Ser 2, Vol 2, pp72-3; Franklin Garrett, *Atlanta and its Environs: A Chronicle of its People and Events*, Athens: University of Georgia Press, 1954, Vol I, p629; Davis, 'The First Golden Age', p703. Davis, *Duel between the First Ironclads*, pp30-3. Brooke, *John M. Brooke*; p240; Dew, *Ironmaker*, pp106, 115-8.

8 Dew, *Ironmaker*, p119; Davis, *Duel between the First Ironclads*, p32. Brooke, *John M. Brooke*, p247.

9 Flanders, *The Merrimac*, p42. Mallory told the President that the labouratory would soon be casting both iron and brass cannon. But there is no evidence that this was accomplished at Gosport. There were in the antebellum South a number of foundries building steam engines for sawmills, shops and small river steamers. The Tredegar plant built engines for two Norfolk warships before the war, but their propeller shafts came from Baltimore; Still, 'Facilities for the Construction', p288; Mallory to Davis, Jul 18, 1861, in *ORN*, Ser 2, Vol 2, p77; Kathleen Bruce, *Virginia Iron Manufacture in the Slave Era*, New York: Century Co, 1931, p349.

10 Mallory to Lee, Mar 24, 26; May 1, 3, 4, 1862; Commander John R Tucker to Mallory, May 8, 1862 in *ORN*, Ser I, Vol 7, pp749–86. For construction at Rocketts and the operation of the James River Squadron, see Coski, *Capital Navy*; pp13-14, 66; and Henry P Beers, *Guide to the Archives of the Government of the Confederate States of America*, Washington DC: US Government Printing Office, 1968, p383; Parker, *Recollections of a Naval Officer*, pp278-9.

11 Ralph W Donnelly, 'The Charlotte, North Carolina, Navy Yard, C.S.N.', *Civil War History*, Vol 5, Mar 1959, pp73–5.

12 Donnelly, 'Charlotte Navy Yard', pp74-8; Mallory to Barron, Oct 2; Capt French Forrest, Chief, Bureau of Orders and Detail to Barron, Oct 6; Barron to Mallory, Oct 30, 1862 in *ORN*, Ser I, Vol 23, pp703-5; Minor to Mallory, Aug 15, 1862 in *ORN*, Ser 2, Vol 2, p250; Minor was succeeded as head of the Bureau of Ordnance and Hydrography by Commander J M Brooke; *Register of Officers*, p22; Brooke to Mallory, Nov 25, 1863 in *ORN*, Ser 2, Vol 2, pp547-8.

13 Mallory to Page, Apr 3, 1863; General Orders No 24, Headquarters, Military District of Georgia, Captain and Acting Adjutant-General George A Mercer, Apr 4, 1863 in *ORN*, Ser I, Vol 13, pp822-3; Mallory to Jones, Mar 15, 1863 in *ORN*, Ser I, Vol 8, p861. For Jones's Confederate service, see *Register of Officers*, p102. for his work with Dahlgren, see Robert J Schneller, *A Quest for Glory: A Biography of Rear Admiral John A Dahlgren*, Annapolis: Naval Institute Press, 1996, pp148–55, 169; Jones's orders to Selma, dated May 9, 1863 are in *ORN*, Ser I, Vol 9, p795. Page relinquished command at Savannah on May 13, 1863. Page to William A Webb in *ORN*, Ser I, Vol 14, p697; Page to Brooke, Dec 8, 1863 in *ORN*, Ser 2, Vol 2, p566; Lt Robert D Minor to Commander Catesby Jones, Mar 23, 1864 in *ORN*,

Ser I, Vol 9, p806. For Ramsay's Confederate service, see *Register of Officers*, p159; Brooke to Mallory, Nov 4, 1864; Mallory to Bulloch, Dec 17, 1864 in *ORN*, Ser 2, Vol 2, pp756, 782; Parker, *Recollections*, pp355-6.

14 A statement listing dates, contractors, amounts and kinds of iron and iron goods contracted for, dated Aug 12, 1862 is in *ORN*, Ser 2, Vol 2, pp248-9. See also Mallory to Davis, Feb 27, 1862; Williamson to Mallory, Aug 15, 1862; Mallory to Davis, Aug 16, 1862; Brooke to Mallory, Nov 25, 1863 in *ORN*, Ser 2, pp150, 151, 240–7.

15 Maxine Turner, 'Naval Operations on the Apalachicola and Chattahoochee Rivers, 1861-1865', MA thesis, Auburn University, 1961, p80.

16 John L Porter to Mallory, Nov 1, 1864 in *ORN*, Ser 2, Vol 2, pp751-3; Turner, 'Naval Operations,' pp99-100; map, 'Confederate Columbus, 1861-1865' in Confederate Naval Museum, Columbus, GA. Brigadier General EF Winslow to Major General James H Wilson, Apr 18, 1865 in US War Department *The War of the Rebellion*, Ser I, Vol 49, Pt 1, pp485-7; Richard B Harwell (ed), *A Confederate Marine*: *A Sketch of Henry Lea Graves with Excerpts from the Graves Family Correspondence, 1861-1865*, Tuscaloosa: Confederate Publishing Co, 1963, p104; Turner, *Navy Gray*, p165; An incident similar to the *Savannah's* engine seizure happened aboard the monitor USS *Weehawken* during her initial trip south. Of monitors like the *Weehawken*, Admiral Samuel F DuPont complained: 'something always breaks', Robert Erwin Johnson, *Rear Admiral John Rodgers, 1812-1882*, Annapolis: US Naval Institute, 1967, pp233-4, 238; James H Warner to J H Alexander, Jul 17, 1865 in National Archives, Record Group 56, Area File 825; Turner, *Navy Gray*, pp153-168, 233-6; James Pickett Jones, *Yankee Blitzkrieg*: *Wilson's Raid through Alabama and Georgia*, Athens: University of Georgia Press, 1976, p144. For British supply of marine engines, see, for example, Robert D Minor to Catesby Jones, Mar 23, 1864 in *ORN*, Ser I, Vol 9, p806; Warner to Alexander, Jun 17, 1865 in National Archives, RG 56, AF 825.

17 See payroll vouchers for Albany Grain Mill, Bakery, Packing Depot and Cooperage in National Archives, RG 45, Entry 422; Paymaster John DeBree, Chief, Bureau of Provisions and Clothing, to Mallory, Nov 14, 1863, Apr 28, 1864; Major William B Cross to DeBree, Apr 14; DeBree to Brigadier General A. R Lawton, Apr 16; DeBree to Mallory, Apr 28, 1864, in *ORN*, Ser 2, Vol 2, pp553, 643, 645-6; Florence F Corley, *Confederate City: Augusta, Georgia, 1860-1865*, Columbia: University of South Carolina Press, 1960, p174; Howell to DeBree, Aug 25, Oct 31, 1863; DeBree to Mallory, Nov 14, 1863; Apr 28, 1864 in *ORN* Ser 2, Vol 2, pp553-8, 643-4; Corley, *Confederate City*, p50; William M Robertson, 'Augusta's Advantages as Arsenal Site Recognized by Confederate Leaders,' Augusta *Chronicle*, Dec 27, 1925; Ruby M Pfadenhauer, 'History of Augusta Arsenal,' *Richmond County History*, Vol 2, No 2, Summer, 1970, p15.

18 Captain S S Lee to Mallory, Oct 31, 1864 in *ORN*, Ser 2, Vol 2, p754.

19 Minor to Mallory, Aug 15, 1862; Brooke to Mallory, Nov 25, 1863 in *ORN*, Ser 2, Vol 2, pp250, 547; Jackson to Major D Graffenried, May 23, 1864 in Adjutant General's Office Records, 1861-65, Georgia Department of Archives and History, Atlanta, GA; Melton, 'Major Military Manufacturing,' p158n; *Register of Officers*, p98; Still, *Confederate Shipbuilding* (1969), p43; Melton, *Confederate Ironclads* pp77-8; N

and A F Tift to Mallory, Oct 14, 1861 in *ORN*, Ser 2, Vol 1, p577. Kennon resigned, joined the Louisiana State Navy, and fought bravely against Farragut's fleet as commander of the gunboat *Governor Moore*. On Aug 20, 1862 he accepted a new commission as lieutenant in the Confederate Navy, *Register of Officers*, p107; Beverley Kennon, 'Fighting Farragut below New Orleans' in Johnson and Buel (eds), *Battles and Leaders*, Vol 2, pp76-89.

20 Still, *Confederate Shipbuilding*, p43. *Register of Officers*, p121; C G Hearn, *The Capture of New Orleans, 1862*, Baton Rouge: Louisiana State University Press, 1995, p241; Fairfax's summary of McCorkle's work is included in George Minor's report to Mallory, Aug 15, 1862 in *ORN*, Ser 2, Vol 2, p250; Brooke to Mallory, Nov 25, 1863; Nov 4, 1864 in *ORN*, Ser 2, Vol 2, pp548, 756; McCorkle to Wayne in Adjutant General's Office Records, 1861-65, Georgia Department of Archives and History.

21 Minor to Mallory, Aug 15, 1862; Brooke to Mallory, Nov 25, 1863 in *ORN*, Ser 2, Vol 2, pp250, 548; Brooke to Mallory, Nov 25, 1863; Nov 4, 1864 in *ORN*, Ser 2, Vol 2, pp548, 550, 757; *Register of Officers*, pp47, 135; Daniel and Gunter, *Confederate Cannon Foundries*, p14; McCorkle to Jones, Jan 25, Mar 8, Apr 14, May 10, Jun 8, Jun 23, 1864 in RG 45, AF 6, National Archives.

22 Brooke to Mallory, Nov 4, 1864 in *ORN*, Ser 2, Vol 2, pp755-6. In June 1863 the Ordnance Bureau sought to establish geographic areas of responsibility for each ordnance works. Richmond was to supply Richmond and Wilmington; Charlotte was to supply Charlotte, Charleston and Savannah; and Atlanta would supply Mobile and the Gulf stations. However, circumstances on occasion required one works to assume the work load of one or several others. Still, *Confederate Shipbuilding*, p43.

23 Brooke to Mallory, Nov 4, 1864 in *ORN*, Ser 2, Vol 2, pp755-6. The difference made by time, and dwindling resources and supplies, is best illustrated by the Army's National Gunpowder Works at Augusta and its Central Ordnance Laboratory at Macon. The Augusta works, begun soon after secession, drew on ample resources of brick, lumber, firebrick, hydraulic cement, heavy machinery and metal castings from sources in Chattanooga, Atlanta, and Columbia, SC, as well as adequate supplies of labour. The factory, built from the foundations up, covered over two miles, in buildings great and small, with sophisticated mills and gothic structures that might have graced the greatest industrial cities. The Central Ordnance laboratory, begun in 1863, had difficulty finding the most basic of construction materials; carpenters and masons were no longer available, and the facility was makeshift, incomplete and functioned on a marginal basis. See Melton, 'Major Military Manufacturing', Chs II and IV.

24 Garrett, *Atlanta and its Environs*, Vol I, p634; Mallory to Davis, Apr 30, 1864 in *ORN*, Ser 2, Vol 2, p638. The date of this report is spurious, as it comments on events throughout the summer of 1864.

25 Mallory to Davis, Sep 24, 1862 in *ORN*, Ser 2, Vol 2, p274; Kenny A Franks, 'McRae, Colin J' in R N Current (ed), *Encyclopedia of the Confederacy*, New York: Simon & Schuster, 1993, Vol 3, p979; McRae to Gorgas, Jul 3; to Mallory, Aug 1, 1862 in *ORN* Ser 2, Vol 2, pp210, 232; William N Still, 'The Construction and

Fitting Out of Ironclad Vessels-of-War within the Confederacy' PhD thesis, University of Alabama, 1964, p70. See numerous entries by McRae and Chambliss in Catesby ap R Jones Letterbook II, Record Group 45, Area File 6, National Archives. For example: letters of McRae to Col J L White, Jan 30, Feb 3, 1863; Chambliss to Major William R Hunt, Mar 2, 14, 1863; Chambliss to Col George W Rains, Mar 21, Apr 6, 1863; Chambliss to J R Anderson & Co (Tredegar Iron Works), Mar 17, 1863; Brooke to Mallory, Nov 25, 1863 in *ORN*, Ser 2, Vol 2, pp548, 550; Jones to Brooke, Jun 15, 24, 28, 29, Jul 14, 1863; to G W Dresen, Jun 20; to Julian Fairfax, Jun 22; to Col J L White, Jun 22; to James Smith, Jun 30; to H W Herbert, Jul 4; to John Adams, Jul 6; to Heath, Jul 9; to Major W R Hunt, Jul 17, 1863 in Letterbook III.

26 Jones to Buchanan, Aug 6, 1863 in Letterbook II; Lt RD Minor to Jones, Mar 23, 1864 in *ORN*, Ser I, Vol 9, p806.

27 Jones to Brooke, Jun 18, 25, 27; Jul 6, 22, 27; Aug 6, 15, 17; Sep 8, 26; Oct 15; Dec 21; to White, Jun 20; Aug 17; Sep 16; to Major General Gideon J Pillow, Aug 27; to Admiral Franklin Buchanan, Sep 10; to Colonel WE Burnett, Sep 11; to McCorkle, Sep 2; to Mallory, Sep 3; to Brooke, Oct 19, 1863, in Letterbook III; Col George W Rains to Jones, Jul 26, 1863 in RG 45, AF 6, National Archives; Jones to illegible, Aug 10; Dr WAW Spottswood, Aug 15; to Dr A Hurt, Aug 19; to RA Talley, Sep 3, 1863 in Letterbook II; Jones to Brooke, Jan 6; to Mallory, Feb 9, 1864 in Jones Letterbook III. Jones's agreement with Ware, dated Feb 6, 1864, is in Letterbook IV.

28 Jones to Buchanan, Jan 8, 1864 in Letterbook III; to Brooke, Jan 11, 1864 in Letterbook IV; for details on Jones's travails in gun casting, see Melton, 'Major Military Manufactures', pp154-74; and Walter W Stephen, 'The Brooke Guns from Selma', *Alabama Historical Quarterly*, Vol 20, 1958, pp462-75.

29 Jones to Brooke, Dec 26, 1863; Jan 6, 13, 20, 1864, in Letterbook III; Brooke to Jones, Mar 3, 1864 in RG 45, AF 6, National Archives; Jones to Brooke, Nov 15, Dec 20, 22, 1864; to Col Eustace Surget, Jan 16, 1865, in Letterbook V. For an account of the battle of Selma, see Jones, *Yankee Blitzkrieg*, pp84-90.

Chapter Five Shipbuilding

1 Thomas P Kettell in *Southern Wealth and Northern Profits*, edited by Fletcher M Green, Tuscaloosa: University of Alabama Press, 1965. For declining shipbuilding in the South during the decade of the 1850s see US Census Office, Eighth Census, *Manufactures of the United States in 1860*, Washington, 1865, pp716-18 and Victor S Clark, *History of Manufactures in the United States* New York: McGraw-Hill, for the Carnegie Institution of Washington, 1929, Vol 1, p470.

A US Navy yard was opened at Memphis, TN in the 1840s, but went out of operation in the next decade. Walter Chandler, 'The Memphis Navy Yard', *West Tennessee Historical Society Papers*, Vol 1, pp70-1.

William N Still, 'Facilities for the Construction of War Vessels in the Confederacy', *Journal of Southern History*, Vol 31, No 3 Aug 1965, pp285-6. William H Russell, *Pictures of Southern Life, Social, Political, and Military*, New York: Gregory, 1861, p9.

2 Williams, *Matthew Fontaine Maury* p381; Memorandum of agreement between Nelson and Asa F Tift, and the Secretary of the Navy, Aug 26; 1861 and AF Tift to Mallory, Sep 11, 12, 1861 in *ORN*, Ser 2, Vol 1, pp571-2.

3 Typescript of a biographical sketch of Willink extracted from *The Times*, [Savannah?], May 31, 1879; Contract between S R Mallory and H F Willink, Jr., Nov 2, 1861 in Henry Willink Papers, Special Collections Department, Robert W Woodruff Library, Emory University. Robert Holcombe, 'The C.S.S. *Macon*: Forgotten Confederate Gunboat', *Middle Georgia Magazine*, Vol 4, No 1, 1994, p30.

4 McRae to Mallory, Aug 1, 1862 in *ORN*, Ser 2, Vol 2, p231.

5 A copy of Johnston's contract, dated Oct 19, 1861, is in the Confederate Naval Museum, Columbus, GA; Turner, *Navy Gray*; p66.

6 Mallory to Messrs Willink and Miller, Jan 14, 1862; Willink to Commander Thomas W Brent, Jul 24, 1862, in Willink Papers.

7 Turner, *Navy Gray*, pp56–75; Still, *Confederate Shipbuilding*, p14; Karen G Wood, 'A Cultural Resource Survey of the Columbus, Georgia Riverfront from the City Wharf to Oglethorpe Bridge,' Atlanta, GA: Southeastern Archeological Services, 1993, p17.

8 Davis, *Duel Between the First Ironclads*, p27; James M Merrill, 'Confederate Shipbuilding at New Orleans', *Journal of Southern History*, Vol 27, 1962, p89. Charles L DuFour, *The Night the War Was Lost*, New York: Doubleday, 1960, p103; Chester G Hearn, *The Capture of New Orleans, 1862*, Baton Rouge: Louisiana State University Press, 1995, pp77–8, Still, *Iron Afloat* (1971), pp45, 98; Melton, *Confederate Ironclads*, p78; N and A F Tift to Mallory, Aug 26, 1862; Mallory to President Davis, Feb 27, 1862 in *ORN*, Ser 2, Vol 2, p152; Senate testimony in *ORN*, Ser 2, Vol 2, pp533–4, 755-6, 803.

9 Senate testimony in *ORN*, Ser 2, Vol 1, p799; Merrill, 'Confederate Shipbuilding,' pp88–9; Hearn, *New Orleans*, pp142-43.

10 Hearn, *New Orleans*, pp146–7, 188 N and A F Tift to Mallory, Nov 21, 1861 in *ORN*, Ser 2, Vol 1, p580; Senate testimony, *ORN*, Ser 2, Vol 1, pp534–7, 597, 604-5, 763, 774-5.

11 Scharf, *History of the Confederate States Navy*, pp145-50; Flanders, *The Merrimac*, pp43, 53; Davis, *Duel*, pp34-5.

12 Flanders, *The Merrimac*, pp32–3, 37 Parker, *Recollections of a Naval Officer*, p278.

13 Mallory to Forrest, Mar 19, 1862; to S.S. Lee, May 1, 1862 in *ORN*, Ser I, Vol 7, pp747, 779; Parker, *Recollections*, p278.

14 For information on building the *Albemarle*, see Elliott, *Ironclad of the Roanoke*, 1994. For others, see Scharf, *History of the Confederate States Navy*, pp303-7, 402-5, 670-2; Still, *Confederate Shipbuilding*, pp11-20, 30-38, 59.

15 Still, *Iron Afloat*, pp62–3; Senate testimony, *ORN*, Ser 2, Vol 1, pp779-81, 783, 801.

16 Senate testimony, *ORN*, Ser 2, Vol 1, pp782, 798; William N Still, 'Confederate Shipbuilding in Mississippi,' *Journal of Mississippi History*, Vol 30, 1968, p292; Still, *Iron Afloat*, p63. *ORN*, Ser I, Vol 18, p640.

17 Since January Brown had been converting steamboats and building ironclads to defend the Cumberland and Tennessee Rivers. The loss of Forts Henry and

Donelson put him out of business. See Senate testimony, *ORN*, Ser 2, Vol 1, pp800-1.

18 McBlair, at least, had located a diving bell and was recovering the sunken armour. Edwin C Bearss, *Rebel Victory at Vicksburg*, Vicksburg: Vicksburg Centennial Commemoration Commission, 1963, pp102–3.

19 Still, *Iron Afloat*, pp63–5.

20 Still, 'Confederate Shipbuilding in Mississippi', p297; William N Still, 'Selma and the Confederate States Navy,' *Alabama Review*, Vol 14 Jan, 1962, pp30–3; J McRae to Mallory, Jul 13, 1862 in *ORN*, Ser 2, Vol 2, p. 638.

21 Mallory to Davis, Apr 30, 1864 in *ORN*, Ser 2, Vol 2, p638.

22 William N. Still, 'The Confederate Ironclad *Missouri*', *Louisiana Studies*, Vol 4, Summer, 1965, pp101–6; Lt Jonathan H Carter to Mallory, Feb 1, 1863 in Letters Sent, Lt Jonathan H Carter, CSN, RG 45, National Archives.

23 John L Porter to Willink, Aug 11, 1862; Mallory to Willink, Aug 11, 1862 in Willink Papers.

24 Turner, *Navy Gray*, p145; Still, 'Selma and the Confederate States Navy', p33.

25 Still, 'Confederate Shipbuilding in Mississippi', pp299-303; Still, 'The Confederate Ironclad *Missouri*,' pp102-4. Carter to Mallory, Feb 1, Apr 14 1863 in Carter Letters Sent, RG 45, National Archives.

26 Still, 'The Confederate Ironclad *Missouri*', p105; Carter to Mallory, Feb 1, Oct 24, 1863 in Carter Letters Sent, RG 45, National Archives.

27 Pay roll for Mobile Station in *ORN*, Ser 2, Vol 1, p319; pay voucher for 'Construction of Four Steam Cruisers of the Class of the Alabama and Florida in C. States' in National Archives, Record Group 365, Miscellaneous Navy Rolls, Entry 67; see also vouchers dated Jun 30, 1864 in Subject File PI, National Archives; Still, *Iron Afloat*, p190; Luraghi, *History of the Confederate Navy*, p289.

28 Wood, 'A Cultural Resource Survey', p24; Joseph B Mahan, *Columbus: Georgia's Fall Line 'Trading Town'*, Northridge CA.: Windsor Publications, 1986, p59; Gordon P. Watts, William N Still, James Lee Cox and Wesley Hall, 'A Reconnaissance Survey of the Chattahoochee River at Columbus, Georgia', unpublished report prepared for the James W Woodruff, Jr Confederate Naval Museum, Columbus, GA, pp13, 20, 33. McLaughlin to Mallory, Jan 24 and Jan 26, 1864; to Brooke, Jan 25, 1864; undated 'Copy of Letter handed Secty – while in Richd.'; McLaughlin to Cmdr John K Mitchell, to Secretary Mallory, Feb 26, 1864 in McLaughlin Letterbook; Confederate Naval Museum, Yard log, entries of Feb 25, 26, 1864 in McLaughlin Letterbook, Mar 13, Jul 15, 16 1864 in Yard log, McLaughlin Letterbook.

29 For information on torpedo craft, see Perry, *Infernal Machines*; Kloeppel, *Danger beneath the Waves*; Sidney H Schell, 'Submarine Weapons Tested at Mobile During the Civil War', *Alabama Review*, Summer, 1994. The editors, 'David C. Ebaugh on the Building of "The David" in *South Carolina Historical Magazine*, Vol 54, Vol 1, Jan, 1953, p33; Perry, *Infernal Machines*, pp81, 122-4, 128-9, 183-4. Halligan's *St. Patrick* was an anomaly, designed with 'a number of ingenious contrivances' which would allow it to be propelled by a small steam engine on the surface, or submerged and cranked by hand. Commander Catesby ap R Jones to Major General Dabney H. Maury, June 16, 1864 in *ORN*, Ser I, Vol 21, pp902-3; Schell, 'Submarine Weapons', p32;

McLaughlin to Graves, Apr 7; to Mallory, Apr 23, May 23; to Hunt, May 17, 30, Jun 10, 20, 1864; to Mallory, May 23, 27, 25, Jun 25, 1864 in McLaughlin Letterbook.

30 McLaughlin to Captain William Davis, CSA, Jun 10, 13, 18, 22; to Mallory, Jun 25, 1864 in McLaughlin Letterbook; Yard log, May 11, 1864 in McLaughlin Letterbook.

31 McLaughlin to Mallory, Jun 25, 1864 in McLaughlin Letterbook. Yard log entries of Mar 23, 24, 25, 31, Nov 19, Dec 22, 1864, McLaughlin Letterbook; Turner, *Navy Gray*, pp216, 223; Apr 16 1865 entry in Yard log, McLaughlin Letterbook, gives a succinct account of navy yard activities during its final day.

32 Luraghi questions whether unseasoned wood was the primary cause of excessive leakage on Confederate vessels. It is probably true that a combination of factors, ranging from scarcity of materials such as copper sheathing and oakum, to substandard workmanship, were responsible. The question, as suggests, needs more study. Luraghi, *Confederate Navy*, p369, n167.

Chapter Six   The Officers

1 Kell, *Recollections of a Naval Life*, pp139-40.

2 Toucey to Semmes, February 15, 1861, quoted in Raphael Semmes, *Service Afloat*, New York, nd, p77.

3 Harold M Hyman, *Era of the Oath: Northern Loyalty Tests During the Civil War and Reconstruction*, Philadelphia, 1954, ppi-iii.

4 Shingleton, *John Taylor Wood*, pp15-19.

5 William N Still 'The Common Sailor, Part II: Confederate Tars,' *Civil War Times Illustrated*, Vol 24, No. 1, March, 1985, p13.

6 Dudley, *Going South*, p8.

7 Bradlee, *A Forgotten Chapter*, pp15-16.

8 Scharf, *Confederates States Navy*, p32.

9 Private Journal of John Newland Maffitt, John Newland Maffitt Papers, Southern Historical Collection, University of North Carolina, Chapel Hill.

10 Durkin, *Stephen R Mallory*, pp146-9.

11 Still, 'The Common Sailor', p13.

12 Scharf, *Confederate States Navy*, p33.

13 Wood to Catesby Jones, August 30, 1862, *ORN*, Ser 2, Vol 2, p256.

14 Shingleton, *John Taylor Wood*, p61.

15 Bradlee, *Forgotten Chapter in Our Naval History*, p17.

16 Coski, *Capital Navy*, pp128-35.

17 Scharf, *Confederate States Navy*, pp773-4. Scharf was himself one of the Confederate midshipmen.

18 Morgan, *Recollections of a Rebel Reefer*, pp206–8.

19 The studies of the midshipmen were sometimes interrupted by combat assignments. Palmer Saunders, stepping into his boarding cutter on the night of the USS *Underwriter* capture near New Bern, NC, glanced up at the sky and remarked: 'I wonder, boys, how many of us will be up in those stars by tomorrow morning!' On the

enemy's deck 'some giant of the forecastle' cut open his head. Saunders became the notable martyr of the midshipmen. Shingleton, *John Taylor Wood*, p100.

20 Wells, *The Confederate Navy*, pp67-73.

21 Shingleton, *High Seas Confederate*, pp24-5.

22 Wells, *Confederate Navy*, p138–9.

23 Durkin, *Stephen R. Mallory*, pp147–8. A list of officers in the provisional navy as of June 1, 1864 can be found in J T Scharf, *Confederate States Navy*, pp819-20. However, the list should be used in conjunction with *Register of Officers of the Confederate States Navy, 1861-1865*, Mattituck, NY, 1983.

24 Wells, *Confederate Navy*, p7, 11-12.

25 Ibid., pp 139-42.

26 Shingleton, *High Seas Confederate*, pp35-7. Maffitt proposed, before the blockade became effective, running into the South large quantities of arms, clothing, provisions, and powerful engines for large warships. A bold proposal was to destroy the New York Navy Yard, which he termed 'not difficult at the period'. None of Maffitt's suggestions were acted on during the summer of 1861 – the window of opportunity for the Confederacy.

27 Wells, *Confederate Navy*, pp142–3.

28 Adjutant and Inspector General's Office, *Uniform and Dress of the Army [and Navy] of the Confederate States*, Richmond, Va., 1861. Reprint Philadelphia, 1960.

29 Still, *Common Sailor*, p38.

30 From a table in Wells, *Confederate Navy*, pp162–5.

31 Still, 'The Confederate States Navy at Mobile, 1861 to August 1864', *Alabama Historical Quarterly*, Vol 30, Fall and Winter, 1968, pp142–3.

32 Scharf, *Confederate States Navy*, p775.

33 Davis, *Rebels and Yankees*, pp 150-1.

34 Horn, *Gallant Rebel*, pp61–2.

35 Shingleton, *High Seas Confederate*, p83.

36 Wells, *Confederate Navy*, pp74–7, 92, 146.

37 Horn, *Gallant Rebel*, p56.

38 The Confederate Navy had better food than the Army for several reasons. Most ships were far from the heavy concentrations of soldiers in the main armies; laws allowing government impressment from farmers and other producers were extended to the Navy; blockade runners often brought in coffee, tea and sugar, which were sent to naval hospitals, naval storehouses, or bartered for other provisions; and the Navy had a better system than the Army. In April 1864 Paymaster DeBree had to propose a board be established to reduce the Navy ration, and that summer the Army began to furnish all provisions to the Navy. Wells, *Confederate Navy*, p80.

39 *Register of Officers of the Confederate States Navy, 1861-1865*, p25.

Chapter Seven Seamen, Landsmen, Firemen and Coal Heavers

1 Wood to Captain Franklin Buchanan, Jan 22, 1862, *ORN*, Ser II, Vol 2, p137.

2 Kennington, 'Gray Jackets', pp59–61

3 Private journal of John Newland Maffitt, Maffitt Papers, Southern Historical Collection, University of North Carolina, Chapel Hill.

4 Kennington, 'Gray Jackets', pp70–5.

5 George W Gift, 'The Story of the *Arkansas*', *Southern Historical Society Papers*, Vol 12 (1884), p50.

6 Kennington, 'Gray Jackets', pp170–5.

7 Daniel B Conrad, 'Capture of the CS Ram *Tennessee* in Mobile Bay, August 1864,' *Southern Historical Society Papers*, Vol 19, 1891, pp76–7.

8 Shingleton, *John Taylor Wood*, pp 92–105.

9 *Register of Officers of the Confederate States Navy, 1861–1865*, pp 15, 57.

10 George W Gift to Ellen A Shackleford, May 28, 1863, George W Gift Collection, Southern Historical Collection, University of North Carolina, Chapel Hill.

11 Conrad, 'Capture of the *Tennessee*', pp72–4.

12 Cited in Wells, *The Confederate Navy*, pp165–6.

13 Robert Watson, 'Civil War Diary' May 10, 1864, Cornell University Library, Ithaca, New York.

14 Wells, *The Confederate Navy*, pp22–4. Wells mentioned two other petty officer ratings, schoolmaster and master of the band, but they were not found to be filled. He also wrote that hospital nurse was a possible petty officer rating. Ibid, p91.

15 *Uniform and Dress of the Army [and Navy] of the Confederate States of America*, Philadelphia, 1960, np.

16 Kennington, 'Gray Jackets', pp 79-81. This first uniform order in England consisted of blue cloth caps, blue flounce overshirts and underwear, wool pea jackets, duck trousers, barnsley sheeting frocks, shoes, woollen socks, cloth jumpers, round jackets and black silk neckerchiefs. Some of these items were interdicted by the blockade.

17 Philip Katcher, *The Civil War Sourcebook* New York, 1992, p239.

18 *Uniform and Dress of the Confederate Army and Navy*, np.

19 From the Office of Provision and Clothing *Circular*, June 3, 1863 cited in Wells, *The Confederate Navy*, p161.

20 Watson, 'Civil War Diary', May 10, Mar 18, Apr 25, Jun 26, 1864.

21 Using the cutlass as a bayonet was not very practicable on muzzle loaders because it interfered with loading. Excited by battle, the loader was likely to pierce or bruise his hand.

Chapter Eight The Marines

1 *Acts and Resolutions of the First Session of the Provisional Congress of the Confederate States held at Montgomery, Ala*, Richmond, Virginia: Tyler, Wise, Allegre and Smith, 1861, 104: No 70, Sec 9.

2 Thomson to 'Dear Pa' Camp Beall, Drewry's Bluff, Virginia Mar 14, 1864. Ruffin Thomson Papers, accession 3315, Southern Historical Collection, University of North Carolina.

3 *Acts and Resolutions*, 103: Sec 5. The company arrangement of the Confederate States Marines was a departure from the organization of the 'Old Corps.' There were no

permanent companies in the US Marine Corps. The constant rotating of detachments between barracks and sea duty was judged to be incompatible with a company system. *Ad hoc* companies were formed only when US Marines were called upon to perform field service, reverting to barracks detachments once their duties were discharged. The Confederate Corps did follow the practice of sending Marines on detached service. However, company affiliation was maintained, and responsibility for the accounts of detached CS Marines remained the province of the company commander.

4 *Acts and Resolutions of the Second Session of the Provisional Congress of the Confederate States, 1861* (Montgomery: Barrett Wimbish, 1861) 39, No 145. Subsequent legislation passed on September 24, 1862 authorized an increase of twenty sergeants, twenty corporals, twenty drummers, and twenty fifers. The two musicians were elevated to 'Principal Musicians.'

5 Donnelly, *History of the Confederate States Marine Corps*, Vol 4. An official count of 539 is reported in Ser 2, Vol 2, p636. As a result of the loss of a large portion of Corps' records at the end of the war, the exact number of enlistments will never be determined. However, a figure of 1,240, based upon a careful count of all the names that appear on extant muster rolls, clothing receipt rolls, medical journals, and other similar records, has been presented in Donnelly, *Service Records of Confederate Enlisted Marines*. This number does not include Marines who were enlisted during Jan–Apr 1865, since records for this period apparently did not survive the war.

6 *Montgomery Daily Mail,* Apr 11, *History of the Confederate State Marine Corps*, 1861.

7 A fourth company of Marines, Captain Hays's Company D, was slated for duty at Pensacola as well, However, Hays was unable to recruit enough men to form a complete company. The twenty-eight men he brought from Memphis in the fall of 1861 were subsequently attached to Companies B and C, while Hays was posted to duty with the Army. Muster Roll of Company B, CS Marine Corps, Sep 1–Nov 1 1861. Van Benthuysen Papers, Tulane University.

8 NA RG 109. GO 70, Jun 10, 1861, and SO. 102, Jun 14, 1861, HQ Troops, CS near Pensacola.

9 NA RG 109, En 19. The Morning Report of the 2nd Brigade dated October 8, 1861, indicates that sixty-nine CS Marines under the command of a captain and two second lieutenants were detached for service with the assault force. US War Department, *The War of the Rebellion*, Series I, Vol 4, p463. Augusta *Chronicle and Sentinel,* Oct 19, 1861, Memphis *Daily Appeal,* Oct 26, 1861; Sayre was subsequently paroled, exchanged and restored to duty, but his wound left one leg shorter than the other and rendered him unfit for field service. He was subsequently assigned to Army duty with the rank of major, PACS.

10 Selfridge to William W McKean, commanding Gulf Blockading Squadron, USS *Mississippi,* off Mobile Bay, Nov 16, 1861. The Papers of Thomas O Selfridge, Sr, and Thomas O. Selfridge, Jr, Library of Congress.

11 Report of Capt A C Van Benthuysen, Nov 26, 1861. Van Benthuysen Papers.

12 *ORN,* Vol 1, p688. Stephenson subsequently served as Orderly Sergeant of the Marine Guard aboard CSS *Georgia.* He returned to the Confederate States in August 1864, and, after serving at Drewry's Bluff and aboard CSS *Fredericksburg,* was paroled

at Greensboro, North Carolina, April 26, 1865. 1st Lt Becket K Howell, CSMC, later joined Semmes aboard CSS *Alabama.* Since no enlisted Marines served aboard *Alabama,* Howell performed the duties of boarding officer, supervised the confinement of prisoners taken from Semmes's victims at sea, and was part of an impromptu gun's crew made up of officers. Following the defeat of *Alabama* by USS *Kearsarge,* June 19, 1864, Howell remained at Liverpool, England until the end of the war.

13 *War of the Rebellion,* Vol 53, p709. NA RG 45. Subfile RL. List of CS naval prisoners, May 1, 1862.

14 *ORN.,* Vol 12, pp295–8. From An Eyewitness, 'The part the Navy Took in the affray at Port Royal,' extracted from the Savannah *Republican,* Nov 12, 1861.

15 *ORN,* Vol 2, p47, Barney to Fendall, CSS Jamestown, James River, Apr 29, 1862, Letter 47, NA RG 45, E 430, *Letters Sent by Comdr. Joseph Nicholson Barney, CSN., December 1861-April 1863,* and Tucker to Henderson, CS Steamer *Patrick Henry,* off Mulberry Island, James River, Apr 25, 1862, Personal Papers of Richard H Henderson, 'ZB' File, Operational Archives, Naval Histroy Division.

16 Van Benthuysen Papers. By this time, Capt J E Meiere had replaced Capt R T Thom in command of Company C and of the Guard aboard CSS *Virginia.*

17 The Marine Guard at the Navy Yard opposite Rocketts was commanded by 2nd Lt Nathaniel E Venable, Feb–May 1863, 2nd Lt John s Van de Graaff, May–Aug 1863, 2nd Lt Samuel E Roberts, Aug 1863–May 1864 and 2nd Lt Henry H McCune, May 1864–Apr 1865. The Richmond Navy Yard Guard was commanded by 2nd Lt David Bradford, Sept 1863–May 1864, and 2nd Lt Lloyd B Stephenson, May 1864–Apr 1865. CSS *Richmond*'s Marines were initially under the charge of O Sgt John W Seymour, Dec 1862–Nov 1863. 2nd Lt James C Murdoch commanded the Guard Nov 1863–Mar 1864, 2nd Lt Samuel M Roberts, Jun 1864–Apr 1865. The Marine Guard of CSS *Virginia II* was commanded by 1st Lt Thomas P Gwynn, May 1864–Feb 1865, and 2nd Lt Edward Crenshaw, Feb–Apr 1865. CSS *Fredericksburg*'s Guard was commanded by 1st Lt David Bradford May 1864–Aug 1864, and 2nd Lt Everard T Eggleston, Aug 1864–Apr 1865.

18 Scharf, *History of the Confederate States Navy,* pp688–9.

19 H M Doak, 'In the War Between the States,' unpublished memoirs, Henry M Doak Papers, Tennessee State Library, p31; Richmond *Examiner,* Aug 7, 1863 and Doak Ms, p32.

20 Doak Ms, pp32–3; *ORN,* Vol 14, p637.

21 *ORN,* Vol 9, pp543–4

22 *ORN,* Vol 15, pp501–2

23 Ibid, p500

24 Franklin Buchanan Letter Book, 1862–1863, Acession 97, Southern Historical Collection, University of North Carolina. Buchanan to Lt John W Bennett, Comdg Officer, CSS *Gaines,* Mobile Jan 26, 1863, and Buchanan to Mallory, Mobile, Feb 1; *ORN,* Vol 19, p591.

25 Henry Kershaw Dubose, *The History of Company B, 21st Regiment, South Carolina Volunteers,* Columbia, South Carolina, 1909, p47. The 21st South Carolina moved to

another position shortly afterward. Dubose never determined whether his comments regarding the Marines proved true.

26 *War of the Rebellion*, Vol 36/2, p996 and NA RG 45, Subfile OV, Quarterly Return of Ordnance and Ordnance Stores, Company C, Confederate States Marine Corps, Drewry's Bluff, for the quarter ending June 30, 1864.

27 Robert E Lee, Jr, *Recollections and Letters of General Robert E. Lee* (New York, 1926), pp131–2. The courier sent by Lee to Early was his son, at that time a captain in the artillery.

28 'Diary of Edward Crenshaw', *Alabama Historical Quarterly*, Vols 1–2, 1930, 1940, pp261–70, 438–52, 52–71, 221–38, 465–82. Entries for July 2–6, 1864.

29 Ibid, entry for July 11, 1864. Crenshaw wrote that news of the destination and purpose of the expedition had reached the enemy. The prisoners had been removed to Elmira, New York and troops had been rushed to Point Lookout to give the raiders a 'warm reception, and no quarter.' The land component of the operation did proceed. Confederate cavalry under Gen Bradley T Johnson galloped north of Baltimore, cutting telegraph lines and burning bridges *en route*. After buring the railroad bridge over the Gunpowder River on July 12, Johnson's troopers were recalled.

30 John L Rapier to 'Dear Tom', US Military Prison, Union Press, New Orleans, Sep 5, 1864. This letter is in the possession of Adelaide Marston Trigg, Rapier's granddaughter.

31 NA RG 45, subfile OO. James D Johnston, 'Admiral Buchanan and the C. S. Ram Tennessee', a speech given before the Georgia Historical Society, nd.

32 Rapier to 'Dear Tom', Sep 5, 1864. Meiere, Raney, Fendall and Rapier escaped from prison on October 13, and returned to duty at Mobile after making thir way through Federal lines.

33 Richard Harwell (ed), *A Confederate Marine: A Sketch of Henry Lea Graves with Excerpts from the Graves Family Correspondence, 1861–1865* (Confederate Publishing Company, Tuscaloosa, Alabama, 1963) pp126–7, and 'Memo for the General Biographical Catalog 1746–1916 of Princeton College, N. J, Edward F. Neufville'. Copy furnished by Mary M Mason, Neufville's granddaughter. The Mariners serving aboard CSS *Macon* at the time of the evacuation of Savannah and others who were collected during the weeks thereafter were ultimately placed under the command of Lt Daniel G Brent at Augusta, Georgia.

34 Doak Ms, p40.

35 Col William Lamb, 'Fort Fisher. The Battles Fought There in 1864 and '65, *Southern Historical Society Papers*, Vol 21, 1893, pp257–90; *ORN*, Vol 11, p444.

36 Freeman Jones, 'A Daring Expedition', George S Bernhard (ed), *War Talks of Confederate Veterans*, Petersburg, 1892, pp231–4 and 'Crenshaw Diary', entries for Feb 3, 1865.

37 Morris Schaff, *The Sunset of the Confederacy*, Boston, 1912, p107, *Confederate Veteran*, Vol 8, No 4 Apr 1900, p170 and *War of the Rebellion*, Vol 46/1, p980.

38 Joseph Warren Keifer, *Slavery and Four Years of War* (2 Vols, New York, 1900), Vol 2, pp208–11. The Marine officers who surrendered at Sayler's Creek were: Capt John D Simms, Capt George Holmes, Capt Thomas S Wilson, 1st Lt Fergus McRee, 1st Lt Thomas P Gwynn, 1st Lt Albert S Berry, and 2nd Lt Eugene R Smith. The survivors of the Naval Battalion were taken to Old Capital Prison at Washington,

and then shipped off to Johnson's Island or Elmira. They were not released from confinement until the summer of 1865.

39 'The Appomattox Parole Lists', *Southern Historical Society Papers*, Vol 15, 1886, p459. 1st Lt Richard H Henderson, 1st Lt Francis H Cameron, 2nd Lt Henry M Doak and 2nd Lt Henry H McCune took their paroles at Appomattox. Major A S Taylor was paroled April 10, and Major Israel Greene at sometime within the next few days.

40 NA RG 45, Subfile RB, 'Prisoners of War, Greensboro, North Carolina'. Marine officers who surrendered at Greensboro were: Maj Richard T Allison, Capt John R F Tattnall, 1st Lt Henry L Graves, 2nd Lt Ruffin Thomson, 2nd Lt Edward Crenshaw, 2nd Lt Everard T Eggleston, 2nd Lt Samuel Roberts, and 2nd Lt Edward F Neufville. Enlisted men numbered twenty-one from Semmes's Naval Brigade and fourteen from Company E.

41 NA RG 45, E 434, Letters sent by the Paymaster of the CSN at Mobile, Jun 1862–Oct 1864.

42 William B Bynum, 'A Confederate Marines' Funeral', *Military Collector and Historian*, Vol 44, No 4, Winter, 1992, p170.

43 CSS *Sumter* Papers, Library of Congress.

44 Lt Col W H Williams, 'A Confederate Marine Corps Button?', *Military Collector and Historian*, Vol 8, No 3, Fall 1956, p81. Description of the buttons on the uniform provided by Thomas Curtis, descendant of Pvt Samuel C Curtis.

45 *ORN*, Ser 2, Vol 2, p5.

46 Ibid and NA RG 45, Subfile OV.

47 Scharf, *History of the Confederate States Navy*, p399.

Chapter Nine Shipboard Life

1 CSN *Regulations*, pp6–7; Kennington, 'Gray Jackets', pp161–8.

2 CSN *Ordnance Instructions*, pp15–18; CSN *Regulations*, pp62–6.

3 CSN *Ordnance Instructions*, pp8–36; CSN *Regulations*, pp6–7, 100–25; Wells, *Confederate Navy*, pp144–9 and appendix.

4 Donnelly, *History of the Confederate Marine Corps*, pp94–8.

5 CSN *Ordnance Instructions*, p32.

6 CSN *Regulations*, pp62, 90.

7 CSN *Ordnance Instructions*, appendix; Wells, *Confederate Navy*, pp146–147; Kennington, 'Gray Jackets,' pp147–9; CSN *Regulations*, pp65–6, 88.

8 CSN *Regulations*, pp65–6.

9 Morgan, *Recollections*, p129; CSN *Regulations*, pp90–4, 61.

10 Kennington, 'Gray Jackets,' pp134–40; Sinclair, *Two Years*, pp18–25, 134.

11 CSN *Regulations*, pp15, 17, 70; CSN *Ordnance Instructions*, 70; Sinclair, *Two Years*, pp58, 72, 95, 104–5, 119, 202, 204.

12 Gift to Lt J Grimball, Jan 21, 25; Feb 4, 1863, Grimball Papers, South Carolina Historical Society, Charleston, SC.

13 Kennington, 'Gray Jackets,' pp39–40; Watson Journal, Aug 6; Oct 2, 10, 1864.

14 Sinclair, *Two Years*, pp117, 171, 210.

15 Kennington,'Gray Jackets,' pp103, 113; Wells, *Confederate Navy*, p82; Delaney, *John McIntosh Kell*, p134; Langley, *Social Reform*, pp243–67; CSN *Regulations*, p136.

16 CSN *Regulations*, p75; Sinclair, *Two Years*, pp83, 146.

17 Horan, *CSS Shenandoah*, pp161–2.

18 Watson Journal, May 10, 1864; Feb 9, 1865 Cornell University Library; Kennington,'Gray Jackets,' p110.

19 CSN *Regulations*, p63; Sinclair, *Two Years*, pp144–5, 202–3; Semmes, *Cruise of the Alabama*, Vol I, pp290, 296–7, 399–400.

20 William N Still, 'Confederate Tars', *Civil War Times Illustrated*, Mar 1985, p19; Sinclair, *Two Years*, p210.

21 Sinclair, *Two Years*, p204.

22 Ibid, pp44–5, 204.

23 Ibid, pp116, 275; Hoole, *Four Years*, p84.

24 Ibid, pp81–2.

25 Ibid, p95.

26 Kell, *Recollections*, p196; Sinclair, *Two Years*, pp53, 100–1.

27 Sinclair, *Two Years*, p83.

28 Semmes, *Service Afloat*, pp420–1; Sinclair, *Two Years*, pp68–9, 109, 130, 148.

29 Sinclair, *Two Years*, p135.

30 Ibid, p184.

31 Ibid, pp166, 206.

32 Semmes, *Service Afloat*, p715; Sinclair, *Two Years*, p67.

33 Ibid, p74.

34 Diary of Midshipman Dubrey Scales, Mar 8, Apr 5, 7 1863, Duke University, Durham, NC.

35 CSN *Regulations*, pp73–5.

36 Ibid, p76.

37 Sinclair, *Two Years*, p205 and muster roll in appendix; Semmes, *Cruise of the Alabama*, Vol 2, pp267–8.

38 Sinclair, *Two Years*, pp130–1; Semmes, *Cruise of the Alabama*, Vol 2, p192.

39 Sinclair, *Two Years*, pp208, 249–50.

40 Ibid, pp237–38.

41 Shingleton, *High Seas Confederate*, pp47–50.

42 Ibid, pp51–5, 75, 78.

43 Horan, *CSS Shenandoah*, p159.

44 CSN *Ordnance Instructions*, p66; Langley, *Social Reform*, pp170–206; Gift to Lt J Grimball, Jan 31, 1863, Grimball Papers.

45 Semmes, *Cruise of the Alabama*, Vol 2, p33.

46 Ibid, Vol 2, pp33, 37.

47 Sinclair, *Two Years*, pp43–4; Semmes, *Service Afloat*, pp511–13.

48 Sinclair, *Two Years*, p34; Semmes, *Cruise of the Alabama*, Vol I, pp392–3.

49 Sinclair, *Two Years*, pp32, 68, 148–9, 184; Semmes, *Service Afloat*, p715.

50 Shingleton, *High Seas Confederate*, pp122–3; Summersell, *Cruise of the CSS Sumter*, p150.

51 Hoole, *Four Years*, p83.

52 Gift to Ellen A Shackelford, Apr 7, 1863; Gift Diary, Feb 6, 1863, Gift Letters and Diary, Southern Historical Society, Charleston, SC.

53 Semmes, *Cruise of the Alabama*, Vol 1, 239; Vol 2, 30; Sinclair, *Two Years*, p70.

54 Watson Journal, Aug 31, 1864.

55 Shingleton, *High Seas Confederate*, pp64–75.

56 Scales Diary, Jan 16, 31, 1863.

57 Ibid, Mar 14, 15, 16, 1863.

58 Hoole, *Four Years*, pp110–14.

59 CSN *Regulations*, pp65, 68.

Chapter Ten Strategy and Tactics

1 Bern Anderson, 'The Naval Strategy of the Civil War', *Military Affairs*, Spring 1962, p11.

2 Durkin, *Stephen R. Mallory*, 1954, p135.

3 Alfred T Mahan, *Naval Strategy*, Greenwood Press, 1975, p17. Mahan's command of the sea doctrine is merely a restatement of Jomini's dictum that 'the organized forces of the enemy are ever the chief objective'.

4 Frank J Merli, 'The South on the Seas', *Civil War Times Illustrated*, Nov 1972, p6.

5 Wells, *The Confederate Navy*, pp11–12.

6 Taylor, *Confederate Raider*, p55.

7 Raphael Semmes, *Memoirs of Service Afloat*, p92.

8 Ibid.

9 Robinson, Jr, *The Confederate Privateers*, p30.

10 Ibid.

11 Harold and Margaret Sprout, *The Rise of American Naval Power, 1776–1918*, Annapolis, 1980, p163.

12 Semmes, *Service Afloat and Ashore*, p82.

13 Merli, 'The South on the Seas', p7.

14 Ibid.

15 John Cameron, *Our Tropical Possessions in Malayan India*, London, 1865, p274.

16 Sprout, *American Naval Power*, p164.

17 Ibid.

18 Archer Jones, *Civil War Command and Strategy* (Free Press, 1992), p141.

19 *ORN*, Ser II, Vol 2, pp67–9.

20 Daly, *How the Merrimac Won*, p63.

21 William N Still, 'Confederate Naval Strategy: The Ironclad', *Journal of Southern History*, Aug 1961, p335.

22 Still, *Iron Afloat*, p214.

23 Jones, *Command and Strategy*, p141.

24 Paul D Lockhart, 'Confederate Naval Strategy and the Ironclad Program at Charleston, 1861–65', *Indiana Military History Journal*, May 1988, p18.

25 Ibid.

26 Still, *Iron Afloat*, p231.

27 Durkin, *Stephen R. Mallory*, p265.

28 Ibid, p279.

29 Perry, *Infernal Machines*, p196.

30 Christopher Chase, 'In Search of the CSS *Hunley*', *Blue & Gray Magazine*, Vol XIII, No 5, pp24–8.

31 *ORN*, Ser I, Vol 6, pp776–7.

32 Daly, *How the Merrimac Won*, p63.

33 Robert Collins Suhr, 'Popular during the Crimean War, the floating battery was revived by hard-pressed Confederates', *America's Civil War*, Jul 1996, p26.

34 Norman C Delaney, 'Raiders of the Seas', *Fighting for Time*, Doubleday, 1983, p138.

35 Delaney, *John McIntosh Kell*, p135.

36 Frank J Merli (ed), 'Lectures on the *Alabama*, June 1864', *Mariner's Mirror*, May 1972, p217.

37 Norman C Delaney, 'The End of the Alabama', *American Heritage*, Apr 1972, pp58–69, 102.

38 Merli, 'The South on the Seas', pp42–3.

Chapter Eleven Operations

1 Beringer, *Why the South Lost*, p57.

2 Still, *Confederate Shipbuilding*, pp6–7, 82; Scharf, *History of the Confederate States Navy*, pp24–5.

3 *Civil War Naval Chronology*, p28; John F Barrett, *The Civil War in North Carolina* (Chapel Hill, NC 1963), Ch. III, note 28.

4 Browning, *From Cape Charles to Cape Fear*, pp17–38. See also Richard A Sauers, 'General Ambrose E Burnside's 1862 North Carolina Campaign', PhD dissertation, Pennsylvania State University, 1987.

5 A number of vessels were captured but only one, the steam sloop of war *Merrimack*, was considered worthy of salvaging.

6 For the battle of Hampton Roads see William N Still, Jr, 'The Battle of Hampton Roads', to be published in a book on famous naval battles by the United States Naval Institute Press. See also Davis, *Duel between the First Ironclads*.

7 It is not clear whether Jones had tactical command of the entire Confederate squadron, but the rest of the squadron followed the *Virginia* when she retired on March 8.

8 Coski, *Capital Navy*.

9 *Civil War Naval Chronology*, Vol I, pp38–40. For the Savannah Squadron see Still, *Savannah Squadron*.

10 Scharf, *History of the Confederate States Navy*, pp656–9.

11 *Civil War Naval Chronology*, Vol 3, pp18–19; Still, *Iron Afloat*.

12 Maxine Turner, 'Davids', in Richard N Current (ed), *Encyclopaedia of the Confederacy*, 4 vols, New York, 1993, Vol II, pp445–6; see also Perry, *Infernal Machines*.

13 For the *Hunley* see Kloeppel, *Danger beneath the Waves* and Ragan, *The Hunley*.

14 For the Wilmington Squadron see William N Still, Jr, 'Southern Ironclad Struggle', *Military History*, Aug 1984, pp62–4, Combs, 'On Duty at Wilmington'.

15 See Elliott, *Ironclad of the Roanoke*; and Bright, *et al*, *CSS Neuse*.

16 For New Orleans and the western rivers see Dufour, *The Night the War Lost*; and Chester G Hearn, *The Capture of New Orleans*, Baton Rouge, LA, 1993.

17 Several of the Confederate vessels such as the *Livingston*, *Maurapus* and floating battery *New Orleans* were up the Mississippi, others not present at the obstructions that day are unaccounted for.

18 Milligan, *Gunboats down the Mississippi*, pp65–77.

19 Confederate warships operated in Texas waters and fought several engagements with Union vessels, but they either belonged to the Army or the Texas Marine Department.

20 For the East Gulf Blockading Squadron see George E Buker, *Blockaders, Refugees, and Contrabands*.

21 Turner, *Navy Gray*.

22 Bergeron, *Confederate Mobile*; Chester G Hearn, *Mobile Bay and the Mobile Campaign*, Jefferson, NC, 1993; Still, *Iron Afloat*, pp187–211.

23 The *Baltic* was considered unseaworthy and did not participate.

24 Spencer, *The Confederate Navy in Europe*; Merli, *Great Britain and the Confederate Navy*.

25 Dalzell, *Flight from the Flag*; Hearn, *Gray Raiders of the Sea*.

26 Summersell, *The Cruise of CSS Sumter*.

27 Read in the *Clarence* captured the *Tacony* and considered her more suitable as a raider. He transferred his crew to her and burned the *Clarence*.

28 Shingleton, *John Taylor Wood*; Kevin Foster, 'Tallahassee' in *Encyclopaedia of the Confederacy*, Vol IV, p1567.

29 For the *Florida* see Owsley, *The CSS Florida*; Shingleton, *High Seas Confederate*.

30 For the *Shenandoah* see Hearn, *Gray Raiders of the Sea*, pp250–301.

31 William N Still, Jr, 'A Naval Sieve: The Union Blockade in the Civil War', *Naval War College Review* (May–Jun 1983) pp38–45. For one squadron and the blockade see Browning, *From Cape Charles to Cape Fear*.

INDEX

Page references in *italics* refer to illustrations, and those in **bold** to diagrams.